FRONTIERS OF LEGAL SCHOLARSHIP

Twenty five years of Warwick Law School

Edited by

Geoffrey P. Wilson
Professor of Law
University of Warwick

John Wiley & Sons
Chichester · New York · Brisbane · Toronto · Singapore

First published in the United Kingdom in 1995 by

Chancery Law Publishing Ltd,
Baffins Lane,
Chichester,
West Sussex,
PO19 1UD

National 01243 779777
International (+44) 1243 779777

Other Wiley Editorial Offices

John Wiley & Sons Inc., 605 Third Avenue,
New York, NY 10158-0012, USA

John Wiley & Sons Inc., Editorial, Administration & Marketing,
7222 Commerce Center Drive, Suite 240,
Colorado Springs, CO 80919

Jacaranda Wiley Ltd, 33 Park Road, Milton,
Queensland 4064, Australia

John Wiley & Sons (Canada) Ltd, 22 Worcester Road,
Rexdale, Ontario M9W 1L1, Canada

John Wiley & Sons (SEA) Pte Ltd, 37 Jalan Pemimpin #05-04,
Block B, Union Industrial Building, Singapore 2057

British Library Cataloguing Publication Data

A catalogue record for this book is available from the British Library

ISBN 0471 96123 X

Typeset in 10/12pt Baskerville by Footnote Graphics, Warminster, Wilts
Printed and bound in Great Britain by Bookcraft (Bath) Ltd

This book is printed on acid-free paper responsibly manufactured from sustainable forestation,
for which at least two trees are planted for each one used for paper production.

CONTENTS

PREFACE

This volume celebrates the first 25 years of Warwick Law School. The contributors all at one time or another taught there. Their work is built into its foundations and is part of its reputation. They do not of course stand alone in this respect. Not everyone asked to contribute was able to do so and not everyone who had been at Warwick could be asked – that number is now large and distinguished. It is difficult to exaggerate what it takes in terms of commitment and important parts of peoples lives to establish a law school and Warwick owes a considerable debt to the contributors and non-contributors alike. And it is not only to the staff – it is also to the students. Some of Warwick's students were given a rough ride when they were called on by sceptical members of the legal profession to explain what was new about the Warwick approach, in ways which revealed a widely shared confusion between taking social problems as a point of orientation, sociology and even socialism. It was to their credit that their qualities have helped to give Warwick a good name not only in the world of scholarship but in the world of the profession and of practical affairs as well, and by no means limited to the world of law.

Although the occasion of this volume is celebratory, this is not a book in praise of Warwick or even Warwick reassessed. The contributors were given a fairly broad brief. The most important part of it was that someone who came to read it would be able to benefit from their experience, whether in terms of the development of a subject area with which they were familiar, or their own personal experiences as scholars working in their chosen fields, or both. Whatever path they chose it was hoped that they would represent in some way the reflections of representatives of a generation, the generation that was at work during the first 25 years of Warwick's existence, but representatives with the special quality that they were willing to take the risk of participating in a radical new venture, the first major shift in legal education since English law was introduced as a subject of study in the universities.

When news got out in 1967 that a new law school with a new approach to legal education was to be established at Warwick there was a good deal of curiosity but also some apprehension. I was frequently asked to give talks to explain what I had in mind. In the end I published one of these in the Journal of the Society of Public Teachers of Law under the title "Getting on with the job". It was basically a plea to be allowed to get on with the job of setting up the law school, and to give a reassurance that it did not pose any threat, that there was no desire to challenge directly the activities of anyone else, but simply a desire to take the opportunity of doing something different. Any one looking at it will see that it is expressed largely in aspirational terms. There is not a lot of detail. It is as much rhetorical as programmatic. It is clearly atheoretical. It is short on footnotes. It does not appeal to or build on any tradition, alternative or otherwise. It was original. It had no ideological or political underpinnings. It was a reaction against the status quo of the world of legal education and not the status quo of the real world. It is not particularly argumentative. It is expressed on a take it or leave it basis.

The Warwick approach has always been a somewhat loose fit and it has continued to be a feature of Warwick's development that its aspirations have largely been expressed in terms of slogans and striking turns of phrase. Had it not been so it would not have been able to provide an umbrella for so long to such a variety of people and approaches, which nonetheless differed in aggregate from those of other law schools. Every effort was made to avoid getting bogged down in the kind of detail which could have destroyed the consensus that was necessary to get the law school up and running and continuing to run.

What this meant was that the burden of filling out and fulfilling the aspirations fell on people like the contributors. The Law School was grateful to them for the contribution they made while they were here. It is equally grateful that they have been prepared to put aside the time to make a contribution to this volume.

Geoffrey P. Wilson, University of Warwick.

Chapter 1

"A WAYWARD, VAGRANT SPIRIT": LAW IN CONTEXT FINDS ITS RICH AND KINDLY EARTH

Professor Ross Cranston*
London School of Economics

The Fortunes of Richard Mahony[1] tells the story of a doctor who travels to one of the goldfields of colonial Victoria. He becomes wealthy and in mid-life, partly for nostalgia, goes home to England, only to be disappointed. He then loses his fortune and on his final return to Australia becomes ill, later mad, and then dies. The novel was Henry Handel Richardson's[2] tribute to her own father, although it was far from being biographical. The fascination is the fate of Richard Mahony as he moves between England and the Antipodes. Constantly Mahony reasons with himself as he struggles in particular to understand his restlessness and failure to settle down and enjoy his wealth. Finally, in his devastation there is reconciliation: "The rich and kindly earth of his adopted country absorbed his perishable body, as the country itself had never contrived to make its own, his wayward, vagrant spirit'' (UT:279).

Richardson helps us to understand Richard Mahony's tragedy at multiple levels. One of the seeds of his destruction is the dissonance between his values and those of society. We see an example early in *Australia Felix*. Mahony is a Victorian gentleman, fastidious, conscious of his superior class and a respecter of established order. The diggers (miners) on the goldfield will have none of it, and Mahony's friend Purdy despairs when Mahony appeals at a diggers' meeting to the loyal subjects of Her Majesty who need "not strife and bloodshed, but a liberty consistent with law and order" (AF:19). As Australians the diggers are convinced that anyone is as good as anyone else and that authority must justify itself before it is accorded respect. Eventually Mahony decides that intellectually

* I am grateful to my colleague Professor Carol Harlow for her comments.

[1] The trilogy consists of *Australia Felix* 1917 (AF), *The Way Home* 1925 (WH), and *Ultima Thule* 1929 (UT). Page references are to the Penguin Modern Classics editions, 1971.

[2] Born Ethel Richardson, Melbourne 1870; left Australia 1888; lived the remainder of her life in Germany and England; died 1946. Recently an English don has argued that *The Fortunes of Richard Mahony* puts Richardson "among the handful of great writers of this century'': K. McLeod, *Henry Handel Richardson* (1985), p 96. See also D. Green, *Ulysses Bound* (1973).

and morally he cannot be at home in Australia. He abandons his successful practice in Victoria to return to what he thinks will be a more congenial England. Yet he finds he cannot stomach the provincialism of mind and snobbishness. "Long residence in a land where every honest man was the equal of his neighbour had unfitted him for the genuflexions of the English middle-classes before the footstools of the great" (WH:41). Thus the final return to Australia.

Richard Mahony is not thoroughly obtuse. He makes an effort to adapt to his context, but one aspect of his tragedy is that this frustrates yet further his moral senses. He has a running debate with himself about money. Unlike other characters in the novel who also make their fortune through the goldfields, he cannot truly enjoy what he possesses. At one level Richardson is pursuing the common theme that there is more to life than the economic. Yet Mahony's very character means that he constantly strives for "a tourney of spiritual adventuring, of intellectual excitement, in which the prize striven for was not money or anything to do with money" (AF:346).

At about the time I was teaching at the Law School at the University of Warwick, the Dean of Cornell Law School was lamenting the lack of the spiritual, and much else besides, in traditional legal education: "Emotion, imagination, sentiments of affection and trust, a sense of wonder or awe at the inexplicable – these soft and mushy domains of the 'tender minded' are off limits for law students and lawyers".[3] My own traditional legal education had led me to share similar sentiments. The quest for a wider view of legal education ultimately led me to law in context, and Warwick.

For many years in this country there had been urgings of a broader perspective than that provided by traditional legal education. One can go back, for example, to *The Treatise on the Study of Law*[4], where logic and history were strongly recommended as background for the lawyer. Another source of that time invoked the memorable comment that the sparks of all sciences are raked up in the ashes of the law, and drew the conclusion that a lawyer needed a smattering of all of them as well as a knowledge of history, natural law and civil law.[5] In a celebrated report of 1846, the House of Commons Select Committee on Legal Education highlighted the need in legal education to teach the scientific and philosophical aspects and deplored the "hyper-critical attention to the technicalities" at the expense of enunciating broad principles.[6] When they have turned their minds to it the leading judges of this country have appreciated that truly to understand the law demands a knowledge of its derivation, operation and moral content. Thus in one of his lectures Lord Macmillan asked rhetorically: "How can the lawyer intelligently appreciate the laws with which he has to

---

[3] Roger Cramton, "The Ordinary Religion of the Law School Classroom" (1978) 29 *Journal of Legal Education* 247, 250.

[4] Anon, *Treatise on the Study of Law* (1797), p 56.

[5] Edward Wynne, *Eunomus* (1767), quoted M. Lobban, *The Common Law and English Jurisprudence 1760–1850* (1991), p 60.

[6] *Report from the Select Committee on Legal Education*, HC 686, 25 August 1846, p xxxix.

work unless he knows how they have evolved, the purposes they have been designed to serve, and the mischiefs which they have been designed to meet?"[7]

Yet the hallmarks of legal education in England, at least from the nineteenth century, have been narrowness and professionalism. It is not a proud history. There was a short flowering in Oxford in the late nineteenth century with those like Bryce, Dicey, Maine and Pollock. Whatever one may think of their conservative sentiments, all of these were in their way more than narrow technicians – Bryce and Dicey with their interest in constitutional development, Bryce and Maine with the historical and comparative approach to jurisprudence, and Pollock with his texts and reflective jurisprudence.[8] But these giants failed to reproduce themselves. The law continued to have a low prestige in Oxford and the intellectually able were still attracted to the Greats.[9]

Similarly in the 1930s the law student at the London School of Economics could not be insulated from the intellectual winds blowing through that institution. With public law in particular Ivor Jennings and W.A. Robson taught and wrote about law against its political backdrop; Harold Laski's classes attracted law students and in his writings he often touched on legal matters, particularly the role of the judiciary.[10] The approach by law teachers at the School was progressive, with a concern with social reform, although atheoretical and apolitical. "[T]hey still found themselves treated as a separate group, and the difficulty remained of persuading others to accept that law should be classified as a genuine branch of the social sciences."[11]

But with a few exceptions English legal education set its face against anything other than a technical approach. Perhaps this is not surprising when the provincial law schools were under the thumb of the local law societies. Not only were the social sciences and humanities seen as irrelevant, or worse dangerous, but law was not even conceived of as a liberal education. Legal writing was both uninspiring and boxed in by conceptual categories. Legal academics, like Sir William Holdsworth, believed that the judges should not be criticised. As Laski said of Holdsworth, academics fell down flat in the face of the Law Lords.[12]

After World War II there was a growing body of dissentients. One of my

---

[7] Lord Macmillan, *Law and Other Things* (1938), p 128.

[8] Bryce, *Studies in History and Jurisprudence* (1901); *The American Commonwealth* (1888); Dicey, *Law of the Constitution*, 1st ed. (1885) *Law and Public Opinion in the Nineteenth Century*, 1st ed. (1905); Maine, *Ancient Law* (1861); Pollock, *First Book of Jurisprudence* (1896), *Possession in the Common Law* (1880, jointly). Anson was not in the same class: even his *Law and Custom of the Constitution* (1886, 1892) is a descriptive survey. Of course Cambridge at this time had the great Maitland. For a different, nonetheless stimulating, interpretation of these scholars: D. Sugarman, "'A Hatred of Disorder': Legal Science, Liberalism and Imperialism", in P. Fitzpatrick (ed.), *Dangerous Supplements* (1991), pp 39ff.

[9] B. Abel-Smith & R. Stevens, *Lawyers and the Courts* (1967), pp 166–8.

[10] *E.g.* Jennings, *The Law and the Constitution* (1933); *Cabinet Government* (1936); W.A. Robson, *Justice and Administrative Law* (1928). On Laski, see especially *Studies in Law and Politics* (1932). On this period at LSE see also J.A.G. Griffith, "The Teaching of Law and Politics" (1982) 16 *Law Teacher* 1, 1–2.

[11] C. Glasser, "Radicals and Refugees: The Foundation of the Modern Law Review and English Legal Scholarship" (1987) 50 *MLR* 688, 695.

[12] Quoted Stevens, *Law and Politics* (1979), p 195.

predecessors in the Cassel Chair at the London School of Economics, L.C.B. Gower, argued that all subjects should be taught in context and by reference to the underlying policies.[13] Glanville Williams edited a volume for the Haldane Society in 1951 which used the American law schools for examples of the importance of studying not only legal history and legal philosophy but the workings of the living law.

> "It may, indeed, be generally said that until the practising lawyer, whether judge or barrister or, though in a less degree, solicitor, is made to realise the urgency of understanding what he does in the light that sciences which fringe the boundaries of law throw upon their activity, they will continue to fail to understand either what they are actually doing or the consequences of what they do."[14]

It would be wrong to paint a picture of history's inevitable progress towards law in context. Most law dons continued to see themselves as teachers of future professionals. But the underlying ferment eventually persuaded even the Society of Public Teachers of Law that a broader perspective was demanded. At the time of the Robbins Committee, it noted that many law teachers believed that law must link with other disciplines and be studied in the light of its underlying policies and effects.[15] The Ormrod Committee took up the theme:

> "[T]he influence of ideas, knowledge and attitudes derived from psychology, sociology and criminology, and the other sciences, must make an increasing impact on the law in practice, and the profession will need to equip itself to use such material in an informed and critical matter."[16]

So quite apart from the American influences[17], there was an English tendency favouring law in context. While there was still resistance, both in the law schools and profession, this approach took triumphant form when Geoffrey Wilson was entrusted with the task of establishing a law school at Warwick in 1967. His manifest success is the occasion for this volume.

In one sense law in context is now taken for granted in legal education. Even black letter teachers feel that they have to genuflect in its direction, although many remain spellbound by the upper court mythology, delight in doctrinal inconsistencies, see law as a series of separate issues without an integrative spirit, and conceive of the law reports as their bible when its most important books also comprise legislation, commentaries and law journals. For many other law teachers, law in context is a positive inspiration. They rightly believe that it is not enough to impart intellectual skills such as conceptual manipulation,

---

[13] L.C.B. Gower, "English Legal Training" (1950) 13 *MLR* 137.
[14] Williams (ed.), *The Reform of the Law* (1951), p 214. See also G. Gardiner & A. Martin, "Legal Education", in Gardiner & Martin (eds.), *Law Reform Now* (1963), pp 283, 286.
[15] (1963) 7 *JSPTL* (n.s.) 110, 111.
[16] *Report of the Committee on Legal Education*, Cmnd. 4595, 1971, para. 96.
[17] R. Folsom & N. Roberts, "The Warwick Story: Being Led Down the Contextual Path of the Law" (1979) 30 *Journal of Legal Education* 166.

orderly reasoning and legal discovery. Law students need also to understand the context – the cultural history of law, its institutional settings, the nature of lawyering and how law actually impacts. They need to learn, perhaps most importantly, not to take law too seriously, not to be over impressed by its rituals, and that even if we could decide on the right rule Paradise would not automatically follow.

The law in context aspiration is not, of course, an everyday reality. Law in context is difficult. It is not simply the addition to doctrinal study of a few thoughts on the setting of a particular subject or of some references to policy. Context is at the heart of the matter and, at least for the subject for which I had responsibility when at Warwick, consumer law, is an organising category. That said, law in context nurtures a diversity of approaches and perspectives. Particular subjects may lend themselves more to the treatment. Moreover, different teachers will naturally have different views of both the context and the ramifications. Pluralism was certainly a feature of my time at Warwick, the approach moving from Patrick Atiyah, with his focus at the time on the historical context of contract doctrine, to the theory laden Marxist approaches at the other end of the spectrum.

Law in context is also hampered by practical problems such as deficiencies in the literature. In straight commercial law there is still a remarkable dearth[18], although the consumer and company law ends of the subject are better served.[19] Moreover, it is hard for even the strongest of us not to be subject to the tyranny of the latest case in our particular areas of study. The cascade of published caselaw makes it hard to resist the descent into trivia as commercial incentive causes the afternoon thoughts of the hard pressed, single judge, and the straightforward applications of existing principle by the Court of Appeal, to be reported at length. One recalls nostalgically the days of Pollock, who as editor in chief of the official law reports between 1895 and 1935 reported judgments with Olympian selectivity.[20]

It is not my task to explore law in context in general, or even law in context at Warwick. Both are covered elsewhere in this volume. The editor of this volume, Geoffrey Wilson, gave me a brief to write something that "might look a bit like an inaugural – though slightly more personal...". Consequently, this essay focuses on some general themes in law in context which were particularly important to me during my time at Warwick – socio-legal studies (by which I mean empirical studies in law), law and economics, legal theory (but only a little on this) and social change through law. Then, before closing, there are a few paragraphs on a particularly contentious current issue in English legal education.

---

[18] Ferguson did some interesting work on sales: see e.g. R. Ferguson, "Commercial Expectations and the Guarantee of the Law", in Rubin & Sugarman (eds.), *Law, Economy and Society 1750–1914* (1984).

[19] Apart from the references in notes 27 and 31, see T. Hadden, *Company Law and Capitalism*, 2nd ed., 1977, sadly out of date; I. Ramsay, *Consumer Protection. Text and Materials* (1989).

[20] Simpson, *Biographical Dictionary of the Common Law* (1984) (note by Professor Gareth Jones).

An early incident in *Australia Felix* brings Richard Mahony in contact with the workings of the law. Mahony is threatened with a law suit for non-payment for goods, which the carrier between Melbourne and Ballarat has made off with. In my consumer law class at Warwick, the students would have analysed this in terms of the application of the Sale of Goods Act. The Melbourne merchant, Bolliver, had fulfilled his obligations to deliver the goods by handing them to the carrier, Mahony's agent. Mahony was clearly liable for the price since property in the goods had passed (a strong point made by the plaintiff's counsel, but unimpressively – AF:99). Indeed Mahony realises that Bolliver's case is at least as strong as his. But my Warwick students would have learnt from day one at the School to appreciate the context of law's operation. Consequently they would not have been surprised that Mahony won the law suit. He has engaged a shrewd young lawyer, Henry Ocock, who mounts a defence of bluff and parades his gentleman client, Mahony, alongside the socially inferior Bolliver. Ocock himself makes a good impression before the judge. "Naturally *I* can afford to pay a better-class man", Mahony reflects, although the result later causes him moral anguish so that even twenty years later he relives it in a dream.

My first major empirical study in law, for my DPhil., was completed and prepared for publication during my early time at Warwick.[21] Like much of the early socio-legal research in England it took as a starting point the gap between law in the books and law in action. To what extent, it asked, are legal norms given concrete expression by the legal system or reflected in the practice of those to whom the norms are directed? Specifically, to what extent was the promise of the raft of consumer protection legislation of the 1960s and 1970s delivered in practice? Critics of gap studies often miss the point that the gap was simply a springboard for enquiry. Explanation certainly did not stop there. In my own case I sought to examine why consumer protection legislation missed its mark by examining the form of the law, the resources devoted to its implementation, and the avoidance strategies adopted by the regulated. An important focus was on the discretion of the regulators – the consumer protection (now trading standards) departments – and on the preference of many of them for advice and persuasion rather than the formal application of the law. Arguably there are certain instances with business regulation where advice and persuasion may achieve more compliance than invoking the criminal process, although even now empirical evidence for this is not great.[22] The moral justification for advice and persuasion was that strict liability ought not to lead to criminal penalty in the absence of fault. Only the morally blameworthy should be prosecuted, it was and is said, where for instance there is a failure to respond to previous cautions. I am afraid that my moral sense revolted at the advice and persuasion philos-

---

[21] Eventually published as *Regulating Business* (1979).

[22] Hawkins, *Environment and Enforcement* (1984) is the classic study. See also *e.g.*, K. Hawkins & B. Hutter, "The Response of Business to Social Regulation in England and Wales" (1993) 15 *Law & Policy*, 199; K. Hawkins, "The Use of Legal Discretion: Perspectives from Law and Social Science", in Hawkins (ed.), *The Uses of Discretion* (1992).

ophy, as did that of some of the consumer protection officers with whom I worked as a participant observer. Not only were some consumer protection offences very close to traditional crime, but like Richard Mahony I was troubled by how the economically powerful could render the law pliable.

In the 1970s black letter lawyers could largely ignore socio-legal studies; it was a marginal activity. Characteristically with some progressive movements the strongest critics emerged from those ostensibly sympathetic.[23] Theoretically uninspired, said one camp, although nothing could have been further from the truth with my immediate contemporaries[24], nor with the three major publications which guided my own research – Kit Carson's seminal article on the factory inspectorate, Skolnick's study of the police, and Paul Rock's marvellous book on debt collection.[25] Too concentrated on rule implementation at the expense of the rules themselves, was a second criticism, again inaccurate in the light even of the then current research.[26] And then, not unexpectedly, the criticism that socio-legal studies were too concerned with Fabian social engineering, and not with "transcending the legal order" – the glib and recurrent war cry of the employed radical. Again I find it difficult to tar all my immediate contemporaries with that brush, although in my own case the Fabian ticket is one to which I have annually subscribed since those days.

Socio-legal studies has now come out of the shadows. Dons at Oxford no longer cross themselves at the Faculty Board when the discipline is mentioned. Large numbers of law schools claim to have some members engaged in socio-legal research, although the bulk is concentrated in a much smaller number, including Warwick.[27] There is a Socio-Legal Studies Association and Oxford University Press has two series devoted to the subject, Oxford Socio-Legal Studies for monographs, and Readings in Socio-Legal Studies intended for undergraduates. Now textbooks regularly incorporate the results of socio-legal research.[28] And socio-legal research has had important policy ramifications: it has thrown light on a range of questions from the efficacy of regulation, through the consequences of family breakdown, to the under-compensation of accident victims.[29]

---

[23] See Bankowski & Mungham, *Images of Law* (1976); C. Campbell & P. Wiles, "The Study of Law in Society in Britain" (1976) 10 *L. & Soc.R.* 547; D. McBarnet, "Pretrial Procedures and the Construction of Conviction", in Carlen (ed.), *The Sociology of Law* (1976), pp 176–177.

[24] Amongst my friends' work: Grace & Wilkinson, *Negotiating the Law* (1978); Paterson, *The Law Lords* (1982); Stewart, *Housing Action in an Industrial Suburb* (1981).

[25] W.G. Carson, "Some Sociological Aspects of Strict Liability and the Enforcement of Factory Legislation" (1970) 33 *MLR* 396; Skolnick, *Justice Without Trial* (1966) Rock, *Making People Pay* (1973).

[26] For example my own doctorate devoted a considerable chunk to characterising the rules; this was shorn from the published version, but provided the framework for *Consumers and the Law*, 1st ed. (1978), most of which was completed while I was at Warwick.

[27] See *Review of Socio-Legal Studies, Final Report*, Economic and Social Research Council (1994). I am grateful to Hazel Genn for showing me this in draft.

[28] In commercial law: Farrar *et al.*, *Company Law*, 3rd ed. (1991).

[29] See D. Harris, "The Development of Socio-Legal Studies in the United Kingdom" (1983) 3 *Legal Studies* 315; R. Cotterrell, "Sociology of Law in Britain: Its Development and Present Prospects" in Ferrari (ed.), *Developing Sociology of Law: A World Wide Documentary Enquiry* (1990).

In commercial law there is some nice work by Hugh Beale and his colleagues on how business people actually use contract law[30], Sol Picciotto's study of international business taxation is pathbreaking in using the public archives[31]; and Sally Wheeler's work on insolvency practitioners demonstrates yet again that what exercises the black letter lawyer is often moons away from the practice of law.[32] Much is to be learnt from the continuing research by Doreen McBarnet and Christopher Whelan on how commercial lawyers and their clients manipulate law and devise avoidance strategies.[33]

Yet we should not delude ourselves about a socio-legal triumph. There is still an uneven coverage. Take civil justice, in which I am currently interested as the academic adviser to Lord Woolf's inquiry into "access to justice". Very little money has been spent on understanding the civil justice process, and despite *Judicial Statistics* there is a paucity of basic information. Access to legal services attracted some important work by Oxford and Warwick contemporaries, although the vagaries of its publication means that it is now largely forgotten.[34] In recent times there has been ESRC funded research on access to legal services in rural areas, and the Lord Chancellor's Department, Law Commission and Legal Aid Board have sponsored some useful work.[35] But other aspects of the civil justice process are sorely neglected and in relation to the higher courts of England and Wales there is nothing comparable to studies elsewhere of delay and efficiency in civil litigation.[36] Moreover, there are no imitators of Alan Paterson's brilliant study, *The Law Lords*, and despite Hazel Genn's work on settlement in personal injury litigation, the lawyering process is still largely *terra incognita*.[37]

Empirical enquiry into the legal system is hard work. Evidence in some areas is almost impossible to obtain. Funding is difficult and often contingent on government having a particular concern in public policy principally, these days,

---

[30] H. Beale & T. Dugdale, "Contracts Between Businessmen: Planning and the Use of Contractual Remedies" (1975) 2 *Brit.J. L.&S.* 45; H. Beale, D. Harris & T. Sharpe, "The Distribution of Cars: A Complex Contractual Technique", in Harris & Tallon (eds), *Contract Law Today* (1989).

[31] Picciotto, *International Business Taxation* (1992).

[32] Wheeler, *Reservation of Title Clauses. Impact and Implications* (1991). See also, Rajak (ed.), *Insolvency Law Theory and Practice* (1993).

[33] D. McBarnet, "Legal Creativity: Law, Capital and Legal Avoidance", in Cain & Harrington (eds.), *Lawyers in a Post-Modern World* (1994); D. McBarnet & C. Whelan, "International Corporate Finance and the Challenge of Creative Compliance", in Fingleton (ed.), *The Internationalisation of Capital Markets and the Corporate Response* (1992).

[34] Partington, *Recent Developments in Legal Services for the Poor: Some Reflections on Experience in Coventry*, CDP Occasional Paper No. 13 (1975); Grace, *Community Need and Law Centre Practice*, Adamsdown Community Trust (1978). See also A. Byles & P. Morris, *Unmet Need* (1977); P. Morris, R. White & P. Lewis, *Social Needs and Legal Action* (1973). A personal concern with "unmet legal need" led a number of us to accompany Warwick law students giving advice at the Bath Place community centre in Leamington Spa: see A. Sherr & J. Webb, "Law Students, the External Market, and Socialisation" (1989) 16 *Brit.J.L. & Soc.* 225, 227.

[35] *E.g.* Blacksell, Economides & Watkins, *Justice Outside the City* (1991).

[36] Cranston, Haynes, Pullen & Scott, *Delay and Efficiency in Civil Litigation*, Australian Institute of Judicial Administration (1985) is a non-American example.

[37] Genn, *Hard Bargaining* (1987). See also her *Personal Injury Compensation: How Much is Enough?*, Law Comm. No. 225 (1994).

reducing costs. This can lead to particularistic, short-term research which lacks strategic vision.

Moreover, there is an intellectual challenge to socio-legal enquiry. Ironically it comes not from the profession, which although it still exercises an important influence on the production of academic legal knowledge is at worst indifferent, but generally welcomes, and indeed sometimes sponsors, empirical enquiry, albeit that it might have an immediate policy focus.[38] Rather the challenge comes from those who argue that legal research should disengage from empirical enquiry and concern with social reform. One strand of this argument is a fear of marginalisation if the researcher strays from conventional legal materials.[39] Socio-legal researchers will not be impressed by such defeatism. Another strand, postmodernism, denies that empirical enquiry can assist a true explanation of matters and indeed claims to have superseded it.[40] Empirical enquirers must concede, of course, that detachment from their subject is impossible and that the very act of describing is in many ways constitutive. Nevertheless, although empirical enquiries will never be able to mirror social reality, they at least enable us to draw better maps of it.

Thus the empirical side of law in context still struggles. The imbalance in legal research remains. Too many legal academics rework the same conventional materials in the same dreary way. A minority of theorists detach themselves from reality and disappear into the ether. Meanwhile, so many aspects of law's operation remain a mystery. So many of those affected by it are in no position to challenge its confiscating hand. Law schools are in default of their responsibility if they do not foster enquiries into the actual workings of the legal process and promote reforms of these.

In an oft quoted remark, Henry Handel Richardson's husband[41] characterised *The Fortunes of Richard Mahony* as a novel from first page to last concerned with money. Certainly money and its correlate, greed, pervade it. In the Proem to *Australia Felix* Richardson paints a canvas of the diggings where each miner is a jealous individualist hoping for a stupendous discovery. Although Mahony's early wealth derived from effort, his later fortune is made for him, quite unexpectedly, by a rise in some ironically named shares, "Australia Felixes". But towards the end of *The Way Home* fraud strikes: Mahony's new broker absconds to the United States with Mahony's fortune. The final blow is when Mahony burns his bonds and share certificates and leaves his family penniless.

Richardson makes us see the contingent nature of Mahony's wealth, in particular its relationship with market fluctuations in the price of shares. But markets

[38] *E.g Entry into the Legal Professions*, Legal Society Research and Policy Planning Unit Study No. 15, 1994; Joanna Shapland, V. Johnston & R. Wild, *Studying for the Bar*, Institute for the Study of the Legal Profession (1993).

[39] D. Jabbari, "Critical Theory in Administrative Law" (1994) 14 *Oxford Journal of Legal Studies* 189, 191.

[40] Cf. G. Teubner, "Regulatory law: chronicle of death foretold" (1992) 1 *Social & Legal Studies* 451.

[41] J.G. Robertson, Professor of German in the University of London 1903–1933.

are not perfectly functioning; non-economic factors might distort their operation. At one point Mahony recounts to his wife the details of a big mining suit:

> " ... This fellow Blake [whom] Purdy swears by was one of the partners in the company formed after old G. had sold his mine – at a dead loss, mind you, and on the express advice of his confidential manager, who, directly after, became a promoter of the new company. When the output suddenly redoubled and the shares began to soar, old Grenville naturally enough thought he had been done, and sued them for fraud. The jury could not agree. Now, there's a rumour of a settlement. If it takes place, it is calculated that the shares will rise in value by two to three hundred per cent. Purdy stands to make his fortune – thanks to having someone at his elbow who was in the swim." (TWH: 235–236)

Mahony regrets that his broker is an old slow coach: "One never gets any inside information from him – for the good reason that he doesn't know it himself". Warwick law students would recognise all this as involving misrepresentation, breach of fiduciary duty and fraud, all overlaid now by statute. But as well they would not be surprised at the intertwining of the legal and the economic.

Since the 1970s law and economics has been a growth area. The American law journals are heavily laden with articles about it and there are specialist publications almost entirely devoted to it, such as the *Journal of Law and Economics*, the *Journal of Legal Studies*, and the *International Review of Law and Economics*. There is even the regular article in mainstream law journals.[42] Indeed the best evidence that the subject had arrived in the English legal world was an article published in 1980 in *The Law Quarterly Review*, co-authored by my doctoral supervisor.[43] In "Contract Remedies and Consumer Surplus", the authors took the decision in *Radford* v *De Froberville*[44] as a starting point, and the lament of Oliver J that there are so few general principles for the award of damages in contract. They argued that the economist's notion of consumer surplus – the subjective value obtained from a "good" over and above the utility associated with its market price – could provide a benchmark for deciding on damages under consumer contracts when considerations like loss of profits or the remedy of specific performance were inappropriate. Consumer surplus could be assessed by means of the reasonable person test – what value would a reasonable person in the promisee's position have put on the consumer surplus which he reasonably expected from performance of the promise?

As this example illustrates, law and economics is imperialistic. Economic analysis is applied to legal phenomena outside the traditional area of markets. The basic concern is how law and legal institutions act as a pricing mechanism, offering incentives or disincentives to behaviour. People are assumed to choose

---

[42] *E.g.* A Ogus, *et al.*, "Evaluating Alternative Dispute Resolution" (1990) 53 *MLR* 57; R. Flannigan, "The Fiduciary Obligation" (1989) 9 *Oxford Journal of Legal Studies* 225.
[43] (1979) 96 *LQR* 581.
[44] [1977] 1 WLR 1262.

rationally to maximise utility. If feasible, parties may trade legal (property) rights to achieve this. A glance at a few of the recent issues of the specialist journals shows that economic concepts have been applied to a wide range of problems in substantive law (contract, tort, crime), legal procedure and the administration of the law.

One puzzle is why law and economics has not had the same popularity here as in the United States. One factor must be the history of English legal education and its generally conservative and anti-intellectual bias. But apart from the long tradition of resistance to innovation, another factor must be that the realists in the United States, by discrediting legal formalism, opened the door to new movements such as this.[45] The importance of Richard Posner's powerful synthesis and statement, *Economic Analysis of Law*[46], in acting as a lodestar, cannot be underestimated. Culturally the United States has always been more wedded to free market ideas than Britain, with its important collectivist tradition. The Reagan years in particular acted as a catalyst for much anti-regulation theorising, although despite Mrs Thatcher there was surprisingly no comparable law and economics boom here. (Indeed, in the United Kingdom the practice of privatisation has not shown much respect for the economic principle of competitive markets.) Finally, there are the practical considerations, notably the large sums of American money available for law and economics summer programmes designed to get law school teachers (some of whom already had undergraduate degrees in economics) up to speed in the subject. What the SSRC provided in this country for its seminars in law and economics was puny by comparison.

In 1976, as a young lecturer at Warwick, I presented a paper at one of these SSRC seminars on law and economics. With all the arrogance of youth I sought to cast doubt on the value of much of the law and economics literature. Although this was interpreted as a general attack on law and economics, it was intended to be aimed specifically – a point which should have been clear by the use throughout the paper of the term "the Chicago approach".[47] Although much of this writing purported (and purports) to be positive rather than normative – simply measuring legal rules, procedures and administration against criteria such as efficiency – much of it contains the very clear policy prescription that there should be a massive withdrawal by government from economic and social life. I could not, and still cannot, accept the jaundiced view that regulation "invariably achieves modest results at significant costs".[48] At an ideo-

[45] See J. Schlegel, "American Legal Realism and Empirical Social Science: From the Yale Experience" (1979) 28 *Buffalo Law Review* 459; J. Ziegel, "What can the Economic Analysis of Law teach Commercial and Consumer Law Scholars?" in Cranston & Goode (eds.), *Commercial and Consumer Law. National and International Dimensions* (1993), p 251.

[46] 1st ed. (1972).

[47] "Creeping Economism: Some Thoughts on Law and Economics" (1977) 4 *British J L & Soc.* 103. A footnote on youthful publishing: the proofs came back without the diagrams, which I again inserted. I never saw them again before publication; the printers got them hopelessly wrong. Always insist on checking any correction that is not straight text!

[48] C. Veljanowski, *The Economics of Law*, Hobart Paper 114 (1990), p 73. On issues such as rent control and the minimum wage (*ibid.*, pp 39, 77) see my *Legal Foundations of the Welfare State* (1985), pp 114–120.

logical level my major objection to the commercialisation of public life which this view has entailed in recent decades has been that it glosses over the distributional consequences.

The 1976 paper was unsophisticated, although I still believe its basic argument to be correct: that the absolute faith which most of the law and economics literature has in the market and the common law is misplaced. In one strand of the literature that faith derives from a belief that markets and courts operate in a manner which maximises efficiency when compared with legal regulation.[49] Another strand speaks of government being infected by special interest groups so that the process is concerned more with wealth distribution than efficiency.[50] This latter argument, which reflects the peculiar reality of the American political process, has been too readily applied outside the United States. In general terms the refutation of the law and economic approach is based on the notions that markets fail, that in cost-benefit terms it might be better to have government regulation than to improve on a market, and that there are important values like justice and fairness which in particular cases trump economic goals such as efficiency. Methodologically too there are flaws with law and economics. The analysis often begins with assumptions which are simplistic and unreal, theories are then built on the basis of these assumptions without regard to the complexity of social matters, and plausible explanations which do not square with the theory are ignored or glossed over. The empirical data which is used to "prove" theories is sometimes quite thin and of an unsystematic, anecdotal nature. Where it is of a detailed statistical nature it often lacks the unambiguous quality with which it is presented, but is massaged to fit the argument.[51]

Nevertheless, my brush with law and economics while I was at Warwick was not entirely negative. It has led me to have an episodic concern with this mode of analysis, even if only to refute its conclusions. Certainly lawyers cannot ignore it; as Richard Mahony's life illustrates, the economic is pervasive. At the technical level there is no doubt that much valuable economic work about the legal system could be done, for example on the issue of the cost of litigation and the legal process.[52] Economics also gives us the important touchstone of efficiency for the use of legal resources. More generally, economics contributes the particular insight that legal choices are not costless. People might respond to a legal change, even if only marginally, in ways that cast doubt on the planned ways of making it. Thus the regulated have an incentive to minimise the effects of government regulation which must be taken into account in its design. But

[49] The public choice end of the literature has highlighted self-interested behaviour in government and in promoting government regulation. The second has, in my own area of interest, been pursued by historians: *e.g.* Kolko, *The Triumph of Conservatism* (1967). As to the former I doubt whether self-interest alone is an especially helpful way to understand political or bureaucratic behaviour.

[50] On common law efficiency see my *Law, Government and Public Policy* (1987), pp 139–140.

[51] In addition to the references in the immediately preceding footnotes, see my "Consumer Protection and Economic Theory", in Duggan (ed.), *Consumer Protection Law and Theory* (1980); and *Law and Economics* (1982), jointly edited with Anne Schick.

[52] See H. Gravelle, "Rationing trials by waiting: welfare implications" (1990) 10 *International Review of Law and Economics* 255.

economics cannot provide the whole truth. As we see on various occasions in *The Fortunes of Richard Mahony* markets are distorted. And, of course, as Richard Mahony's life testifies, while people strive for the economic there are other values which move them as well.

In the prime of his life, and with his newly acquired wealth, Richard Mahony retires from medical practice and builds up a large library. He decides first to read all the works of "the great moderns: those world-famous scientists and their philosophic spokesmen who dominated the intellectual life of the day" (TWH:138). After weeks of this Mahony is troubled:

> "Riding on the crest of the highest wave of materialism that had ever broken over the world, they themselves were satisfied that life and its properties could be explained, to the last iota, in terms of matter; and, dogmatically pronouncing *their* interpretation of the universe to be the only valid one, they laid a crushing veto on any suggestion of a possible spiritual agency." (TWH, 139)

Like Mahony I too am troubled, in my case by some of the "great moderns" of legal philosophy. My concern is not because I am unsympathetic to legal theory. As Holmes correctly said, it is the most important part of the law, as the architect is the most important person in the building of a house. I tutored in the subject at Warwick and in two law schools have used what influence I had on developments in the curriculum to ensure legal theory was a compulsory subject.[53]

Perhaps one of my problems is simply keeping pace with the latest intellectual fashion when theory is necessarily a sideline to other time consuming tasks. When I was at Warwick, apart from the classics, Marx, Weber and Durkheim, two names on everyone's lips were the alliterative Poulantzas and Pashukanis. Tragically, Poulantzas cut short his own life not, it seems, to become an icon. One had no sooner mastered Pashukanis' attempt to put legal form centre stage than the opinion makers in modern legal theory declared him to be ahistorical.[54] Foucault came and faded, although like Mahony's Australia Felixes his stock seems yet again to be on the rise.[55] And one now struggles with feminist legal theory and other aspects of post-modernism, afraid that at any moment one's current, inconclusive reading will be declared passé.

A second, practical problem with theory is posed by the students. Many find legal theory indigestible, yet simplifying for them is ridden with traps. Moreover, many students are what J.W. Hurst used to call "bastard pragmatists", impatient with anything which does not equip them for the here and now of passing the examinations and practising law. Talk theory to them in commercial law and they turn off. Nevertheless, students are importantly functional to legal theory, as to other academic writing, for much of it would remain unread without being assigned reading.

---

[53] As chair of the curriculum committee at the Law School, ANU and Dean of the Faculty of Laws at Queen Mary and Westfield College.

[54] Pashukanis, *Law and Marxism* (1978, originally 1929).

[55] Hunt & Wickham, *Foucault and the Law* (1994).

A third problem with theory is that it rather than law can become the organizing charter of the academic's work. Geoffrey Wilson has noted this tendency to concentrate on what were originally "preliminaries" to such an extent "that the general effect has been centrifugal and what began as a preliminary study has ended up a study for its own sake with little direct relation to law". [56] Impressionistically this disease seems to have stuck some American law schools, when the agenda is set by theories from economics, literature, philosophy and so on as if law itself has nothing general to say and no agenda of its own. The unfortunate corollary of all this is that the law schools are increasingly divorced from the concerns of lawyers, judges and law reformers. Not only do the latter find themselves in difficult currents without any scholarly assistance, but they feel an undertow in the law schools distinctly hostile and to be avoided.

Mahony found an absence of the spiritual in his "great moderns". This is not one of my major concerns with modern legal theory, although it does make my memory race back to the Marxist reading groups I observed at Warwick in the mid-1970s and their similarity to the Sunday School bible classes of my childhood. But the dogmatism and absolute certainty which Mahony detected in his "great moderns" do have a definite resonance. One does not object so much to claims by the proponents of a particular approach that it is pathbreaking; that is only natural. What sticks in the craw is the disparagement of any other approach by those who have discovered the holy grail (albeit that the holy grail changes from year to year). Of course one should simply be resigned by now to periodic repetition of the canard that law in context is atheoretical and cannot provide the framework for a true understanding.[57] Stripped of the rhetoric, the substantive scholarship produced by those of that view often has remarkable similarities with what law in context aims to achieve.

Perhaps puzzlement is my instinctive reaction to some of the "great postmoderns". Law in context has always sought to move legal scholarship away from the centrality of the text, and here it is back in the limelight. The focus is, of course, different. The black letter scholars are rationalisers: they want to state and explain the law, criticise its inconsistencies and wrong turnings, and organise doctrine into a coherent and understandable picture. By contrast the deconstructionists are concerned with what the text does not directly express – they wish to understand its code, retrieve the "other" (what is not expressed), supposedly with the aim of achieving a political or ethical reconstruction.[58] While some is incredibly dense, other post-modern work of this genre is both stylish and coruscates with images. But some post-modern work lies on the other side of the boundary from the law in context quest for understanding, solutions to social problems and some greater certainty in an uncertain world. While life's complexities can never be reduced to any one theme, even law in

---

[56] G. Wilson, "English Legal Scholarship" (1987) 50 *MLR* 818, 825.

[57] P. Ireland, I. Grigg-Spall & D. Kelly, "The Conceptual Foundations of Modern Company Law" in Fitzpatrick & Hunt (eds.), *Critical Legal Studies* (1987), p 149.

[58] *E.g.* Cornell *et al.* (eds.), *Deconstruction and the Possibility of Justice* (1992).

context's broad church finds it difficult to encompass the disconnectedness of some post-modern theory.

Social change runs through Richardson's novel. In *Australia Felix* we hear of the diggers' stand against the authorities at the Eureka stockade. They fail, but their failure becomes emblematic in the development of an Australian radical consciousness.[59] At a personal level we see social change. Thus many on the goldfields do well. Henry Ocock becomes Sir Henry Ocock, the lawyer's social mobility contrasting with Mahony's eventual social descent. From being a market gardener and alcoholic, Devine becomes a member of the Legislative Council, part of the colonial Establishment, along with Mahony's brother-in-law.

Embedded in law in context is a concern with social change, in particular with legal and social reform. While the focus of much of this concern in the non-criminal area has been with topics such as legal services, welfare provision and civil rights, some 20 years ago Maureen Cain put into words a constant theme of my own work, that attention needs to be given also to matters such as commercial behaviour, corporate organisation, and business regulation.[60]

Here let me mention just one aspect of the general theme, the belief still shared by many who could be labelled contextualists, that lawyers and the courts can be instruments of social change. For some, especially north Americans, this is because law itself embodies a moral order, a set of normative standards which can found transformative goals. For others, and this tends to be the dominant view in this country, the courts are part of the political process, institutions which cannot be isolated from community pressures. Interest groups can and should use the courts, just as they might use the legislature or the executive, to obtain their goals.[61]

There is no doubt that courts are part of the political process, engaged in the "authoritative allocation of values" and deciding "who gets what, when and how".[62] In exercising their power, the courts are not simply applying precedent or implementing legislative decisions, but are playing a creative and independent role in evolving common law and interpreting the often vague legislative mandate. Although a particular decision will involve only a limited number of parties, it may have a broader impact because others in similar positions use it to guide their behaviour. A court can change the impact of legislation by its interpretation and, as we have seen with the growth of administrative law in recent decades, can invalidate executive acts.[63] Yet despite all this, the courts' capacity to effect social reform should be viewed sceptically.

In my own approach to this issue the *Bank Nationalisation Case*[64] seared my

---

[59] Clark, *A History of Australia* (1978), Vol. 4, pp 61–83.

[60] M. Cain, "Poor Man's Law Rich Man's Law" (1975) 2 *British Journal of Law & Sociology* 61.

[61] See Harlow & Rawlings, *Pressure Through Law* (1993).

[62] To use the famous analysis of Lasswell, *Politics, Who Gets What, When and How* (1936).

[63] But *quaere* the impact of the latter on government behaviour: see my "Reviewing Judicial Review", in Genn & Richardson (eds.), *Administrative Law and Government Action* (1994).

[64] *Bank of New South Wales* v *Commonwealth* (1948) 76 CLR 1. See Crisp, *Ben Chifley*, 1960, pp 323–342, a book which greatly influenced me when I was about 15 or 16.

consciousness. That was the decision of the High Court of Australia which struck down the attempt of the post-war Labour Government in Australia to nationalise the banks. In that and subsequent decisions the High Court used the relevant section of the Constitution, designed to ensure a common market in the Australian federation, as a charter for private enterprise.[65] As a student at Harvard I caused consternation to the professor and American class by casting doubt on their collective belief that the courts were a useful instrument to achieve welfare rights. But even in that heyday of liberal decision-making by courts in the United States, every *Goldberg* v *Kelly*[66] was more than matched by a *San Antonio Independent School District* v *Rodriguez*.[67] I was bemused – despite the beguiling *Brown* v *Board of Education* – that Americans should have any other view than my own when over a long period their Supreme Court had struck down social legislation, such as health and safety regulation, before it changed tack in the 1930s to uphold New Deal legislation following, as Mr Dooley had put it, "th' iliction returns" and Roosevelt's court packing threat. Subsequent research in the United States into using courts to bring about social change confirmed my sceptical view.[68]

That view is more fully developed elsewhere, notably in my *Legal Foundations of the Welfare State*. A few words only are appropriate here. First, it is not primarily because judges are influenced by extra-legal views. In fact it is too simplistic to think of social commitment as always, or even mainly, a factor in judicial decision-making, even where the case being considered has clear implications for public policy.[69] A judge's decisions are shaped by a complex combination of the trend of precedent, legal craftsmanship, the peculiarities of the case, as well as his or her general disposition to any policy issues involved. The way these factors operate differs between judges, and for a particular judge can change with time, since judges, like other people, are not monolithic or necessarily frozen in their approach.

As important are the institutional limitations to social change through litigation. A claim must be capable of formulation in legal terms, it must be presented through the adversary process and the evidence which can be submitted is limited in scope. A judicial decision must be justified in terms of precedent, or the language of a statute, and be generally acceptable in terms of the canons of legal reasoning. The remedies of courts are limited when compared with those of the legislature and the executive. Put crudely, courts do not have the administrative machinery to implement complex decisions but must rely on

---

[65] See my *Law, Government and Public Policy* (1987), pp 136–137. See also Galligan, *Politics of the High Court* (1987).

[66] 397 US 254 (1970), where the Supreme Court held that procedural due process demanded a hearing before benefits were terminated.

[67] 411 US 1 (1973), where the Supreme Court rejected an equal protection challenge to what was clearly the unequal funding of public education in Texas.

[68] *E.g.* Horowitz, *The Courts and Social Policy*, 1977; Yackle, *Reform and Regret* (1989); Rosenberg, *The Hollow Hope* (1991).

[69] Of course it is one factor, a point made by a former Chancellor of the University of Warwick and a leading judge: Lord Radcliffe, *Not in Feather Beds* (1968), pp 212–216.

voluntary compliance by the parties or the assistance of the executive. Finally, the legislative and executive arms of government might reverse an adverse decision by statute, regulation or administrative act. All these factors limit what courts can achieve in the way of social reform, even if they are favourably disposed.

Legal education is not generally speaking a subject to raise the passions. On the whole it is a matter of indifference to practitioners. There are always grumbles, of course, that law graduates are deficient in basic skills such as gathering and marshalling facts, and effective communication. And occasionally the backwoodsmen of the profession or its bureaucrats march in and do great damage. Likewise, the average legal academic has only a passing interest in the subject, being too busy with his or her own special interest. If pressed most legal academics will defend a liberal model of legal education, where students pursue a deep understanding of matters, discover things for themselves, and develop an ability critically to evaluate, generalise from and apply material.[70] The trade school mentality will generally be rejected, where law is taught as a set of definite rules, to be learned rote without any reference to its intellectual derivation, social context or moral content. But beyond that the legal academic will have thought little. My own experience is, I suspect, typical – until recently only one article on legal education, and that a proselytizing piece on law in context.[71]

Recently my passions were aroused, however, when I was forced to take an interest in the Common Professional Examination.[72] The story of the CPE can be briefly recounted. The Ormrod Committee, established in December 1967 to examine the whole of legal education, recommended that the normal mode of entry into the profession should be by way of a law degree. However, it accepted that other classes of candidate should be eligible, although in most cases a university degree should be a prerequisite. In general its philosophy was that schemes of training should not be unnecessarily rigid or over-demanding in time, lest abler persons should be discouraged from entering the profession, nor should standards be so high that the profession would be deprived of valuable members. Consequently the Committee recommended a common professional examination for non-law graduates which should include five "core" subjects together with at least three optional subjects to be studied in the main over a two year period.[73]

In 1979 the Benson Royal Commission endorsed the Ormrod recommendation that the law degree should be the normal mode of entry to the profession, but also agreed that there was a need to continue with non-law graduate entry,

---

[70] See D. Oliver, "Teaching and Learning Law"; W. Wilson & G. Morris, "The Future of the Academic Law Degree", in Birks (ed.), *Reviewing Legal Education* (1994); R. Goode, "The Academic Stage of Legal Education: A Non-Vocational View", *Law Society's Gazette*, No. 13, March 30, 1988, p 12.

[71] "Law and Society: A Different Approach to Legal Education" (1978) 5 *Monash LR* 54.

[72] As Vice-President, then President of the Society of Public Teachers of Law. I drafted the SPTL report *The Future of the CPE* (1992), from which some of the following is taken.

[73] *Report of the Committee on Legal Education*, Cmnd. 4595, 1971.

which it said produced a number of promising recruits with valuable knowledge of other fields. It observed that the Lord Chancellor's Advisory Committee on Legal Education had thought that a year was all that was necessary for the common professional examination. The Commission then concluded that bearing in mind that students would already have studied a degree for three years, it was reasonable "to restrict the topics covered in order to enable the course to be dealt with in one year".[74] It seemed that financial, not academic, considerations were the basis of this conclusion. Thus when the CPE began formally in 1979 it was of one year's duration, with six "core" subjects and no options. The CPE mode of entry ballooned from the 1980s because of political pressures, because of what was perceived as a shortage of lawyers and because financial pressures forced many law schools to raise money other than through LLB teaching.

There has never been any detailed consideration subsequent to the Ormrod Report as to whether one year's study provides an adequate foundation of legal knowledge, nor as to why the one year CPE differs in its length from what is required in every other jurisdiction for non-law graduates who wish to become lawyers. For a time the view was widespread that CPE graduates performed better than law graduates in professional courses necessary to qualify as either a solicitor or barrister. Detailed examination of the statistics which are available reveals, however, that basically there is no difference between CPE and law graduates.[75] Anecdotal evidence, and the views expressed in questionnaires returned by a very small sample of solicitors' firms, indicate that practitioners are relatively satisfied with CPE graduates.[76] It seems fair to say that one reason for this satisfaction has nothing to do with legal knowledge, but is because of their maturity as compared with the average law graduate. No law firms have monitored the performance of CPE graduates in any systematic way. There is now clear evidence that on the whole they come from the wealthier classes, which is not surprising given that most have to fund what is an expensive year themselves given that public money is not generally available.[77]

My personal view is that CPE lawyers, who in many cases are very bright, do not on the whole have the fundamentals of a good legal education. One year is not enough time to study the core itself, for with skills based vocational training there is not an adequate opportunity for maturation and for building on the foundations. Moreover, there is the threat to the diversity of law schools as options are devalued, and there is also the impoverishment of legal science because of the implicit assumption that difficult questions are easily answered.

---

[74] *Royal Commission on Legal Services*, Cmnd. 7648, 1979, v.2, p. 633.

[75] See *The Future of the CPE*, Appendix (by Sharon Bowles).

[76] *Ibid.*, pp 18–22. With hindsight this research was profoundly inadequate in another way, besides the small sample. It is not apparent on the face of the report, but those who replied to the questionnaire were, in the main, the training officers of the law firms contacted, not those at the coal-face of legal practice. While training officers will be able to say something about the relative performance of the two types of graduate, they will not have a full view.

[77] *Entry into the Legal Professions*, Law Society Research and Policy Planning Unit Study No. 15, 1994.

Law in context is as threatened as traditional legal education by this quick fix to what reveals itself to be a lawyer surplus, not shortage.[78]

There is, however, another law in context point here. That concerns what seems to be true: that CPE lawyers do as well in practice as full-time law graduates. One also recalls Posner's arresting illustrations for his assertion that the greatest figures in American law have been those who have transcended the traditional conceptions of the lawyer's craft.[79] One obvious reason for the success of CPE graduates is that until recently they were the very best graduates of other disciplines. Another is the specialisation in the large City law firms and in important parts of the Bar, so that all new lawyers start on a relatively equal footing when it comes to matters such as capital markets or shipping law. And finally, it must also have something to do with the nature of modern lawyering. In the big City firms, for example, this has as much to do with consummating deals as with legal analysis, for we are in the age of the lawyer-businessman. At partner level lawyering is in large part about attracting and retaining clients and organising the work of others. For many partners and associates much modern lawyering in City firms is also mass process, routine work – the drafting of documents, or at least the adaptation of documents from the precedent bank – although there will always be unique legal issues associated with some aspects and real creativity demanded. The nature of modern lawyering is a matter which urgently needs research; it is a matter fitted for law in context studies.

Henry Handel Richardson spent only the early part of her life in Australia, but it marked her indelibly. She escaped the provincialism of English education of the time, and avoided in her writing the inward looking, socially narrow range of most contemporary English novelists.[80] Society needs its non-conformists and outsiders if it is better to understand and change. In my days at the University of Warwick the law school was peopled by intellectual iconoclasts like Geoffrey Wilson and Patrick Atiyah, and those such as William Twining and Patrick McAuslan who had had their horizons widened in the United States and Africa. There was also the occasional North American and Antipodean to leaven the mix yet further.

In this post-modern world I still remain rooted in the cluster of concerns I had around my time at Warwick. I have touched on some of them in this chapter. Can anyone deny that we are still grossly ignorant of the workings of the legal system and legal institutions, and need more socio-legal research? As well as furthering our understanding empirical studies in the law can suggest ideas for law reform and can base a critique of law's values. Law and economics has proved a damp squib in Britain and much of its literature is, in my view,

---

[78] P. Birks, "Shortcuts", in Birks (ed.), *Reviewing Legal Education* (1994).

[79] Posner, *The Problems of Jurisprudence* (1990), p 452. Posner mentions Justice Jackson who did not graduate from law school, Cardozo who left before taking a degree, Learned Hand who failed in practice, and Holmes. The point about transcending law is surely correct. See also p 425.

[80] Possibly for the same reason she was not taken up by the English literary world, although she spent most of her life in this country. Certainly she was not part of the self-promoting, gossipy set, which as in academic life gives some second raters an unwarranted credibility.

flawed. But we cannot escape its great insight; that law functions to affect choice – to put it another way, that law is never costless. Then there is legal theory: without constant, systematic reflection about law and the legal system, we will be unconscious prisoners of unarticulated premises and unable to comprehend multi-layered reality. The danger is in pursuing legal theory for its own sake: a move too far in the direction of theory will result in the voice of the legal academic being confined to the academy and even there being heard by an ever diminishing band. Finally there is the paramountcy of a liberal legal education. We must resist anything which devalues it or which pushes law schools in the direction of trade schools. It is the law schools which enlighten our understanding about law, which gives birth to new ideas for the legal system, and which educate many of society's leaders. Training for immediate professional practice would negate the obligations for law schools which each of these entail. Law in context is a key element of liberal legal education; Warwick law school is its beacon.

Chapter 2

LEGAL EXPLORATIONS IN DIFFERENT LANDS

Professor Michael Chesterman
University of New South Wales

This chapter draws on my experience as a law teacher in the School of Law at Warwick University ("Warwick") for five years, between 1973 and 1978, and in the Faculty of Law at the University of New South Wales ("UNSW") for more than twelve years (1979–83, 1987 to the present day) to discuss some themes about newly-created, exploring, "rebellious" law schools within the common law world.

During the 1960s and 1970s, numerous academic lawyers in England and Australia conducted a minor rebellion against a seemingly overpowering orthodoxy. At that time, most long-established law schools focused their teaching almost exclusively on the positivist inculcation, primarily through lectures, of "the legal principles" (or, as they were sometimes called, "the concepts"), in order, so it was thought, to cater for the educational needs of the practising profession. Scarcely anything else seemed to be attempted by legal educators in these two countries.

The rebellion involving Warwick and UNSW was not, of course, the only rebellion going on inside academe, let alone outside it. Marxism and allied political philosophies flourished within a broader reaction to a long post-war period of conservatism. But this mini-rebellion is the academic movement most relevant to the founding and the first 20 or 25 years of the Law Schools at Warwick and UNSW.

1. Warwick: The "Contextual Path"

In the case of Warwick, the infusion of radical politics into academic law may in fact have seemed *déjà vu* to some observers. The phenomenon of newly established law schools offering radical challenges to the intellectual hegemony of older ones had already occurred, for example, when the Law Department at the London School of Economics challenged Oxbridge orthodoxies during the 1920s and 1930s.[1] The establishment during the 1960s of the "plate glass" universities, of which Warwick was one, provided another breeding ground in which a new school could make its mark by challenging prevailing views.

A further influential factor specific to the Warwick Law School was the fundamental rethinking of the goals of law teaching that several of its founding and comparatively early staff (including myself) had been impelled to carry out through having taken advantage of the opportunities then available to spend some time teaching in one of the newly-created law schools of post-colonial Africa. Whether that law school was avowedly radical, like Dar es Salaam (where a number of early Warwick staff had been) or comparatively conservative, like Nairobi (where I had spent a year), the first-hand view that one obtained of the results of the imperial imposition of common law principles and institutions on alien cultures inevitably prompted profound questionings of (amongst other things) the basic role of university legal scholarship. In addition, one was inevitably stimulated by working alongside both indigenous African law teachers and teachers from other common law countries, notably the United States.

Curriculum content

At the time of my arrival there, Warwick (the Law School, that is) was about six years old. It was clear by then that while the educational rebellion occurring there called for sustained intellectual exploration and innovation in the development of subject syllabuses and teaching materials, it did not take the form of a rigorous pursuit of specific, rigorously defined educational goals. The legal education sought to be offered at Warwick could principally be defined by what it was not. At all costs, it was not to be "black letter". If there was a word that described what it was supposed to be, the word was "contextual" though even this inherently vague term was seen by some as suspect, because it was compatible with only superficial re-ordering of traditional legal material.

For me at least, this made the early months at Warwick a far from relaxing experience. It was a place where your colleagues might (for instance) be "contextualising" Family Law by teaching it against a background of genetics[2] or addressing the theme of corporate governance by devoting a segment of the Business Organisations course to the operation of worker-controlled enterprises in Yugoslavia. It was easy to feel paranoiac when preparing teaching materials at a photocopier. A colleague might pass by and utter the fateful words: "Hmm ... looks rather BLACK-LETTER to me...".

It was also very exciting. All teachers in the School, whether experienced or

[1] See *e.g.* C. Glasser, "Radicals and Refugees: The Foundation of the Modern Law Review and English Legal Scholarship" (1987) 50 *MLR* 688.

[2] I remember being somewhat taken aback by seeing an exam question in this subject which required the students to formulate family law principles that would be appropriate for a species of mythical troilistic being in which the co-operation of three of them was necessary to conceive a baby.

comparatively junior, had virtually sole responsibility for the subjects (or, in some cases, sections of subjects) that they were teaching. They were free, indeed strongly encouraged, to experiment with whatever interdisciplinary approach they had decided to adopt.

In hindsight, I have no doubt that the ethos of Warwick over the last 25 years (and of a few other like-minded British law schools during the same period), requiring continued exploration of law's interrelation with other modes of study (history, sociology, political theory, economics, genetics, whatever else one might choose), was of very great value in advancing law's claim to be treated at last as a genuine academic discipline in England – perhaps as a social science, possibly one of the humanities. Later, I will touch briefly on the question whether this status has in fact been achieved.

Teaching and assessment methods

For someone who had chiefly worked in a fairly traditional law school, the approach to assessment adopted at Warwick was also innovative and refreshing. As was appropriate in a law school which was trying to develop new perspectives on legal subject-matter, students were strongly urged to conduct their own explorations, both in the library and by means of empirical investigations. Research essays were a major form of assessment, though traditional problem-based examinations were also used.

In mild contrast, teaching methods were generally not (as I recall them) particularly innovative. The familiar programme of lectures supplemented by tutorials for each subject operated, though on account of the School's concern to promote academic exploration by maintaining the autonomy of individual teachers within their own subjects, these were generally conducted by the same person.

Relationship to other schools in the University

Because the Warwick Law School pursued interdisciplinary perspectives (and also because it was located in a social sciences building, it built up reasonably good links with academics in related fields, such as sociology and social history. In 1979, a joint Law–Sociology degree course was created, including a couple of subjects each of which was jointly taught, with genuinely interdisciplinary aims, by a member of each school.

Relationship to legal practice and other external constituencies

Warwick's attitude to the practising legal profession was interesting. Unlike some radical law schools of the time, it did not teach a subject or carry out research submitting the profession (its structure, regulatory practices, ethics etc) to critical scrutiny. Nor was it overtly antagonistic to the profession and its members. It seemed rather to ignore them. This was consistent with its concept of law as primarily a subject for academic scrutiny within an appropriate disciplinary context. Preserving this autonomy was all the easier because the imperatives imposed on the LLB degree by the rules governing admission to practice went no further than requiring some sort of coverage of the "Ormrod Six" – Contract, Tort, Land Law, Criminal Law, Constitutional Law and Trusts.[3]

There was a degree of concern within the School at the fact that its graduates, including many of the best ones, did conspicuously poorly when, in order to gain admission as solicitors, they had to face a gruelling set of closed-book, "black-letter" questions on "practitioner subjects" (Conveyancing, Succession etc) in the Law Society Part II Examination. I am not sure, however, that anything much was done within Warwick's LLB programme to alleviate this problem. It was considered that equipping students to handle this particular type of anti-intellectual ordeal was not a proper function for a university education in law. The students were left to find out for themselves how best to adapt the study techniques developed at Warwick for the very different exercise of passing Part II.

In one specific sense, Warwick did engage with legal practice. It was one of the few English law schools to establish a clinical subject, in which students obtained credit towards their LLB degree by acting as legal advisers and (within limits) legal representatives for real-life clients. It had recourse to local community law centres and legal advice centres to provide the necessary cases. But by the standards of at least one other clinical programme of the time, at the University of Kent, Warwick's offering in this area was fairly modest. It was also typical of Warwick, in that, at least in the early days, the mode of assessment was a research essay based on some social or theoretical topic emanating from one or more of the cases handled by the student, or on some theoretical aspect of the solicitor–client relationship. Warwick, in short, sought to "contextualise" legal practice, along with virtually all the other legal subjects that it taught.

Other external legal constituencies – for example, public sector lawyers, in-house corporate lawyers, law reform agencies – were also generally outside Warwick's range of interactions. Its location outside London, indeed outside a major city (the comparatively few miles between the campus and the Coventry business centre constitutes a long way in this context), encouraged this sense of remoteness from places where law was administered or determined in a large-scale way.

---

[3] See Report of the Committee on Legal Education (The Ormrod Committee), Cmnd 4595, HMSO, 1971, para 108.

2. UNSW: One of Australia's "Second Wave"

When the Law School at UNSW commenced teaching in 1971, it was only the second university law school in New South Wales.[4] The first such school, at the University of Sydney, had since its establishment in 1890 maintained a comparatively small full-time staff. Much of its teaching, particularly in the later years of the LLB, was done by visiting practitioners.

The potential for dominance of practitioner imperatives was, and still is, further assisted by the fact that the LLB was expected to cover all the subjects that an incoming barrister or solicitor could be expected to have studied. There was, and still is, no equivalent of the Law Society's Part II Examinations. This produces, amongst other things, a strong reliance on half-year subjects, which make endeavours like "contextualisation" difficult because there is less teaching time in a subject to expose students to relevant non-legal material.

On the other hand, law was, and still is, generally studied in Australia as a second degree, or as the second component in a double-degree programme lasting at least five years (for example Arts–Law, Economics–Law, Science–Law). Potentially at least, this provides scope for interdisciplinary treatment of legal material in the LLB, as well as for study at a more advanced level than in England. The students are well experienced in tertiary study by the time they reach the later stages of the LLB.

UNSW, like Warwick, thus had close to hand a similar model of traditional legal education to rebel against. But the style of its rebellion was different, in interesting ways, from that of Warwick.

Curriculum content

Although it had a firm determination to react against traditional modes of teaching "black-letter law", UNSW had no universally held commitment to interdisciplinary broadening, or "contextualising", of the content of its LLB syllabuses. In a number of specific subjects, this did occur: new and interesting perspectives, sometimes politically radical ones, were energetically pursued. But there was no collective ethos putting such endeavours high on the list of School priorities.

On arriving at UNSW in 1979, I had first-hand experience of this. The Trusts course which I had developed at Warwick in an effort to "contextualise" this subject was markedly different from the UNSW one, in which a relatively traditional case-book provided the material for Harvard-style case-method teaching. In contrast to Warwick, where Trusts was *de facto* compulsory because of Ormrod requirements, it was an elective at UNSW. After a period of

[4] On legal education in Australia, see generally M. Chesterman and D. Weisbrot, "Legal Scholarship in Australia" (1987) 50 *MLR* 709.

occasionally tricky negotiation, it was agreed that the students who wished to do Trusts should be able to make an informed choice between the two available versions.

A "second wave" law school in Sydney which more strenuously sought, like Warwick, to include interdisciplinary perspectives in the teaching of law was Macquarie Law School, established in 1975. It became riven, however, by academic dispute, in which "trad" and "rad" views were in bitter opposition. One of the numerous reasons for this was, in my view, that those "rad" School members who were committed to sweeping curriculum innovations in the LLB adopted a distinctly less pluralist approach than was to be found at Warwick. At Warwick, it was not a matter of "anything goes", but exploration ("contextualisation") of any sort was given at least a provisional green light by most if not all School members.

Teaching and assessment methods

Having, as I said earlier, found aspects of Warwick's teaching and assessment to be innovative and refreshing, I was surprised to discover that in this area its efforts were outstripped by UNSW. Here, there were firm and enduring School resolutions and practices which:

- outlawed monologue lectures (and with them small tutorials),
- maintained classes at a size (initially 25–30, now for resource reasons 35–40) which in the view of the School permitted genuine student discussion,
- enjoined students fairly firmly to read prescribed materials (reproduced in large quantities by a very active and efficient School printroom) before they attended class,
- strongly encouraged (indeed, for a while, virtually mandated) teachers to include a mark for student participation in class discussion,
- encouraged a wide range of other assessment techniques (to be used in combination as the subject teacher(s) proposed), including moots, take-home exams, research essays and drafting exercises, so as effectively to outlaw 100% examinations,
- encouraged teachers to set open-book rather than closed-book examinations,
- required teachers to submit to the Head of School, before the start of each semester, an outline of the objectives and content of their subject, an outline of the proposed assessment strategy and a statement as to how this strategy conformed with the stated objectives,
- maintained from early days a standing School committee concerned explicitly with the improvement of teaching and assessment techniques.

UNSW's reaction against traditional law teaching thus focused more clearly on pedagogy than on content. No doubt, its divergence in this regard from other "rebellious" schools like Warwick was partly attributable to American influences, which overall tend to weigh more heavily – in numerous aspects of life, not merely legal education and scholarship – in Australia than in England. Often, the Harvard–Langdell socratic mode was said to describe what UNSW used, or at least aspired to, though my impression is that even from the outset its approach was distinctly softer and more eclectic than this implies.

An interesting illustration of the strength of UNSW's commitment to this approach to teaching occurred in 1989, when unintended over-enrolment of students and scarcity of resources led the School to propose for the following semester the introduction of "large" classes (65 or thereabouts, unsupported by tutorials) for a significant proportion of the LLB subjects. The students mounted an ultimately successful campaign of resistance, in which the principal industrial tactic was a strike of silence. They attended classes, but collectively refused to answer questions or participate in any way in class discussion. The degree of upset to the School and its self-image was palpable. There was probably no more effective way of striking at the School's sense of its own educational worth.[5]

Relationship to other schools in the University

At UNSW and elsewhere in Australia, as mentioned above, an LLB is taken either on graduate entry or as the second part of a double degree programme (BA/LLB, BCom/LLB etc). A double degree structure such as this would seem to encourage interdisciplinary collaboration between relevant schools. But in fact the Law School at UNSW has not pursued this. By and large, the two degrees that a "double degree" law student takes are studied in separate compartments. This fact is partly attributable to hostile location: the Law School is the lone academic unit in the upper floors of a tower block. But it also illustrates further the proposition that, in terms of curriculum content, UNSW has not sought to explore and innovate to the same extent as Warwick.

Relationship to legal practice and other external constituencies

As the second law school in Australia's largest city, UNSW was under stronger pressure than Warwick to define its relationship to the practising legal profession, i.e., not merely to appear to ignore it. Overall, this relationship was somewhat equivocal.

[5] For completeness, I should add that Macquarie Law School's "rebellion", as well as focusing explicitly on curriculum content, also embraced small group discussion-style teaching. It took this aspect of its work very seriously and has, on the whole, maintained smaller class sizes than UNSW. A former Head of Macquarie Law School has however publicly expressed the view that Macquarie probably took the lead from UNSW in this regard and that UNSW in fact brought about a "revolution" in Australian law teaching.

Initially, this relationship had, or was interpreted to have, distinct elements of confrontation. Some three years after it commenced teaching, UNSW introduced a compulsory single-session LLB subject, called Law, Lawyers and Society, which provided a distinctly critical outline of the structure, regulatory practices and ethics of the legal profession. Again, it was following American models to some extent. A substantial book of cases and materials was published shortly afterwards by the creators and teachers of the subject.[6] On a number of occasions, members of the NSW profession, which was generally in a somewhat defensive mood at this time of heady radical politics, denounced both the subject and the textbook as unfairly critical if not downright subversive. As late as 1983, recognition of Law, Lawyers and Society as satisfying the Legal Ethics component in the prerequisites for admission to the NSW Bar was temporarily withdrawn, apparently for this reason.

There were, however, contradictory tendencies. In particular, the evolving LLB at UNSW came to contain a number of elective subjects with a clearly practical orientation. These include two subjects focusing in different ways on trial advocacy, a subject, until 1981, offering experience of supervised placement in a legal office and, since 1981, clinical experience in a community legal centre founded and run by the School. As at Warwick, clinical legal education is not seen just as an introduction to practitioner skills and to the experience of taking responsibility for clients' legal problems. Its aims include deepening the students' understanding of legal principles and exposing them to the interaction of these principles with social and institutional realities. A significant difference, however, from Warwick's clinical subject is that the assessment at UNSW is pass/fail assessment based essentially on the student's performance in advising and assisting the centre's clients. The idea of a research essay in which the student is required to discuss his/her experience with client's cases within some broader theoretical context has never been adopted.

Other aspects of the law student's experience at UNSW reinforce this connection with his/her likely future career in some sort of law-related occupation, though not necessarily in private practice. These include a well developed compulsory LLB component on legal research skills (predictably, this focuses increasingly on computer retrieval) and a very active student-run programme of mooting. Overall, the transition to post-degree practical training and thence to practice has not been problematic for UNSW graduates, once the opposition to the perceived "subversiveness" of Law, Lawyers and Society started to die down.

When the relationship with external legal constituencies other than the practising profession is considered, there is again a clear contrast between UNSW and Warwick. Staff and indeed students at UNSW have maintained over many years a strong tradition of involvement with law reform programmes and agencies. Two out of a number of examples involving students may be cited. With

---

[6] J. Disney, J. Basten, P. Redmond and S. Ross, *Lawyers*, (1st edn, 1977, 2nd edn, 1986). The other leading critical study of the profession in Australia – D. Weisbrot, *Australian Lawyers* (1990) – also emanated from UNSW.

staff support, students took the lead some years ago in mounting a campaign to abolish imprisonment for fine defaulters in New South Wales. More recently, they established Australia's first regular newsletter on human rights, the *Human Rights Defender*. Staff are regularly engaged on a part-time basis writing or otherwise assisting with law reform submissions or reports for government or quasi-governmental agencies (such as the Family Law Council and the Australian Institute of Judicial Administration) or *ad hoc* official committees (such as the Prime Minister's Republic Advisory Committee). In several instances (the first was in 1976), they have obtained leave without pay for an extended period (typically, three years) to take up a full-time post as a law reform commissioner (Commonwealth or State) or some similar appointment. Accompanying these activities is a very high media profile: it is most unusual for a week to go by without at least one UNSW law teacher appearing somewhere in the Sydney media.

The Australian constitutional structure supplies 13 Commonwealth or State Houses of Parliament (plus some Territory ones), together with associated bureaucracies, to govern about 18 million people. The opportunities for a law school to engage in official or semi-official law reform are therefore much greater than in a comparatively sparsely-governed country such as England. UNSW has not been alone among Australian law schools in taking up these opportunities. But its involvement, both in absolute terms and measured per head of academic staff, would seem clearly to exceed that of any other school.[7] It constitutes one of the school's trademarks, one of the channels into which its "rebellious" energy has flowed.

I was fortunate enough to obtain one of these full-time appointments: I went on leave from UNSW to the Australian Law Reform Commission for three-and-a-half years, between 1983 and 1986. It required a relatively easy transition from the law reform ethos of UNSW. I have no doubt also that the prodding that I had received at Warwick to look continually for the relation between legal knowledge and other perspectives on social phenomena constituted very good preparation.

3. Some Themes from Two Rebellions

I am not sure that a great deal, in the way of general conclusions, can be drawn from this piecemeal comparison of two generally progressive law schools in whose work I happen to have participated. But a few specific observations may be justified.

---

[7] There have for instance been eight appointments from the School to full-time law reform commissionerships, if you include as one of them a long-term School member who applied for the post within 18 months of moving to another law school. The next highest number from a single school is three.

Scholar lawyers and "arguing" lawyers

First, it is interesting to compare the different models of a graduating lawyer that seem discernible in the different LLB programs that the two schools developed, each in reaction to traditional post-war black-letter law teaching.

The Warwick model, as I would define it, was first and foremost a scholar, whose understanding of the law was never unduly cribbed and confined by the law's own internal logic, but was situated as consistently as possible in some sort of understanding of society as a whole. While my description above may at times seem to imply that the activities of lawyers in society, such as Warwick's own graduates would mostly become, were tacitly deemed to be irrelevant to this sort of broad understanding of the law, it is probably more accurate to say that their relevance resided mainly in the light they cast on the development and changing dynamics of the law.

At UNSW, the model, arguably, is that of an "arguing" lawyer – arguing, that is, not just in the narrow sense that a barrister might do for a client, but in a broader sense that takes full account of the fact that neither the "is" nor the "ought" of law is ever fixed and certain, but is instead the proper subject of engaged and continuing debate. Within this model, which I see as rooted in UNSW's very conscious concern with active student learning, the relevance of practising lawyers and their activities is clear and direct. The UNSW model does indeed overlap greatly with the professional lawyer, provided that this term is given a broad connotation, extending well beyond the traditional private practitioner.

As already suggested, part of the explanation for these different emphases lies in the different situations of the two schools – the one, a comparatively small school in a provincial university, not bound by professional requirements to cover the "practitioner subjects" and therefore operating mainly in whole-year subjects; the other, a largish school in a capital city, effectively bound to offer in single-semester units a largish set of subjects ranging (in terms of "practitioner relevance") from Legal Theory to Conveyancing. There is also the empirical fact that the founding head of the former had been a Cambridge academic, while his equivalent in the latter was a Sydney QC.

A "teenage" rebellion?

In invoking the metaphor of rebellion to describe the innovative elements in the early work of these two law schools, I have at times been tempted to add the adjective "teenage". The implication would be that the reaction against traditional educational practices was vigorous, more or less necessary for growing up, perhaps excessive (depending on one's point of view and, no doubt, one's age) and bound in due course to subside into a more mature accommodation of the old and the new.

I believe that subsequent events suggest that the word "teenage", as so defined, is indeed applicable to some aspects of the "rebellion" of UNSW. I am referring in particular to the strident critiques of, and deliberate distancing from, the legal profession that characterised the early years of UNSW, Macquarie and some other newly-founded Australian schools during the 1970s.

The reasons for this are not hard to find. At the time of UNSW's establishment in 1971, the dominance of practitioner imperatives was remarkably strong in Australian legal education: it was challenged only by the efforts of a small handful of theorists such as Julius Stone. Until 1968, a non-university law course, conducted by professional admission boards, actually generated more admissions to legal practice than the Law School at Sydney. Part-time practitioners did a large part of the teaching, at this School and at other capital city law schools, since no genuine cohort of career academics in law existed, or indeed had ever existed. To illustrate this last point, when Australia's first association of professional law teachers had been created in 1946, it had only 13 members drawn from five law schools. It declared itself prepared to accept as a "law school" any appropriate institution that had as few as three full-time members.

It follows that in New South Wales (as elsewhere in Australia), the arrival of a second law school in a State capital city was an essential step in the creation, for the first time, of a sufficient critical mass of full-time law teachers to permit any sort of breakaway from the educational dominance of the local legal profession.

It was thus virtually inevitable that when a school such as UNSW came into being at a time of general political radicalism, it would want to challenge, more or less head on, the "parent" tradition of practitioner-dominated education. This was at least until academic lawyers as a group had sufficient size, maturity and self-confidence to confront practitioners as an independent body of legal experts who happened to be working in a domain of law other than practice.

I am not saying that this status of academic lawyers as an "independent but equal" group of legal experts has in fact been acknowledged by practitioners. But there is no doubt that their status, along with their numbers, has grown significantly within the legal world. I was strongly aware of this during my time at the Law Reform Commission, where the commissioners included senior practitioners and present and former judges as well as academics. Consequently, accommodation with, rather than confrontation of, practitioners describes the present-day attitude of UNSW – as indeed of other Australian law schools, whether they be older or younger than UNSW. In this sense, the "teenage" phase of UNSW's "rebellion" seems to have come to an end.

I am less sure about the epithet "teenage" for Warwick for three reasons. First, I know less about recent developments at Warwick than at UNSW. Secondly, Warwick's establishment was not part of the phase in England where the concept of a career as a law teacher had to be created: this had already occurred. Thirdly, as I have said, Warwick ignored rather than confronted the practising profession. Instead, it chiefly confronted traditional legal academe, a constituency which felt much less like an authoritarian, overbearing parent.

Focus on undergraduate study

My third comment draws attention to an important point of similarity between the two schools: namely, that each of them acted out its rebellion and made its mark through the development of an undergraduate degree programme. I suspect that this is the most common way in which new law schools in the common law world establish individuality. It may well be the only way, in contrast to other disciplines in which it could easily be a new research degree or school research programme that performed the same function.

If it is indeed the only way, or at least the only practicable way, one probably cannot say, to return to a question briefly addressed above, that law in the common law world has become a fully-fledged academic discipline. Law would appear to have had this status since "time immemorial" in continental Europe. It was always a learned scholarly field, side by side with such disciplines as philosophy and theology. But as appears clearly from the well-told tale of the common law's intellectual domination since the earliest days by the Inns of Court[8], there has been no such academic ascendancy on the part of the common law.

A pessimist might argue that this means that law has by now missed its chance to obtain this form of academic recognition. Given the current pressures on universities to cut costs and demonstrate national economic relevance in virtually everything they do, legal study is likely to have to continue sustaining its right to exist not in predominantly academic terms – as a true member of the family of humanities or social sciences – but on account of its vocational role. This provides little hope for a pronounced switch of emphasis towards high-level research. In contrast to medicine, law is not a field where practice, even at the most sophisticated and advanced level, requires significant postgraduate education, either of the research or coursework variety. A coursework masters in law may, in Australia at least, have become a standard "professional upgrade" qualification for those seeking partnership in a top city firm. But academically it falls far short of a medical college fellowship.

The optimistic counter-argument would point to such factors as increasing credentialism in legal practice and allied environments – the rise in practitioner demand for coursework LLMs may be only the first stage – the increasing specialisation of law and, perhaps most significant, its increasing internationalisation. Whether it be towards Europe, Asia or The Hague, lawyers in England and Australia are nowadays compelled, to an unparalleled extent, to look outwards from their own countries. Enhanced study of international and comparative law may well create a new need for advanced research, focusing on wide-ranging theoretical and cultural issues of a type that can be passed over when the sole focus of attention is the common law.

If this more optimistic view is right, it will be the scholarly model of a lawyer aspired to at Warwick, rather than the "arguing lawyer" of UNSW, that proves the more valuable notion in the long term. This is not, however, to deny the

[8] See *e.g.* R. Dawson, *The Oracles of the Law* (1968)

value of the pedagogical insights developed at UNSW and other similar law schools. Indeed, to deny the element of what I call argumentation in the formation of legal principles is to miss an important aspect of a full scholarly understanding of the phenomenon of law.

Tolerance and pluralism

My final comment again relates to a point of resemblance between Warwick and UNSW. Although both of these schools had a distinct collective commitment to "rebel", to do something new within legal education, they both (fortunately) escaped the dangers of collective authoritarianism. Through allowing significant leeway for staff members and, indeed, students to develop their own individual models of scholarship, teaching and learning, they averted the internecine conflicts that plagued a few other energetically innovative academic departments (both within and outside the field of the law) during the politically radical period of the 1960s and 1970s. From the point of view of a law teacher employed within both schools at different times, the different opportunities offered, experiences gained and challenges posed in them were therefore not only mutually complementary and distinctly educative, but also highly enjoyable.

Chapter 3

AN AUTOBIOGRAPHICAL FRAGMENT

Professor Patrick Atiyah
University of Oxford

Although I only spent four years at the University of Warwick (and in fact only three actually teaching there), the Law School and some of those who played a prominent part in helping to establish it as a place with a distinct ethos, played quite a crucial role in my own life and work as an academic. In particular, my book, *The Rise and Fall of Freedom of Contract*, was conceived and mostly written during my time at Warwick. But my earlier book, *Accidents, Compensation and the Law*, also owed something to a leading Warwick figure, if not to Warwick itself.

Sometime in 1967, when I was a tutorial fellow at New College, Oxford, I received a visit from my old friend, William Twining, then Professor of Jurisprudence at Belfast University. William and I had first met at Khartoum, where he had joined the Law Faculty a couple of years after I did. He was keenly interested in various problems of legal education and, together with another Oxford friend, who had migrated to Yale, Robert Stevens, he had persuaded the publishers Weidenfeld & Nicolson to launch a new series of legal books. These were designed, William told me, to be law books with a difference – instead of just concentrating on explaining what the law actually was, they were intended to include discussions of the law in its context. The context could be historical, social, economic, political, or a combination of all these, but the essential point was to provide some link between the world of law itself, and the world beyond it. I agreed at once with William in thinking that educationally this was a very desirable objective. For too long legal education had tended to be very narrow in England. Although at Oxford a course in law did involve papers in legal history, Roman law and legal philosophy, so that it appeared to be a broad-based sort of course, in fact it was, in many respects, just as narrow as most other law courses. The problem was that even the legal history, the legal theory and the Roman law courses were studied in rather a narrow technical legal way: there was no serious attempt (for instance) to link the study of legal history with non-legal history, nor to connect the study of Roman law with the way in which it subsequently came to be adopted as the basis of modern European legal systems. The legal history course at Oxford was entirely concerned with the history of legal doctrine, and proceeded through several centuries of development and change without any reference to what was happening in the country or the social and political changes which were taking place. Similarly, the study of ordinary legal subjects was extremely narrow and technical, involving little contact with the world outside the law itself.

At the time of William's visit I had begun to develop a keen interest in the contextual study of one particular area of law – the law of tort. By that time, all academic lawyers knew in a vague and general sort of way that most awards of damages in ordinary tort actions (for instance, actions arising out of road accidents) were paid for by insurance companies, and not by those who were legally responsible for the damage; and law students were beginning to be told by their teachers that this fact of insurance explained many things which were otherwise puzzling about tort liability decisions. Nobody, however, had yet made a serious study of the relationship between legal liability in tort and insurance, and this was something which was increasingly taking my attention. I had first begun to look at this subject when doing my book on vicarious liability, but it was clear to me then that the subject was a large one, and demanded far more attention than could be devoted to it in that particular book. So when William invited me to write a book on contract law for the new *Law in Context* series of legal books I immediately replied by saying that I would like to do a book on tort law for the series. This took William by surprise, and his first reaction was to suggest that the existing books on tort law were already quite good and reasonably contextual. I explained to him that what I had in mind was something very different from anything done in the existing books, and William promised to think over my suggestion. Eventually my proposal was accepted.

For the next two or three years I devoted my energies to research on this question. I found that the Americans were far ahead of us in England in studying the relationship between insurance and legal liability. Indeed, there had already been several American studies, and also one Canadian survey, into the effectiveness of tort law and liability insurance. These studies had shown that this was a pretty unsatisfactory way of compensating injured people. In the first place, only those who were able to prove that someone else's fault had caused their injuries were able to recover any compensation at all. That meant that the majority of accident victims never received any compensation in the form of damages. But in addition, it transpired that this method of insurance was very slow in operation as well as very costly, because a large part of the insurance premium was swallowed up by legal and administrative costs. This kind of third party insurance was much more expensive than ordinary insurance, such as householders' or life insurance, where legal and administrative costs were far lower. So Americans had started wondering whether it would not be more sensible to try to shift the emphasis of the system from third party to ordinary (or first party) insurance. This meant getting rid of legal liability, either wholly or at least partly. At first sight that seemed a very drastic thing to do, because most people feel instinctively that the right to sue someone who does them an injury is an absolutely fundamental legal right. But in some cases, at any rate, especially perhaps in road accident cases, it seemed to make good sense because the system of compulsory third party insurance meant that the person who was responsible for the accident never actually paid for the damage anyhow. So the right to sue him was really the right to claim from his insurance company; and if the accident victim was going to be given an insurance claim, it seemed sensible that the kind of insurance provided should be efficient and speedy in operation. So there was beginning to be pressure in some American states to introduce a system of insurance for road accidents under which an injured person would claim compensation from his own insurance company rather than from the other party's.

Another major aspect to the problem I now began to study in earnest was that there were so many different avenues by which an accident victim could recover compensation. Apart from the possibility of suing another person, the victim might have a claim against his own insurance company in some cases, he might have a claim to a wide range of social security benefits, or he might have a claim against the State under the Criminal Injuries Compensation Scheme, which had been set up in 1964. In addition, of course, he might receive limited compensation (or what came to the same thing), have some of his bills taken care of in other ways – the NHS, for instance, looked after his medical costs in most cases, and if his injuries were relatively short-lived (as most were) his employers might continue to pay his salary or wages. Now it had not been customary to look at all these methods of compensation together, as part of one whole legal system; and when they were looked at as a whole, the total picture began to look amazingly anomalous and haphazard. Whether an injured accident victim received any compensation, and if so, how much, and by what methods, all began to seem to me increasingly arbitrary and irrational. All the different systems of compensation had their own ideological underpinnings, and these often conflicted violently. In theory the right to sue was different from other methods of compensation because it depended on being able to prove that the accident was due to the fault of the person being sued. Once it came to be seen, however, that it was an insurance company which was going to pay, then the difference between the right to sue, and other forms of compensation tended to melt away. They were, in effect, all based on the principle of insurance. Then it began to seem much less obvious why the question of fault should matter. When a person insures his house against fire he doesn't expect to be denied a claim, merely because a fire starts which was partly his fault. What was more, looking at all the different methods of compensation as a whole brought to light the facts that many accident victims received very little compensation while others were compensated several times over.

It so happened that a case raising an important point of law, and involving some of these complications, came before the House of Lords while I was working on my book. In this case (*Parry* v *Cleaver*) a policeman injured in a road accident was claiming damages from the other driver involved, and the question concerned the amount of damages to which he was entitled. He had had to retire from the police force as a result of his injuries but had been given a police pension by way of compensation. The question that arose before the courts was whether the value of this pension should be taken into account in reducing the damages. Traditionally, it had been argued that such payments should not reduce the damages, because the damages were payable by the person who was to blame for the accident, and there seemed no reason why he should benefit from the police pension. I found myself challenging this sort of argument on the ground that it was unreal and artificial to treat the damages as though they would be paid by the negligent driver. In fact everyone knew they would be paid by his insurance company, and the insurance is really paid by the public through their premiums in very much the same way as a tax. The public were also paying for the police pension, so I argued that it was absurd for the injured person to be able to claim two lots of compensation for the one injury. When *Parry* v *Cleaver* reached the House of Lords I happened to see Lord Wilberforce at a New College dinner, and I asked him about the case. He told me that the other four law lords had already written their speeches, and that two were in favour of allowing the appeal, and two for dismissing it, so that his would be the deciding vote. I thought this would be my chance to influence the development of the law, so I gave Lord Wilberforce the benefit of my views. It would be agreeable to record that I persuaded Lord Wilberforce to decide against the injured plaintiff, but in fact he decided the other way. However, I did have the satisfaction of seeing the House of Lords move somewhat away from the majority decision in *Parry* v *Cleaver* in two cases in the 1980s, in which the reasoning of the judges appeared much closer to that for which I had argued.

This was a small part of the story I was getting to grips with in 1968–9. My work on that aspect of the problem remains, I believe, relevant today though in England very little reform has occurred. Another aspect of the problem was, I now think, seen by many people, including myself, from a particular perspective in the 1960s – and the perspective was a rather liberal left-wing perspective in which we saw accidents as not being really the fault of those who caused them, and we also saw the State as a kind of universal insurer. These two ideas eventually led many academics in the 1970s to think that all claims for damages for personal injuries could be abolished, and the State could run a general accident insurance system, so that anybody injured in an accident could recover compensation on the same lines. In New Zealand, which had already developed a far more elaborate and extensive welfare state than England, a compensation system along these lines was eventually introduced, as a result of a very far-reaching report by Mr Justice Woodhouse. In essence, it meant that actions for damages for personal injuries were abolished, and replaced by State compensation. The compensation was not as generous as damages at law were, but they were much more generous than ordinary social security benefits. What was more – and this was the key point – they were available to all accident victims, not just those whose injuries were somebody else's fault. Today, a scheme of that kind probably looks rather left-wing and bureaucratic, and plainly the tide of movement is against this kind of massive social welfare scheme. Indeed, even New Zealand itself is in process of dismantling its Woodhouse scheme. In the 1960s, when the welfare system was constantly being expanded in all directions, it did seem that this was the ultimate goal to which everything else was gradually moving. Of course I was an academic writer, not a law reformer; I did not see my task as that of advocating a particular type of change, but rather as discussing, analysing and reviewing the way the law worked, so that anomalies and inconsistencies could be brought to light. All this might point to some need for reform, and I was at that time broadly in favour of a New Zealand type of scheme, but that was not my essential purpose.

I began to plan out my new book for the *Law in Context* series, with the intention of covering all the different ways by which an accident victim might be compensated. But I first wanted to visit the United States and Canada, to meet some of the people who had been most active in research and writing on these issues. With the aid of Robert Stevens, Williams' co-editor in the *Law in Context* series, I secured an invitation to spend a semester at Yale in the Spring of 1968. There I taught a short advanced course (on contract law) to earn my money, and I had also secured a small grant from an American legal research foundation to cover my travel costs to a number of other universities where I wanted to visit some leading academics. I visited Robert Keeton, then at Harvard, later to become a federal judge, and co-author of the leading work on no-fault compensation, Harry Kalven at the University of Chicago, Al Conard at the University of Michigan, who had been responsible for the largest survey to date on the effects of road accident compensation, several academics at Temple University in Philadelphia, and, in Toronto, Professor Allen Linden with whom I became very good friends. Linden had done a small survey of road accidents in Toronto, and we discussed its results and methods. On many subsequent visits to Canada, I never failed to visit Toronto. Allen Linden was eventually made a judge of the Ontario Supreme Court and later the Court of Appeal and also served for a term as chairman of Canada's Law Reform Commission. On one occasion, many years later, when he was visiting England as secretary of an Ontario Legislative Law Reform Committee on road accident compensation, he wanted me to give evidence as an expert to his committee, but I myself was due to leave England for Canada and the US the day after they arrived in England. He therefore arranged – at the committee's expense – for me to spend the night (with Christine) at the Churchill Hotel, he took us to dine at the Mirabelle, and in return I talked to his committee the next morning before catching my plane from Heathrow! After experiences of that kind I began to feel like a Victorian poor relation in my contacts with North American academics.

In Yale itself I was also able to meet Guido Calabresi, who can claim to be the founder of the law and economics "school" of academic thought. Calabresi had an economics background as well as a legal training. In fact he had read PPE at Magdalen College, Oxford, at the same time that I (and Ronald Dworkin) had been doing law in the same college, and he had begun to write a powerful series of articles, which culminated in his book, *The Costs of Accidents,* on which he was then working. Calabresi's argument, which now seems trite enough, was then highly original: he argued that the law of civil liability was an essential part of the free market economic system. His idea basically was that most accidents are preventable by a sufficient injection of money – although many accidents may seem unpreventable, that is not necessarily true if they are viewed in a broader time perspective. But the money will not be spent if those who are liable to cause accidents are not held legally liable for the consequences. So it is desirable that legal liability should be maintained in order to ensure that adequate money is spent on safety. What is more (Calabresi'ssuccessors, anyhow, have argued) the amount to be invested in safety can also be decided by reference to the law of legal liability. Companies who may be held liable at law for accidents will have an economic incentive to spend money up to the point that the expenditure exceeds the amount of their potential liability – or their insurance premiums. Of course all this assumes that the law of liability in tort is the chief way, or even the only way, in which society and the law tries to prevent accidents – which is obviously untrue. There are many other laws for the same purpose; the criminal law, for instance, as well as licensing and regulatory laws. Calabresi's theories were later seized upon by a new generation of very right-wing academics in the United States, who disliked licensing and regulatory laws as bureaucratic and inefficient, and who wanted, as a matter of ideology, to treat legal liability as the sole way of controlling the levels of expenditure on accident prevention. Of course there are terrible troubles with the extreme versions of this theory, though I have come to think that, within limits, and in some areas, we need to pay attention to the basic idea that legal liability is a kind of market mechanism for controlling the levels of accidents.

But in 1968 I found myself somewhat out of sympathy with these theories, and I thought that England was at that time so far removed from America, in its economic system and in its ideology, that Calabresi's theories had little to offer us of value. I was, however, concerned to learn whether Calabresi thought that his theories were an obstacle to a New Zealand type of national compensation scheme, and I had a number of conversations with him which satisfied me that they were not. In theory, even a national compensation scheme of the New Zealand kind could pay due regard to the economic deterrence arguments which the economists have developed. To do this it is necessary to ensure that those who cause accidents are liable to pay premiums to the national compensation scheme, just as they now pay premiums to private insurance companies. In fact the New Zealand scheme did make some allowance for the possibility of levying premiums in this way, although in the event this aspect of the scheme was never implemented. At any rate, my concern at this time was to study, to learn, and to think about the possible alternatives, and I learnt much from Calabresi.

My visit to Yale was the first of many visits to the United States, and although for family reasons, it was the least successful, I was enormously impressed by a number of things which I began to identify with American law schools – by the energy, and optimism which I saw all round me, as well as by the teaching methods which I had first heard about from my Oxford tutor, John Morris, and now saw at first-hand. American law schools differ very much from English law faculties, and on the whole they are more impressive. They have of course the great advantage of being graduate institutions, so the students have already done four years of college, they are much older and more mature than English students and it is possible to pitch the level of sophistication in law teaching correspondingly higher. Further, the method of instruction is in many ways vastly superior to English-style lecturing. As is well known, most law teaching in America is done through the Casebook, and at its best and most effective, the class hour is spent in Socratic question and answer style. The students are expected to, and (at any rate in their first year) they do prepare for class very thoroughly, so that the teacher can ask a series of searching questions, going from one student to another. In this way, answers emerge slowly and – if the exercise is done with real skill – the reasons for them emerge as the answers themselves emerge. What is more, the student is made to see that there are always alternative possible answers, and he is made to examine the advantages and disadvantages of each possible answer.

This method of instruction makes teaching more rewarding for the teacher as well as the student. A class conducted in this fashion is rarely dull, and no one class ever repeats itself. At the same time, the system is very efficient in its use of the teachers' time. A teacher can take a class four or five hours a week for a semester of 15 or 16 weeks, so that the class meets for perhaps 70 or 80 hours to cover a subject like the law of contract or tort. At Oxford, by contrast, with its much vaunted tutorial system, the average student got perhaps eight tutorials a term in which he was expected to cover the same quantity of material, and half of that time was often occupied in the student reading out his essay or other written work. It was true that the student might also attend some lectures on the same subject, but lectures were largely optional, and were not well integrated into the teaching programme. At the same time the Oxford teacher was expected to teach for anything up to 15 hours a week (and his teaching involved a highly repetitive process) instead of perhaps six or eight hours a week which his American counterpart would be teaching. There was no doubt, in my mind, that the student got far better value for his money out of a course in a top law school like Yale than at Oxford, nor was there any doubt in my mind that teaching in the American style was much more enjoyable for the teacher.

The main failure of the American system was that it involved no teaching in writing skills, and in order to overcome this problem many American law schools have been forced to include separate courses themselves devoted to teaching writing skills. Unfortunately these courses usually take the form of teaching the students to write American style legal "briefs", a singularly bloodless and tedious form of legal writing, which hardly encourages literary skills. The result is that most American law graduates are far more articulate than English graduates in speaking, but much less able to communicate in writing.

Back in Oxford after my visit to Yale, I pressed ahead with my book, and completed the first draft by the following year, when I submitted it to William for his comments and criticisms. The book was eventually published in 1970 under the title, *Accidents, Compensation and the Law,* and it launched the new *Law in Context* series, which has now been going successfully for 25 years. The book was well received, and indeed, it set a fashion by enabling some law schools to run new courses on the subject of accident compensation as a whole. I did three editions of the book before handing it over to Peter Cane in 1986 for the fourth edition. By that time I was devoting so much of my energies to the law of contract that I simply had no time to prepare a fourth edition. I was also worried that the book had almost outlived its utility. The revival of the free market ideal, and the withering of the idea that the State could or should run huge bureaucratic welfare schemes meant that the message of the book had become outdated by the late 1980s. Although I still thought that the law of legal liability was full of anomalies, and that it was useful to study compensation systems as a whole, I would not have written the same sort of book in the 1980s as I wrote in the 1960s.

When the book was finished I decided that I would try to see whether an academic could actually achieve anything personally in the way of law reform. I launched a sort of mini campaign of my own with this end in view. I knew that the issues were too vast and cut across the work of too many government departments to think it possible that the kind of reforms I had in mind could ever be proposed in the routine course of departmental work. Any New Zealand-type reform would have such profound implications for the work of the social security department, the legal profession and the judges that several major departments of the government would be bound to be involved. So I hit on the idea of campaigning for a Royal Commission to take a broad look at the whole field. I opened my campaign with a letter to *The Times* which (rather to my surprise) immediately attracted editorial support. I next drafted a brief memorandum addressed to the Lord Chancellor, Lord Gardiner, urging the appointment of a Royal Commission. I sent this to a number of prominent academic and practising lawyers, and some judges and politicians with some interest in the law or in the social security system, and invited them to sign it. I collected about 35 pretty distinguished signatures, the memorandum was itself published in *The New Law Journal* and it was duly despatched to the Lord Chancellor.

The memorandum attracted some publicity in legal circles, and the Industrial Law Society (which was interested because of the implications of my proposals for workmen injured in industrial accidents); organised a public debate in London, at which the Lord Chancellor agreed to preside. Eventually the Lord Chancellor turned my proposal down, though he made it clear to me in a private letter that he was not unsympathetic to the idea of a Royal Commission, but was concerned that the legal profession simply could not absorb the massive legal changes already being thrust upon them in those years of Harold Wilson's Labour Government.

In the event, the Royal Commission was established four years later, under the chairmanship of Lord Pearson, mainly under the impetus of the thalidomide tragedy. The Commission proved an unmitigated disaster, and I came to regret that I had ever advocated it. Its report, published eventually in 1978, was a mass of political compromises with a complete lack of underlying principle, and almost from the beginning it was clear that its proposals were doomed.

My work on the *Accidents* book had placed me firmly alongside the new generation of academics who, under the leadership of Geoffrey Wilson, had tried to establish a new kind of law school at Warwick with a strongly contextual orientation. So when a few years later, after an interlude in Australia, I sought to return to England it was not surprising that I was especially attracted to the Warwick law school. The appointment of the Pearson Royal Commission had naturally also attracted my interest, as had the fact that William Twining had by this time left Belfast for Warwick. So in 1973 I returned to England to take up a chair at the Warwick law school.

Unfortunately, I spent my first year at Warwick suffering from acute depression as a result of some family problems which had blown up in Australia, but I still managed to do a certain amount of writing. I did a second edition of the book on *Accidents* which had sold sufficiently well to get the *Law in Context* series off the ground and encourage the publishers who at one time had ben inclined to cancel the whole venture. I had also done a serious piece of research developing out of my work for the Australian (Woodhouse II) Committee of Inquiry, to which I had been appointed by Prime Minister Gough Whitlam.

In Toronto, on behalf of the Australian Committee, I had spent three days studying at first hand the workings of the Ontario Workers' Compensation Board, which had a high reputation for fairness and efficiency in handling this one major type of accident. This Board had adopted a fairly sophisticated system of varying the levies they charged to employers in accordance with their accident experience, and I had looked at this system particularly closely. The Toronto officials who I had spoken to were all convinced that their system operated to reduce accident rates but when I questioned them closely about the way it worked they admitted that they had never actually sought to monitor it, by (for instance) comparing the accident rates of those subject to penalty levies and those companies not so subject. At my suggestion they had made a limited inquiry into the efficacy of these rates by examining the statistical record of a small number of companies, and they had sent me the results of this inquiry.

Back in Warwick, I now subjected these figures to a close examination which made me very dubious of the efficacy of the whole system of penalty rating adopted by the Ontario Board. I published these results in an academic journal and sent a copy to Lord Pearson. He invited me to lunch at the House of Lords, a novel experience for me, but the peer's lunchroom looked distinctly unaristocratic. Indeed, I noticed a very unlordly tin can on the carpet designed to collect the raindrops percolating through the roof!

Later I received an invitation to give "evidence" to the Royal Commission and did so, though it was a somewhat depressing experience. Lord Pearson made it evident that the Commission took a very narrow view of their terms of reference, and he also explained to me that the trade unions (who at that time seemed almost as strong as the Government) had told the Royal Commission that they expected to surrender nothing in the way of privileges or special benefits available for industrial accident victims, though they certainly expected to improve the position of accident victims generally. Their attitude, as well as Lord Pearson's view of the Commission's terms of reference, appeared to preclude any general solution to the problem of compensation for accident victims. I carried on a desultory correspondence with the Commission's statistical staff on one or two points arising out of my Toronto paper, and I also corresponded with Professor Prest, the only economist on the Commission, over a few issues, but I do not think I had much influence on their deliberations.

I thus managed to keep myself busy during that first year at Warwick though my depression was severe enough to prevent me doing any truly original or novel work. William Twining was constantly encouraging me to do a major book on the law of contract, perhaps for the *Law in Context* series, but at that time I simply did not see how this could be done. Early in my second year, the depression began to lift, and I suddenly found myself deeply, and indeed passionately excited by a new project. The catalyst was the appearance of a new short book on contract law by an American professor, named Grant Gilmore, called provocatively, *The Death of Contract*. Gilmore referred in this book to some casual remarks which I had tossed out in my own *Introduction to the Law of Contract*, suggesting that the nineteenth-century foundations of English contract law had been profoundly affected by the economic theories generally known as "classical economics" widely taken to have been founded by Adam Smith. At the time I had written this, the thought had no originality, and was not based on my own research. It was, in my student days, a cliché to say that English contract law was influenced by the *laisser-faire* ideas of the classical economists. But Grant Gilmore's little book reminded me that I had at one time thought seriously of pursuing this relationship, and I began, tentatively and cautiously at first, to browse in the library on the economic origins of the law of contract in the eighteenth and nineteenth centuries.

I rapidly became deeply engrossed in this subject, and soon discovered that I had all-unknowingly hit upon a gold mine for legal research. There was a huge mass of material of every kind about the historical relationships between law and economics (even more, law and economic thought) in the last two centuries, most of it totally unknown to legal historians or contemporary academic lawyers. I soon realised that what I was studying was the whole history of a massive intellectual movement – the movement known as freedom of contract, or more broadly, *laisser-faire* – which had its foundations in post-Reformation England, but developed only slowly until the time of Adam Smith. In a sense, indeed, what I was studying were the historical foundations of the idea of the free market, and its association with the law. My work seemed particularly timely because 1974–75, when I first began to get involved seriously in this research, appeared to mark the absolute nadir in England of the whole concept of the free market. The return to office of Harold Wilson's second administration in

1974 had led, even among Conservatives, to a rather despairing belief that the days of the free market appeared over. Planning – by government and unions – appeared to control all economic activity. At the same time, the legal concept of freedom of contract was at its lowest point. Almost every kind of contract was subject to legal and statutory intervention which overrode the freedom of the parties on scores of vital issues. Indeed, whole areas of contract law had disappeared altogether, and were replaced by administrative mechanisms. All this meant that I was faced with a fascinating piece of history – a remarkable swing of a remarkable pendulum. Subsequent events indeed confirmed that this was a particularly good moment for this study, because after Mrs Thatcher's election win in 1979, it soon became clear that the same pendulum was beginning to swing rapidly in the opposite direction again. As I watched the political events of the 1980s I was often amused to recollect how closely the renewed upward swing of the pendulum matched the earlier swing of the period from about 1750 to 1850. This meant that I had caught the movement precisely at the moment of its changing direction, and thus had a neat historical story to tell – the story of the rise and later the decline and fall of freedom of contract as an economic ideal and a legal concept.

I now found that Warwick University was a very good place for this research. Unlike most universities which have separate law libraries, Warwick had taken the deliberate policy decision of integrating the law library with the rest of the social sciences material. This was an enormous advantage to me, because it meant that I often stumbled across non-legal material on the shelves which would otherwise have remained unknown to me. I began to look at the shelves more closely in certain areas, and found all sorts of fascinating material about the history of economic thought, and its relationship to contract law. What was so particularly exciting – as it always is to the academic – was the feeling that I was treading such virgin soil. Lawyers had simply never studied this material at all, and even English legal historians, with one or two isolated and uninfluential exceptions, had never shown any interest in the relationship between legal development and its social and economic environment. Indeed, English legal historians were far more interested in the mediaeval history of legal doctrine than they were in the nineteenth century. The Warwick library had also made a speciality of government publications, an area of particular importance to my research. In these respects I found Warwick a congenial place to work.

I soon realised that I had a major project on hand, and began to sketch out the bones of a very wide ranging book. I had at first intended to study the relationship of economics to contract law, as a contemporary theoretical matter, as well as in its historical context, and my reading was designed to produce a two-part book, the first historical and the second, contemporary. The research alone was a massive exercise. Because I was primarily interested in studying the relationship between economics (or economic thought) and the law, much of the material I sought was buried deep in historical literature which often had very little about the law. I found myself searching for needles in haystacks. I often had to read a whole book for a single worthwhile reference, and became adept at skimming a book in the course of an evening. As the research progressed, my depression lifted, and was replaced by a prolonged burst of manic energy. I threw away my anti-depressant pills and had instead to ask my doctor to prescribe me sleeping pills to enable my restless mind to get some sleep. I worked as I had never worked before. I brought home books to read every evening and every weekend. I carried around with me little reference cards on which I jotted down my notes, and for a year or two, I am afraid I neglected my family and virtually all other interests. I was obsessed with the work, and begrudged time spent in any other activity. Doing the work in this obsessive way was probably an advantage in the end, because it was so concentrated in time, and I was so engrossed in it, that I carried much of the material and the ideas in my head during this period. This was invaluable, because the most interesting and most original part of what I sought to do, was to relate these disparate sources of material into an integral whole. I needed to keep the material and the ideas continuously in the forefront of my mind so that I could constantly make mental notes of how the different pieces of my gigantic jigsaw all fitted together. Had I spent ten years over the task – which one could easily have done – and kept all my notes on computer-retrievable discs, I am quite certain that I would never have noticed many of the detailed relationships between my sources which kept obtruding on my mind because of the way I worked.

By 1976 my work was sufficiently far advanced for me to apply to the Social Science Research Council for a personal research grant which would free me from all teaching responsibilities for the year 1976–77, to enable me to start writing. My application was approved, and my grant included a generous expense allowance to enable me to visit a number of scholars in the United States who I wanted to meet and talk to before I settled down to write my book. This was my first academic visit to the United States since 1968, when I had been completely unknown there, and I was rather surprised to discover that I now had something of a reputation. At Yale I was invited to give a lecture to the first year students, and to everyone's astonishment (including mine) the response was so great that the venue had to be changed twice to accommodate the audience. At Harvard I had been invited to present a paper to a group of social and legal historians, and had written a rough account of some of the main themes I intended to work into my book. This too went down very well and my sponsors, Professors Morton Horwitz and Duncan Kennedy were especially enthusiastic.

Both Horwitz and Kennedy were keenly interested in the nineteenth century history of contract law, and its relationship with social and economic conditions and ideals, though both of them took positions with which I was not myself much in sympathy. Horwitz adopted a more or classic Marxist analysis of the history of contract law, and attempted to demonstrate in his writings that, at least in America, the lawyers and judges had pursued a conscious policy of subsidising industry by externalising many costs onto the shoulders of workers or other third parties. While there may have been truth in this analysis in America, conditions in nineteenth-century England were very different and I was convinced that the story was much more complex than this. Apart from anything else, it was apparent to me that English nineteenth-century judges did not simply associate themselves as members of the "governing classes" against the labouring class. They saw themselves rather as arbitrators, mediating between the industrialists and commercial classes, and the rest of society – which included both the labourers and also the aristocratic landowners.

Duncan Kennedy wrote less than Horwitz, and his position was often difficult to grasp, but he was a wonderful person to listen to. His ideas poured out of him like the waters of Niagara Falls, and listening to him was very much like being under those Falls! The waters surged out, submerging rocks and difficulties, sweeping aside obstructions, sparkling with aphorisms, gems and quotations or references to writers and theorists, many of them unknown to me. On one occasion I spent an evening with Kennedy and a young visitor to Harvard, called Richard Danzig who attempted for a couple of hours to stem the tide of Kennedy's brilliant talk, much more successfully than I could. It was an extraordinary evening of academic talk, such as I had never previously encountered, and I confess that I felt overwhelmed by it. For the first time in my life, I also felt I was growing old – I simply did not have the speed of mind to keep up with these two able and nimble intellects. Kennedy was one of the founders of the movement which became known as "Critical Legal Studies" and I got to know him, and the movement better when I spent a year as visiting professor at Harvard in 1982–83.

I returned from America excited, invigorated, and full of energy for the task ahead of me. I collected my notes, I arranged my desk, and a table by the side of it, so that I had plenty of room to work, and I settled down to write. It was all done on a manual typewriter – this was before word processors became commonplace amongst academics – and I typed with two or three fingers. But the work soon surged ahead. I often wrote as much as 8000 words in a day. I wrote very fast, partly because I had sketched out the general story in my mind already, and partly because, as I had written my notes, I had often written them in a form which enabled me to incorporate them bodily in my text. Indeed, I had often kept even mental notes of the way I wanted to express things, and such was the speed at which I had been working that my mind was brimming over with all this material. I was also going through one of my "manic" phases, so that my mind raced ahead of my writing, and my nights were once again often restless as I composed sentences and paragraphs of my next chapters in the early hours of the morning, while still lying in bed.

By Christmas I had already written a large part of the book, and by the Spring of 1977 the back of the whole work had been broken. I had soon realised that my original idea of the two-part work, embracing both the historical and the contemporary studies, could not possibly be realised within the one volume. I concentrated therefore on my historical material, and the book took shape under the title, *The Rise and Fall of Freedom of Contract*. It was completed in 1977–78 and published in 1979. But by that time I had left Warwick and returned to Oxford as Professor of English Law.

Chapter 4

A NOBEL PRIZE FOR LAW?

Professor William Twining*
University College, London

The date of birth of a law school and its coming of age are both indeterminate. In recent years there has been a spate of birthday celebrations by law schools around the Commonwealth. Among those with close associations with Warwick, the law faculties of Dar es Salaam and Lagos celebrated their 25th anniversaries in 1989; in the same year the Faculty of Law of the University of Hong Kong commemorated its 20th birthday and in 1993 the Centre for Socio-Legal Studies in Oxford chose the less fashionable 21. In 1987 The *Modern Law Review* marked its 50th year with a special issue. Each of these events resulted in a substantial publication.[1] For Warwick to celebrate its 30th anniversary with a symposium devoted to legal scholarship suggests a pleasing maturity.

Of course, the timing of these celebrations is not entirely fortuitous. The 1960s and 1970s saw a massive expansion of legal education throughout the common law world, typically as part of more general developments in higher education. During this period established law schools grew larger and many new ones were set up. Local legal education in former colonies typically started just before or after independence as part of the process of decolonisation. In England and Wales law expanded largely in step with higher education: it got off to a slow start, but over time increased its share of the total. The modern

---

* This essay builds on and develops themes that are dealt with at greater length in previous writings, especially Blackstone's *Tower: The English Law School* (1994) (hereafter BT); Llewellyn's *Unfinished Agenda: Law in Society and the Job of Juristic Method* (Chicago Papers in Legal History, 1993); a shorter version was published in 48 *U. of Miami L.Rev.* 119 (1993) (hereafter JJM); "Remembering 1972", in D. Galligan (ed.) *Socio-Legal Studies in Context* (1995) (hereafter RN); and *Rethinking Evidence* (1990, 1994) (hereafter RE). I am grateful to Terry Anderson, Hans Nijboer and Reiner Hegselmann for helpful comments on an earlier draft. I have also benefited from conversations with Geoffrey Wilson and with colleagues at the Netherlands Institute for Advanced Study (NIAS), where this was written.

[1] Shivji (ed.) *The Limits of Legal Radicalism* (Dar es Salaam, 1987); Omotola and Adeogun (eds.) *Law and Development* (Lagos, 1987); Wacks (ed.) *The Future of Legal Education and the Legal Profession in Hong Kong* (Hong Kong, 1989); Galligan (ed.) *op cit* n 1; W.T. Murphy and Simon Roberts (eds.) Symposium on legal scholarship in the common law world (1987), 50 *MLR* No. 6.

English law school, like its university home, is essentially a post-World War II creation.[2] It has been estimated that the scale of the academic legal enterprise is about 20–25 times what it was in 1945 and, almost as significant, nearly four times what it was when the Ormrod Committee reported in 1971. For legal scholarship this had several implications: the number of full-time teachers increased from about 130 in 1945, to 974 in 1974–75 to nearly 2000 in 1994.[3] Expansion made space for specialisation, innovation and above all diversification in respect of ideas, methods and perspectives. Legal scholarship today is generally more varied, more lively, more sophisticated and more self-confident than it was at the start of the period of expansion. A new pluralism in academic law has become established.

It is not surprising to find in these anniversary volumes a mixture of nostalgia, self-congratulation, critical stock-taking and prescriptions for the future. What are birthdays for except to give some licence to retrospection, introspection and prospective speculation? One underlying theme is that law schools have changed out of all recognition in the past thirty years, that most of the developments have been positive, and that there are many substantial achievements to celebrate. However, there is also a strong undercurrent of dissatisfaction and self-criticism. Like many other disciplines, especially those that are unsure of their full acceptance within the academy, law is endemically plagued by self-doubt. Much of this is articulated in terms of disagreements and ambivalences about objectives, priorities and functions within formal legal education. Such problems of identity are caught by Thomas Bergin's title of 1968 "The law teacher: a man divided against himself".[4] The gender-balance in academic law has changed in the past 25 years, but the theme persists. What began as an educational problem has tended to spill over into legal scholarship.[5] Here self-doubt is sometimes expressed in the idea that there is no Nobel Prize for law.[6] This has sometimes been explicitly discussed in print, but doubts about the nature, achievements and prospects of legal scholarship are much more wide-spread. The actual Nobel Prize is in many respects an idiosyncratic, historically contingent and controversial institution. But it provides a convenient symbol for its stated aspiration of recognising extraordinary contributions that benefit mankind.[7] In this context, the question becomes: what, if anything, can legal

---

[2] BT Chap 2.

[3] *Ibid.*

[4] (1968) 54 *Virginia Law Rev.* 637.

[5] This paper assumes a close interdependence between teaching and research in English law schools, not least because teaching still provides the main economic base for scholarship. For an excellent discussion of the relationship between teaching and research in law, see *Law and Learning* (The Arthurs Report, Ottawa, 1983), passim, esp. Chap 7.

[6] *E.g.* the passages from Atiyah and Conard, quoted below.

[7] One may discount the peculiar history and idiosyncrasies of the actual Nobel institution; but it is worth noting that two recent Nobel Laureates in economics, Ronald Coase and Gary Becker, derived some of their inspiration from legal examples and their close association with the University of Chicago Law School. And some lawyers, for example Sean McBride and Nelson Mandela, have been honoured as activists for their contributions to human rights, environmental protection or World Peace.

scholarship contribute to human welfare or human understanding?

It is not difficult to find some negative answers, for example:

(a) "... I have heard it said by a Professor of the Harvard Law School (not himself a lawyer) that the reason why there is no Nobel Prize for lawyers is that common lawyers have no respect for original thought. The system of precedent, urged this Professor, means that in a common law court you can destroy your opponent's arguments by showing that nobody has ever thought of them before. This is no doubt an exaggeration, but he definitely has a point."[8]

(b) "The predominant notion of academic lawyers is that they are not really academic ... Their scholarly activities are thought to be unexciting and uncreative, comprising a series of intellectual puzzles scattered among 'large areas of description'".[9]

(c) "A more fundamental obstacle to awarding a Nobel Prize for law is the difference between what scientists and artists do for humanity and what lawyers do. When a scientist discovers a means of making rice fields more productive, he adds to the food supply without taking food from anyone. When a poet provides us with a new insight, he makes us wiser without making anyone more ignorant.

Law, on the other hand, is largely concerned with taking from one person to give to another."[10]

(d) "[I]t is not easy to see that law is a discipline in the usual sense. What truths do lawyers come up with? What are the great legal discoveries of the past ten years, or fifty years, or even a hundred. There do not seem to be any."[11]

(e) "Insofar as intellectual disciplines can be identified, this is usually done in terms of distinctive methods, distinctive subject-matter or theory, or distinctive scientific or scholarly objectives. None of this applies to the 'discipline' of law, which possesses no methods unique to legal study, no theory which is other than an application or development of social, political or ethical theory of some kind, and no distinctive scientific or scholarly objectives. All attempts to mark law off from other knowledge fields are bound to fail."[12]

(f) "The character of English law and the English legal system, judge led, pragmatic and undoctrinal ... [is] neither sufficiently scholarly to be attractive to scholars nor sufficiently legal to be attractive to lawyers. If putting 'legal' in front of 'scholarship' was like putting plastic in front of 'cup', then adding 'English' is like adding 'disposable'. The words 'English legal scholarship', though high sounding have a similar function to the words 'disposable plastic

---

[8] Atiyah, *Pragmatism and Theory in English Law* (1987) at p 7.

[9] Becher, *Academic Tribes and Territories* (1989) p 30, discussed BT, Chap 6.

[10] Alfred A. Conard, "The Nobel Prize for Law" (1985) 18 *Michigan Journal of Law Reform* 226.

[11] Simpson, *Invitation to Law* (1988) at p 178.

[12] Roger Cotterrell, "A 'Post-disciplinary' Perspective on Law", (unpublished outline for seminar, 1991, quoted with permission of the author). Cotterrell has since developed some relevant themes in print without using the phrase "autonomous disciplines", *e.g.* "Sociological Perspectives on Legal Closure", in Norrie (ed.) *Closure or Critique: New Directions in Legal Theory* (1993) Chap 10.

cup'. Each adjective strengthens the message that one can not expect much in terms of quality or long-term utility from it."[13]

These six quotations are by respected contemporary scholars with whom I do not often disagree. Most of the statements can be interpreted as reporting views, which may be quite widespread, rather than endorsing them. However, I would suggest that all of them, at least if taken at face value, are fundamentally misleading, largely because they are based on indefensible assumptions about the nature of contemporary legal scholarship or scholarship in general or both.

For example, to suggest (a) that lawyers are not interested in new ideas because they argue from precedent, deals with only one small part of the practice of law and of legal scholarship, the construction, presentation and criticism of arguments on disputed questions of law. It also mischaracterises the activity. Ronald Dworkin's Hercules might be a strong contender for a Nobel Prize for law. So might some actual judges in our tradition.

Similarly to suggest (b) that legal scholarship is mainly taxonomic or descriptive implies that exposition is the only kind of legal scholarly activity. Furthermore, it misconceives the nature and functions of legal dogmatics.[14]

Thirdly, it is surely misleading to suggest (c) that all Nobel prizewinners are involved in win-win activities, whereas law is mainly concerned with redistribution. Even if both assumptions were true, a case could be made for claiming that if someone could devise a just, efficient and cost-effective system for distributing risks, this might deserve to count as an extraordinary contribution to human welfare – and possibly also to human understanding.

To suggest (d) that law is not really a scholarly discipline because there have been no great legal discoveries, omits the processes of invention, interpretation, and construction of ideas that are normally considered as central to the humanities and social sciences. Do historians, novelists, literary theorists, economists or sociologists make great discoveries in ways which jurists do not? A lawyer may discover a forgotten precedent in much the same way as an archaeologist may discover a new site or a lost manuscript, but such findings do not on their own win Nobel prizes, and scientists and scholars do not discover theories, concepts, interpretations, insights, or more controversially, facts. Sharp distinctions between discovery, construction, interpretation and invention in the physical sciences are now doubted by both philosophers of science and sociologists of knowledge.[15] Cannot legal practice and law-making as forms of problem-solving take credit for some significant inventions, such as the trust or the letter of credit or the Mareva injunction or public interest litigation, to say nothing of monumental achievements such as Justinian's *Institutes* or Blackstone's *Commen-*

---

[13] Geoffrey Wilson, "English Legal Scholarship" (1987) 50 *MLR* 818 at p 819. Wilson is, here it seems, talking more about the achievement of English legal scholarship than its potential. He concludes on a slightly more optimistic, if ambivalent, note: "One cause for optimism for the future of legal scholarship is that so little has been tried." (id. at p 851).

[14] This argument is developed at length in BT, Chap 6. Differences within "legal dogmatics" in the civilian tradition are explored in Nijboer and Wemes, *Rechtspraak, domatiek en dogmatisme* (1990).

[15] *E.g.* Gilbert and Mulkay, *Opening Pandora's Box: A sociological analysis of scientists' discourse* (1984).

taries or the United States Constitution or the Uniform Commercial Code or some of the international conventions on human rights?[16]

To suggest (e) that law as a discipline is not autonomous because it has no unique or special subject-matter or methods or forms of knowledge (which some would doubt), is to set a standard of autonomy which would disqualify most other disciplines. Is psychology or history or statistics or literature or politics or sociology autonomous in ways that law is not? Is it not strange to imply that social, political and ethical theory are autonomous disciplines?

Finally, even if one accepts (f) that the pragmatic, sometimes anti-intellectual tendencies of the common law tradition makes much of our academic activity fit the disturbing image of a disposable plastic cup, this metaphor hardly fits the work of Blackstone or Maitland or Hart or Kahn-Freund or Dworkin in our tradition, to say nothing of legal scholarship in other legal cultures. If there were a Nobel Prize for law, there would be some strong candidates, even from England.

If I were concerned here to take on some of the fundamental theoretical questions about the nature of scholarship in general and legal scholarship in particular, it would not be adequate to take a few quotations out of context and dismiss them so peremptorily. But my purpose is to comment on the current scene in the United Kingdom at a less fundamental level. It is to consider some of the concerns that underlie this poor image of legal scholarship and to suggest an alternative.

As a start, it is worth dealing briefly with a possible semantic confusion about the terms "discipline" and "scholarship". Debates about the autonomy of disciplines typically centre on philosophical questions about forms of knowledge. From an epistemological point of view, if any disciplines can be said to be autonomous in a strong sense (which I doubt), I agree that law is not one of them[17]; but nor are most of the subjects that are generally accepted today as being part of the humanities and social sciences. If on the other hand, one views a discipline as a form of organised or institutionalised activity ostensibly directed to the advancement and dissemination of learning, then the idea of discipline marks out the intellectual division of labour which is historically

[16] The potential of a technological perspective on law – viewing legal praxis as a form of institutionalised problem-solving – is explored in JJM. A great many legal inventions are the work of teams or anonymous practitioners or incremental development over time rather than the work of named individuals. If one wants to look for examples of "creative lawyering" or "imaginative problem-solving" one is most likely to find it in lawyers' offices and chambers, where largely anonymous individuals and teams use their ingenuity and skill to solve thousands of practical problems, not least to prevent conflict, typically under a cloak of confidentiality. Many, of course, may be serving particular interests rather than the general welfare. Insofar as legal culture may be less inclined to assign credit for its main advances to individuals, it may be less wedded to a Great Person view of science than some other disciplines. On concerns about allocation of credit in the physical sciences see Latour and Woolgar, *Laboratory Life* (1979) Chap 5. Nobel Prizes, other than the Peace Prize, are given only to individuals.

[17] BT Chap 7. Richard Posner, in his much-cited article, *op cit* below n 33, uses autonomy in a weak sense to refer to "a subject properly entrusted to persons trained in law and nothing else" (at p 762).

contingent and may vary according to time and place.[18] In our system, the study of law has been largely institutionalised into separate departments, faculties or schools which have developed more or less distinctive academic cultures. English law schools today might be said to be semi-autonomous: on the one hand during the past twenty years they have been treated by governments and administrators as part of the humanities and social sciences and to a significant degree have been assimilated into and share in a common academic culture. On the other hand, for complex reasons, law schools tend to have a culture that is in some respects different from that of history or sociology or English departments – with many individual variations. This is as much to do with differences of function and tradition as with the intellectual content of the activities that take place within them. There have, of course, been recurrent attempts to develop inter-disciplinary studies, "to break down the artificial barriers between disciplines", and "to mitigate the rigidities of the departmental system". Such attempts have met with mixed success, partly because of cultural differences, but also because of the internal political economy of universities.[19]

Similarly, "scholarship" is an activity that goes on mainly, but not exclusively, in universities. In contrast to the situation in Continental Europe, English legal scholarship antedated our university law schools by several centuries. In ordinary usage the term "scholarship" is notoriously vague. For example, the *Oxford English Dictionary* defines it as:

> "1.a. The attainments of a scholar; learning, erudition; esp. proficiency in the Greek and Latin languages and their literature. Also the collective attainments of scholars; the sphere of polite learning …
> b. Applied by unlearned speakers, etc., to educational attainments of a more modest character."

In the present context doubts about legal scholarship can be interpreted as raising questions about its standing and whether it measures up to the standards of other disciplines. There are clearly some legitimate reasons for concern. For example, it is well known that research training in law is less developed than in most other disciplines and in some other countries. Data from Halsey's 1989 survey of British academics indicate that at the time only 11.5% of law teachers had doctorates compared with an average of 58.4% in other disciplines.[20] Secondly, academic lawyers have many opportunities to participate in

[18] Such a ethnographic perspective deals with "the social aspects of knowledge communities and the epistemological properties of knowledge forms and how the two influence one another". Becher, *op cit*, p 1.

[19] W. Twining, "Law and Anthropology: A Case Study of Inter-disciplinary Collaboration" (1973) 7 *Law and Society Review* 561. In my experience attempts to develop genuinely inter-disciplinary degrees have more often run into difficulties because of questions of cost than because of intellectual or cultural difficulties.

[20] This is based on a preliminary analysis of data kindly provided by Professor Halsey. See further, BT 200–205. This was the most significant deviation by academic lawyers from the norm in respect of Halsey's indicators. The recent ESRC report on *Socio-Legal Studies* (1994) identifies research training as a priority need for the development of the field. See further, William Twining, "Postgraduate Legal Studies: Some Lessons of Experience", in Birks (ed.) *Reviewing Legal Education* (1994) 93.

extra-curricular activities which are either not academic or which fall on the borderline of "research" and "scholarship".[21] Thirdly, the main audiences for legal writing – practitioners, vocationally oriented law students, and law reform bodies – exercise a strong gravitational pull towards applied work, towards *recherches ponctuelles* rather than *recherches sublimes*, as they say in Quebec.[22] Fourthly, law has not attracted, and academic lawyers have not sought, as much outside research funding as most other disciplines, and such funding as is available tends to favour applied rather than fundamental research.

These concerns are real, but they need to be balanced against some other points considerations. A good deal of work that is recognised as scholarly is produced by practitioners, judges, law reform bodies and others outside the universities; for, at least in the upper reaches, the law has some claims to being called a learned profession. It would indeed be churlish to disqualify the more thoughtful, well-researched, and innovative products of practising lawyers and judges as not being scholarly just because they were undertaken for practical purposes. A great deal of specialist work that is undertaken by academic lawyers in other jurisdictions is done by barristers, law publishers and government officials in England. This may reduce the opportunities and temptations for academic lawyers to be diverted away from serious scholarship. As part of the process of assimilation of law into universities, for purposes of appointment, promotion, research assessment and terms of employment, most academic lawyers are treated in much the same ways and are judged by comparable criteria to colleagues in the humanities and social sciences. There is a certain amount of evidence that today academic lawyers are on average no less productive than their colleagues in other disciplines.[23]

Another factor that may underlie these negative images is the point that law has traditionally been seen as one of the cheapest subjects. This is an international phenomenon. A strong case can be made that this inhibits the development of legal scholarship, especially in areas which require fieldwork, foreign travel or expensive equipment. This perception of the subject is very difficult to change, as the Heads of Law Schools found in 1983.[24] Even if the unit costs of law were increased, it is quite likely that most of the extra revenue would be invested in higher academic salaries for law teachers rather than in support for research, as has happened in the United States.[25] It could be argued that law is well-equipped to deal with economic adversity just because law school culture is less dependent on outside research funding and has not developed expensive tastes. However, in the long-term, modest expectations are likely to lead to modest performance.

Negative images may also be a symptom of disappointed expectations. Many

---

[21] Arthurs, *op cit*, Chap 5.
[22] *Ibid*; see further BT Chap 6.
[23] For details, see BT, Appendix.
[24] Heads of University Law Schools, *Law as an Academic Discipline* (1983); the bulk of the report was published in the S.P.T.L. *Newsletter*, Summer (1984).
[25] Bok, *The Cost of Talent* (1993) Chap 8.

of the new law schools in the Commonwealth began life during a period of academic euphoria, and many of the post-war generation of law teachers shared in a general mood of idealism, optimism and political commitment. The boom period for universities did not last long. What Halsey has called the "decline of donnish dominion" began in the late 1960s and has continued in fits and starts ever since.[26] Issa Shivji's well-chosen title, *The limits of legal radicalism*[27] wryly catches the sense of frustration and disappointed expectations of many of those who started their academic careers in the 1960s or even the 1970s. Its significance extends beyond Tanzania and academic law. Our discipline may be larger, better integrated into the university and more self-confident than it was 30 years ago, but self-doubt and a sense of promise unfulfilled persists, as is illustrated by the passages quoted above.

Let us consider some examples. In the 1960s some of us launched an attack on the dominance of "blackletter law" or "the expository tradition" in both legal education and legal scholarship, complaining that it was narrow, conservative, illiberal, unrealistic and boring.[28] The orthodox student textbook was selected as the target which symbolised the tradition. This was a challenge to a near monopoly rather than an outright assault on exposition as such. More radical critics challenged the validity of the methods of expositors or dismissed their writings as bourgeois mystification. As is common with such polemics there was an element of artificiality in the battles and a tendency to caricature. In curriculum discussions traditionalists fought rearguard actions, often with bitter resentment, but rarely did they join issue intellectually. Leading expositors tended to use the time-honoured technique of Ignoring and just got on with the job.[29]

Like most such battles there were no clear victors. On the one hand, academic law has diversified and the near-monopoly of exposition has been broken. Some kinds of broader approach, such as socio-legal studies and economic analysis of law, have become established, alternative kinds of legal literature have developed, and there is a much greater variety in legal theory.[30] Perhaps because of the tendency to pluralism, no clear alternative genre of legal literature has developed as a rival to traditional textbooks and treatises. The expository text has survived. Indeed the taught tradition may be tougher and more sophisticated as a result of these attacks. It may become even tougher as more expositors undergo the discipline of preparing expert systems. In 1987 Lord Goff could say: " ... we live in the age of the legal textbook".[31] In the United States Judge Harry Edwards has sharply attacked law schools for failing to perform their traditional role of providing "practical doctrinal scholarship"

---

[26] Halsey, *Decline of Donnish Dominion* (1992).
[27] *Op cit*, n 2.
[28] BT at pp 141ff.
[29] A notable exception was T.B. Smith, "Authors and Authority" (1972) 12 J.S.P.T.L. (N.S.) 1.
[30] On the new pluralism in academic law, see BT Chap 6 and RN.
[31] Robert Goff, "Judge, Jurist and Legislator" (Child and Co. Lecture) (1987) *Denning Law. Jo.* 79, at p 92.

for the practising profession and the judiciary.[32] Even Richard Posner, another academic turned judge, has gone so far as to say that "[d]isinterested legal-doctrinal analysis of the traditional kind remains the indispensable core of legal thought".[33] Exposition has survived, perhaps with its dominance and prestige reduced, but it is here to stay, not least because expositors have been assigned a useful, if modest, role as participants in the legal system.[34] Even those who consider exposition to be a form of divination or jugglery concede that there is a steady demand for its products.

Let me illustrate the theme of disappointed expectations more concretely by reference to two areas that are of special interest to me: evidence and "legal method". When I came to Warwick I was asked what field of law I proposed to rethink or to "Warwickise". After some thought, I settled on evidence. My choice was fortunate, for it has recently become a very lively area. In the 19th century, evidence as a subject attracted some of the best legal minds: Bentham, Stephen, Thayer and Wigmore, for example. But in the 20th century it suffered a period of recession as an academic subject. In the United States it was difficult for scholars to break out of the shadow of two giants, Thayer and Wigmore. In England, during the formative period of university law schools, it was eccentrically treated as "a barrister's subject" and was hardly studied at all. When Rupert Cross made the subject academically respectable, he followed American tradition in concentrating on the technical rules of evidence and ignoring the rich heritage of theoretical writings on proof and of work in other disciplines. In the last fifteen years there has been a series of developments which have been, somewhat grandiosely, labelled "the New Evidence Scholarship". It is an intellectually diverse movement involving scholars from philosophy, psychology, statistics, diverse semiotics, and history, as well as law. It treats the law of evidence as one, relatively small, part of the subject of evidence and proof; how small is a matter of controversy. Some of us believe that the importance of the formal rules is diminishing, that their importance has been greatly exaggerated and that over-concentration on them has distracted attention from subjects which are of greater practical and theoretical significance such as the logic of proof.[35] Although this area has been widely recognised as a significant academic development, it seems so far to have made a very modest impact on the teaching of evidence, and on the ordinary discourse and practices of practitioners. Some attention has been paid to psychological findings in debates on law reform, although this is not often reflected in actual legislative changes.[36] From

[32] Harry T. Edwards, "The growing disjunction between legal education and the legal profession" (1992) 91 *Michigan Law Review* 34; see also the responses and comments in (1993) id. No. 8.

[33] Richard Posner, "The Decline of Law as an Autonomous Discipline: 1962–1987" (1987) 100 *Harvard Law Review* 761 at p 777.

[34] BT at pp 135–141 and Atiyah, *op cit*, passim.

[35] RE Chap 6. There has, of course been a long, though spasmodic, tradition of studying proof in continental Europe from a variety of perspectives, as is illustrated by the work of Mittermaier, Muensterburg, Le'vy-Bruhl and Perelman.

[36] See, *e.g.* the symposium on the Royal Commission on Criminal Justice in 21 Journal of Law and Society, No 1 (1994).

time to time one may feel frustrated by the continuing failure of colleagues to take facts seriously and to embrace these developments. But perhaps one is being too impatient. Evidence as a field of study is unrecognisably different from what it was 20 years ago; there is a very active international network of scholars pursuing a variety of lines of enquiry and there is a burgeoning literature. Some expository works have begun to take notice of these new ideas.[37] Similar developments can be reported in a number of fields; family law, regulation, administrative law, for example. Scholarship is a collective enterprise which develops incrementally and in an area like this perhaps one should expect it to take a generation for new ideas to become part of the mainstream.

Perhaps "legal method" provides a better example. In its lowest form this term is widely interpreted to encompass not much more than the doctrine of precedent, the so-called "rules" of statutory interpretation and a few bits of information that beginning law students need to know. That is a crude misnomer. Even in more sophisticated books and courses with this title two ideas are regularly conflated and confused: purported (typically misleading) accounts of the methods of reasoning of judges in appellate cases and the task of developing certain elementary skills – legal method as the skills of the law student. Teaching about the thought processes of one kind of functionary is a very different operation from getting students to learn how to think. Learning about the rules of precedent is tangential to both.[38]

A slightly more sophisticated interpretation of "legal method" is to equate it with "thinking like a lawyer" or, more narrowly, with "legal reasoning". These at least have the merit of focusing on method and linking the subject of study to a relatively developed body of theory. But "legal reasoning" is still almost universally equated with reasoning about disputed questions of law, typically in "hard cases". In 1964, Julius Stone coined the phrase "lawyers' reasonings".[39] This correctly implies that lawyers are involved in a wide range of operations which ostensibly involves different kinds of ratiocination in a variety of contexts. Negotiating, arguing about disputed questions of fact, pleas in mitigation, sentencing, criticising particular laws, institutions or practices, recommending reforms are all examples of professional activities that involve, or purport to involve, reasoning. So do many activities of other legal actors. Unfortunately, Stone followed tradition in concentrating almost exclusively on questions of law. But to confine "lawyers' reasonings" to one kind of argumentation is, once again, to treat one small part as if it were the whole. Clearly this fits the narrow conception of academic law that is confined to legal doctrine; part of the point of "broadening" legal studies is to break out of such confines.

No doubt there are many factors that have contributed to what seems to me to be an elementary and persistent form of narrowness. One obvious reason

---

[37] Ligertwood, *Australian Evidence* 2nd ed (1993).

[38] On the elementary distinction between the doctrine and techniques of precedent, see Twining and Miers, *How To Do Things With Rules* 2nd ed (1991) at 299ff.

[39] Stone, *Legal System and Lawyers' Reasonings* (1964).

why it persists is that no one has yet constructed an alternative, broad theory of "lawyers' reasonings" to set against the traditional narrow one. There have, of course, been some developments in relevant areas: the new rhetoric to some extent transcends the division between questions of fact and questions of law[40]; the debates on probabilities and proof[41], the currently fashionable concern with story-telling[42]; the application of game theory to negotiation[43], the suggestion that most or all lawyers' skills can be subsumed under the rubric of "problem-solving"[44] are just some examples. One striking aspect of these particular developments is that they have resulted in separate bodies of literature that have grown up largely independently of each other.

At first sight, it seems fairly straightforward to sketch an agenda for a general theory of lawyers' reasonings which would subsume all of these various activities and discourses under one head. For example, do not negotiation, appellate advocacy, arguments about questions of fact, law and disposition, law reform and constitution-making all involve the application of the same general principles of practical reasoning? Insofar as questions arise about the uses and limits of "rationality" and competing conceptions of the rational, these would form part of the task of constructing such a theory. An agenda for constructing a normative theory of lawyers' reasonings might include: in respect of what kinds of activities, in what contexts, do lawyers typically purport to use reason? What constitute valid, cogent and appropriate reasonings in each context? What are the similarities and differences between each of these various kinds of reasoning and how are they related to each other? Are they all examples of some generalisable notion of practical reasoning? Can they all be subsumed under some general theory of problem-solving? What conception(s) of rationality are presupposed by such theories? Can such conceptions be defended against sceptical attacks and, if so, how?

A general theory of lawyers' reasonings which provided a coherent set of answers to such questions would indeed be broader than standard theories of legal reasoning such as those of Levi, Llewellyn, MacCormick, Dworkin or Alexy. But maybe this is all too simple. First, many of our stock of theories in this area are more or less explicitly limited to common law reasoning and, as such, are closer to particular than to general jurisprudence. It is clear that what is thought to constitute a valid, cogent and appropriate argument on a question of law or fact or sentencing varies from legal system to legal system and within legal systems, depending on context, standpoint and so on. Yet questions about

---

[40] Perelman, *The Idea of Justice and the Problem of Argument* (1963); Neil MacCormick, deals briefly with questions of fact in *Legal Reasoning and Legal Theory* (1978) and in subsequent writings about coherence. There is an extensive philosophical literature on "practical reasoning" and "informal logic", see *e.g.* Hamblin, *Fallacies* (1970), Walton, *Informal Logic* (1989)

[41] This is, of course, one part of "the new evidence scholarship". For an excellent survey of recent debates and writings about inference and probabilities in several disciplines, see Schum, *Evidential Foundations of Probabilistic Reasoning* (1994).

[42] *E.g.* Jackson, *Law, Fact and Narrative Coherence* (1988); RE Chap 7.

[43] *E.g.* Raiffa, *The Art and Science of Negotiation* (1982).

[44] *Op cit,* n 17 above.

the validity and cogency of arguments are meant to transcend particular cultures and contexts; they purport to provide general principles of reasoning. How does one reconcile the claims to universality of principles of logic with the apparent cultural relativism implicit in comparing and contrasting forms and styles of legal reasonings?

Secondly, this is a philosophical minefield in which it would be naive to expect consensus. There are many theories of deduction, induction, probability and so on and many conceptions of rationality. There is no agreed base from which to start to construct a normative theory of lawyers' reasonings as an application of some more general theory; and there is no escaping the philosophical difficulties.

A third concern is empirical. What is the relationship between normative theories of rational argument and psychological theories of decision-making or other kinds of empirical study, such as discourse analysis or jury studies? If broadening involves going beyond the study of rules and particular systems, being more "realistic" includes getting closer to the actual behaviour of real participants. This general problem of the puzzling relationship between normative and empirical aspects of decision-making is illustrated by a relatively recent development in respect of fact-finding: psychological studies have convincingly shown that juries and other triers of fact in coming to decisions about particular past events typically either construct stories or choose between competing stories presented to them. Stories typically form coherent wholes, while standard theories of argumentation about both questions of fact and questions of law tend to be based on versions of propositional logic. The contrast is sometimes made between the "atomism" of standard accounts of reasoning and the "holism" of the psychological accounts. There is thus a seeming tension between normative theories about how people ought to think and empirical theories about how they in fact think. If psychologists could show, as they may well do in respect of certain kinds of operation (*e.g.* facial recognition), that people in fact make better judgements when they think holistically, this may pose important challenges at the normative level to standard prescriptive theories of reasoning and some conventional conceptions of rationality. A great deal of writing about judicial processes hovers uneasily between logic, psychology and heuristics. We are only just beginning to come to grips with such issues in legal theory. These examples may at least illustrate one point: broadening the study of law involves raising one's intellectual sights. Far from being "soft" ("cauliflower scholarship" or "Sunday Supplement law", as some denigrators call it), the movement to broaden the study of law points in the direction of an ambitious intellectual agenda. If that is the case, one mistake of those who denigrate the achievements of legal scholarship, English or otherwise, may be that they have underestimated the magnitude of the task, a repetition of the error made in the 1930s by some "scientific" American Realists.[45]

---

[45] Karl Llewellyn, "The Theory of Legal 'Science'" (1941); 20 *North Carolina Law Review* 1; Twining, *Karl Llewellyn and the Realist Movement* (1973, 1985) 188–196.

The current situation is, of course, open to multiple interpretations. From the standpoint of one who remains committed to the development of broader approaches to the study of law, I would construct a story of modest achievement and unfulfilled potential rather than of failure. Some progress has been made, but there is still an unfinished agenda. Academic law has considerable potential, but it has some way to go before it can hope to be reinstated as one of the great humane studies.

How might one construct this rather more optimistic scenario? In respect of the past, the story of academic law in England can be plausibly told in terms of late development in rather unfavourable circumstances. After a slow start, the pioneering generation of law teachers in the late 19th century had to struggle to establish the respectability of the subject in the eyes of two sceptical constituencies: colleagues in other disciplines and the practising profession. The leaders adopted the strategy of arrogating to themselves the role of systematisers of the common law; their first scholarly priority was the preparation of basic undergraduate texts.[46] The jurist as Expositor sidelined the Censor and the Craftsman and, hijacked the title of "Scientist" (despite the fact that exposition was particular and science is general), so that the roles of the external observer, as exemplified by historical jurisprudence, sociology of law and comparative law, were largely marginalised.

It took a long time for law in the universities to attract able students in large numbers; it was not seen to be entirely convincing either as a vehicle for general education or as a preparation for practice. The most significant changes took place in the 1960s and 1970s, when high demand, the acceptance of the law degree as the normal route to professional qualification (though by no means always to practice) enabled law to share in the general expansion and belatedly to achieve critical mass. The post-Ormrod settlement assigned universities a clear, "academic" role and facilitated their assimilation into the universities; but it also confined their contribution to the first stage of a four-stage process of professional formation. The result was that they were largely sidelined not only in respect of vocational training but also of more advanced studies, such as the training of researchers, specialists and the judiciary. Unfortunately, the period of expansion largely coincided with a period of almost perpetual economic crisis in higher education.

During the 1970s and 1980s university and polytechnic law schools were, with few exceptions, essentially undergraduate teaching institutions and much of the early efforts of innovative academic lawyers were invested in designing new courses and preparing new kinds of educational materials. This produced some

[46] David Sugarman, "Legal Theory, the Common Law Mind and the Making of the Textbook Tradition", in Twining (ed.) *Legal Theory and Common Law* (1986) Chap 3. It is too simple to say that a new pluralism in legal scholarship replaced a monolithic orthodoxy which conceived of exposition of legal doctrine as the beginning and end of "legal science". This does not do justice to the individuality, the tradition of dissent, and the cosmopolitanism of many of the very small band of pioneers who helped to establish law in the universities in the late 19th century and in the inter-war period. Nor does it allow for the survival and increased sophistication of expository work.

excellent scholarship[47], but development was constrained by the limited role of law schools and the economics of publishing: despite the recent increased involvement of university presses in law publishing, most academic law books have still to be addressed to a student market which is based on a restricted curriculum.

For a period university and polytechnic law schools fell between stools in that they were neither treated as genuine professional schools, as in the United States, nor as full-fledged academic departments, providing a general education for undergraduates and specialised advanced studies at postgraduate level, as happened in the better law faculties in continental Europe. Instead they were viewed and used by their clientele as little more than primary schools for the profession. In the 1980s law schools began to diversify their roles and their clientele. Postgraduate studies expanded; more and more institutions became involved in the second or vocational stage of professional formation; and there was a significant increase in mixed degrees with a European component. The skills movement has so far concentrated on elementary teaching of basic skills – another form of primary education – but it represents a significant step in the direction of becoming more grown up; it has also stimulated some promising new lines of research.

By the early 1990s there was an increasing feeling among academics that university law schools had by and large outgrown the three year undergraduate degree at 18+. Changes in legal practice and increased competition for entry to the legal profession created a potential crisis in universities: if the undergraduate law degree continued to be regarded as mainly vocational and law schools were essentially undergraduate teaching institutions, it was possible that demand for legal education might fall and that at least some law schools would be in danger of losing their economic base. Faced with this situation, law schools collectively need to consider a number of options: to diversify their clientele, their functions and their sources of funding; to make the undergraduate degree more credible as a vehicle for general education in order to compete more seriously for students with disciplines such as history and English; or to contract. Whether this is a genuine crisis or an opportunity to develop further in the direction of being multi-functional institutions dealing with all aspects of law in society at a variety of levels was, by 1994, an open question.

In the light of this story, perhaps we should be impressed rather than depressed by what has been achieved in legal scholarship in the past thirty years, not least in respect of diversification. And, more than most academics, lawyers have some grounds for optimism: the subject-matter of our discipline is ubiquitous, important, intellectually challenging and accessible; it has a rich mass of constantly renewed primary sources that have to date been generally underexploited by scholars, including legal scholars.[48] It is constantly fed by

[47] Geoffrey Wilson, *op cit* at p 821.
[48] BT Chap 5.

problems and materials from outside the discipline – what some people call "the real world". Its economic base is reasonably secure because of high demand, alternative markets for legal education, association with a generally profitable and powerful occupational group, and because it has relatively low overheads, even if it is not quite as cheap as its traditional image. The community of legal scholars is strengthened by the contributions of practising lawyers and judges, at least some of whom can genuinely be said to be learned. There are signs that law is becoming more part of the intellectual mainstream. Above all, the modern English law school is a very recent creation, which has only recently been assimilated into the university and is only just in process of coming of age. Whether or not there should be a Nobel Prize for law is unimportant, not least because the advancement of learning is a collective enterprise, often involving teamwork, multi-disciplinary perspectives and the gradual accretion of contributions by many participants, most of whom remain anonymous. But there is no reason why law as an institutionalised discipline cannot make significant contributions to human welfare and human understanding.

Chapter 5

POLICY ISSUES IN LAW AND THE FAMILY

Professor John Dewar
Griffith University, Brisbane

Over the last 25 years, the study of Family Law has come to exemplify the Warwick ethos of legal scholarship. It has become axiomatic that the subject can only be understood in its social context, a context that has been illuminated both by empirical study and a plundering of the allied disciplines of sociology, social administration and social and critical theory. This has transformed our understanding of the subject, and has shaped views of what the subject is. Socio-legal research, in particular, has illuminated the working of the law and legal processes, has assisted in identifying problems and in devising solutions. Analysis of theory and policy has become more sophisticated. The traditional object of legal scholarship, the reported case, has been removed from centre stage.

This chapter is an attempt to identify some of the most important themes presently dominating the study of Law and the Family and to give an overview of the state of scholarship in this field. It is neither theoretical, nor merely a report of empirical research: instead, it seeks to occupy a middle ground between the two, drawing on both.

1. Background

Like social policy in the United Kingdom, legal policy with respect to the family over the last 25 years been characterised by a number of differing, and sometimes competing, objectives.

Three features characterised legal policy in the wake of the divorce reforms of 1969 and 1970. The first was that divorce should be more easily available than previously (both in terms of the substantive grounds and state funding of proceedings), and that the courts should have a wide ranging discretion to redistribute family assets and to make orders for income transfers on divorce. Second, marriage occupied an almost unquestioned centrality in lawyer's thinking about family matters: there was very limited provision for unmarried couples and the concept of illegitimacy was not to be removed from the law until 1987. Finally, the social security system, sometimes acknowledged as the "third system" of Family Law, continued to be grounded on the post-war consensus that the role of the state was to guarantee the well being of family members to a basic level. The 1973 Finer Committee Report on One Parent Families, for example, did not regard it as politically unacceptable to propose new forms of state assistance for single parents, a group identified as facing particular economic hardship.

The shortcomings of this state of affairs became increasingly apparent during the 1980s. Divorce rates continued to rise with disastrous financial consequences for women and children, something which the divorce court, even when armed with its wide order-making powers, was powerless to prevent. Research[1] showed that for many couples, the divorce court's jurisdiction to make financial provision was a luxury afforded by only a few; for increasing numbers of divorcing couples, the reality of divorce meant making the most of the state benefits available, particularly supplementary and related benefits (and especially the payment of mortgage interest). The courts colluded in this form of benefit planning, taking the view that men should support their new rather than former families.[2] It became common practice for men to trade property for reduced child support[3]; and although in theory such orders were not binding of the DHSS, there was a low level of recovery of support from "liable relatives". Further, it became apparent that never married mothers were an increasing and significant group of social security claimants, mirroring the rise in extra-marital cohabitation and non-marital births.[4]

These developments had an impact on the public purse in two ways. The first was the growing cost of benefits paid to single mothers; the second was the rising cost to the Legal Aid budget of paying for a growing number of family disputes. The coming to power in 1979 of a Conservative government committed to reducing public expenditure meant that it was only a matter of time before this state of affairs came under official scrutiny. It duly did so, most obviously in the shape of the Government White Paper on Child Support (1990) and a later Green Paper on Divorce and Mediation (1993); less obviously in the shape of a steady erosion in legal aid eligibility and a restructuring of the state safety net by the Social Security Act 1988. These cost cutting measures were accompanied by an increasingly vehement rhetoric of parental (and individual) responsibility and a condemnation of 'abnormal' family lifestyles. Single mothers and feckless fathers were demonised.[5]

Three trends in government and other official thinking appeared during the 1980s. The first was the growing recognition for legal purposes of family forms

---

[1] See Eekelaar and Maclean, *Maintenance after Divorce* (OUP, 1986).

[2] See, *e.g. Delaney* [1990] 2 FLR 457, per Ward J.

[3] *Hanlon* v *Hanlon* [1978] 2 All ER 889.

[4] Volume 2, *Children Come First* (Government White Paper on Child Support), Tables 1–4.

[5] See L. Fox Harding, "'Alarm' versus 'liberation': Responses to the increase in lone parents" [1993] JSWFL 101 and 174; Abbot and Wallace, *The Family and the New Right* (Pluto, 1992).

outside marriage. Growing diversity in patterns of family living forced a recognition that the creation and enforcement of effective support obligations would have to depend on something other than marriage. This, when coupled with other policy developments (outlined below), led to the recognition of legal relationships (and especially obligations of support) that had nothing to do with marriage.

The second was that the traditional means of resolving family disputes were called into question: they were easily portrayed as expensive, unnecessarily elaborate for the majority of clients and likely to produce bad consequences for the welfare state. The third, linked to the second, was the disenchantment with the discretionary modes of decision-making that have come to characterise decision-making in family law in post-war years. This is seen to be productive of uncertainty and, thus, of inefficiency and injustice.

It could be argued that these trends were prompted exclusively by a desire on the part of the government to curb public spending; but there are two reasons why this argument should be treated with caution. The first is that public spending has exerted a grip over family law for some time. The introduction of the "special procedure" in 1977, which arguably did more than the Divorce Reform Act 1969 to alter the nature of divorce, was prompted by a desire to remove legal aid from undefended divorces.[6] Second, it is unlikely that these policy changes would have taken root if they did not reflect existing disenchantment with the system, or other policy shifts pointing in the same directions. The shift from marriage, for example, could be attributed as much to a policy of recentring legal concern on the child, rather than on the marital status of the parents, as to concern with the social security bill. The disenchantment with traditional methods of adjudication could be attributed as much to the conciliation/mediation movement, and to research on the behaviour of judges and lawyers in the context of traditional litigation, as to concerns about the costs to the state of legal aid. The scepticism about discretion comes as much from a feminist perspective (especially discretionary decision-making in children and money cases) as from the perspective of justice and efficiency.

2. The Decline of Marriage

In the late- 1970s, Eric Clive argued that marriage was a logically redundant concept for legal purposes: the same ends could be achieved by other legal means.[7] Redundancy in theory would be followed by increasing obsolescence in practice. Twenty years later, marriage, although not entirely redundant, is certainly less significant than it was. Instead, a powerful new legal status is developing around parenthood. What is the evidence for this, and why has it come about?

---

[6] C. Gibson, "Divorce and the recourse to legal aid" (1980) 43 *Modern Law Review* 609.

[7] E. Clive, "Marriage: An unnecessary legal concept?" in Eekelaar and Katz (eds), *Marriage and cohabitation in contemporary societies: Areas of legal, social and economic change*, Ch 8.

Starting with financial obligations of family members, marriage now adds very little to the obligations of parenthood. Studies have shown that income transfers after divorce between former spouses are almost entirely confined to cases where there are children.[8] As Eekelaar and Maclean have put it, post-divorce support is effectively child support.[9] Further, the support obligation is no longer confined to marriage: the Child Support Act 1991 now extends that obligation to any absent parent, irrespective of that parent's relationship with the parent with care.[10]

It could nevertheless be argued that marriage continues to make a difference in two ways. First, it creates a support obligation between adults, which parenthood does not. Second, only a former spouse is able to claim a substantial transfer of property or of a lump sum in the divorce court. Yet while these points must be conceded, their weight should not be overstated. It could be argued, for example, that the CSA formula in effect recognises a support obligation between adults, by including the parent with care's personal allowance as the biggest single element in the maintenance requirement. The absent parent is recouping the cost to the state of supporting not just the child, but its carer as well.[11]

As to the second point, the significance of marriage in this context will depend on the wealth of the parties. If there are substantial assets, then a former spouse will be able to make claims to property that would have been unavailable otherwise, save on proof of ownership. She may even be able to claim support in her own right, if the absent parent is wealthy enough to meet the CSA requirements and still have enough for her. Marriage clearly makes a difference in this sort of case. Yet the significance of marriage is less visible where the parties' assets are limited. For example, if the parties' only significant asset[12] is a tenancy, then the court's powers to transfer property between parents "for the benefit of" the children under Schedule 1 of the Children Act 1989 would appear sufficient to make an outright transfer of the tenancy from one parent to the other whether the parties are married or not.[13] The impression is that parenthood is being fashioned into a poor (wo)man's (quasi-) marriage law. This is confirmed by recent case-law which sets firm limits to the capital settlements that may be awarded under Schedule 1 against wealthier parents.[14]

---

[8] See Eekelaar and Maclean, *Maintenance after Divorce* (OUP, 1986); J. Gregory and K. Foster, *The consequences of divorce* (HMSO, 1990).

[9] "The evolution of private law maintenance obligations: The common law" in Meulders-Klein and Eekelaar (eds), *Family, state and individual economic security* (Story Scientia, 1988), Ch 6.

[10] Child Support Act 1991 s 1.

[11] It could (and has been) argued that the maintenance requirement is merely a starting point for calculating the absent parent's liability, and that we should not read too much into how it is constructed. This argument would be stronger if the absent parent's liability were related directly to the number of children, as it is under the Australian scheme. Under the CSA, that liability is affected only marginally by the number of children, at least until the higher rate of payment is reached.

[12] Apart, that is, from future earnings, which, as we have seen, are available for redistribution regardless of marital status.

[13] See *K* v *K* [1992] 2 FLR 220.

[14] *A* v *A* [1994] *Fam. Law* 368.

Parenthood, perhaps, is being offered as a solution to the problems of the working class relationship breakdown, while marriage continues to be a middle and upper class option.

All of this suggests that, at least for some sections of the community, marriage is all but superfluous as a legal concept. Why has this come about? At least two different factors have been at work. The first is the increasing child-centred nature of private law, according to which the marital status of the parents is irrelevant. It has been official policy for some time, evidenced in successive Law Commission reports[15], to eliminate the legal distinctions between children whose parents are and are not married. The logical unfolding of this policy has entailed assimilating the property and financial claims of children against their parents on relationship breakdown, whether the parents are married or not.

The second has operated at the level of recent state policy towards the family. Here, the primary concern has been with reducing dependence on state welfare by family members at a time when family members no longer behave according to traditional patterns. This has entailed the construction of legal obligations of support (notionally, at least, towards children) that turn on concepts other than marriage. Child-centredness emerges again, with parenthood as the key term, but this time from a different logic.[16]

Marriage continues to have a significance in other respects: in tax law, for example, and in some aspects of property rights during marriage. The CA 1989 also distinguishes married from unmarried parents when it comes to acquisition of parental responsibility (a term which, incidentally, does not include responsibilities of support, which follow biological parentage). Even so, it is not hard to foresee the fading away of marriage even from these areas: the married couple's income tax allowance is likely to be allowed to wither on the vine; the review of cohabitant' property rights seems likely to produce some degree of assimilation between the married and the unmarried of the position during an ongoing relationship; and it may not be long before English law adopts the recommendation of the Scottish Law Commission that unmarried fathers should acquire parental responsibility automatically.[17]

This turn from marriage to parenthood demands careful evaluation, not least in its impact on women, for whom it could be seen as both a threat and an opportunity. It is a threat because it renders women visible in Family Law only as mothers and not as bearers of rights as individuals. As mothers, women's claims are likely to become weakened as they are mediated through professional evaluations of what is best for the children.[18] It is an opportunity, because it allows for the construction of alternative ways of making claims: for

---

[15] Law Commission Reports Nos. 74 (1979), 118 (1982), 157 (1986).

[16] See Parker, *Informal Marriage, Cohabitation and the Law, 1750–1989*, Ch 6 for a similar argument.

[17] Scottish Law Commission *Report on Family Law* (No 135), paras 2.36–2.51.

[18] See Fineman, *The illusion of equality: The rhetoric and reality of divorce reform*, Part II; "Dominant discourse, professional language and legal change in child custody decision-making" (1988) 101 *Harvard Law Review* 727; C. Smart, "Power and the politics of child custody" in Smart and Sevenhuijsen (eds) *Child custody and the politics of gender*, Ch 1.

example, claims rooted in care rather than in rights (such as a primary carer presumption: see below), claims which (because of the sexual division of labour) are likely to be stronger in the hands of women than of men.[19]

3. Family Justice

An important premise of legal policy has been that family litigation is merely a specialised version of ordinary civil litigation. Most of the procedural rules[20] concerned with the progress of proceedings and the disclosure and discovery of evidence would be recognisable to any civil practitioner; and until very recently there has been little serious questioning of the central role of the court and of legal professionals, especially solicitors, in the handling of divorce and family proceedings. There was talk of a family court, but, in some versions at least, this would merely be a specialised version of the traditional court model.

Central to the current system of family justice are solicitors. They have successfully established and maintained a monopoly over the management of the divorce process, a process which remains essentially a legal one in which adjudication in court remains an ultimate (but largely theoretical[21]) possibility. But solicitors are more than just gatekeepers of a court-centred system: they are the most significant means by which family disputes are settled, drawing selectively on a range of court-related strategies in a process described by Richard Ingleby as "litigotiation".[22] Ingleby's study of solicitors in divorce concluded that solicitors are far more settlement minded than is often supposed and that court proceedings are initiated in only a minority of cases.[23] Thus, it is the process of "litigotiation" between solicitors that is the most significant dispute resolution process in divorce.

This model of family justice has recently come under serious scrutiny, and there are already signs that it is being dismantled. The Children Act, which itself goes a long way to establishing a specialist judicial body for children cases, has fundamentally altered the role of courts in cases arising under the Act by requiring it to take a proactive role in matters of timetabling of proceedings

---

[19] K. Bartlett, "Re-expressing parenthood" (1988) 98 *Yale Law Journal* 293; C. Smart, "The legal and moral ordering of child custody" (1991) 18 *Journal of Law and Society* 485.

[20] Family Proceedings Rules 1991.

[21] "For most divorcing couples, a decision of the court is as remote a prospect as the summit of Mount Everest viewed from base camp": Davis, Cretney and Collins, *Simple Quarrels* (OUP, 1994), p 253.

[22] Ingleby, *Solicitors and Divorce* (OUP, 1992), quoting M. Galanter "Worlds of deals: Using negotiation to teach about legal process" (1984) 34 *Journal of Legal Education* 268: "the negotiation of disputes is not an alternative to litigation. It is only a slight exaggeration to say that it *is* litigation. There are not two distinct processes, negotiation and litigation: there is a single process of negotiating in the vicinity of official tribunals that we might call *litigotiation*, that is, the strategic pursuit of settlement through mobilising the court process".

[23] A less sanguine view of the process is taken by Davis *et al* in *Simple Quarrels* (above) who conclude from their study of the divorce process that, more often than not, settlement is a result of delay and stagnation rather than "purposeful settlement seeking".

and submission of evidence, as well as (though this is more controversial) in the supervision and implementation of the orders it makes. The development, so far on a voluntary basis, of mediation and conciliation (discussed further below) has provided a choice of dispute resolution processes.

More significantly, the Child Support Act 1991 has removed, save in limited cases, the jurisdiction of the courts to make orders for child support. Instead, the extent of liability is determined according to a statutory formula by a Child Assessment Officer, whose decisions are subject to a statutory system of reviews and appeals. It is only on points of law, and issues of parentage, that the courts retain a continuing role. This has led to concern that the courts' ability to achieve a satisfactory "package" of property and money orders will be seriously undermined, and in particular that many fathers will be unwilling to part with their share in the home if they cannot be "compensated" by a nominal child support award.[24]

Although the CSA 1991 takes away a substantial jurisdiction from the courts (and thus from lawyers), it poses no serious threat to lawyers' professional dominance. Indeed, it is possible that the CSA will be a further source of advisory work for lawyers[25], and that the operation of the formula and the Agency will be readily assimilated into the current model of professional practice. A more serious threat comes from the Government Green Paper, *Mediation and the Ground for Divorce*, in which a more radical review of family justice, at least in the divorce context, is proposed.

A central feature of the proposals is the state-assisted expansion of out of court mediation services, hitherto confined largely to the voluntary sector. This would be coupled with financial incentives to use mediation rather than solicitors. "Incentives" may be the wrong term, though, given that the availability of legal aid would depend on the client adopting a "reasonable" attitude towards mediation.[26] An "incentive" of this sort can easily become compulsion for those without the means to employ a solicitor. The scale of mediation envisaged in the Green Paper, when coupled with the crude system of financial sticks and carrots, implies a very reduced role for lawyers. For the first time, the dominance of lawyers in the divorce process is under real threat.

What has this transformation in thinking about family justice come about? Again, it is possible to identify a number of contributory factors. The first is government concern at the alarming escalation in the matrimonial legal aid budget.[27] Much of that budget is spent on lawyers' time, and lawyers (in common with other professional groups) are able, by controlling both the supply and demand for legal services, to demand a comparatively high level of

---

[24] J. Eekelaar, "Child support – An evaluation" (1991) *Fam. Law* 511.

[25] There is nothing to prevent those who can afford it from obtaining legal advice – possibly from a solicitor – on the impact of the CSA. Computer programmes are available which, their makers claim, enable the user to predict the likely level of CSA assessment: see, *e.g.* Mostyn, *Child's Pay*. Only limited legal aid funding is available for this purpose.

[26] *Looking to the future*, Ch 9.

[27] See LAG, *A Strategy for Justice: Publicly Funded Services in the 1990s* (LAG, 1992), Ch 3 which shows that matrimonial cases are the single largest category of legal aid expenditure.

remuneration for those services.[28] It is therefore an entirely logical step to seek to remove from lawyers as much of the work of processing family disputes as possible. Although this may not have been the prime motive behind the CSA 1991, there is little doubt that it is a major objective of the Green Paper proposals.

A second factor has been the growth in conciliation and mediation as alternative ways of resolving family disputes. The impetus towards conciliation can itself be attributed to a number of different factors[29]: a concern at the growth in the numbers of children involved in a parental divorce, and the inability of legal procedures to address the needs of such children directly; a perception that divorce requires a therapeutic rather than merely legal response; the desire to "empower the parties" by helping them to resolve their own differences; the need to find ways of diverting the growing number of family disputes into another forum, so as to focus scarce adjudicative resources on those cases that cannot be resolved in any other way; and evidence that solicitor handling of family disputes is characterised by delay and inefficiency.[30] Not all of these can stand together: "child saving", for example is not easily squared with "party power", since leaving it to the parties can easily lead to a demotion of the interests of children.[31] Even so, the power of the mediation idea is such that it is difficult to be against it; and the government has now yoked it to its own expenditure policy, having been persuaded that mediation is a cheaper way to settle disputes.[32]

These trends have two important implications. The first is the emergence of a two-tier system of family justice: it seems, quite literally, that there is to be one system for those on legal aid or income support, and another for the rest. Under the CSA, for example, a parent with care on benefit has no alternative but to use the Child Support Agency.[33] Indeed, she is in danger of losing benefit if she refuses to identify the father. For those not on benefit, by contrast, a wider range of choice presents itself. Although it is no longer possible to go to

---

[28] See Abel, *The legal profession in England and Wales*, Ch 1.

[29] See Dingwall and Eekelaar (eds) *Divorce mediation and the legal process* (OUP, 1988), Ch 1; Piper, *The Responsible Parent: A study in divorce mediation*, Ch 1.

[30] See Davis *et al*, *Simple quarrels: Negotiating money and property disputes on divorce.* This criticism was not made in the other major study of solicitors in divorce, by Richard Ingleby (*Solicitors and divorce*), who found that solicitors were not inclined to prolong disputes. Davis *et al* would not deny the settlement orientation of solicitors, but would attribute the achievement of settlement as much to stagnation as to purposeful settlement seeking. However, the sampling technique employed by Davis *et al* is open to question: they looked only at those cases in which an application to court had already been made. This has two consequences. The first is that cases settled without such an application were not represented in the sample; the second that the sample probably contained an over-representation of legal aid cases, since an application to court is an essential prerequisite of legal aid eligibility. Even so, the findings suggest that legal aid clients may sometimes receive a low quality service.

[31] See R. Dingwall and D. Greatbach, "Who's in charge?: Rhetoric and evidence in the study of mediation" (1993) JSWFL 366.

[32] The evidence for this is not overwhelming. Recent research has found it hard to find firm evidence of cost savings through mediation and concludes that the major cost in divorce remains solicitor time: see *Mediation: The making and remaking of co-operative relationships: An evaluation of the effectiveness of comprehensive mediation* (Relate Centre for Family Studies, University of Newcastle), Ch 9.

[33] CSA 1991 s 6.

court for a contested order, it is still possible to seek a consent order in the terms of a previous written agreement, or simply to reach a private agreement.[34] For the very rich, top up orders are available from the courts where the formula maximum has been surpassed, as are orders for school fees.[35]

The two-tier structure emerges even more clearly from the proposals on mediation. As we saw above, legally aided clients will be prevented under the proposals from seeing a solicitor at state expense unless they have behaved "reasonably" in relation to mediation, a question determined in the first instance by a civil servant. Privately paying clients will be able to seek legal advice at their own expense, but will be subject to less draconian cost penalties if found (again, by a civil servant) to be acting "unreasonably" in relation to mediation.[36]

A class-based system of family justice is nothing new. The Finer Committee identified three different systems of Family Law at work in the early 1970s, each serving a particular clientele: those dispensed by the High Court, the Magistrates and the DHSS. The social exclusivity of the first has been ameliorated by the brief post-war flowering of legal aid and the policy of redistributing the High Court jurisdiction in family matters to the lowest reaches of the system; but as pressure on the legal aid budget has proved too intense to sustain political support, so the class basis of the family justice system seems set to reassert itself.[37]

There may be a case for offering simpler regimes of family justice where the issues to be settled are relatively straightforward. The current system was designed to deal with the problems of one social class, but is for the most part applied to another; and the evidence suggests that there is a close relationship between the complexity of a case and the length it takes to resolve it: the simpler, the longer.[38] The concern, though, is that the trends identified here are not concerned solely with simplifying family justice as an end in itself, but with reducing public expenditure; and that the net result could be worse, rather than better, for families.[39]

The second point is that the trends identified here are likely to reinforce pre-existing inequalities between parties, especially where one is legally aided and the other is not. Because Family Law is still characterised by wide discretion,

---

[34] Although this would not be binding on the Agency: see CSA 1991, s 9.

[35] CSA 1991, s 8.

[36] *Looking to the future*, paras 9.20–23.

[37] The disproportionate reliance of women on legal aid and income support makes this a gender issue as well.

[38] See Davis *et al*, *Simple quarrels*, Ch 11.

[39] For worrying evidence of the impact of the CSA 1991 on parents with care and children, see Garnham and Knights, *Putting the Treasury first: The truth about child support* (CPAG, 1994), pp 106–122; NACAB, *Child support: One year on* (1994). Neither report found much evidence that parents with care have gained from the Agency's operations. This may be because the overwhelming majority (96%) of cases taken on by the Agency have been "benefit cases" where any child support received merely reduces entitlement to income support (see Social Security Select Committee Report on the Child Support Act). Indeed, some parents with care are worse off because they are floated off income support and lose so-called passported benefits, such as free school meals.

there remains an advantage to be gained from professional assistance: a discretionary framework requires specialists to predict the results it might produce.[40] Those denied access to that specialist advice, and to professional adjudication, may be faced with having to deal with their former partner in ignorance of the shadow, or shadows, cast by the law.[41] So long as discretion retains its central place in Family Law, it would be unfair to place obstacles to obtaining legal advice in the path of some parties and not others. The question of what constitutes a legal need is a difficult one[42]: but there is more to eliminating the causes of such a need than simply blocking access to lawyers.

If it is the discretionary nature of Family Law that creates a need for legal services, then we need to switch attention to the arguments for and against retaining a discretionary system.

4. Rules and Discretion

Discretion occupies a large place in Family Law. It appears in the statutory framework governing division of property on divorce[43], applies to the resolution of disputes concerning the upbringing of children[44] and permeates the law on domestic violence and civil injunctions.[45] This amounts to more than just a weak discretion (ie, deciding how to apply a standard in a particular case) but extends to discretion in the strong sense (ie, deciding which standards to apply).[46]

---

[40] For the argument that discretion serves the interests of the legal profession, see R. Ingleby, "Recent Australian developments: Discretion discredited" in Weitzman and Maclean (eds) *Economic consequences of divorce: The international perspective*, Ch 4.

[41] The image of parties bargaining "in the shadow of the law" comes from R. Mnookin and L. Kornhauser, "Bargaining in the shadow of the law: The case of divorce" (1979) 88 *Yale Law Journal* 950; Ingleby concludes from his research that the law casts many shadows.

[42] See Philip Lewis, "Unmet legal need" in Morris, White and Lewis (eds) *Social needs and legal action* (Martin Robertson, 1973). For the argument that women in particular fare worse in informal dispute resolution procedures than in formal ones, see A. Bottomley "What is happening to family law?: A feminist critique of conciliation" in Brophy and Smart (eds) *Women in Law: Explorations in Law, Family and Sexuality* (London, Routledge), p 162; L. Weitzman, "Gender differences in custody bargaining in the United States" in Weitzman and Maclean, *Economic consequences of divorce* (OUP, 1992), Ch 23. For evidence the other way, see J. Pearson, "Ten myths about Family Law" (1993) 27 *Family Law Quarterly* 279 at p 283. Davis *et al* suggest that women do best in trials and less well in lawyer-mediated settlement: see *Simple Quarrels, op cit*, p 261–2.

[43] This discretion was increased in 1984 when the Matrimonial and Family Proceedings Act 1984 removed the only (albeit manifestly unachievable) objective specified in the original MFPA 1970, namely that the courts should seek to place the parties in the position in which they would have been had the relationship not broken down. It was replaced with two (probably incompatible) objectives: priority to the welfare of children and the clean break: see the Matrimonial Causes Act 1973, s 25A.

[44] CA 1989, s 1 (welfare of the child to be the court's paramount consideration when making decisions about the child's upbringing).

[45] This is not expressly stated in legislation; indeed, the legislation says almost nothing about the criteria governing, for example, ouster orders or attaching powers of arrest. The discretion here, then, is frequently a discretion to decide what the law is.

[46] C. Schneider, "The tension between rules and discretion in Family Law: A report and reflection" (1993) 27 *Family Law Quarterly* 229. As Schneider points out, the distinction between rules and discretion is not absolute: rules often entail some degree of discretion – if only in interpretation – and discretions often harden through repeated exercise into rules.

Discretion, nevertheless, is increasingly being replaced by rules or firm guidelines[47] both in the UK and in other jurisdictions. The Child Support Act 1991, which applies throughout the UK, sets child support levels according to a rigid formula, and reduces discretion almost to vanishing point[48]; similar legislation has been passed in Australia[49], and uniform child support guidelines have been promulgated in the United States.[50] The division of assets on divorce is also increasingly governed by firm guidelines: in Scotland, for example, the relevant legislation lays down five principles (the first of which is the equal division of matrimonial property)[51]; a similar starting point has been proposed in Australia[52]; and a number of American states have moved from separate property regimes to community property and presumptions of equal sharing on divorce.[53] The recent Law Commission proposals on Domestic Violence and Occupation of the Family Home seek to constrain or remove judicial discretion in a number of areas.[54] There is even doubt about the welfare criteria as the appropriate standard for resolving custody disputes. Firm presumptions, such as the primary carer presumption, are proposed in its place (see further below).

A number of different factors explain the demise of discretion. From the point of view of the state, a discretionary system cannot be relied on to pay sufficient regard to governmental priorities, especially concerning welfare expenditure. We have already seen, for example, that the willingness of judges to collude in the "benefit divorce" provided a powerful impetus for the CSA 1991; and the consequent routinisation of the issue of child support requires a formula amenable to bureaucratic implementation in which discretion is reduced to the minimum. Further, discretion can increase the cost to the state of settling disputes, whether in terms of judicial time or public assistance for litigants. A discretionary regime of individualised decision-making offers parties an incentive to spend time (or their lawyer's time) on searching out more and more information from each other, and promotes uncertainty about the eventual outcome.[55] This in turn prolongs disputes.

---

[47] The distinction between rules and discretion is sometimes characterised as reflecting a philosophical distinction between rights and utility: see S. Parker, "Rights and utility in Anglo-Australian Family Law" (1992) 55 *MLR* 311; or a distinction between a rights and needs based approach: see Jackson *et al* "Financial support on divorce: The right mixture of rules and discretion?" (1993) 7 IJLF 230.

[48] For a description and analysis of the UK system, see M. Maclean and J. Eekelaar, "Child support: The British solution" (1993) 7 *IJLF*, 205–229.

[49] See S. Parker, "Child support in Australia: Children's rights or public interest?" (1991) 5 IJLF 24.

[50] H. Krause, "Child support reassessed: Limits of private responsibility and the public interest" (1990) 24 *Family Law Quarterly* 1.

[51] Family Law (Scotland) Act 1985, s 9; see J. Dewar, "Reforming Financial provision: The alternatives" [1984] JSWL 1 for discussion.

[52] Australian Law Reform Commission, *Matrimonial Property*, Report No 39.

[53] L. Weitzman, "Marital property in the US: Its transformation and division", in Weitzman and Maclean (eds), Ch 5.

[54] *E.g.*, there will be more structured criteria for "occupation" (ouster) orders, and a presumption in favour of exclusion in certain cases, as well as presumptions in favour of, *e.g.* attaching powers of arrest. See now the Family Homes and Domestic Violence Bill.

[55] See Davis *et al*, *Simple quarrels*: "along with discretion goes uncertainty; the elevation of professional judgement ...; an almost limitless need for information about family finances ...; and the demand for almost limitless amounts of professional time" (p 259).

From the individual's point of view, the issue of cost is also relevant, even to the legally aided litigant who may find herself bound by the statutory charge. Moreover, it has been pointed out that a discretionary regime fails to redress, and may even exacerbate, inequality between parties.[56] Further, a discretionary system promotes dependence on expensive legal professionals. Their skills are required to obtain, interpret and present the information necessary for discretionary decision-making, and to predict the behaviour of the professional adjudicator.

Another criticism of discretion is that it leads to like cases being treated differently. In his study of District Judges, John Eekelaar found wide differences of opinion between the judges as to their general objectives when deciding ancillary relief cases: "when asked to articulate a general goal towards which they are working, the [district judges] are unable to produce a cohesive model. This is not surprising as the law has provided none".[57] One of the arguments put forward in the White Paper on Child Support for what is now the CSA 1991 was that the court based discretionary system led to like case being treated differently, especially when child support was calculated as a percentage of the absent parent's net income.[58] Such variations can be portrayed as infringing fundamental principles of the rule of law.

The criticisms of discretion are applied also to custody disputes. Studies suggest that women are disadvantaged when they negotiate child custody against the backcloth of a "best interests" standard. Women, it is argued, are less willing than men to regard children merely as part of a package for negotiation, and may be willing to concede other financial claims to avoid the threat of losing their children.[59] There should, it is argued, be firmer rules to protect women from the threats of this sort, such as a primary carer presumption which favours granting custody to the parent who has done most of the caring in the past.[60] Similarly, it has been argued that the best interests standard has allowed professional experts in the "psy" disciplines to colonise the decision-making process, and thereby to introduce values disguised as social science: values which often work to the disadvantage of mothers.[61]

---

[56] *Op cit*; in particular, unequal tolerance of postponed resolution, unequal ability to manipulate or conceal resources, unequal responsibilities for child care and inequalities in the quality of legal advice.

[57] *Regulating Divorce* (OUP, 1991), p 62. Nevertheless, Eekelaar found greater consistency of approach to detailed questions concerning use of the courts' distributive powers: see generally Ch 4.

[58] *Children Come First*, Vol 1 para 1.5; Vol 2, Table 13, p 27.

[59] L. Weitzman, "Gender differences in custody bargaining in the United States" in Weitzman and Maclean (eds), Ch 23; C. Smart, "The legal and moral ordering of child custody" (1991) 18 *Journal of Law and Society* 485.

[60] Fineman, *op cit*, pp 180–184. Fineman herself advocates a primary carer presumption as a way of resisting the encroachment of "psy" discourses into legal decision-making.

[61] Fineman, *op cit*, Part II. For the (opposite?) view, that law distorts the lessons of child welfare science, and that child welfare law should be delegalised, see King and Piper, *How the law thinks about children* (Gower, 1990). For a sophisticated defence of the best interests standard, see J. Eekelaar, "The interests of the child and the child's wishes: The role of dynamic self-determinism" (1994) 8 IJLF 42.

In defence of discretion is the evidence suggesting that women appear to do better financially under discretionary than fixed division regimes[62]; and the fact that rules compelling equal division may lead to a forced sale of the family home, which may be contrary to children's interests.[63] This suggests that the law is likely to retain a substantial discretionary element for the foreseeable future. Even so, English law is currently in a curious state: while child support is fixed according to a rigid formula, all other money and property issues continue to be resolved under the most discretionary of regimes. Parker's suggestion[64] that Australian Family Law is currently experiencing "an uneasy oscillation between rights and utility" could equally be applied in an English context.

5. Children: Displacement and the "Dual Logic"

Legal policy with respect to children is now dominated by the Children Act 1989. The Act was the culmination of a reform process pursued in parallel between the Law Commission and the DHSS, drawing together the strands of public and private law. It is an impressive achievement: its theoretical framework is rooted in widespread consensus following extensive consultation, all the more impressive given the prevailing political culture of the time.

Even so, critical reaction to the legislation insisted on seeing it as an extension of government policy. It was described as effecting a "privatisation" of the public interest in children, a withdrawal of legal regulation, of rolling back the state to children's detriment and as installing instead a specifically conservative view of parental responsibility according to which parents rather than the state are "responsible" for children.[65] As evidence, these commentators pointed (*inter alia*) to the reduced role for the courts in divorce[66], the presumption against

[62] See Weitzman, "Marital property in the US: Its transformation and division", in Weitzman and Maclean (eds), Ch 5.
[63] See Jackson *et al*, "Financial support on divorce: The right mixture of rules and discretion?" (1993) 7 IJLF 230. It is possible to conceive of fixed rules that would not disadvantage women or harm children. Much depends on the content of any rule and its scope of application. For example, it has been suggested that the fact that women fare better under discretionary regimes is an illusion created by the limited range of property rights available for distribution. If "new property" rights were included, such as pension rights, educational and professional qualifications and future earning potential, then women do remarkably badly, and would do better under a presumption of equal shares. Alternatively, a presumption in favour of the family home passing to the primary carer would both meet children's needs and (on the assumption that she is the primary carer) ensure protection of the wife's position: see Fineman, *op cit*, pp 175–180; Weitzman, "Marital property in the US" (above).
[64] S. Parker, "Rights and utility in Anglo-Australian Family Law", above at p 328.
[65] See A. Bainham, "The privatisation of the public interest in the welfare of children" (1990) 53 *MLR* 206; S. Cretney, "Defining the limits of state intervention: The child and the courts" in Freestone (ed) *Children and the Law* (Hull UP, 1990), Ch 3; J. Eekelaar, "Parental responsibility: State of nature or nature of the State?" (1991) JSWFL 37; S. Edwards and A. Halpern, "Parental responsibility: An instrument of social policy" (1992) *Fam. Law* 113.
[66] MCA 1973, s 41 as amended.

making court orders[67], the removal of voluntary care[68] and the tougher conditions for care and supervision orders.[69]

Although it is true that there is a strong "pro-family" theme to the legislation, it is wrong to reduce such a complex document to one set of political principles.[70] Instead, and from the point of view of legal policy, it could be said that there are two themes at work, both of which are obscured by the "privatisation" hypothesis. The first concerns the changing nature of legal regulation itself; the second relates to the emergence of a new logic of judicial intervention (ie, regulation in the conventional sense used by the privatisation theorists).

The first point, then, is that, contrary to the "delegalisation" or "privatisation" hypothesis outlined above, the Act is very much concerned with regulation through law, but in a displaced form. For the privatisation theorists, "regulation" through law seems to mean judges sitting in court making orders; and, indeed, regulation in this sense is to some extent reduced by the Act. But this obscures two important features of the new regime. In the private sphere, the Act erects a presumption of equal and shared parental responsibility between parents following divorce[71]: in effect, a presumption of what used to be called joint custody. This installs the legal backdrop against which private negotiations (often through mediation) over custody take place: often, it has been suggested, to the detriment of women.[72] Merely because there need be no court involvement in these negotiations (ie, regulation in the traditional sense) does not lessen the impact of the legislation on the outcomes arrived at.[73] Traditional regulation has been displaced by informal dispute resolution governed by legal norms.

A similar point may be made about the public law aspects of the Act. Here, it has been suggested that, in stark contrast to the "privatisation" hypothesis, the Act marks an extensive legalisation of child care, especially of social work practice. The courts, for example, have a more interventionist role in the cases coming before them than used to be the case.[74] Even when not in court, social work is now circumscribed by extensive regulation, guidance and official statements of shared principles and good practice.[75] There is now much greater

[67] CA 1989, s 1 (5).
[68] CA 1989, Part III.
[69] CA 1989, s 31.
[70] The subtleties are well explored by Fox Harding in *Perspectives in Child Care Policy* (Longman, 1992).
[71] See CA 1989, s 2.
[72] L. Weitzman, "Gender differences in custody bargaining in the United States", above; J. Brophy, "Custody law, child care and inequality in Britain", in Smart and Sevenhuijsen (eds) *Child custody and the politics of gender* (Routledge, 1989), Ch 9.
[73] Christine Piper has shown how the rhetoric of responsible co-parenting is invoked by mediators to persuade parents to accept certain joint post-divorce parenting arrangements: see *The Responsible Parent: A study in divorce mediation*, pp 191–4.
[74] Except, possibly, in wardship proceedings.
[75] Ten volumes of Official Guidance have been issued by the Department of Health to supplement the primary and secondary legislation; and a further document, entitled *Principles and Practices in Regulations and Guidance*, seeks to fill any remaining gaps.

emphasis on procedures, on consistency and the elimination of arbitrariness. Although not law in a traditional sense, much of this regulatory activity is informed by a spirit of what Parton has termed "legalism" and the rule of law.[76]

The second trend, also obscured by the "privatisation" hypothesis, concerns the logic of judicial intervention itself. Here, there has not been, as suggested, a straightforward withdrawal of judicial resources. Instead, there is now a more precise targeting of those resources, creating what Thery has described as a "dual logic of abstention/intervention".[77] In private law, for example, the presumption of no order ensures that courts will become involved only where there is a dispute: otherwise, party control reigns.[78] The early signs are that, in practice, this dual logic will lead to the routinisation of some children cases but an intensification of litigation in others.

In public law, the Act presupposes a distinction between parents who are "dangerous" on the one hand, and those who merely need help, on the other. The former are subject to legal procedures, while the latter are dealt with outside the court system, a process described by Parton as "bifurcation" according to which the "role of the state is not so much reduced as redirected".[79]

These twin trends, of displacement of legal regulation and the dual logic of intervention/abstention, are best understood as marking the confluence of different strands of thought, not all of them merely reflective of prevailing political ideology: the rise of family rights and a distrust of untrammelled state intervention in family life[80]; an ideological commitment to a limited but "strong" state; scepticism about the curative potential of the welfare state and the effectiveness of legal procedures in protecting children's interests; an emphasis on party control over dispute settlement and on partnership between parents and state agencies; and a concern to reinforce the private sphere of the family as the proper locus for both decision-making about children and for the discharge of care for children.

The Children Act thus holds in suspense a number of different philosophical positions, not all of which are compatible. This presents a problem for the judges, for whom the task is to render the legislation workable and coherent. It

---

[76] Parton, *Governing the Family: Child care, protection and the State* (Macmillan, 1991), Ch 7; "The contemporary politics of child protection" (1992) JSWFL 100; S. Gibson, "Social work, law jobs and the form of modern law: The Children Act 1989" in Maclean and Kurczewski (eds) *Families, politics and the law: Perspectives for East and West Europe*, Ch 12.

[77] I. Thery, "'The interest of the child' and regulation of the post-divorce family" in Smart and Sevenhuijsen (eds) *Child custody and the politics of gender* (above), Ch 4.

[78] This fact has intensified debate about the proper role of mediators with respect to children: should they play an active "child saving" role and protect the child's interests in mediation, or should they confine themselves to assisting the parties to reach their own agreements? Compare M. Roberts "Who's in charge? Reflections on recent research on the role of the mediator" (1993) JSWFL 372 with Dingwall and Greatbach "Who's in charge? Rhetoric and evidence in the study of mediation" (1993) JSWFL 367. Piper's evidence, above, suggests that some mediators may fail to see the difference.

[79] "Contemporary politics", above.

[80] See J. Eekelaar, "Families and children: From welfarism to rights" in McCrudden and Chambers (eds) *Individual rights and the Law in Britain* (OUP, 1994).

is already possible to identify judicial disagreements that go to the heart of the relationship between state agencies, individuals and the courts.[81] In this sense, the 1989 Act effects another form of displacement by which political issues of this sort are diverted from traditional political processes to the courts.[82]

6. Looking to the Future?

Family Law was a latecomer to the undergraduate curriculum. The first student text appeared in 1958[83] and confined itself to the traditional private law concerns of marriage and status: the public law aspects, especially child protection, were thought by its author to be beyond the book's scope and properly dealt with in courses on social administration.[84] As this chapter has shown, Family Lawyers no longer acknowledge such self imposed boundaries: attention now extends well beyond legal doctrine to include the behaviour of the lower (and unreported) reaches of the judiciary, legal practitioners and state officials.

As we have seen, it has been empirical work that has helped Family Lawyers chart this expanded terrain; Family Law in turn has provided a rich seam for socio-legal researchers. Yet this "socio-legal turn" in Family Law is itself a phenomenon that requires explanation. Is it that the doctrinal content of Family Law is so small, or so shot-through with discretion, that the subject's academic interest or credibility depended on expanding the frontier? Or that it is an area in which the boundaries between law and social life are so thin as to make for an especially promising site of socio-legal investigation? Or is it that the invasion of law into the private domain provokes such incommensurable conflicts of interest between genders, generations, individuals and state, that the "objectivity" of socio-legal research appears to provide an apparently value-free route to policy formation?

Whatever the answer (and it may be none of these), there is increasing scepticism about the influence of empirical work on official policy formation. Ruth Deech, for example, has been critical of formulating legal policy on the basis of empirical research: this, she argues, has led to "wholly inaccurate predictions" of the effects of the divorce reforms of 1969. She also deplores the draining away of family law's normative content as a threat to the civil liberties of family members.[85] Katherine O'Donovan detects signs in the most recent Law

[81] Consider, for example, the difference between the Court of Appeal and the House of Lords in the interpretation of the key threshold criteria for care and supervision orders in *Re M* [1994] 2 WLR 200, [1994] 3 WLR 558; or the differing views expressed in, for example, *Re B* [1993] 1 FLR 543 and *Kent CC* v *B* [1993] 1 FLR 308 on the power of the court to review or supervise local authority care plans.

[82] For some, this greater reliance on "impartial regimes of truth", such as the courts, is a characteristic response to a perception that welfare states are limited in their capacity to affect human behaviour: Offe, *Contradictions of the welfare state*, Ch 2.

[83] Bromley's *Family Law*, now in its 8th edition.

[84] *Op cit*, Preface.

[85] "Divorce law and empirical studies" (1990) 106 LQR 229, at p 245.

Commission proposals on divorce[86] of "an abandonment of law's claims to knowledge and to judge human behaviour". She suggests that – in the face of difficulties in predicting the impact of laws on behaviour ("a lack of knowledge") and the lack of consensus about legal norms governing family life ("unagreed values") – family lawyers should renew their concerns with basic questions of justice in its widest sense (and not just in the procedural sense I used above): in O'Donovan's words, "a family law that values liberty and equality".[87]

The pre-eminence of discretion over the last 25 years has meant that the conflicts of interest endemic to family law have been held in suspense. Now that the trend seems to be away from discretion, and towards firmer norms (as discussed above), it is right to heed O'Donovan's call. Indeed, there are already signs of growing interest in philosophical questions amongst Family Lawyers, particularly in connection with children's rights.[88]

All of this signals an interesting time ahead for Family Lawyers. As the Warwick Law School enters its next 25 years, it is particularly well placed, through the appointment to a Chair in 1992 of a prominent family lawyer[89], to play a leading role.

---

[86] Law Commission Report No 192, *The Ground for Divorce* (1990, HMSO).

[87] *Family Law Matters* (Pluto, 1993), p 115. See especially O'Donovan's discussion of Susan Moller Okin, *Justice, Gender and the Family* (Basic Books, 1989).

[88] See, for example, Alston, Parker and Seymour (eds) *Children, rights and the law* (Oxford, 1991). John Eekelaar's writings seem to have followed a similar path: compare, for example, the first and second editions of *Family Law and Social Policy* (Weidenfeld, 1978 and 1984) (I owe this point to Stephen Parker).

[89] Professor Judith Masson.

Chapter 6

CONSTITUTING CRIMINAL LAW

Professor David Farrier

University of Wollongong, NSW, Australia

1. Introduction

I would like to make a few simple points about the way we approach criminal law as a field of study[1], and in the process question some of the assumptions which have traditionally underpinned scholarship in this area:

- The field of rules which we collectively refer to as criminal law is disparate rather than unitary, so disparate that we may in fact be talking about not one but a number of quite different forms of regulation. The parameters of some of these are outlined.
- The version of criminal law emanating from the appeal courts and the legislature needs to be set in the context of the criminal process. Here we will find other versions of criminal law, which, in practice, may frequently compete successfully with the "official" version.
- Commentators on criminal law must be at least as concerned with policing the borderland of criminal law as the detailed structure of core offences.
- "Criminal law is not the civilising cement which holds society together and prevents the anti-social unleashing of egoism and plunder that 'human nature' would otherwise dictate.'[2] Rather, it supplements and interacts with other forms of regulation, many of which operate very successfully on a non-institutionalised level.

---

[1] I first made many of the points considered in the early part of this essay in Farrier, *Drugs and Intoxication* (Sweet and Maxwell, 1980), especially pp 1–6; 130–139 and Ch 6. For more recent discussions, see Lacey, Wells and Meure, *Reconstructing Criminal Law* (Weidenfeld, 1990), Ch 1; Brown, Farrier, Neal and Weisbrot, *Criminal Laws* (Federation Press, 1990), Ch 1; Farrier, "The Distinction Between Murder and Manslaughter in its Procedural Context" (1976) 39 *MLR* 414; Farrier, "In Search of Real Criminal Law" in Bonyhady, *Environmental Protection and Legal Change* (Federation Press, 1992). I am particularly grateful to David Brown and David Weisbrot for helping me to clarify my thoughts on many of these points.

[2] Brown, Farrier, Neal and Weisbrot, *ibid.*, p 15.

2. The Broader Context of Criminal Law

Writing in 1979, Professor Colin Howard, at that time the leading Australian academic authority on criminal law, had these comments to make about the inclusion of chapters on drugs offences, public order offences and motor traffic offences in a recently published book of teaching material[3], which represented the first real attempt to place the substantive criminal law in a broader social, historical and procedural context:

> "These are important topics, particularly to the practitioner, and raise wide and fundamental questions about society. Nevertheless ... they seem more appropriate to consequential or specialist courses than to the sort of basic criminal law concepts to which the great bulk of the book is devoted. The space used on these matters might better have been devoted to more thorough coverage of such topics as theft and arrest. Moreover, interesting though drugs, public order and automobiles may be in the larger context of the ordering of society, in themselves they throw little or no light upon the general principles of the criminal law as a body of law."[4]

Experience in teaching drugs offences and road traffic offences at the University of Warwick from the mid-1970s onwards suggested that Howard was quite right if he was suggesting that the study of these areas of the law would not assist in a positive way by helping to explicate the "general principles" of criminal law. However, a focus on these offences certainly would have a negative impact on any such enterprise, by raising questions about whether emphasising the general rather than the particular was going to be a helpful point of departure for students of such a diverse body of rules and practices.

There are, for example, relatively serious offences of drugs possession in the United Kingdom for which liability is in part, at least, strict[5], despite the fact that strict liability has traditionally been depicted as exceptional and unacceptable in relation to serious offences. Drugs offences also give the lie to what has traditionally been presented as the crucial distinction in the law of attempts between non-criminal acts of preparation to commit a crime and subsequent activity which crosses the threshold of criminal attempt. Drug offences such as possession look very much like preparatory activity; so does supply, at least when it is defined expansively to include "offering to supply", and "receiving for supply", as it is under New South Wales legislation.[6] This same legislation makes short work of the problem of impossible attempts, over which academic criminal lawyers and the courts have long agonised: if someone represents a substance to be a prohibited drug for the purpose of supplying it to someone else, then it is deemed to be a prohibited drug even if it is in fact quite innocuous.[7]

---

[3] Bates, Buddin and Meure, *The System of Criminal Law* (Butterworths, 1979).
[4] Book review (1980) 3 *UNSWLJ* 444, 446.
[5] *Warner* v *Metropolitan Police Commissioner* [1969] 2 AC 256; *Lewis* (1988) 87 Cr App Rep 270. This is no longer the position in Australia: *He Kaw Teh* (1985) 157 CLR 523.
[6] Drug Misuse and Trafficking Act 1985, s 3(1).
[7] *Ibid.*, s 40(1).

Nor do drugs offences appear to raise any problems of causation. Unlike offences against the person, drugs offence definitions do not require proof that a harmful consequence has been caused by the accused. Indeed, frequently, there is nobody who would perceive themselves as a victim. If drug users are the victims of drug suppliers, we have the atypical situation of the victim being labelled and penalised as an offender.[8]

What is the assumed but unspecified harm which has merited such a concerted assault on alleged principle? There is certainly a good deal of written material about the effects of drug use, and in particular about the difficulties of causal attribution, but this does not appear in the legal literature and is not regarded as raising issues of criminal responsibility on which scholars of the criminal law have traditionally feasted. This material does raise a number of questions about what would appear to be the crucial issue of whether the criminal law has any business in this context in the first place. But the issue of the appropriate limits to criminal law has not traditionally been defined as falling within the brief of criminal law scholars. Indeed, why should it, if the meat of criminal law is homicide, assault, rape and theft, social problems which few would dispute merit its attention?

What a discussion of drugs offences indicates is that the existence of general principles of criminal law cannot be taken for granted. If they do exist, they have to be shown to exist. More recently, Norrie has drawn attention to the inconsistencies of approach which are present in practice even in relation to what are supposed to be central organising principles within core areas of criminal law.[9]

Beyond this, if criminal lawyers are to have any purchase in policy debates about appropriate responses to social problems, the application of alleged principles must be assessed and sustained in the context of specific sites rather than by appeals to broad notions of responsibility and punishment. What the shape of drugs offences shows is that legislatures do not regard criminal law as a package response to social problems, but as an institutionalised instrument of social control which is sufficiently flexible to allow it to be moulded to the contours of the specific problems which they have identified. These adaptations are the legitimate subject of scrutiny by commentators on criminal law, but it is no longer adequate, if it ever was, simply to make departure from principle the thrust of the critique. An adequate critique must tease out and clarify the precise nature of the perceived problem, and assess the adequacy and the sensitivity of the detailed legal response.

As teachers of criminal law, we must be sensitive to the fact that laying out our field of study is not simply a matter of convenience. The way in which we constitute the subject-matter of our study plays a crucial role in determining the lines of inquiry we pursue. The first step in the contextualisation of criminal law is the relatively simple one of finding room in a crowded curriculum to teach

---

[8] See generally, Brown, Farrier, Neal and Weisbrot, *op cit.*, Ch 9.

[9] Norrie, *Crime, Reason and History* (Weidenfeld, 1993).

offences other than those which have long been taken for granted as forming the core of criminal law: offences against the person, particularly homicide, and property offences. It is to place the narrow field of inquiry currently constituted as criminal law, in the context of the broad body of rules officially labelled "criminal law".

3. Versions of Criminal Law

Many statutory criminal offences are hopelessly ambitious if intended to be more than symbolic. In New South Wales, it is an offence to cause waters to be polluted unless you have a licence, with "waters" and "pollute" very broadly defined.[10] On the face of it, every farmer is guilty of a criminal offence if excess fertiliser is washed off land into streams by heavy rain. In practice, the enforcement agency has concentrated its efforts on regulating point-source pollution and largely ignored diffuse agricultural run-off.

Other statutory criminal offences are helplessly vague. Under New South Wales legislation[11], it is an offence for an employer to breach a duty to "ensure the health, safety and welfare at work of all his employees". Further clarification offers little enlightenment. For example, we are told that there will be a breach where there is a failure "to provide or maintain a working environment for his employees that is safe and without risks to health and adequate as regards facilities for their welfare at work". Not only is the statutory provision itself neither use nor ornament, but the reality is that it will be clarified through decisions of courts of first instance rather than appeal courts. If an appeal court decision is the criterion of relevance, offences like this will never be studied by students of criminal law.

Even where the appeal courts have had a go at clarification, the "rule" enunciated may be so vague as to invest the other players in the criminal process with a considerable degree of discretion. So, for example, the New South Wales Court of Criminal Appeal, in trying to help us to understand what it means to behave in an "offensive" manner in a public place, has told us that it covers behaviour which is "offensive in the sense of giving, or of a nature to give, offence; displeasing; annoying; insulting".[12] In these circumstances, the assumed gulf between legal rule and administrative discretion largely disappears. The law-making function is effectively delegated to other players in the criminal process. This offence is widely advocated by Australian police on the grounds that they need to have adequate powers to protect members of the public from being harassed in the streets. In practice, however, it has been systematically used to discipline members of the public in their interactions

[10] Clean Waters Act 1970, ss 16, 5.
[11] Occupational Health and Safety Act 1983, s 15.
[12] *Smith* [1974] 2 NSWLR 586, 588.

with the police. The police have defined themselves as victims, and, for practical purposes, largely modified the actus reus of the offence.

While enforcement agencies are not in a position to insist that somebody is labelled as a criminal, they can make decisions routinely to withhold the designation from actors in particular circumstances. Studies of some strict liability offences have found that specialised enforcement agencies working in industrial contexts frequently impose their own fault requirements as a precondition for prosecution. In the field of pollution control, these relate to such factors as whether there has been a persistent noticeable failure to comply or whether an incident has caused substantial and noticeable damage.[13]

In these circumstances, the definition of the offence is mediated through its application in the criminal process. This is not done in the *ad hoc*, personalised way frequently contemplated when we talk of discretion; decisions are structured and institutionalised. Nor is it simply a discrepancy between the law in the books and the law in practice. It is not obvious that the latter needs to be brought into line with the former. Claims by enforcement agencies that the use of prosecution as a last resort is more likely to induce compliance with pollution regulations have to be taken seriously. What we are dealing with is an alternative and, in some cases, competing version of the criminal law. This suggests that we cannot fully understand criminal law except when it is located in the broader context of practices within the criminal process.

It is not only enforcement agencies who develop versions of the criminal law which may compete with the official version. So do members of the public. In some situations, the question for victims and witnesses is not simply whether they will bother to report behaviour which they clearly identify as a criminal offence, but whether they will define ambiguous behaviour as a breach of the criminal law in the first place. A woman who is violently coerced into having sexual intercourse may decide not to report what to her is an indisputable breach of the criminal law because of the ordeal which she perceives that she will undergo within the criminal process. A woman who is "date-raped" may, until recently at least, have defined her experience as involving a crude form of seduction rather than a criminal offence. Even if such matters do go to trial, a jury has the power to bring in what from one perspective is a "merciful", from another a "perverse", verdict. Verdicts of this kind may play a crucial role in the reform of official versions of criminal law. So, for example, in Australia, jury reluctance to convict of murder battered women who kill their partners while their backs are turned, played a crucial role in the reform of the law relating to provocation.[14]

---

[13] Hawkins, *Environment and Enforcement* (Clarendon 1984) p 201; Richardson, Ogus and Burrows, *Policing Pollution* (Clarendon 1982), pp 198–199; 130–145; G. Richardson, "Strict Liability for Regulatory Crime: the Empirical Research" [1987] *Criminal Law Review* 295; M. Weait, "The Letter of the Law? An Enquiry into Reasoning and Formal Enforcement in the Industrial Air Pollution Inspectorate" (1989) 29 *Brit. J. Crim.* 57; K. Hawkins and J. M. Thomas, "The Enforcement Process in Regulatory Bureaucracies" in Hawkins and Thomas, *Enforcing Regulation* (Kluwer-Nijoff 1984); W. G. Carson, "Some Sociological Aspects of Strict Liability and the Enforcement of Factory Legislation" (1970) 33 *MLR* 396.

[14] Brown, Farrier, Neal and Weisbrot, *op cit*, pp 745–747.

4. Reaffirming Fundamental Values

The practice of criminal law is only one of many processes which strive to influence the values we have and the way we conduct ourselves. If we are to understand criminal law, we must set it in the context of the many other forms of regulation which operate in society.

Some of the criminal law's messages are far from novel. They reflect norms dispersed and sustained by other forms of regulation operating beyond the law and having a more immediate and continuing effect. These are the moral, religious and social codes propagated by families, schools, the media and other socialising agencies. Whether or not there is, empirically, a complete consensus of values, it seems safe to assume that the vast majority of community members do not kill or commit burglary because of the existence of criminal prohibitions. As long ago as 1975, Jock Young commented:

> "However much the new deviancy theorist talked of diversity and dissensus in society, the ineluctable reality of a considerable consensus over certain matters could not be wished away. This was particularly noticeable, moreover, in the widespread and uniform social reaction against various forms of deviancy (and, especially, against crimes against the person and certain crimes against property)."[15]

To the extent that there is a consensus, criminal law is substantially parasitic on other forms of regulation. We cannot assume that by labelling morally neutral behaviour a criminal offence and processing it as such, we will necessarily attract community condemnation. From this perspective, the substantive criminal law is first and foremost a codification of fundamental values espoused by non-legal forms of regulation.

This is what the Canadian Law Reform Commission was referring to when it described the "real function of criminal law" as "an instrument of last resort for reaffirming values" – fundamental values[16]:

> "In its own way the criminal law re-enforces lessons about our social values, instils respect for them and expresses disapproval for their violation. This ... is the moral, educative role of criminal law."[17]

---

[15] Jock Young, "Working Class Criminology" in Taylor, Walton and Young, eds., *Critical Criminology*, (Routledge, 1975), p 71, cited by David Brown and Russell Hogg, "Essentialism, Radical Criminology and Left Realism" (1992) 25 *ANZJ Crim.* 195, 197. Note, however, that Young's extrapolations from this are very different from those developed here. Compare Alan Norrie, *op cit*, pp 30–31, who posits a class-based conflict model. While this may be appropriate in relation to certain property crimes, we must remember that here the lower class are disproportionately represented not only as offenders, but as victims. See, generally, Brown and Hogg, *op cit*, pp 196–203, discussing "left realism". Insofar as there is conflict about appropriate sexual behaviour, it is largely gender-based. In this context I would hypothesise that there would *at least* be a consensus when it comes to sexual assault involving physical injury, and it is likely that agreement would go beyond this.

[16] Report, *Our Criminal Law* (1976), p 17. Note that the serious contravention of a fundamental value is a necessary, not a sufficient condition for use of "real criminal law". See also Lacey, *State Punishment: Political Principles and Community Values* (Routledge, 1988), pp 100–112; 176–181.

[17] *Ibid.*, pp 5–6.

While this model of criminal law sees its primary function as being communication rather than initiation, it would be misleading to depict it simply as a mimic. Threats of detection, conviction, punishment and stigmatisation emanating from the criminal process will operate sporadically at the fringes, when disjunctions between values and behaviour begin to emerge in particular individuals. Yet we will marginalise criminal law, if we focus attention on its impact on the few who are tempted to deviate, rather than the many who strive to conform to values and behaviours recognised as fundamental.

I have, however, argued elsewhere that we can take this model a stage further, and, in the process, acknowledge the role criminal law plays in addressing the broader social audience.[18] For it becomes readily apparent once we attempt to identify fundamental values, that criminal law needs to be much more than the rubber-stamp conveyed by the notion of "reaffirmation". Values propagated through non-legal forms of regulation are frequently imprecise, sometimes ambiguous and occasionally conflicting. Once we move away from core instances of murder and theft, for example – from the contract killer to those who commit euthanasia and from those who snatch and grab to those who keep things given to them by mistake – it is apparent that there is going to be significant dissensus. If criminal law is to reaffirm fundamental values, then it must first of all elaborate and clarify them. The hypothesis might then be that criminal laws, enunciated by the Parliament and the courts, mediated in day-to-day application by the discretionary activities of enforcement agencies, refined by trial courts in individual cases before being applied in typically dramatic fashion by juries, and vetted by the appeal courts, are the vehicles through which fundamental values are elaborated and clarified, prior to being reaffirmed. In this guise, criminal law would be much more than peripheral, much more than an adjunct to other non-legal forms of regulation.

The process of clarification must necessarily be a fluid and a continuing one. The details of criminal laws reflecting fundamental values are by no means set in concrete. They are culturally and historically specific. They are continually subject to renegotiation. The historical and continuing struggles between and within legislatures, the courts, law reform bodies and enforcement agencies over where manslaughter ends and murder begins, and the more recent controversy over the definition of rape, provide telling illustrations of how some of the most fundamental of our values are not immune from this process of renegotiation. The agencies of the criminal process do not simply apply rules derived from other forms of regulation. They are more than mere ciphers. They must continually explore the limits of relatively incoherent values and settle their contents at any one point of time.

We can hypothesise that as long as the agencies of the criminal process can lay a legitimate claim to being engaged in the task of clarifying and reaffirming fundamental values, the rules in question will attract the uniquely persuasive pressure which stems from the claim that they have their source in values

[18] Farrier, "In Search of Real Criminal Law", *op cit.*

emanating from other non-legal forms of regulation, widely perceived as playing a basic role in the constitution of contemporary society, and guaranteed by criminal law. Once particular rules are perceived as trespassing beyond this source – once members of the community begin to develop alternative, conflicting versions of criminal behaviour – then criminal law will begin to lose its distinctively persuasive value, not only in the particular context, but throughout its range.[19]

Some such model of criminal law as clarifying and reaffirming fundamental values may underpin and inform the world view of those who sight criminal law through the lenses of homicide, assault and rape. It is here where such values have probably been located historically. Such a model cannot, however, legitimate an exclusive focus on the elucidation of key internal principles of criminal responsibility. A crucial message is that abuse of criminal law through inappropriate use by the legislature and the courts, will fundamentally dilute its persuasive powers in core areas. Those who assume this model must therefore be as vigilant in policing the boundaries of criminal law as they are in tending its internal principles.

5. Criminal Law as Long-stop

This model of criminal law as clarifying and reaffirming fundamental values is but one possible model of regulation through criminal law. It is a model in the sense of being an "ideal type" or artificial accentuation of reality.[20] The aim is simply to help clarify the often confused debate about the functions of criminal law.

Other models can be teased out of the existing practice of criminal law. One of them underpins one of the versions of criminal law discussed above: the version developed by specialist enforcement agencies faced with the task of regulating activities perceived to have positive social utility but which produce spillover effects, such as polluting externalities. Here, the introduction of new fault requirements into offence definitions is only the tip of the iceberg. What we have here is criminal law being employed as a "long-stop" within a system of administrative regulation which relies primarily on licences or permits, reinforced by the powers of enforcement agencies to issue individualised directions.

In this context, prosecution and sanctioning become sparsely used weapons of last resort rather than shock troops. The underlying assumptions are that most applicants will be drawn within the administrative system by applying for a licence or some other kind of permission, and that the primary issue relates to the conditions to be attached to a grant of permission, rather than whether permission to carry out the activity should be denied altogether. Because agencies possess limited information about the technology available and what is

---

[19] John C. Coffee, Jr., "Paradigms Lost: The Blurring of the Criminal and Civil Law Models – And What Can be Done About It" (1992) 101 *Yale Law Journal* 1875, 1877; Abraham S. Goldstein, "White-Collar Crime and Civil Sanctions" (1992) 101 *Yale Law Journal* 1895, 1899.

[20] Packer, *The Limits of the Criminal Sanction* (Stamford U.P., 1968) pp 152–154.

feasible in terms of the commitment of financial resources, these conditions are frequently fixed through a process of negotiation and compromise rather than directive. When it comes to breaches of condition, these are generally dealt with through a combination of administrative warnings and a continuation of the bargaining process. The focus is on devising means to bring industry into compliance and the operative assumption is that this is what industry itself is committed to.

The primary function of criminal law within this model is to set the ground rules defining the market in which bargaining takes place. The existence of a criminal prohibition against polluting without a licence denies any right to pollute, which might otherwise have to be purchased in the open market. It effectively reweights the bargaining process in favour of the administrative agency by creating a community right not to be polluted. This is a very different role for criminal law from that which sees it as clarifying and reaffirming fundamental values. Its main function is not to condemn, but to define the parameters within which agreements are made between the state and the individual or corporation, in situations where a balance needs to be struck between the beneficial and detrimental effects of an activity which is currently morally neutral.

6. The Significance of Sanctions

It is all too easy to slip into the assumption that penalties drive compliance with the criminal law. Rather than an instrument of coercion, the model of criminal law as long-stop sees criminal law as a vital component of the machinery for inducing a realistic consensus between regulator and regulated. In this context, sanctions assume a relatively insignificant role. While they are there to be applied to the midnight dumpers who operate outside the administrative system altogether, and in exceptional instances of prosecution for breach of condition, the model operates under the assumption that legitimate industry will bring itself within the licensing system and strive to comply with licence conditions for reasons which have nothing to do with the threat of sanctions.

Similarly, sanctions play a marginal role where criminal law has the function of reaffirming fundamental values. The successful operation of the criminal process, in at least some instances of breach, culminating in the conviction and punishment of the guilty, may play an important part in reassuring members of the community that crime does not pay, but it is not the reason why they generally conform to the norms in question or why they feel guilty if they do breach them. A commitment to the norms reaffirmed by criminal law is the product of subtler pressures than the threat of criminal sanctions.[21]

In a third model of criminal law, however, sanctions do have a crucial role to play. This is criminal law as "command backed by threat". Here, there is no

[21] See generally, Farrier, *Drugs and Intoxication*, *op cit*, pp 227–235; Lacey, *op cit*, pp 81–83; 91–93; 181–186.

assumption of any commitment or allegiance on the part of significant sections of the community to the norm in question. Rather, compliance is to be gained through deterrence, in the narrow sense of fear of being caught, convicted and punished. Crucial to the effective operation of such a strategy is a perception among those subject to it that the threat is immediate. This perception must be regularly reinforced by successful prosecutions and significant penalties.

Contrasting with this is the model of criminal law as "symbol". Once again, there is no suggestion that the values espoused by an offence currently represent fundamental values to which there is substantial commitment; they may indeed conflict with values which are held by significant sections of the community. This is a much subtler form of social engineering than command backed by threat. The objective is to use the aura of the criminal law in an attempt to make adjustments to fundamental values. In the short term, the struggle is primarily over the official meaning of language – for example, the word "rape" – although the expectation is that in the longer term this will be reflected in changes to value systems. There is no intention that changes in meaning be forced upon people by the use of commands backed by threat. The potential difficulties of drawing on this model of criminal law have been identified above. If official definitions of criminal behaviour attempt to stretch the imaginations of community members too far, then the backlash against a particular offence definition may be generalised to the criminal law as a whole, undermining its distinctive authority.

These are but ideal types. In reality, different practices within the existing criminal law lie along a continuum, frequently reflecting the features of more than one of these models in an uneasy state of tension. Moreover, particular rules will always mean different things to different people. Although there may be a substantial consensus about the fundamental nature of certain norms, it is unlikely there will ever be unanimity, even at the level of values, let alone behaviour. Consequently, some people will always confront criminal laws designed to reaffirm fundamental values as commands backed by threats, and the threat of penalty must be a real one. Similarly, rules designed primarily to act as long-stops within administrative systems must also have a significant deterrent potential for those who are tempted to operate outside the system. Many may be sceptical of claims by special interests that new criminal laws represent fundamental or desirable values, and interact with them as commands backed by threats. At the other extreme, some few may perceive any rule labelled criminal law as automatically representing a fundamental value and comply with its demands, regardless of the efficiency of the sanctioning process.

7. Conclusion: In Search of Distinctively Criminal Law?

One possible conclusion from this is that we need to trim down the body of rules which we dignify with the label "criminal law", hiving off what is left into other legal categories. In the United States, "civil penalties" are widely available to specialist regulatory agencies as alternatives to criminal proceedings. In many situations, they can be imposed by the agency itself in administrative, as distinct from judicial, proceedings. Both Mann[22] and Coffee[23] have argued that prohibitions backed by civil penalties should entirely replace criminal law in some areas. Mann has called for the development of a middle ground between criminal punishment and civil remediation, involving explicit recognition of the punitive function served by civil penalties. Procedural protections would be related to the severity of the sanction, but would fall short of those traditionally associated with criminal prosecution. Coffee, on the other hand, suggests that a penalty, extracted by the State, is non-punitive, albeit deterrent, if it is designed simply to reflect the social costs imposed by externalities stemming from an activity which the State wants to regulate rather than to prohibit altogether. While it is non-compensatory because the penalty does not go to the victims, it is non-punitive because it does no more than force those engaging in the activity to internalise social costs. As a result, it does not have to be delivered through the criminal process, with its attendant procedural inhibitions. Criminal law can be reserved for prohibiting conduct which society defines as lacking in any social utility. Here, Coffee talks loosely of the "nondeterrent functions" of criminal law, "the criminal law's socializing role as a system for moral education" and "the criminal law as an instrument for shaping preferences".[24] This is reminiscent of both the criminal law as clarifying and reaffirming social values, and the criminal law as symbol. But he also equates the prohibiting function of criminal law with "total deterrence".[25] Certainly Coffee would have us use a system of civil penalties to replace the criminal law's role as long-stop.

At this stage, I do not want to get involved in a debate about what the essence of criminal law "is" and what distinguishes it from other forms of regulation through law.[26] I am, however, very interested in the possibility that the ragbag of institutionalised social prohibitions which we call criminal law, and the diverse range of pathways which we loosely refer to as criminal justice

---

[22] Kenneth Mann, "Punitive Civil Sanctions: The Middleground Between Criminal and Civil Law," (1992) 101 *Yale Law Journal* 1795.

[23] *Op cit.*

[24] *Ibid,* p 1877. See also, by the same author, "Does 'Unlawful' 'Mean Criminal'?: Reflections on the Disappearing Tort/Crime Distinction in American Law" (1991) 71 B.U.L. Rev 193, 193–194, where he refers more obviously to the role of criminal law in reaffirming fundamental values, depicting it as a "system of moral education and socialization", and suggesting that it is obeyed "not simply because there is a legal threat underlying it, but because the public perceives its norms to be legitimate and deserving of compliance ... the criminal law is a system for public communication of values". At a later point, he refers to the criminal law as "a uniquely effective medium for communicating a communitarian ethic" (p 224). *Cf.* Abraham S. Goldstein, *op cit,* pp 1896–97, who distinguishes between the theory of criminal liability which emphasises social control, and which is prepared to utilise objective standards, and the theory of criminal liability which stresses personal culpability.

[25] *Ibid,* p 1884.

[26] For an early attempt to identify the distinctively criminal law, see Farrier, *Drugs and Intoxication, op cit.,* Ch 6.

or criminal procedure, represent not simply a mishmash which needs to be sorted out and brought into line with principle, but rather a number[27] of alternative, albeit at this stage inchoate, forms of regulation through law, each with a potentially legitimate contribution to make to influencing attitudes and behaviour.

In this context, there are steps which can be taken to clarify and improve the practice of criminal law which fall short of producing a blueprint. We should insist that legislatures, and the policy-makers which stand behind them, think more carefully and act more self-consciously when it comes to designing policy instruments. By all means think creatively, and approach with a degree of scepticism broad assertions that because we are dealing with criminal law and criminal punishment, then the principles of criminal law and the traditional safeguards associated with criminal procedure, must apply. But spell out precisely what a particular policy instrument is designed to achieve, and let us debate in this specific context the adequacy of procedural safeguards, criteria of responsibility and justifications for any sanctions to be imposed. Do not pretend that there is a consensus of values where none in fact exists.

More careful thought needs to be given to the function to be performed by criminal law when standards of individual criminal responsibility are being determined. If, for example, the objective is to make a symbolic statement about the need to take much greater care in sexual relationships, in the hope that it will eventually be seen as reflecting fundamental values, then there is less reason to be concerned about criminalising as rapists those who have nonconsensual intercourse, genuinely but unreasonably believing that consent has in fact been given. The situation might be very different if it is envisaged that the criminal law is to take the form of command backed by threat.

Enforcement agencies need much greater guidance when it comes to questions of enforcement policy. Are they dealing with a rule which is intended to be largely symbolic, or a mere back-stop, or should they allocate significant resources to its enforcement in an effort to make the rule into a command which is difficult to resist? The South Australian Soil Conservation and Land Care Act 1989, for example, provides that soil conservation boards, in implementing and enforcing the legislation, must "endeavour to do so as far as possible on the basis of first seeking the co-operation of owners of land within the district".[28] Here is a clear indication that criminal law is to play only the role of long-stop.

Acceptance of the proposition that what we know as criminal law legitimately comprises a number of different forms of regulation does not involve us in accepting the appropriateness of any particular form as a way of responding to particular behaviour. As scholars of criminal law, we must continue to be vigilant in our hunt for injustices, but we must extend the range of our critique

[27] Unlike Coffee and Mann, I think that the current practice of criminal law comprises more than the two forms of regulation which they assume.
[28] Section 29(1)(a).

beyond assertions of conflict with principle, and apply it to specific manifestations of criminal law as they are applied, in a particular social and historical context, to activity which somebody has claimed ought to be defined as a social problem.

Chapter 7

IMPLEMENTING THE SOCIO-LEGAL: DEVELOPMENTS IN SOCIO-LEGAL SCHOLARSHIP AND THE CURRICULUM

Professor Martin Partington*
University of Bristol

> "It is just as plausible, however, to regard the current developments [in the study of Law in Society in Britain] as fortuitous and perhaps transitional ..."[1]

> "Socio-legal scholarship in the broadest sense is the most important scholarship presently being undertaken in the legal world."[2]

1. Introduction

This paper seeks to offer a personal reflection on the impact of socio-legal scholarship both on legal education as well as on the wider world. The focus will be primarily on past achievement, but there will also be some consideration of the future prospects for socio-legal research in this country. This paper[3] falls into five parts. The first raises important definitional issues about the nature

---

* This is a substantially revised version of a lecture delivered at the Annual Conference of the Society of Public Teachers of Law, held at the University of East Anglia, in September 1994.

[1] C. M. Campbell and Paul Wiles, "The Study of Law in Society in Britain" (1976) *Law and Society Review* at p 547.

[2] Roger Cotterrell, "Socio-Legal Studies: Between Policy and Community", Address given to the Annual Meeting of the Socio-Legal Studies Association, Exeter, March 1993.

[3] In preparing this essay I have drawn heavily on work done for the recently completed ESRC, *Review of Socio-Legal Studies: Final Report* (1994) (2 volumes) (ESRC, Swindon). The Executive Summary is reprinted in a special edition of the *Socio-Legal Studies Association Newsletter* (No 13) (SLSA, 1994). A limited number of copies of the full report is available from Penny Smith, Editor, SLSA Newsletter, Law School, University College, University of Wales, Cardiff.

and scope of "socio-legal studies". Part two gives a personal view of the development of socio-legal studies over the last 30 years. The significant findings of the ESRC survey and review of socio-legal studies are summarised in part three together with an indication of possible future developments. Part four considers some of the issues involved in the relationship between socio-legal research and policy development. Part five makes some concluding remarks about the contribution of socio-legal research to the development of the legal curriculum.

2. Socio-Legal Studies: Problems of Definition

The precise parameters of what falls within the scope of "socio-legal studies" are still the subject of debate and uncertainty. For some, socio-legal studies are synonymous with the sociology of law. Others assume that all socio-legal studies are necessarily empirically based. Yet others regard socio-legal research as applied research, relating exclusively to the development of social policy. There are those who regard socio-legal research as overlapping with criminology and who thus find it hard to distinguish between the two.

I adopt here the definition used by the ESRC, for the purposes of its review, of the nature and scope of socio-legal studies.[4] There it was stated that socio-legal studies represented an *approach* to the study of law and legal process, which sought to explain the impact of law in society. Socio-legal studies encompass, in summary:

- analyses both historical and contemporary – of the social, economic and political factors leading to development of the law and legal processes;
- examination of the operation of the law in formal contexts, for example, the courts, or informal contexts, for example, the law office;
- analyses of the processes of decision-taking by those responsible for the administration of the law;
- analyses of the experience of those affected by the process of law; and
- more generally, theoretical and empirical analyses of the nature of law and its relationship to society and the State in the context of a rapidly changing world.

Thus a wide range of scholarship and research falls within this definition of the "socio-legal", including much that individual scholars might themselves neither conceive as nor claim to be socio-legal. The essence of "socio-legal" scholarship is that it seeks to look beyond the detailed and technical analysis of the rules of law themselves – important, complex and difficult though that may often be – and to offer an account of how or why those rules developed and/or the impact they are making on society.

[4] *Op cit,* above n 3.

Two specific comments should be emphasised: first, while much socio-legal research has been empirical in nature, such research is not exclusively empirical; and second, while much socio-legal research has been related to matters of policy and law reform, such work is not exclusively policy related.

3. The Development of Socio-legal Studies

Socio-legal studies, as an approach to research and scholarship in the law, has developed in the United Kingdom over the last 30 years or so. From tentative and rather narrowly focused beginnings it has become, now, a substantial and wide-ranging intellectual enterprise. The reasons why "socio-legal" studies thus began to emerge are many and complex, and require a more detailed history than is possible here.[5] Personal recollection suggests a number of factors which can be identified.

The Early Years: 1965–1980

First, there were in the early 1960s clear feelings of uncertainty – vividly recorded, if overstated, by Professors Abel-Smith and Stevens[6] – about the place of the law school in the academic community. Reflecting this mood, a number of influential law teachers had – even then – begun to urge the adoption of a broader vision for both research and teaching law.[7] Their views were reinforced by other scholars who had visited law schools in the United States and returned to the United Kingdom impressed with the scope of legal education and research being conducted there. Thirdly, pioneering work was actually beginning to be done which – however modest it may now appear – began to provide examples for others to follow, criticise and develop.[8]

These individual initiatives were supported by significant institutional developments. As early as 1965 a research unit to consider the study of law in a social science context was established at Bedford College in London. At about the same time two new law schools – at Warwick and Kent – were created, committed in their different ways to the development of a new contextual approach to the teaching of, and thus research and writing on, law. During the same period,

[5] Professor David Sugarman at Lancaster University is currently working on a detailed history of the development of legal education and scholarship in the UK.

[6] Stevens and Abel-Smith, *Lawyers and the Courts* (Heinemann, 1967) 68–69 stated at 69 that "University Law faculties ... lacked prestige [both] with other university faculties and with the [legal] profession".

[7] L. C. B. Gower, "English Legal Training: A Critical Survey" (1950) 18 *Modern Law Review* 137; O. Kahn-Freund, "Reflections on Legal Education" (1966) 29 *Modern Law Review* 121.

[8] For example, Abel-Smith and Stevens, *op cit* and Campbell and Wiles, *op cit.* See also M. Zander "Promoting Change in the Legal System" (1979) 42 *Modern Law Review* 489, for a summary of much of the early empirical work he had published.

the Young Members Group of the Society of Public Teachers of Law provided a forum for critical discussion about the scope and purpose of the legal curriculum.[9]

Additional interest was also shown by the then still very newly established research funding bodies. The Social Sciences Research Council (SSRC) – predecessor to the Economic and Social Research Council (ESRC) – was established in 1965. While initially legal studies were regarded as outside its remit, the Council decided early in its existence to create two research units – one on race (now ethnic) relations, the other on industrial relations. Since both involved areas where the impact of law was considerable, it was agreed to establish a panel, under the chairmanship of Mrs Jean Floud, to review the position of legal studies more generally. The panel recommended the creation of a Committee on Social Sciences and the Law, initially chaired by Jean Floud, succeeded in turn by Lord Kilbrandon, and later Professor Geoffrey Wilson from the University of Warwick.[10]

The Committee was able to offer general support for the development of socio-legal research by providing a series of summer schools, sponsored by the SSRC, run for academic staff already in post, in social science research methods, and also law and economics. It created a number of post-graduate studentships for both taught courses and research in the socio-legal area. The Committee also commissioned a number of literature reviews of work done in the socio-legal area to guide the development of further research developments.[11] 1972 also saw the establishment by the SSRC of the Centre for Socio-Legal Studies in Oxford.[12]

The results of the work of socio-legal scholars began to be discussed in the meetings of the Socio-Legal Group which was founded in 1974. It also began to be published in journals such as the newly founded *British Journal of Law and Society*[13] and new book series, notably the *Law in Context*[14], and the *Oxford Socio-Legal Studies*[15] series.

---

[9] For brief accounts of its work, see *e.g.* reports contained in the *Journal of the Society of Public Teachers of Law*, 1966–1972.

[10] In addition, the Nuffield Foundation gave early support to a number of initiatives, including the founding of the Legal Action Group which, from the outset, has brought practitioners and academics together to debate questions of reform of legal aid, and change to the legal system.

[11] See, *e.g.* Wilson, *Socio-legal Research in Germany* (1980); McAuslan, *Review of socio-legal research on Planning, Housing and the Environment* (1981); Veljanowski, *Review of Economics and the Law* (1984); Partington, *Socio-Legal Studies and Social Welfare* (1986); and Rawlings, *The Complaints Industry: A Review of Socio-Legal Research on Aspects of Administrative Justice* (1986).

[12] For an account of the contribution of the work of the Oxford Centre to the development of socio-legal scholarship in the UK see, *e.g.*, D. R. Harris, "The Development of Socio-Legal Studies in the United Kingdom" (1983) 3 *Legal Studies* 315; see also the collection of essays celebrating the first 21 years of the Centre's existence Special Issue, *Journal of Law and Society* (1994).

[13] Now the *Journal of Law and Society*; for a review of the first 20 years of publication, see Jenny C. Wiltshire, *The Journal of Law and Society: A Twenty Year Review*. Other journals which now regularly publish work that can properly be characterised as socio-legal include the *Journal of Family and Social Welfare Law*, the *Modern Law Review*, the *Civil Justice Quarterly* and *The Industrial Law Journal*.

[14] Originally published by Weidenfeld and Nicolson, now Butterworths.

[15] Originally published by Macmillan.

The early years of the socio-legal research enterprise were characterised by some often fierce debate about its intellectual scope and direction. There was too much intellectually arid empiricism, it was claimed; and insufficient theoretical grounding. Some of this debate – sometimes conducted in rather bruising fashion – is captured in the seminal article by Campbell and Wiles.[16]

Expansion and consolidation: 1980–the present day

While the scope of the research agenda was, perhaps, initially drawn rather narrowly – concentrating in particular on questions such as aspects of the criminal trial process, and the unmet need for legal services[17] – and despite the setbacks and insecurities that were felt, at least by some of us at the time, nevertheless from the late 1970s and early 1980s onwards a steadily growing body of work was beginning to appear from an increasingly experienced body of researchers.

(a) The changing role of the ESRC

During the 1980s some of the institutional support began to change. The Social Science and the Law Committee of the SSRC was transformed into a sub-committee of the Law and Government committee of the ESRC in 1982, and wound up altogether in 1985. By the mid- to late-1980s the arrangements changed again as the ESRC management was forced to react to increasingly difficult financial settlements from Government. In 1987 the ESRC further refined its structure. The Law and Government Committee was itself wound up and its work incorporated into one of three new Research and Development Groups – the relevant group for socio-legal studies being the one on society and politics. The ESRC's 1987 restructuring was followed, in 1992, by a further round of change. The "subject based" groups were replaced by five "generic" Boards concerned with each of the principal activities of the Council: Research Centres, Research Grants, Research Programmes, Research Resources and Postgraduate Training.

There were always those who felt that socio-legal research attracted inadequate ESRC support. Many interpreted these moves at the time as a down-playing of that commitment, especially as during the same period it had become clear that core funding for the Oxford Centre was to become time-limited. However, in my judgment this is too simplistic a view. During this period, the ESRC developed a number of new research programmes in related areas: they included research into the Police and Criminal Evidence Act, Procedures for the Redress for Citizens' Grievances and a research programme on Crime and Criminal Justice. It has to be said that at least part of the reason – perhaps a

[16] See above n 1.

[17] It should be remembered that much of the choice of topic reflected the political climate of the time: those were the days of the rediscovery of poverty, a shift from "discretion" to "rights" as the basis for the delivery of entitlements in the area of social policy, the assumption that the primary provider of welfare – broadly defined – would be the state. It is not surprising that much of that early work should reflect those issues, which were then high on the political agenda.

major part – that socio-legal studies did not receive as much research funding from the ESRC as the research community might have liked was that the research community itself did not ask for it.[18]

(b) The Socio-Legal Studies Association

One specific development deserves mention at this point. Notwithstanding all the structural changes outlined above, and some sense of pessimism engendered by reductions in government money for research, nonetheless a new vitality and self-confidence in the research community began to be demonstrated.[19] For a number of years, the annual conferences of the Socio-Legal Group had attracted rather sparse attendance. However, this trend was dramatically transformed by the conference held in Oxford in 1988[20] which was extremely well attended and very lively. Its success and that of the conference in Edinburgh the following year led to the proposal[21] to establish the Socio-Legal Studies Association as a formal learned society to represent the interests of the socio-legal research community.

The new Association replaced the informal SLG when it was formally established in 1990.[22] Since then, it has taken a number of initiatives to strengthen the profile of socio-legal scholarship. Building on the success of the Oxford and Edinburgh conferences, the SLSA now regularly attracts around 200 delegates to its annual conferences. Its membership has grown rapidly and is likely to exceed 500 in 1995. It publishes a termly newsletter, designed to encourage debates about current research issues, as well as providing information about conferences and other activities. Recognising the importance of developing the level of research skills in the community, it has organised annual conferences for post-graduate students in socio-legal studies. It has sponsored a number of study days on research methods and teaching for staff in post. It is currently organising a conference for research students' supervisors. In addition, a Scottish Branch of the SLSA has been established which runs conferences on socio-legal research in Scotland. It has published two editions of its research directory, which, from 1995, will be published annually by Butterworths. In 1995 the SLSA also published a list of post-graduate courses and research programmes in socio-legal studies. The Oxford University Press has, in association with the SLSA,

[18] This was certainly true during my period as a member of the Law and Social Sciences Committee, from 1979–1982. It is a criticism that can still, though to a lesser extent, be made today.

[19] The extent to which this change of mood may be attributable to the start of the Research Assessment Exercises, conducted by the universities' funding bodies, is hard to assess; but in so far as the acquisition of research grants, and the employment of research fellows and assistants were in some sense regarded as "performance indicators", there is certainly evidence that some heads of department began to regard socio-legal research in a new light.

[20] Organised by Professor Hazel Genn.

[21] Advanced initially by Professor Genn and myself.

[22] I chaired the steering group that developed the formal proposals for the establishment of the Association; Professor Genn was elected as the first chair of the Association, a post to which I was elected in 1993. Although the Association is now self-financing, it received a most generous initial loan from the Nuffield Foundation, which played an essential part in its launch.

launched a new series of student readers in socio-legal studies. OUP have also sponsored a prize for outstanding scholarship which will be awarded for the first time in 1995 now supplemented by a prize from Dartmouth.

4. The ESRC Review of Socio-Legal Studies

The ESRC started a series of strategic reviews of area-sponsored research activity in 1990. The decision to review socio-legal studies was taken in principle in 1991. However the structural changes to the ESRC, mentioned above, combined with the fact that a final review of the work of the Oxford Centre was carried out in 1992, meant implementation of the review of socio-legal studies did not start in earnest until early 1993.

The review was conducted during 1993 by a panel[23] appointed by the ESRC, under the chairmanship of Mary Tuck.[24] In addition, Lee Bridges[25] was invited to act as research consultant to the review; he undertook the main empirical survey of the state of socio-legal research in the United Kingdom. The ESRC also organised a day seminar at which a number of background papers were discussed.[26]

The results of the review were derived in part from the empirical survey – which analysed factors such as the level of socio-legal research funding and the sources of funding, numbers of research projects and numbers of staff engaged in socio-legal research – and in part from the judgment of those members of the review panel who offered views as to the quality of past achievement and considered the basis for future activity.

Principal findings

The survey by Lee Bridges was based on responses to a relatively open-ended questionnaire circulated to all universities. The information obtained from particular institutions did vary in quantity and quality.[27] I set out here a selection of what I regard as the most significant findings:

- socio-legal research was being undertaken in 46 law departments, and 53 other departments from other disciplines[28];

[23] Apart from the Chair, see following note, the members of the review panel were: Professors Galligan, Genn, Morgan, Partington and Wiles; Lee Bridges, Dr A. Sanders, Ann Millar, Carole Willis, Glyn Davies and Susan Blair.

[24] A member of the Council of the ESRC; Mary Tuck was formerly director of the Home Office Research Unit. She was an assessor on the Woolf Inquiry.

[25] Director, Public Law Project, Institute of Advanced Legal Studies, University of London.

[26] M. Partington and H. Genn, "Socio-legal Studies: A Review by the ESRC"; N. Lacey, "Conceiving Socio-Legal Studies"; P. Hillyard, "Some Reflexions on Socio-Legal Studies".

[27] The caveats about the data are set out in detail in ESRC (1994) *op cit* pp 22–24.

[28] The predominance of socio-legal research being carried out in law departments is in contrast to the situation in other countries, notably the USA, where socio-legal scholarship is seen as primarily an intellectual activity carried on outside the law school.

- 265 members of staff were identified as engaged in such research, on the basis of funds provided either by the ESRC or from other research funding sources;
- a further 199 researchers were doing such work without any apparent funding;
- 14 departments (9 law, and 5 others) had developed a substantial research presence with more than 6 staff involved in funded socio-legal work[29];
- two thirds of the 46 law departments responding and 58% of other departments had some funded research, and
- seven law departments and four non-law departments were, in 1992–1993, conducting their socio-legal research with funding from more than six separate sources.[30]

The figures indicate that there is now an impressive range of socio-legal work being undertaken within a wide variety of departments. Notwithstanding the fact that the ESRC itself had only specifically sponsored one research centre, there was now a group of departments which had established a very impressive research portfolio.[31] These figures are the clearest possible indication of "the spread of research interest and skill in obtaining funding in this sector over the past 20 years or so".[32]

What is also noteworthy is the fact that, although the Oxford Centre undoubtedly attracted over the period a good proportion of the resource available from the ESRC[33], nevertheless other departments have been able to develop substantial funded research portfolios. Indeed, at the time of the survey, the ESRC was funding less than 10% of the reported 93 funded projects.

What both the empirical data and the more descriptive analysis show is that the scope of research areas had broadened significantly.[34] For example, in the area of civil justice, work on access to legal services has expanded to embrace work on the operation of the courts, dispute resolution, and the administration of civil justice, the legal profession, and law and the family. Regulation, public law and administrative justice were also identified as areas with – now – a sub-

[29] Oxford (CLSS), Sheffield, Bristol, Brunel, Dundee, Strathclyde, UWE Bristol, Warwick, Cardiff (all law), Cambridge (Criminology), Cambridge (Land Economy), Bristol (Dartington Social Research Unit and Department of Social Policy), Glasgow (Housing), UC Wales, Cardiff (Social and Administrative Studies).

[30] Universities of Birmingham, Bristol, Brunel, Leeds, Sheffield, Warwick, Strathclyde (all law), Cambridge (Criminology), Glasgow (Housing), Newcastle (Family and Community Dispute Centre), UC Wales Cardiff (Department of Social and Administrative Studies).

[31] At least part of the explanation for this important development was the fact that many former members of staff and research students from the Oxford Centre had moved on to posts in other institutions.

[32] *Op cit* p 25.

[33] In 1992, 35% of the ESRC's support for socio-legal research went to the Oxford Centre. In that year it received about £500,000.

[34] This impression is also confirmed by the substantial, but by no means complete, bibliography of published socio-legal scholarship, reproduced at Appendix VII of the Review.

stantial research literature. Also noted was a significant literature on women and law. On the criminal law and criminal justice side there was also a substantial literature[35], much of which has been very influential in terms of policy development.

The methodologies of socio-legal studies had also expanded. While the early studies relied heavily on somewhat crude statistical data collection, more recent studies employed econometrics, oral histories, case studies, qualitative observational studies and documentary analysis – used usually appropriately and often with a high degree of sophistication and expertise. Equally important was the fact that the objects of study had broadened from a focus on the powerless and disadvantaged, with access now obtained to a number of considerably more powerful groups in the community – not least the Law Lords, but also other players such as firms of accountants and solicitors, and industry.

Notwithstanding the evident developments, the Review was also of the opinion that there were potential areas for socio-legal research that had not yet been fully exploited. The Review itself identified the areas of the environment and planning, business and the economy, and historical studies as areas ripe for further development. In addition there were substantial research gaps in the area of civil justice.[36]

The report made it clear that the termination of the core funding of the Oxford Centre represented potentially a substantial reduction in the level of funding for socio-legal research. It is money that the socio-legal community will have to argue for collectively, in competition with other subject and disciplinary areas. However, the ESRC is committed to maintaining its support for socio-legal research[37], and has taken steps to assist.

It has created a Socio-Legal Research Users' Forum, with representatives from government, industry and the professions, to consider the implications of the review. Second it has been agreed that a bid should be developed for a new research programme in socio-legal studies, which if successful could result in a significant injection of resource in the academic year 1996/7 onwards.[38] It has also agreed to consider further training needs in the light of increased demand for socio-legal research from a number of sources, and a fear that there may be inadequate numbers of properly trained researchers available to undertake the work required. Although the precise terms of reference of the Research Programme bid have not, at the time of writing, been settled, it is likely that it will be in the general area of civil justice and reflect such developments as the enactment of the Courts and Legal Services Act 1990, and the Woolf Inquiry into Access to Justice. It is also likely that any research programme should help

---

[35] Though notwithstanding the difficulties of defining the "socio-legal" not as dominant as might have been expected: see p 26.

[36] Family law was excluded from this comment.

[37] See *e.g.* the address of the then Chairman of the ESRC, Professor Howard Newby, to the 1993 Annual Conference of the SLSA, reproduced in *Socio-Legal Newsletter* No 9, Summer 1993.

[38] I was asked to undertake the work involved in the preparation of the bid, in conjunction with the Research Users' Forum, and with the support of the academic community and others.

to strengthen interdisciplinary links, in particular those between lawyers and economists.

5. Implementing the Socio-legal: the Impact of Socio-legal Research on Policy Formation

Having considered the development of socio-legal scholarship, I turn now to the questions of implementation. Two points should be stressed at the outset: first, as already noted, socio-legal research is not exclusively policy related research. There are many who resist the pressure to undertake narrowly policy related research. I would defend that view. There must be a danger that the more that funding is directed towards specific policy objectives, a wider range of questions will come to be ignored. Indeed, the ESRC review itself noted that there was need to widen the intellectual framework within which socio-legal work is carried out[39]; second, even where research is commissioned with a view to informing the development of policy initiatives, it is my view that – on the whole – the researcher should always keep the question of the research and the policy separate. The policy maker has a function in the policy making process, quite distinct from the researcher. The researcher may be disappointed if particular ideas are not taken up or are distorted by policy developers, whether inside government, or elsewhere. But the roles are distinct, and this should be remembered.

The inherent tensions between researcher and policy-maker[40]

It has to be accepted, however, that there can be tensions between the researcher and the policy maker. These arise for the following reasons:

- many, perhaps most, policy initiatives are driven by political considerations, not research ones;
- much research is – quite properly – undertaken for purposes quite other than the development or advancement of policy initiatives;
- the timetables of policy makers are often at sharp variance with those of the scholar;

[39] *Op cit.*, Ch 7.
[40] The following sections of this essay adopt much of the text of the ESRC review on these issues, in relation to which I, with Carole Willis of the Law Society, provided initial drafts. The theme of the tension between researchers and policy makers was the subject of debate at the Scottish SLSA Conference, held in Edinburgh in September 1994.

- there can be deep suspicion between the researcher and the policy maker. In extreme cases, the former may fear that involvement with policy will compromise critical objectivity; while the latter may fear that all research will be destructive and therefore embarrassing for both politicians and bureaucrats alike.

Nevertheless, because much socio-legal research looks at the interactions between law and policy, there is the potential for a closer link between the outcome of much socio-legal research and its application in policy and practice than in some other areas of academic endeavour. There is no doubt that there is still considerable concern in some sections of the academic community about the relationship between research and policy development. Nevertheless, if only for pragmatic reasons, research which can be said to have some policy relevance is often more likely these days to attract funding than that which does not. While some will deplore this, my own view – which I know is shared by many others – is that if good research can assist in the development of policy, that is broadly a good thing.

A classification of research

The nature of the links between socio-legal research and policy development is extremely complex. Questions of implementation are, therefore, not straightforward. The links between any given piece of research and any policy outcome can vary enormously. The extent to which implementation takes place may depend on the essential characteristics of the research. At least eight different types of research can be identified.

(a) Background research

Background research is research specially commissioned by policy makers to provide basic information to be used as the background against which policy may be developed. The research commissioned by the Lord Chancellor's Department for the civil justice review is one example. The bulk of the research commissioned or undertaken by the Law Society's Research and Policy Planning Unit is another.

(b) Linked research

Linked research is policy related research specifically linked to the development of new policy ideas and initiatives, or to ideas which have already been adopted where research allows such ideas to be fleshed out. Recent examples of this category of research might be the Legal Aid Board's research into franchising, and the development of transaction criteria; or the Law Society's and the Bar's research commissioned in relation to their new professional qualification courses.

(c) Issue-defining research

Issue-defining research involves the identification of issues that have perhaps been hitherto unrecognised by officials, but which once published helps to determine new policy directions. Judith Masson's research on wardship and Mervyn Murch's research on the length of care proceedings might be given as examples.[41]

(d) Critique-research

Critique-research is research which has the effect of so undermining policy ideas that may have been floated, for example in official consultation papers of Green Papers, that the government abandons or substantially modifies its ideas. Such research will often be commissioned by bodies other than sponsoring government departments. One example of this might be the ESRC funded research into Legal Services in Rural Britain by Kim Economidis and colleagues. The outcome of this research project had, *inter alia*, the effect of demonstrating that proposals from the Lord Chancellor's Department that all initial advice under the Green Form scheme could be handled in Citizens Advice Bureaux would simply not work, as the distribution of legal services in rural areas was much more dependent on the location of lawyers' offices than had previously been realised. In this instance, policy developed in a rather different direction from that which had initially been anticipated.

(e) Evaluative research

Evaluative research is focused not so much on policy development, as on policies, perhaps introduced without much initial research, which need evaluation to determine whether or not they are working in practice as it was hoped they would in theory, and thus whether or not they need amendment. Often, again, this will be research that is sponsored not by government departments, but by other funding bodies. The ESRC sponsored research by the Policy Studies Institute into the operation of the Social Fund might be one example. The Nuffield Foundation sponsored research by Baldwin *et al* into Social Security Appeal Tribunals might be another.

(f) Opportunistic research

Opportunistic research is research undertaken for quite other purposes than policy development, which is nevertheless used – almost opportunistically – by policy making agencies for the purposes of policy development. Into this sixth category a number of studies on racial discrimination in the criminal justice system may be placed, including most recently the study of the work of the

[41] Noted by Brenda Hoggett, *Socio-Legal Newsletter*, No 8 p 3.

Crown Court by Dr Roger Hood, which has been used to inform the training policies of the Judicial Studies Board and the monitoring of ethnic minority experiences in the criminal justice system by the Home Office.

(g) Fundamental research

Fundamental research is research which, though not leading to immediate policy initiative, nevertheless has the effect of changing the nature of the debate so that ideas and opinions begin slowly to change. The work of the Oxford Centre into accidents is an example. This did not lead to the rapid adoption of no-fault compensation schemes, but has informed the, admittedly slow, development of thinking on the appropriateness of the tort system in the compensation of accident victims.

(h) Unused research

Finally, there is a distinct category which may have started out under one of the earlier heads but is ultimately *unused research*. Though commissioned by a government department or other policy making agency, such research is not in the end used by that body or which influences policy in ways other than might be expected. The major report for the Lord Chancellor's Department, by the Genns on the Effectiveness of Representation in Tribunals is perhaps one example. Given the impact of representation on outcome found by the study, one clear policy implication of that research was that more legal aid should be available in tribunals, and was essential if there was to be equality of outcome at tribunal hearings. Official policy on legal aid for tribunals has remained unchanged, however. Nevertheless, the research also identified the value of representation by persons other than professionally qualified lawyers; this has influenced a number of developments in relation to tribunal representation outside the formal legal aid structure.[42]

A more recent, and very controversial, example has arisen in the context of the Royal Commission on Criminal Procedure, where a number of major research findings concerning court processes and procedures – the product of research sponsored by the Royal Commission – have been ignored in the report itself.

The ESRC review provides many more detailed examples of the impact of research on policy development: in family law, legal services, legal education (especially professional legal education), alternative dispute resolution and conciliation, and many aspects of criminal justice.[43] There will be plenty more examples in the years ahead. If those who work in the universities claim – as they should – to be at the cutting edge of research and development, this must embrace a willingness to consider the policy implications of work they have carried out.

---

[42] Though see the recent Green Paper on the Future of Legal Aid which has resurrected this research.

[43] *Op cit.* Ch 4.

The limitations of the impact of research

Despite all the examples provided above, it has to be acknowledged that the contribution of socio-legal research to policy developments has only been partial. Many, perhaps a majority, of the main policy developments have been introduced without preliminary research or proposals to monitor and evaluate the consequences. For example, in a legal context, despite the major impact that the Courts and Legal Services Act 1990 is likely to have on the work of the practising branches of the legal profession, and on the relationship between those two branches and other professional groups that may seek to enter the legal services field, there is no major research enterprise that is seeking to analyse the precise effects on the profession of this changed context. Given the changes in policy that have already been decided, this is an area which would more than justify evaluative study.

Factors promoting the relationship between socio-legal research and policy

Merely publishing research will not, of itself, lead to implementation. Over the recent past scholars have come to appreciate that implementation is dependent on other factors as well. For example, one of the factors likely to influence the degree to which research can assist the development of policy is the development of research activity within government departments and other agencies. Many government departments, and other policy making bodies have specifically commissioned socio-legal research for policy development purposes. Of these, the Home Office's Research Unit is the most long-standing, having been established over thirty years ago. It is this department which in the past has signalled most clearly the importance of research in the development of policy.

The Lord Chancellor's Department itself never established a research unit as such – though there are now indications that this may change – but it has commissioned a number of socio-legal research studies in recent years. More recently, the Legal Aid Board has been developing research specifically linked to the policy initiatives it has been making in the context of legal aid franchising. The Lord Chancellor's Advisory Committee on Legal Education and Conduct is also developing a modest research programme. For the legal profession, the Law Society has both established a Research and Policy Planning Unit, and has used the product of that research in its policy development. The Bar has commissioned research on specific matters, for example the new Bar Finals course, but does not have an internal research resource.

Where policy making bodies have invested in an internal research function, it is possible to estimate the value placed on research by those bodies. Such research units work properly when they help policy makers to recognise when they need research, and enable them to commission rigorous objective research providing good value for money. They can also show policy makers how to use research and remind them of research findings which may suggest certain solutions to policy questions. Their presence can also prevent problems developing between researchers and policy makers, since they can turn policy questions into research specifications and translate research reports into policy related summaries.

One of the successes of socio-legal scholars during the past two decades has been to develop an awareness of the possible relevance of socio-legal research to policy making in bodies which have not considered this before. The involvement of a number of agencies in the Oxford Centre's research on the uses of discretion is perhaps one example. Another is the involvement of the Sheffield Centre in aspects of local authority complaints procedures.

Other mechanisms for a constructive interchange between research and policy might also be developed. For example, the input of research into policy development need not arise exclusively in the context of academics producing reports, which are then utilised by officials. It is possible to envisage more collaborative models of participation. The example of the work recently undertaken by Mavis Maclean for the Lord Chancellor's Department in the development of its policy on child support is one example[44]; that by Rod Morgan for the Woolf Inquiry is another.[45]

The series of conferences sponsored by the Scottish Office and the ESRC into research on the work of the Scottish courts is another type of context in which policy makers and academics can be brought together to discuss the relationship of research to policy making.[46] The Law Society's own annual research conference is another such context.

A final observation

There is one danger that can arise when contemplating the links between research output and policy development. In so far as research is commissioned or funded by policy makers themselves, their interest will be a limited one focusing on their immediate policy needs. Important gaps may be allowed to emerge on issues on which policy makers do not see the value of research or on which, more significantly, they do not wish an independent and critical spotlight to be thrown. Yet these may be just the policy areas which do need research attention. One of the challenges facing the socio-legal research community in the coming years will be to ensure that sources of funding remain available to allow the investigation of the kinds of politically sensitive and potentially embarrassing research which may not be valued in the short term by policy makers, but may nevertheless be vital for good long-term policy development.

---

[44] *Socio-Legal Newsletter*, No 5 p 2.

[45] *Ibid*, p 3.

[46] SLSA Newsletter, No 4 Autumn 1990 p 5.

6. Implementing the Socio-legal: Impact on the Curriculum

In this final section, I wish to consider briefly the effect of socio-legal research on the curriculum. Here it is necessary to be somewhat impressionistic, but it has to be said that in the context of legal education, the integration of the output of socio-legal research into the curriculum has been very patchy[47]; and in the context of other disciplines, very limited indeed.

Casual empiricism suggests that – with rare exceptions – even those law teachers anxious to adopt a socio-legal or contextual approach to the teaching of their courses, set the scene with a bit of policy context at the beginning and then – as the students start to get restless – abandon all that and plunge into the cases and statutes for the rest of the year.

There are signs, however, that things may have to change. The newly published Law Society guidelines on the Foundations of the Law Degree stress the importance of teaching students about the social, political and economic background to the law they are studying. Furthermore, the Lord Chancellor's Advisory Committee on Legal Education and Conduct's recent consultation paper on Legal Education stresses the desirability of a truly liberal education in the law, rather than a narrowly rule bound one. Now that the boundaries of socio-legal research have expanded into the core curriculum there will really be no excuse for law teachers to ignore the potential contribution that this area of research permits.

There were those who argued that when law schools such as Warwick or Kent were established they were offering an alternative to traditional law courses, less dominated by the profession. At present there is a considerable body of opinion that, paradoxically, the future of the legal profession will be enhanced by the provision at the initial university stage of the broad, liberal, critical approach to the study of law envisaged by those with a socio-legal perspective.

The difficulties of delivering such an approach without sacrificing a rigorous introduction to legal doctrine as well are considerable. It may, however, be anticipated that a socio-legal approach to legal education will cease to be regarded as a deviation from the norm, but rather the paradigm model for legal education in the 21st century.[48]

---

[47] See the comments in the HEFCE *Subject Overview Report: Quality Assessment of Law 1993–1994* (HEFCE, 1994) para 8.

[48] See P. A. Thomas, "Socio-Legal Studies in the United Kingdom" in *Precaire Waarden; Liber Amicorum voor Prof. mr. A A G Peters* (Gouda Quint, 1994) pp 229–246.

Chapter 8

CLINICAL LEGAL EDUCATION AT WARWICK AND THE SKILLS MOVEMENT: WAS CLINIC A CREATURE OF ITS TIME?

Professor Avrom Sherr
University of London

This chapter provides an account of the development of the clinical law programme at Warwick University during its first 25 years. It then goes on to question some issues relating to that programme, its place at Warwick and the importance of clinical legal education more generally within the English university environment and internationally. The questions posed are whether clinical legal education was a creature of a particular epoch, or whether it has universal importance for all time. And does the progress of the "skills movement", itself a spin-off of clinical legal education, now negate the importance of clinical programmes?

1. The Legal Practice Programme at Warwick

"On 6 October 1975 a new type of law course began at the School of Law at Warwick University. The course was designed to enable students as a part of their work for the LLB degree, to handle cases on behalf of clients in the local community. This work, which was to be carefully supervised by the teaching staff, was to be used as an experiential basis from which the students and teachers could learn more about the ways in which the law works in practice.

The two sets of proposals on papers placed before the law faculty in 1974 set out the aims of the programme as building on the existing Warwick emphasis of 'law in action' and 'law in context'. A course with somewhat similar aims had started and foundered within a year at the University of Kent at Canterbury. The reasons for this infant mortality were probably more closely related to the success of that enterprise, as intended, than its failure. 'Clinical' programmes, as they were called, had begun in the late sixties in North American law schools largely funded by the Ford Foundation through the Council for Legal Education in Professional Responsibility. By 1975 there were therefore a number of models from which Warwick could choose. Law teachers, law students and a local law centre lawyer worked on the original proposals. The 'clinical' courses, as a result of a compromise in nomenclature which seemed to mean little at the time, were to be known as the 'Legal Practice Programme'.

The Programme has gone through three main phases. The early years of the Legal Practice Programme could be described as the 'Age of Generalists'. A number of members of staff, proficient in their own study area, were interested in the course. Students with cases in those subject areas would go to those teachers for their supervision on those cases. An overall convenor administered what was happening with cases and set up rotas for attendance at advice centres. The teaching element of the course in subject areas such as 'office methodology', 'court procedure,' 'interviewing,' 'negotiation' and 'advocacy,' as well as practice, procedure and law relating to housing, unfair dismissal, supplementary benefit and family law were all treated as a separable programme not integrated with the case handling work.

The supervision system was a relic of the prior period during which those supervisors had worked on cases coming from the legal advice centre, but outside of a recognised law course. Each supervisor had a different approach to the work. Some would attend and interview the clients and conduct almost the entire case themselves whilst the students watched and took notes. Others allowed the students more responsibility. A few, whilst having a very good knowledge of law, knew little of practice and procedure. The more 'laissez-faire' atmosphere of the classroom affected the approach to handling clients' cases. The students also felt a need for more integration between the different elements of the course.

In the next phase of the programme's development there was a move to more centralised control. Case work took on a 'practitioner mode,' in which there was a set system for control and 'diarising' of cases, specialist secretaries to type letters and pleadings and more of the formalities of the normal law office. The main supervision was carried out by two or three individuals and an accent was placed on a more 'businesslike' approach to the case work. At the same time the viewpoint of the programme became clarified. Its main object was not to provide legal assistance to advice centre clients, but to provide a special form of legal education to law students. Recognition of this was the most important factor in the transition to the next era of the programme when the 'teaching and understanding' aims of the programme were to take precedence. Whilst clients' cases were to be dealt with as closely as possible in a way a good lawyer would deal with them, the object of all this was to teach the students how to behave as lawyers, so that they could understand better the way the law operates, and can be operated, in the real world.

As the programme became more integrated it became more closely taught by one or two teachers who combined supervision on cases with the more formal teaching roles. With clarity of objective came clarity of the means by which those objectives could be met. In order that the students could learn properly from their experiences of acting as lawyers, and in order that they could provide a good service for clients in doing so, they needed to be taught first, and as quickly as possible, what was involved in acting like a lawyer. This was rather different from the main aims of a university law school which concentrated on teaching how to 'think like a lawyer'. Secondly, the students needed a small but adequate case load to be carefully supervised from an educational, as well as a 'professional' point of view. Thirdly, the

> students needed an academic background and intellectual framework within which they could review their experience and place it in perspective. Lastly, they needed some forum or occasions in which theory and practice could be well integrated."[1]

This is how the early years of the Legal Practice Programme at Warwick were described in 1986. The third phase of the development of clinical courses continued until about 1991. The teaching of skills and concepts strengthened with an expanding literature and the growing years of experience of education in that manner. The Legal Practice Programme had wider effects on learning within the curriculum as a whole. Legal Practice students brought some of the experiences and skills that they had learned into other subjects and enriched both seminars and project work there. During this period also the elements of the course which concentrated on the theory of the profession were strengthened and students were guided more clearly through theoretical perspectives in a process of evaluation of their experience in legal work and of other actors in the legal process.

The main Legal Practice Course, Legal Practice I, had always been oversubscribed from the beginning. It was felt by the teachers that no more than some 22–25 students a year could be accommodated on a programme which involved such intensive one-to-one supervision by members of staff on individual cases. Students were selected on the basis of an application form and their results in examinations. This approach was justified by the need to ensure that clients were well served and that the negligence insurance premiums would not rise (in 18 years of operation no claims needed to be made on the insurance). But this approach was never popular and legal practice teachers also felt some unease about its operation. By 1988 the pressure to take larger numbers of students became irresistible and in that year for the first time some 45 students were accommodated on Legal Practice I.

Inevitably, without extra staff, the nature of the course changed somewhat, but it was possible to retain the crucial process of individual responsibility for client work which was the main educational strength of the course. By 1992, the increased numbers began to tell both on teaching staff and methodology. In the current phase of the development of legal practice at Warwick the main course is taught through simulating the elements of client work. Supervising the number of cases that became necessary to provide an adequate caseload for the increased number of students was not possible without a large increase of staff. Simulation of client work provides the majority of the experiences previously available under the Legal Practice Programme, although the special significance represented by the needs of a real client is missed. On the other hand, an organised programme of simulation allows for a more structured and standardised experience for each of the students taking Legal Practice I, and allows a much larger number of students to benefit from the special characteristics of the course.

---

[1] Sherr, *Client Interviewing for Lawyers* (Sweet and Maxwell, 1986) vii–ix.

Assessment on Legal Practice I also went through some developments over the same period. From phase 2 onwards assessment was 50% based on students' performance on client cases and in class exercises, 25% on a written project and 25% on an examination based largely on the more theoretical elements of the course. The project was another occasion to try to marry the practical and theoretical parts of the course together.

This account so far deals largely with the main course, known as Legal Practice I. Legal Practice II also became available in phase 2 of the development outlined above. Legal Practice II was a half course which could be taken in the summer break between the second and third years and was based on a placement lasting for at least six weeks with a legal venue organised under supervision from Warwick. Work at the placement was subsequently written up as a project under supervision at Warwick, which identified some specific areas of interest arising out of the placement and followed those through in the written work. There was also a report from the placement venue on the student's performance there. Legal Practice II was available to any student and Legal Practice I was not a prerequisite for taking this course.

From 1982 onwards it was also possible for students who had taken Legal Practice I in their second year to take a Legal Practice III half course in their third year. By its nature, this course could only be taken by a small number of students and each individual's project and programme for this half course was unique. In one instance it involved setting up a new venue for client advice in a nearby community centre and on other occasions it included the supervision of students carrying out work on Legal Practice I cases. Assessment on this course always involved written project work reflecting on individual course experience.

2. Tensions Underlying the Programme

This largely factual account of changes in the Legal Practice Programme at Warwick belies some of the underlying tensions created by its existence. Such tensions exemplified at Warwick, were also reflected in the development of clinical legal education internationally. A first tension lay simply between "theory" and "practice". As in the United States where clinical teachers were still not fully accepted as tenure-track professors, and clinical legal education was looked at as a form of training for practice and therefore less intellectually valuable, so did some among the faculty view the concept, at least at its inception. But Legal Practice at Warwick was unlike most American clinical programmes. Its major objective was to provide students with a real understanding of the workings of the legal system and legal practice through experiencing it by a form of ethnomethodology from inside the system as a worker within it. This was no pious hope, but a structured aim supported by the educational method, content and teaching of the course. Though some students may have wished to take the course simply to find out what it would be like to work as a practising lawyer, they would soon find that those motives were mobilised to satisfy their personal objectives but based on an intellectual framework and clear academic structure. The programme was about the development of an understanding of legal practice and the operation of legal professionals within the legal system, not about training students how to be lawyers. The programme produced a good deal of its own research and students felt involved and privileged to be involved, in an understanding of how socio-legal method could be used to record and analyse their experiences on the course.

A second, but related, tension was the feeling that since the Legal Practice Programme dealt with "practice" it was "un-Warwick" in its approach and did not really belong in a law school which was clearly not traditional. But, in many respects, legal practice "out-Warwicked" many of the other parts of the curriculum. The objective was to study law in context and what could be a clearer or more obviously real context than the context in which law itself was actually practised?

Another tension caused by the Legal Practice Programme related to the amount of work involved in conducting client cases. For students this might well involve a far greater workload and more concentrated effort than in other courses at particular times such as preparation for trial. The workload was also different for the teachers. The amount of individual supervision of case preparation meant that "live client" work had to be accorded a different weighting as far as teaching credit was concerned on the staff matrix. This particular tension would have been alleviated by the movement to simulated client work in 1992.

A fourth tension which was not so evident at Warwick, but certainly occurred in most law schools in the United States resulting from clinical legal education programmes, related to a movement towards clarity of teaching objectives. In devising the curriculum for clinical programmes, teachers were forced to analyse clearly more direct teaching methods for the skills and forms of legal practice involved.[2] Aims, objectives and teaching outcomes were a clear part of the new pedagogy arising out of Jerome Bruner and the "experientialist" movement in education generally.[3] This clarity of approach was thrown back at regular law teachers in American law schools as a challenge to explain the aims, objectives and intended outcomes of more traditional methods of teaching in substantive law. This tension partly served to underline some of the existing dichotomy between "education" and "training".

A last tension which occurred elsewhere concerned the political nature of early clinical activists and their own relationship with the "Reggies"[4] in the United States and the law centre movement in this country. Early clinical teachers were heavily committed to a liberal or left-wing approach to the provision of legal services to the under-privileged, to the use of the law as a liberating force and to educating new lawyers in the work of individual clients and the less privi-

---

[2] Perhaps this is what Wilson was referring to in G.P. Wilson, "The Concept of a Law Degree: Getting on with the job" (1968) 10 *Journal of the Society of Public Teachers of Law* 114 p 117.

[3] Bruner, *The Process of Education* (Harvard University Press, 1962).

[4] Reginald Huber Smith appointments to legal services posts – see A. Ashman "The New Private Practice" (1972) NLDA.

leged, rather than the more traditional areas of property and commerce. This approach, in North American law schools, was often different from the viewpoint of the more traditional, substantive law educators, and it often placed the clinic and clinical teachers in a different political camp from those who ran the law school. Interestingly, there was to be some development in this position as the clinical movement itself developed.

These were among the major tensions which underlay the development of clinical legal education internationally. Warwick's pioneering approach and general difference in outlook allowed the creativity of those tensions to operate whilst not undermining the central function of the clinical programme.

3. Why Warwick?

The progress of clinical legal education in the United States has been well charted from the effects of the Watergate scandals, Chief Justice Warren Burger's approach to legal ethics[5], the foundation of the Clinical Legal Education for Professional Responsibility[6] as a result of money from Ford Foundation and how a generation of clinical law professors was hired, acclimatised and in due course attempted to assail the monolith of the socratic method, case method and appellate court supremacy over legal education.[7] In order to place the development of clinical legal education at Warwick within this context it is necessary to study the conditions under which CLE blossomed there.

There is a temptation first to analyse why the early Kent "praxis" experiment did not last beyond its second year. That is a temptation which this author will resist because the two sets of circumstance seem to be very different. The praxis programme began a year before Warwick started its Legal Practice courses. Kent's approach was far more wide ranging than Warwick's and its intention was to affect the entire law curriculum, rather than being a separate but integrated part of the overall undergraduate programme. Some practical and personality issues seemed to cause great difficulty at Kent, as well as issues of principle, and Warwick was able to learn from these in fashioning this second attempt at CLE in the United Kingdom. Although the comparison may not be fruitful, Kent's pioneering course must be seen as one of the important conditions for the inception of the Warwick programme. Perhaps partly as a result, Warwick's programme was less holistic and wide ranging, less public and openly principled, used less university resources and used the cover of external community based organisations in order to run its cases. The latter was a significant help when cases were taken against local authorities and the university itself. The university could not then be "blamed" for taking cases against itself or against other local public bodies with whom it needed to have a good working

[5] (1973–74) 42 *Fordham Law Review* 227.
[6] Pincus, *Clinical Education For Law Students* (Meilen, 1980).
[7] See eg. Freeman, W. and Weinhofen, H. "Cases and Text on Clinical Law Training" West, 1972, and the works of David Barnhizer and Meltsner and Shrag.

relationship. Similarly, cases taken against local commerce or industry would also not affect the name of the university in its dealings with them.

The "cover" of neighbouring community organisations was not a cynical and otherwise unconnected usage of their names and facilities. The main community organisations used had been fostered and organised and sometimes staffed by members of the School of Law in their private capacities. Work within those organisations as lawyers was therefore a natural progression on previous involvement. To have used the aegis of the university in such circumstances would have been less appropriate to the objectives of both staff and students.[8]

The second important condition for Warwick's Legal Practice Programme was the climate of interest within the law school itself. There were strong connections with law teachers at Kent, deep commitment to the objectives of the community organisations among staff and students, an interest in American approaches to legal education and an openness towards new methods and ideas. It has already been stated that support was not universal immediately. But the major concerns of those who saw clinical legal education as being too practical, as opposed to being theoretical, and too based within a traditional model of professional orthodoxy served well to help fashion the particularity of Warwick's approach as a "laboratory of legal practice" rather than a trade school for lawyers. This climate of interest was based both on particular individuals and the shared objectives of a collegiate faculty, in so far as they could be articulated. Individual law teachers of influence within the Law School had been involved in teaching in East Africa, the United States and Canada. These opportunities had given them insights into the purpose and method of legal education which would not have been available only within the English experience at that time. Most were strongly committed to the idea of educating lawyers who would be able to serve the "underprivileged" and who would wish to do so. Some individuals had already begun to theorise legal skills and legal education itself. Others had begun to theorise issues relating to the legal profession; and all were committed to an approach often referred to as "law in context" which encouraged studying the operation of the law within its practical context. Each year the Law School brought over a "visiting American" who would typically have just completed a law degree at a prestigious university in the United States and were on their way to taking up a teaching post over there.[9] Their presence enriched the Law School's experience by bringing across a constant stream of the latest ideas within legal education in the United States factored through the involvement of one of the latest recipients of those ideas. Their reactions, both positive and negative to the progress of clinical

---

[8] Where legal need could not be sufficiently covered by the irregularities of student attendance, the community organisations, together with law school staff made application for funds for separate services to be established and this occurred in at least two major areas of legal work in Leamington Spa.

[9] R. Folsom & N. Roberts, "The Warwick Story: Being Led Down The Contextual Path Of the Law" (1979) *Journal of Legal Education*, Vol. 30.

legal education in the United States assisted the climate of interest and informed it in very specific ways.

A third condition which seemed to be important was the presence of one or two members of the Faculty with recent experience of professional legal work and a desire not to accept given models of orthodoxy within it. As had occurred in the United States, it became necessary to hire specifically with this person specification in mind. It was useful, though probably not essential, to combine the experiences of someone who had worked as a solicitor as well as someone who had worked as a barrister. It was also useful to combine the experiences of someone who had worked at a law centre and someone whohad worked in commercial practice. But actual knowledge and experience of handling cases and clients was imperative in providing both a client service and a responsible education.

At first, those who had been in practice saw as distinct the systems of legal education and handling client cases. Progression towards an approach in which the two became integrated and each was achieved through the other took some time. During the developmental period of the Legal Practice Programme a number of recent practitioners joined in the teaching for varying periods of time. Most had great difficulty in ceding the responsibility for handling the case over to the students themselves. For the educational purposes essential to the programme the students had to feel that they had real responsibility. Most lawyers so recently out of practice (and so imbued with the hierarchical structure of practice) found it extremely difficult to hand over even the perception of responsibility to young undergraduates, let alone real responsibility. It needed some personal confidence, the evolution of a system of safety-netting and supervision, and a clear commitment to the educational, rather than client-serving, aspects of the work before the appropriate transition could take place. Somebody could be a great practitioner or a great educator but this work seemed to need a level of competence in both.

A fourth condition was exposure for those involved in teaching the course to other clinical legal educators and similar programmes elsewhere. Warwick soon became a natural draw for those interested, and involved in, clinical legal education in the United States, Canada, Australia and New Zealand. Although not inundated with such visits, each year brought a number of short-term and sometimes long-term visitors to the Law School who would sit in on the programme and allow an effective comparison with what was happening elsewhere. Warwick often became part of a circuit through which clinical legal educators would pass bringing a wake of up-to-date information behind them. Longer term visitors helped to develop a feeling of confidence about the programme which was essential to prevent any feelings of isolation. Warwick was not in any way behind – it was often in front of – developments elsewhere. But it was important for the Programme to feel confident with reference to its nearest comparators and these contacts enabled it to do so. In addition these contacts and exposure enabled a more clear differentiation to emerge between the objectives of an experiential and research-based programme as compared with the trade school or apprenticeship approach which had often been adopted elsewhere.

Finally, and most likely with strong effect also on all the conditions mentioned previously, in retrospect the era seemed important. The atmosphere of the 60s which had washed over into the universities of the 1970s clearly encouraged and informed the idea of serving the needs of the underprivileged and a concept of education based on experience and emotion as well as rationality and openness.

4. Politics or Skills?

The influence of "the 60s" and the legacy of attitudes which derived from that period then almost certainly had an effect on the other preconditions which existed with the inception of the Warwick Legal Practice Programme. It then becomes necessary to ask whether that particular set of traditions, orthodoxies and views which can easily be herded together under the description of "the 60s" was in some way a necessary factor for clinical legal education or whether it could exist independently of that form of influence.

This question becomes increasingly important when one of the main objectives of clinical legal education has probably become fulfilled in rather different ways in common law countries in general and most recently in England and Wales. One of the major objectives of clinical legal education was to achieve a direct teaching of the legal skills involved in legal practice. Indeed, this became the defining characteristic of all clinical legal education programmes in the United States, many of which were not live client programmes and therefore taught legal skills through the simulation of practical work. The teaching of skills, which had previously not been part of the law curriculum, such as interviewing, fact finding, negotiation, drafting and advocacy, was effected through clinical legal education programmes in the United States partly because of the general absence of the apprenticeship stage of formal legal education, training and qualification.[10]

Other common law countries such as England, Scotland, New Zealand, Australia and Hong Kong all had systems of compulsory vocational training, compulsory apprenticeship or both. It was therefore not very surprising that clinical legal education should start in the United States where there was almost entirely an absence of these elements of legal education which would have provided a practical training. It is also understandable that the organised United States Bar should have been strong enough to force that education into the law curriculum at university, rather than adding an extra period beyond graduation, because law in the United States is a postgraduate study. Students were therefore older, already studying for a period of approximately seven years, more vocationally oriented in the approach to their studies since none saw it as

[10] See Chief Justice Warren Burger, *op cit.*

a general foundation degree and therefore more keen to learn at university about legal practice.

The progress of the skills movement in these contexts should therefore not be seen as surprising but some elements of its content merit further study. To some extent elements of skills had always been taught in the law school. Legal writing, legal analysis and appellate court advocacy were a strong part of the indirect teaching objectives of any law school. Although it has been more fashionable to break down legal analysis and reasoning into sub-skills of case handling, rule handling[11], statute handling, policy issues etc, these have all, to a greater or lesser extent, always been an indirect part of the curriculum. Similarly, legal research and writing was necessary for the preparation of classes and preparation of written material and for examinations. Even if there were not a formal mooting element within, or extramural to, the curriculum the approach of case study and Socratic dialogue within the classroom, as well as the examination question based on a given set of facts, was usually directed to the subject-matter and methodology of appellate court advocacy. It would therefore be wrong to assume that such skills, or any practical legal skills, were given no attention in the pre 1960s–70s law school classroom in North America or elsewhere in the common law world.

The difference that came about with the revolution of clinical legal education was that the skills were now taught in a more direct manner and that other skills were added to them. All teaching had until then been at the level of what was necessary for the appellate court advocate. It did not cater for the general work of those lawyers who were not involved in this particular level or type of work. The importance of the work of Frank[12], Llewellyn[13] and other realists was to demonstrate that the bulk of lawyers were not involved in appellate court work, and even those who were so involved under the American system, were not involved in it all of the time. It was therefore necessary to ascertain and then teach what it was that other lawyers did and how cases which got to court were prepared, how trial court advocacy operated and everything else which led up to the appellate court. Although theories of evidence existed[14] it was much later that factual investigation skills were studied, analysed and put together.[15] More common elements of legal work starting with the first client interview began to be analysed[16], researched and written up in such a way that they could be taught. But until all of these items could be placed carefully under the microscope of academic observation and findings reproduced in textual form, the

---

[11] See, *e.g.* Twining and Miers, *How To Do Things With Rules: A Primer of Interpretation* (Weidenfeld & Nicolson, 1991).

[12] J. Frank, *Why not a Clinical Law School?* (1933) 81 U Pa L Rev 907.

[13] *E.g.* Llewellyn, *Jurisprudence: Realism in Theory and practice,* (University of Chicago Press reprinted 1971, 1962).

[14] Wigmore, *Evidence in Trials at Common Law,* (Little, Brown, 1961).

[15] Binder and Bergman, *Fact Investigation: From Hypothesis to Proof* (St. Paul, 1984); Anderson, Twining & David, *Analysis of Evidence, How to Do Things with Facts* (Weidenfeld & Nicolson, 1991).

[16] Binder & Price, "Legal Interviewing and Counselling" West, 1979; Sherr, A.H. "Lawyers and Clients – The First Meeting" 1986 MLR and *"Client Interviewing for Lawyers"* (Sweet & Maxwell, 1988).

most simple approach to teach these elements was within the experientially based clinical legal education programme. The experience of behaving and acting as a lawyer would itself provide some of the necessary clues to the development of these skills. Careful monitoring and supervision by teachers would further hone each student's abilities. Hence the major, and necessary, purpose of clinical legal education at least until texts could be developed in skills areas, was the teaching of skills themselves. In addition, the behavioural nature of work in clinical legal education lent itself to the teaching of skills which were often as much behavioural as intellectual and the experiential method was therefore a much stronger method of inculcation than the teaching system in substantive law subjects based on lectures, readings and discussion. Skills teaching was therefore a rational, necessary and useful major element of the clinical legal education process.

But skills teaching, outside of North America, has now moved house away from the innovatory source of the undergraduate curriculum and into the functional environment of the vocational courses. Encouraged and monitored by professional organisations everywhere as "the new orthodoxy", it starts to look different from the political idealism of its originators. Now that skills teaching has been incorporated into the work of vocational courses and formal training in apprenticeship in so many other parts of the common law world, is there still a place for clinical legal education at all? One might strongly argue that skills teaching which did not include some "real" or simulated element would not be as effective, but it seems as if the vocational courses have borrowed the clothes of the law school and it may therefore be difficult to see what purpose might yet be served by clinical legal education in these circumstances.

But was there then something rather different about clinical legal education, and clinical legal education at Warwick, from merely being a skills training school? It has already been suggested that Warwick's programme was at least as much involved in research and understanding of the legal profession and its work, as in teaching the skills which would enable law students to be in a position to experience those issues. But this element was not universal. Much stronger was the ethos which clinical legal education brought with it in providing a political standpoint and some energy to encourage the teaching of legal issues relating to the underprivileged and a view of law and its practice which would encourage students to feel able to move into that work area.

Additionally the ethos, which probably also gave rise to the critical legal studies movement[17], was internally critical of areas of law, the legal profession, the law school itself and the perpetuation of traditional models of practice. For many these elements were an essential part of what was different about the CLE approach. It was a part of the law school where students could express their own anti-authoritarian views, where underprivileged clients could be served even if students were to end up in large commercial firms; where the form of the law school itself could be examined and attacked. The critical legal studies

[17] See, *e.g.* Unger, *The Critical Legal Studies Movement* (Harvard University Press, 1986).

movement has already been mentioned. Could one say that this movement has taken over the energy and position previously engendered and occupied by the clinical legal education movement, with similar acronym and identical feel? Is it possible to take the politics out of clinical legal education? Can they be left with the theoreticians of the critical legal studies movement and can legal skills be taught, sanitised of the ideology and devoid of the emotion? Why should not there be a set of legal skills for doing commercial work? Is it right that the clinical teachers clandestinely operated their own political agenda?

5. Conclusion

The progress of skills teaching in the last ten years in North America, and more recently elsewhere, has exposed exactly these issues. In many law schools skills teaching is a functionally embedded part of a formal process taught by skills educators, but extracted out of the world of legal need of the underprivileged. The 80s engulfed the anti-authoritarian clinical movement and brought in a new wave of young teachers who knew not Reginald Huber Smith, but did know about skills. Their analytical writings have filled for a long time the back pages of the *Journal of Legal Education.* They are analytically strong but often politically absent. Conference meetings of old and new clinicians often show a clear contest of culture and style. Skills and skills teaching have progressed immeasurably and the new clinician is a perfect technician, mirroring the development within the legal profession itself.[18] But skills can be employed in all areas of client service and the commercial need has financial strength far above that of the legal aid client. Skills and clinic have been formalised and some of the heart, energy and politics taken out of them.

Whilst clinical legal educators should be proud of the universal success of the skills movement there was, and still is, much more to clinic, much more to legal education and much more to the practice of law than just skills. The inheritors of the new orthodoxy and the new imparters of this creed need to be aware of the richer provenance of the functional training in which they are now involved. Understanding, emotion and imagination and the ethics of justice for all were, and are, equally at the heart of clinical legal education and of excellence in legal professional practice. Studying legal skills outside of their natural context needs today the same form of health warning which Warwick Law School gave to the study of substantive law outside its context 25 years ago.

---

[18] See A. Sherr, "Come of Age" (1994) *International Journal of the Legal Profession* p 1.

Chapter 9

"OUT ON THE WEEKEND": REFLECTIONS ON EUROPEAN UNION LAW IN CONTEXT

Professor Francis Snyder*
European University Institute, Florence

1. Greeting

Logic, in this post-modern age, is problematic. Theories of linear development are even more suspect. To suggest that either is the basis of a series of scientific contributions over a long period of time makes little sense, even if one focuses solely on public manifestations of thought in writing, which are usually taken to be one's intellectual footprints. Nor is it a simple matter, even if hypothetically it were possible, to indicate with any precision one's own contribution to academic research. This is doubtless an apt subject for empirical study. But to do so with any credibility – either for oneself or one's colleagues – presupposes a degree of objectivity to which few would lay claim.

This chapter is more modest. My aim is to illustrate one way of studying the law of the European Union, namely by means of a contextual approach, which places European Union law in its social, political, economic and cultural contexts. "Studying" is shorthand for a long and continuous process of learning, expressed in writing of various forms. "The law of the European Union", despite its complexity, is considerably more straightforward: here it designates the legal institutions, substantive law and legal processes of the Western European economic integration scheme encompassing the three Communities (ESCS, Euratom, EEC) established in the 1950s and their development up to and including the creation in 1993 of the European Union.[1] This paper

* The author wishes to thank Christian Joerges, Emir Lawless, Rossa Phelan, Wolf Sauter, Anne-Lise Strahtmann, William Twining, Nuno Venade, Geoffrey Wilson, Song Ying and Neil Young (who provided the title) for their contributions to this article. He alone, of course, is responsible for the contents of this article.

[1] The Treaty on European Union was signed on 7 February 1992 and came into effect on 1 November 1993. For the complete text, see OJ C224/1. On suggested terminology, see "Names after Maastricht" [1994] 1 CMLR 4. Throughout this article, and for the sake of convenience, I use "European Union" and EU to denote, not only the EU narrowly conceived, but also the three previously existing Communities: the European Community (EC), the European Coal and Steel Community (ECSC) and the European Atomic Energy Community (Euratom or EAEC). EC or EEC is used to refer specifically to the European Community, which prior to the Maastricht Treaty was known as the European Economic Community (EEC).

does not pretend therefore to be objective, comprehensive or representative.

A primarily personal account of the development of European Union law in context might nevertheless be of wider interest. As yet there are relatively few contextual studies of European Union law. I have recently described these elsewhere[2], so that another account of the development of the contextual approach to the study of European Union law or a survey of the field could easily be superfluous. A more personal view, however, may offer different insights or add a new perspective; it supplies part of the context of more academic work which is usually neglected. In addition, it may be suggested with some diffidence, my own work has been among the main contributions thus far to the contextual study of European Union law. To some extent it has established novel themes or, in the form of an academic journal, helped to create at least one new institution in the field of European law in context. Instead of being limited solely to the experience of one person, it may therefore serve to some extent as a convenient shorthand for broader developments in the field.

If the delineation of the main lines of a *cursus academicus* is difficult, the presentation of the fruits of study and research poses its own problems. The past may re-present itself in different ways when viewed from the standpoint of the present. Two extremes of the spectrum, however, might identify a jumble of unconnected and random events, on the one hand, and the uninterrupted, if not always obvious, elaboration of a single idea, a guiding thread, on the other hand. The present case, like most, is situated between these two extremes, though the reader, not the writer, is best able to judge where.

Chronology forms a convenient skeleton. It at least has the merit of giving a structure to what otherwise might seem to be marvellously like a letter, bits and pieces, some chat. There is more to the skeleton, however, than mere chronology. Chronology by itself has no sense in the present context: it is impossible to think of a time in the past without also recalling what happened then; the two are inextricably interwoven, and inevitably each is defined at least partly in terms of the other. But identifying "what happened" implies choices, not only expressly about level of discourse and nature of themes, but also implicitly about relationship and direction.

I propose two general themes: first, the tension between concentration and dispersion; and, second, the tension between power and relativity. Concentration means having a single or main focus; dispersion refers to disaggregation, fragmentation, perhaps even incoherence. Power involves competition, hierarchy, domination and subordination, ideology, relations between structure and agency, and negotiation. Relativity refers to the two dimensions of time and space. If you like word games, you will recognise that these themes are intimately related; indeed, from some perspectives each can be considered to be a transformation of the other. As will be seen, these themes run through the development of my work on European Union law in context; they may also

[2] See my "Introduction", in each of the two volumes of Snyder (ed), *European Community Law* (Dartmouth, *International Library of Essays in Law and Legal Theory*, 1993), Vol. I, pp xiii–xxvi, and Vol. II, pp xiii–xxviii.

represent broader trends in the field. We can use these themes, together with chronology, to structure the discussion.

So what is the menu?

There are five courses. Let us start with an antipasto, intended to whet the appetite: a mixture of law and other social sciences should do the trick. We move on to the next course, delicately flavoured, beautifully coloured, and prepared with a light touch for the modern reader: long-term empirical anthropological and historical research, with unforeseen ramifications. The principal course[3] is today's speciality: the law of the European Union in context. Because we are among friends, we can relax and enjoy the meal and the conversation, and things we already know well can be passed over quickly. Even so, this course will occupy most of our attention. After such a repast, dessert might be too much, but something tantalising may not come amiss: hence a glance at the future. It is worth recalling, however, the caveats with which the paper began: the glance at the future does not provide a crystal ball; like the past, it is subject to chance so much more than we usually care to admit.

2. Antipasto

The seeds of any intellectual interest are never entirely intellectual; indeed it may be suggested that rarely are they mainly intellectual. If I had to look back to the origins of my current work, several factors stand out.[4] Superficially, and in many ways in substance, they seem far removed from the study of European Union law in context. Nevertheless, at least from this subjective viewpoint, they form part of its genealogy.

First, my father was a scientist, initially a professor of geology, then a practising geologist and later a consultant, while my mother was a part-time secondary school teacher of foreign languages, particularly French, German and Spanish. I recall my father saying once that among the reasons why he liked geology was that it was the most historical of the natural sciences; perhaps he also thought it the social science that most closely resembled the hard sciences. Taken together as individuals, and also as archetypes, my parents embodied a concern for time and space, for detailed analysis and broad comparison which I have often carried forward in my work. They also represented, of course, the tensions, conflicts and sometimes contradictions between these dimensions.

Second, at least partly because of my father's work, as a child I moved from one city or town to another very frequently. As an adult, I am now aware of the

---

[3] The two of the world's cuisines which are of most relevance to this article have no main course: see Hazan, *The Classic Italian Cookbook* (Macmillan, 1981), p 5; and Lo, *Chinese Food* (Penguin, 1972), pp 7–8.

[4] The method of analysis is roughly inspired by Marx's method of political economy: see Marx, *Grundrisse: Introduction to the Critique of Political Economy*, trans. M. Nicolaus (Penguin Books, 1973), especially pp 100–108. See also Carver (trans. and ed.), *Karl Marx: Texts on Method* (Blackwell, 1975). For an earlier attempt to experiment with this method, see my unpublished paper, "Vers une généalogie de la migration capitaliste: Les Jola-Banjal", presented at the International Seminar on Migration in Tropical Africa, Leiden, The Netherlands, 21–25 November 1977.

destructuring effects of such mobility on children. Be that as it may, in my case it also had two other possible effects, and I stress "possible" because this is to some extent an attempt at intellectual autobiography, far removed from even the uncertain "science" of psychology. On the one hand, frequent moving, for a child (and also an adult, but then it is perhaps easier) may be a continual consignment to being an outsider. Negatively, it can lay the foundation for a later pattern of recurrent removal and reintegration. Positively, it may form the basis of what one might call *un regard anthropologique*, an anthropological perspective, in which one instinctively brings to bear on any situation, even those in which one participates, the perspective of an outside observer.[5] On the other hand, it may be suggested that, in addition to its socio-spatial aspect, this pattern of removal and reintegration had a relativising influence. In this sense: that continually dealing with differences in geographical space and social time (for each community has its own temporality) tends to incline one toward a sense of cultural relativity.

Third, in fact, I would now go further and put these two points together: in my consciousness of my own development and work processes, I have noticed what seem to be a cycle or alternation between concentration and diffusion. By this I mean, so far as scientific work is concerned, a concentration on a specific topic, geographical area or, more precisely, task; followed by a diffusion in the sense of a proliferation or plurality of different foci which do not appear to be linked by any underlying logic and together do not seem to have any coherence; followed later by concentration; and so on. If one is more or less unconscious about oneself, such an alternation can be a cause for serious concern, but with some effort to be self-conscious it may be a source of pleasure and, in any case, employed fruitfully in one's own personal and intellectual development.

Fourth, comparative research and an interest in methods of comparison have long been part of my intellectual baggage. As an undergraduate at Yale I specialised in comparative politics; as a student at Harvard Law School I concentrated mainly (in addition to the required courses) on comparative law, including law in different societies, cultures and time periods; as a PhD student in Paris I participated in intensive bi-weekly seminars on comparative African land systems; during my PhD and later field research in Senegal I did a good deal of reading in economic anthropology and comparative economic systems; subsequently at the beginning of my teaching career I regularly taught comparative law and anthropology of law.

The fifth and final point concerns an interest in and research on very different cultures. After my penultimate year at Yale, I was awarded a Summer Travelling Fellowship in French, which I used to carry out research in West Africa, particularly Senegal and Mali, on the origins of political parties in Mali during the 1930s and their development until independence in 1960.[6] While a law student at Harvard, I worked as a research assistant, part-time during the

[5] See, *e.g.*, Lévi-Strauss, *Anthropologie structurale* (Plon, 1958); Powdermaker, *Stranger and Friend: The Way of an Anthropologist* (Norton, 1966); Nader (ed), *Law in Culture and Society* (Aldine, 1969).
[6] Published in revised form as *One-Party Government in Mali* (Yale University Press, 1965).

academic year and full-time during the summers, to Professor Jerome Cohen, the founder of the study in the United States of modern Chinese law[7]; this involved not only Chinese law but also the legal systems of other East Asian countries, particularly 19th century Vietnam and 20th century Korea, as well as research in comparative and historical sociology of law. As part of my PhD research and work that developed from it, I lived in a village in Senegal for more than two years.

The intellectual crunch, as I recall, came in October 1970. Having arrived at Yale Law School as one of the first three Research Fellows in the Programme on Law and Modernisation[8], I remember looking at the mass of notes and other materials from research in Senegal, all of which then seemed to concern space categories and ritual, and asking myself, "What does this have to do with law?"[9] Years later, after giving a paper on my research on European Community legislative processes to an audience of English law teachers, I was surprised to be asked the same question. The contextual approach to European Union law aims to provide an answer.

3. Primo Piatto

After such a substantial *antipasto misto,* which probably amounted to more than you expected, a *primo piatto* might seem superfluous. For the sake of the balance and the continuity of our narrative, however, as well as to preserve the coherence of our theme, I propose to pause briefly for some delicate spring rolls. We can perhaps consider them to be a Chinese analogue of Proust's *madeleines.* With them, I would like to evoke more than a decade of empirical research. Though the research has long been finished, or at least what is likely to be written up has been written up, this decade was by no means an isolated period of time. Instead, it had its roots firmly in the past, and its branches and leaves spread, usually unpredictably, into the future.

Beginning with my PhD field work in Senegal which started in 1969, there followed a decade of detailed empirical research on the legal and economic history of a former kingdom in southern Senegal.[10] Following the PhD fieldwork,

[7] See Cohen, *The Criminal Process in the People's Republic of China* (Harvard University Press, 1968); Jerome Alan Cohen, "Introduction", in Cohen (ed), *Contemporary Chinese Law: Research Problems and Perspectives* (1970). For a general account, see Stanley Lubman, "Studying Contemporary Chinese Law: Limits, Possibilities and Strategy" (1991) *American Journal of Comparative Law* p 293.

[8] I had carried out legal and anthropological research in Africa. The other two Fellows were Tom Heller, now at the Law School and the Institute for International Studies of Stanford University, who had conducted legal and economic research in Latin America, and Marc Galanter, now at the Law School of the University of Wisconsin-Madison, who had conducted research in law and sociology in India.

[9] This conundrum was reflected in my "A Problem of Ritual Symbolism and Social Organisation among the Diola-Bandial", Yale Law School Program in Law and Modernization, Working Paper No. 2 (1971).

[10] The principal publication from this research, in addition to numerous articles, was Snyder, *Capitalism and Legal Change: An African Transformation* (Academic Press, 1981). An offshoot was *Law and Population in Senegal: A Survey of Legislation* (with the collaboration of M.-A. Savané) (Afrika-Studiecentrum, 1978). These two books illustrate nicely the continuing relationship between concentration and dispersion, as well as my interest in both law and context and studies of legal doctrine.

most of the research was conducted during the period of a joint appointment in law and social science at York University in Toronto. There I taught mainly comparative law and property law at Osgoode Hall Law School and the anthropology of law in the Division of Social Science as well as (together with Phil Gulliver) in the Graduate Faculty of Social Anthropology. The natural history of the Senegal project has already been published.[11] Based on a case study, the research was designed to answer two questions. What changes in legal forms occurred during the subsumption of a precapitalist society into the world economy? What relations obtained between legal forms and economic changes during this period of historical transition? The research thus was a study of relations between legal ideas and economic organisation. Here I wish to mention only some general lines of force which developed from (or were strengthened by) this work.

First, though not conceived initially in these terms, the Senegal project became increasingly historical and interdisciplinary in nature. Without seeking a causal explanation, suffice it to say that this research consolidated my concern for change and comparison through time. My interest in history did not of course begin with this research. However, some of the historical themes with which the project dealt were followed up in later research. They include the nature of culturally specific histories[12], the relationship between law and the creation of a market economy[13], the creation of a labour force[14], the historical development of different state structures[15] and the ways of making sense of specific social and cultural configurations in the past and how one configuration was transformed into another.[16]

A second strand of development was comparison across space, that is, cross-

[11] See Francis G. Snyder, "Land Law and the Transition to Capitalism: The Natural History of a Senegalese Case Study", in Luckham (ed), *Law and Social Enquiry: Case Studies of Research* (Scandinavian Institute of African Studies, and International Center for Law in Development, 1981), pp 76–109.

[12] See my "Note on the Study of African Legal History", unpublished (1968), and "The Use of Oral Data in Legal Anthropology: A Senegalese Example" (1973) 17 *Journal of African Law* p 196.

[13] See my "Land Law and Economic Change in Rural Senegal: Diola Pledge Transactions and Disputes", in Hamnett (ed), *Soeial Anthropology and Law* (Association of Social Anthropologists Monograph No. 14) (Academic Press, 1977) pp 113–157, trans. as "Le droit de la terre et le changement économique au Sénégal", in Le Roy (ed), *Etudes sur le droit de la terre en Afrique Noire* (Laboratoire d'Anthropologie Juridique de Paris, 1975), Vol. 2, pp 1–43. See also my "Colonialism and Legal Form: The Creation of 'Customary Law' in Senegal", in Sumner (ed), *Crime, Justice and Underdevelopment* (Heinemann, 1981) pp 49–90; longer version in (1981) 19 *Journal of Legal Pluralism* p 49.

[14] See my "Labour Power and Legal Transformation in Senegal" (1981) 21 *Review of African Political Economy* p 26; and my (with Douglas Hay), "Comparisons in the Social History of Law: Labour and Crime", in Snyder and Hay (eds), *Labour, Law and Crime in Historical Perspective* (Tavistock, 1987).

[15] See my "Legal Innovation and Social Change in a Peasant Community: A Senegalese Village Police" (1978) 48 *Africa* p 231; and Hay and Snyder (eds), *Policing and Prosecution in Britain, 1750–1850: Social History of the Criminal Law* (Clarendon Press, 1989).

[16] See my "'Folk Law' and Historical Transitions: Some Conceptual Issues", in Allott and Woodman (eds), *People's Law and State Law: The Bellagio Papers* (Foris Publications, 1985) pp 263–274. See also Jan Vansina, "The Use of Process Models in African History", in Vansina, Mauny and Thomas (eds), *The Historian in Tropical Africa (Studies presented and discussed at the Fourth International African Seminar at the University of Dakar, Senegal, 1961)* (Oxford University Press for the International African Institute, 1964) pp 375–389.

societal comparisons within the same time period. This is the *locus classicus* of comparative law and comparative politics. It was reflected later in numerous conference papers and, more substantially, in an interest in the transplantation of legal systems. It was sustained by my continued participation, during the 1970s, in the Laboratoire d'Anthropologie Juridique de Paris.[17] However, my own published research has never really dealt directly with problems of comparison or comparative law as such. Instead, it has borrowed from anthropology what Max Gluckman used to call the method of "implicit comparison".[18]

Third, these two strands were united in a strong interest in theories of development and underdevelopment. During my research in Senegal Professor Samir Amir was the Director of the UN Institut Africain de Développement Economique et de Planification (IDEP) in Dakar. My own research and conversations with him stimulated wide reading on development theory, which by definition is concerned expressly with social and often macro-historical change and often implicitly involves comparative studies. This work resulted in a major survey of the literature, which was published in a special issue of the American journal *Law and Society Review* on "Current Issues in Law and Social Science".[19] Its concern for the nature of the state, relations between the state and the economy, relations of domination and subordination, and the interaction between national and global processes was followed up in later research.[20]

A fourth element brings us back to our repast: food and agriculture. For the Senegal research I remember reading Grist on *Rice*.[21] The content of this book proved indispensable then, but more germane to the present purposes is the fact that its title symbolised a host of concerns. In fact, the ramification of these concerns spread energetically like so many deep roots to underlie the next two decades of my work, periodically bursting forth in published form, as if to remind me that something organic and continuous, yet often hidden from view, knit together apparently disparate endeavours. The latter include an interest in food and agricultural policy, a concern for roots in the historical sense, a method of analysis that gave special attention to *filières* or networks of economic

[17] See generally my "Anthropology, Dispute Processes and Law" (1981) 8 *British Journal of Law and Society* [now *Journal of Law and Society*] p 141; reprinted in Sack and Aleck (eds), *Law and Anthropology* (Dartmouth [International Library of Essays in Law and Legal Theory], 1992); trans. in (1982) *Bulletin de Liaison du Laboratoire d'Anthropologie Juridique de Paris* p 1; revised version published in Thomas (ed), *Law and Social Science* (Dartmouth [International Library of Essays in Law and Legal Theory], 1995).

[18] Max Gluckman, "Concepts in the Comparative Study of Tribal Law", in Nader (ed), *Law in Culture and Society* (Aldine, Chicago, 1969) pp 361–362; see also Sally Falk Moore, "Comparative Studies: Introduction", in *ibid*, pp 337–348, and Paul Bohannan, "Ethnography and Comparison in Legal Anthropology", in *ibid*, pp 401–418.

[19] See my "Law and Development in the Light of Dependency Theory" (1981) *14 Law and Society Review* 723; reprinted as Warwick Law Working Papers, Occasional Monograph No. 1, 1980.

[20] See especially Ghai, Luckham and Snyder (eds), *The Political Economy of Law: A Third World Reader* (Oxford University Press, 1978). This book grew out of the LLM in Law in Development, of which Yash Ghai, Patrick MacAuslan and I were among the founders at the Warwick Law School during the 1980s. More recently, see my "Integrità e frontiere del diritto europeo: Riflessioni sulla base della Politica Agricola Comune", Working Paper LAW No. 94/6, European University Institute, Florence, 1994.

[21] D.H. Grist, *Rice* (Longman, 5th ed. 1975).

relations[22], a sensitivity to the interconnections between aspects of life, often in different parts of the globe, simply because they occurred at the same time: in other words, the diverse themes which development theorists have sometimes identified as relations between centre and periphery[23], sociologists have approached in terms of systems theory or functionalism, and Jung called synchronicity.[24] Many if not all of these were variations on the theme of relationships: causal, systemic, symbolic, temporal and other. In my case, at the core lay the production of food – but, as we all know, food is far more than mere sustenance.[25]

4. Secondo Piatto

It should not be surprising, therefore, that food occupied so much of the next phase; in suggesting this, I have one foot outside the frame of our meal. On moving to Warwick Law School in January 1979, I started teaching European Community law as my main subject; my additional courses usually comprised law in development and socio-legal research methods and periodically included property, trusts, consumer law, and jurisprudence. After finishing the book on Senegal, I began, in the framework of my teaching duties, to read about the EC's Common Agricultural Policy (CAP). All EC lawyers know that the CAP has been for years the EC's main common policy, accounting until recently for about three-quarters of all EC legislation, judicial decisions and financial commitments. Nevertheless, it had been singularly neglected by lawyers and legal scholars, especially in England. Thanks in part to the congenial, supportive and stimulating academic community at Warwick, this came to form a central pillar of my research for the next decade.

Law of the Common Agricultural Policy[26] was written as an intellectual experiment.[27] It was an attempt to deal in a contextual way with one of the toughest nuts of EC law, that is, one of the most legally technical, economically complex and politically intractable areas. Whether or not the book was successful is not for me to judge, but I found it one of the most stimulating and rewarding pro-

[22] See Lauret, "Sur les études de filières agro-alimentaires" (1983) 16 *Economies et Sociétés, Cahiers de l'ISMEA* (mai) 721.
[23] On the legal aspects, see generally my "Law and Development in the Light of Dependency Theory" (1980) 14 *Law and Society Review* 723. For a recent survey, see Adelman and Paliwala (eds), *Law and Crisis in the Third World* (Hans Zell Publishers, 1993).
[24] On the last, see C.J. Jung, "Synchronicity: An Acausal Connecting Principle" and "On Synchronicity", in Jung, *The Structure and Dynamics of the Psyche*, trans. R.F.C. Hull 2nd ed. (Routledge 1969, reprinted 1991) 417–519 and 521–523, respectively.
[25] *E.g.*, see Visser, *Much Depends on Dinner* (McClelland and Stewart, 1986).
[26] Sweet and Maxwell, London, "Modern Legal Studies" series, 1985; trans. *Droit de la Politique Agricole Commune* (Economica, coll. "Coopération et Développement", 1987), *Diritto Agrario della Comunità Europea* (Giuffrè, coll. "Giuristi stranieri di oggi", 1990). I was pleased that it was possible for a translation of the book to be published in these two distinguished series.
[27] Oddly enough, so was *Capitalism and Legal Change: An African Transformation* (Academic Press, 1981), though in a different respect. Only in retrospect, however, have I noticed that the two books have this in common.

jects in which I have been involved. What excited me can be conveyed best by recalling four aspects of the book.

The first was the attempt to identify and theorise models of the EC legislative process. Dissatisfied with lawyers' concentration solely on formal procedures, I distinguished five ideal types of CAP legislative process. While two types corresponded closely to formal procedures, three others were defined more in sociological and political terms. They included "the marathon session", "logrolling" and "stonewalling". As with all ideal types, these types of legislative process do not exist as such; the adoption of EC legislation usually involves a combination of several ideal types.[28] This simple analytical device helped me to understand how EC law, especially regulatory law, was initially enacted and continuously renegotiated.

The second aspect was the analysis of controls on surplus production as a form of regulatory policy, involving distinctive economic instruments and legal measures, especially in the context of the polycentric problem presented by the dairy sector.[29] Economic policy rather than law thus provided the point of departure. In addition, following usual EC practice (but rare among lawyers), I classified legal measures according to economic criteria, in particular whether they were intended to operate with regard to supply or to demand. Finally, my analysis identified why potential solutions to the over-production of dairy products were so difficult to agree and to put into practice. It set out four key variables: the production of dairy products in the Member States as compared to their varying national requirements; the shares of the different Member States in total EC production; the importance of dairying in the various Member States' national economies; and the size, extent of concentration and average yield of dairy farms in the various countries. On the basis of this quantitative exercise, I concluded that, in relation to any particular legislative proposal, the different interests in the dairy sector overlap and cut across each other. They did not coalesce in favour of any policy except the status quo.

A third aspect of the book was the treatment of EC structural policy in the context of the historical internationalisation of the food and agricultural sector.[30] My conceptual framework for establishing the context drew directly, albeit unobtrusively, on my previous work in Senegal. It emphasised macro-sociological changes over a long period of time, international economic

---

[28] See *Law of the Common Agricultural Policy*, pp 47–51. This led eventually to my "Thinking about Interests: Legislative Process in the European Community", in Starr and Collier (eds), *History and Power in the Study of Law* (Cornell University Press, 1989) 168–198, of which a revised version was published as Chapter 2, "'Interests' and the Legislative Process", in my *New Directions in European Community Law* (Weidenfeld & Nicolson, 1990).

[29] See *Law of the Common Agricultural Policy*, Chap 6, pp 122–151; on the dairy sector in particular, see especially pp 142–151. The distinction between economic instruments and legal measures was borrowed from T.C. Daintith, "Legal Analysis of Economic Policy – I" (1982) 9 *Journal of Law and Society* 191.

[30] See *Law of the Common Agricultural Policy*, especially pp 157–159. I am very pleased now to have a PhD student at the European University Institute who, having taken up my point that the CAP lacks a coherent definition of "agricultural holding", is elaborating the implications of this point in a stimulating and original way.

relations, changing relations of domination and subordination within and across national borders, and the role of the state in the economy and, in particular, its use of law.

In my view, these aspects of the book represented a novel approach to EC law. They also illustrate the contextual approach. The first aspect involved an attempt to bring social science theory, in particular a concern for the development of conceptual models, to bear on EC law. The second aspect represented a first effort (for me) to think about economic regulation with regard to a polycentric, indeed inherently unsolvable problem. The third aspect was an attempt to place law in its broader historical context involving conflict, competing ideologies, and change, partly but not only through law.[31]

A fourth aspect of the book was more traditional: its concern for policy. The book made some contribution to the broader debate concerning whether or not agriculture should continue to be treated as a special sector in EC law.[32] The debate is significant from the constitutional standpoint: to what extent should a specific economic sector, namely agriculture, have a special status in the EC Treaty? It is also important economically, politically, socially and financially: for example, this special constitutional status is closely related to the amount of money devoted to the CAP, as well as to why it is so difficult to reform. As stated in a later work, my view was that agriculture should no longer be recognised in EC law as an entire economic sector with a special legal status; instead, we should focus on improving the basic conditions of life and the decision-making power of disadvantaged individuals and groups.[33]

"CAPLaw", as I nicknamed it, represented the culmination of a period of concentration, which had been initiated by coming to Warwick. Just as each ending is a new beginning, however, it stimulated a phase of dispersion. The next few years saw the publication of the results of a variety of quite different projects. All involved co-operation with colleagues, and some resulted in lasting friendships. Among the many fruits of the Warwick LLM in Law in Development was a set of teaching materials, which, once published, was used in many law schools throughout the world.[34] The organisation of an international and inter-

---

[31] The links between this vision and the research that led to *Capitalism and Legal Change* are obvious. What is not so obvious was that I found this long-term perspective so exciting, and still do. In the field of EC law, it was also novel.

[32] See *Law of the Common Agricultural Policy*, especially pp 23–24. I developed this theme further in a paper presented first at the 13th European Society for Rural Sociology in Braga, Portugal, in 1986: see "L'agriculture et l'industrie dans le droit de la CEE" (1987) 5 *Droit et Société* 23, which provided the stimulus for "The Special Legal Status of Agriculture: Assumptions and Contradictions in Economic Law", chapter 4 of my *New Directions in European Community Law* (Weidenfeld & Nicolson, 1990). Further work on this theme was presented in my Special Course at the Academy of European Law in Florence in 1991, which was published as "The Common Agricultural Policy in the Single European Market", in *Collected Courses of the Academy of European Law, 1991*, Vol. II, Book 1 (Martinus Nijhoff, 1992) 303–336.

[33] See my "The Special Legal Status of Agriculture: Assumptions and Contradictions in Economic Law", chapter 4 in my *New Directions in European Community Law* (Weidenfeld & Nicolson, 1990) 145.

[34] Ghai, Luckham and Snyder (eds), *The Political Economy of Law: A Third World Reader* (Oxford University Press, 1987).

disciplinary conference during my period as director of the Legal Research Institute at Warwick spawned two volumes edited together with a social historian.[35] The organisation of another conference, part of a continuing interest in and co-operation with French universities since the 1960s, helped in a modest way to stimulate comparative law with regard to the international law of development.[36] These various projects have common themes which cannot be dealt with here; for the present purposes, they serve to illustrate a personal rhythm or cycle, as well as some of the diverging shoots of a single root.

In Autumn 1987 I moved from Warwick to the Faculty of Laws, University College London. The two institutions differ greatly, but for our limited purposes the most striking contrast concerned my own mandate. UCL is a large faculty with a high degree of specialisation, and my task was simply (or not so simply, as it turned out) to teach and carry out research in EC law. In other words, the move can be seen as the beginning of a phase of concentration, an attempt to rationalise and draw together some of the numerous shoots which during the past few years had burgeoned, at times apparently without logic and coherence.

The move to UCL is so close in time, and more importantly it is so inextricably intertwined with a personal journey, that it is difficult to have a clear perspective on my work since then and whatever implications it may have had for the field of European law. A list of publications and a curriculum vitae are woefully inadequate in conveying the sense of disintegration, discovery and gradual reintegration which, for me, have been such a feature of the period since 1987. Nevertheless, the writer of an academic account may perhaps be excused for sticking to the letter of the law, even though, as in this case, he is more well aware than most that in life, as in law[37], the context is determinative.

While being interviewed for the post at UCL, I was asked what my priorities were in the development of teaching and research in EC law. My reply was:

> Teaching and research on European Community law in the United Kingdom and other countries thus provide the foundation for a two-fold development. The first aspect is the continuation of certain established lines of enquiry. This includes the tradition of highly sophisticated scholarship concerning legal doctrine in fields such as European Community institutions, procedures and competition law. The second, building on this work, is the study of European Community law in its social and economic context, using insights from the political economy of law and critical theory. This development would integrate the study of European Community law more fully into the highly fruitful lines of enquiry which have marked the best legal scholarship in other fields during the past several decades.
>
> Special emphasis, in my view, needs to be given to four different themes. They are

[35] Snyder and Hay (eds), *Labour, Law and Crime: An Historical Perspective* (Tavistock, 1987); Hay and Snyder (eds), *Policing and Prosecution in Britain, 1750–1850: Essays in the Social History of the Criminal Law* (Clarendon Press, 1987).

[36] See Snyder and Slinn (eds), *The International Law of Development* (Professional Books [now Butterworths], 1987).

[37] It should be obvious that the distinction between life and law is made here for expository purposes only.

(i) institutions, rules, ideologies and processes; (ii) law, economy and society; (iii) the international political economy; and (iv) state forms and legal pluralism, including the relationship between European Community law, the law of the Member States and the laws, customs and practices of local communities, firms and other organisations.[38]

Though I did not really appreciate its import at the time, this reply has served me ever since as a kind of charter. In the following paragraphs I refer to it sometimes as a research agenda, but in fact it resembled a mythological genealogy more closely than anything else.[39] Instead of being a checklist, it was a source of inspiration for later research and an intellectual marker against which it could be charted.

It may be helpful to mention some ways in which I have tried, not always consciously, to put this programmatic statement into practice. In fact, the account could stop here, for subsequent developments might be seen as simply an elaboration of this statement. This would be a considerable over-simplification, however, if only because general guidelines often do not tell us much about detailed rules or specific practices: the reader thus might go away hungry. In this specific instance, to cut the account short would neglect in particular the recent emergence of two different strands (or shoots, to continue the horticultural metaphor). One of these current projects concerns European Union constitutional law, while the other refers to European Union trade law, in particular customs law and commercial policy. Each represents a specific instance of a general theme, a particular example of the implementation of the charter. But implementation is a process with its own life and logic, distinct from the policy statements it is intended to put into practice. So also each of these shoots has its relative autonomy and special features. In addition, as in the case of policy implementation, each has been influenced decisively by its context.[40]

The process of putting programme into practice has in my view been aided by two factors that surfaced in 1988–89. Both might appear as substantial disruptions of the narrative so far, but in fact they shaped the next few years in profound, though unpredictable, ways.

On the one hand, in the autumn of 1988 I was approached by the Law Department of the European University Institute (EUI) in Florence about the possibility of joining them. Having moved to UCL only recently, I initially declined. Eventually, however, this led to my appointment as a part-time pro-

[38] Snyder, *New Directions in European Community Law* (Weidenfeld and Nicolson, 1990) 14. This printed version differs very little in substance from my notes made in preparation for the interview. It was originally elaborated for presentation in draft form at the European Law workshop at the first Critical Legal Conference, University of Kent, Canterbury, September 1986, and then published simultaneously in (1987) 14 *Journal of Law and Society* 167 and in Fitzpatrick and Hunt (eds), *Critical Legal Studies* (Blackwell, 1987).

[39] For a classic example of the genre, see Griaule, *Dieu d'Eau: Entretiens avec Ogotemmêli* (Fayard, 1966).

[40] Sometimes (and, in my view, most importantly) in ways which remain outside the scope of this account.

fessor of European economic law, together with Christian Joerges from Bremen, starting in September 1989. This venture proved to be incredibly stimulating, and at the time of writing it still is. The international and research-oriented environment of the EUI, based on fundamental research and postgraduate seminars, is ideal for developing a contextual approach to European Union law.[41]

On the other hand, in May 1989 I was invited to give the required course on European Community [now Union] institutions in the English stream at the College of Europe in Bruges.[42] This challenging opportunity had, I think, two facets. It required me to prepare a set of cases and materials and to teach a very intensive, detailed course at a high level to a relatively large group (usually about 60) of highly motivated students, which I did then and have continued to do by the so-called socratic method; though initially threatening, this rapidly proved to be very enjoyable. In addition, it quickly oriented me away from agriculture and towards EC institutions and constitutional and administrative law; this provided a solid foundation for similar teaching in London as well as for later research.

Though both postgraduate institutions with excellent students, Florence and Bruges can be viewed as representing two extremes. One is an international research institute, emphasising basic (and sometimes policy) research from a variety of perspectives, but involving full-time staff recruited on limited-term contracts and concerned only partly with European affairs. The other is a hot house, with a rather technocratic teaching programme, dealing mainly with European issues, but with few full-time academic staff and with little research orientation until very recently. For me, concerned as I was with EC (and now EU) law, which was a core subject at both institutions, what might possibly seem to be a strange combination proved an ideal stimulus to develop and try out new approaches, ideas and materials on EU law in context. By this means and others, particularly the recruitment of students and joint research projects, I have also tried to create links between the two institutions.

The three institutions – UCL, EUI and Bruges – encouraged or at least permitted this new orientation; at the same time they were to some extent influenced by it. Gradually the EC law in context project – for in the institutional framework of the EUI it soon became a project – assumed a definite shape. My purpose was to clarify my own ideas about how European Community law was made and operated in practice. Then, using these hypotheses, I planned to

[41] My seminars have concerned topics such as European Community law in context; European economic law; regulation in Europe after 1992; interests, policy and the law in the European Community; and constitutional law of the European Union. I have usually taught at least one seminar each year in conjunction with other colleagues from the Law Department and the Department of Social and Political Sciences. In addition, I have supervised a relatively large number of LLM dissertations and PhD theses on a broad range of topics in European Community law.

[42] Then, as now, the Bruges course in Law (then called the Law Dominant, now the Law Department) includes four compulsory courses: the law of EC (now EU) institutions (one semester), the European courts (one semester), European competition law (entire year), and European internal market law (entire year). When I started, students were required to take one semester-course and one year-course in French and one each in English.

explore a limited set of important themes in more detail and more systematically in order to arrive at broader theoretical generalisations. In order to do this, I envisaged a series of works: first, a book of essays, which, though written for various purposes and at different times, revealed in fact not only a common thread but also a clear theoretical argument; second, a collection of readings, based on a thorough search of the periodical literature and presenting the best essays so far written on EC law in context; third, a textbook or book of cases and materials on EC law, making use of the theoretical approach set forth in the book of essays; fourth, a study of the EC in the international arena; and, fifth, an empirical case study, bringing theories in other social sciences to bear on EC law.

This project and my earlier charter soon developed a complex relationship, somewhat like that of twins who are similar but not identical. This was so even though the charter was prior in time (for the most part) and thus helped to shape the project. Each was a research agenda, a framework, a skeleton, which surfaced periodically to confront, orient and (I hope) enrich the other. But the two distinct creations differed in content, level of generality and the extent to which they could be put directly into practice. Put another way, the charter identified the themes, while the project spelled out how they could be elaborated in the form of research projects and publications.

For convenience of exposition, and without distorting the actual process of research, it may be helpful to describe in more specific terms how the two were related. This may illustrate one way of doing European law in context, as well as illuminating to some extent how the field has developed.

First, the book of essays was to deal substantively with all four elements of the charter, so as to illustrate how each element could be approached from a contextual standpoint. Its principal theoretical concern, however, was to be the relationship between institutions, rules, ideologies and processes. Second, the collection of readings was also to focus on all four elements by drawing together already published material. It was designed to exemplify work already accomplished on European law in context, to help to consolidate the contextual approach, and to provide a set of materials which could be used to supplement traditional textbooks in teaching EC law. Third, the textbook was initially conceived as dealing with all of EC law, or at least the main elements of constitutional law and administrative law (institutions) and economic and social law (substantive law). The scope proved too vast, however, in particular with the very rapid development of EC (and later EU) law in the late 1980s and early 1990s. Consequently, as described later, this book was eventually split into different parts. Fourth, the international element came to be represented mainly by a book, now in progress, on EU trade law, mainly customs law and commercial policy.[43] As will be seen later, it also influenced other work on EC and EU external relations. Fifth, the case study was to bring all four elements together

[43] This is scheduled to be published in 1995 as Hawkes and Snyder, *Customs and Trade Law of the European Union* (Butterworths, "Commercial Laws of Europe" series).

in a specific example. For this I had in fact started to gather material in 1986 while still at Warwick. The research for this project is now virtually completed, and only the writing up remains to be done.

The first of these works to be published was *New Directions.*[44] It set forth six simple hypotheses. First, we can understand most adequately the meaning of EC law and its operation in practice if we place legal institutions, ideas, rules and processes in their social, political, cultural and economic context. Second, the structure, function and operation of EC institutions, on the one hand, and the enactment, application and implementation of EC law are closely related. Third, the meaning of EC law and its operation in practice are the result of social processes of negotiation. Fourth, these processes of negotiation involve diverse, often conflicting perspectives or ideologies. Fifth, these ideologies are based upon different objective or subjective interests. Sixth, the social meaning of EC law and its operation in practice are almost inevitably contested, at least in important matters, and hence are often the subject of social and legal conflicts. These hypotheses provided a general methodological and theoretical statement for the development of EC/EU law in context.

The second book was a two-volume collection of readings on *European Community Law.*[45] As a glance at the table of contents will show, it was based squarely on the charter. It included 38 articles grouped according to the following headings: Volume I: Perspectives on European Integration, Federalism and Legal Pluralism, Institutions and Ideologies, and Rules and Processes; Volume II: Law and the Market, Social and Regional Policies, Economic and Social Regulation, and The International Political Economy. The book was the result of an exhaustive search of the English language literature[46] in numerous disciplines on EC law. It aimed to present a set of interdisciplinary readings which exemplified what seemed to me to be the best published work on EC law in context. The research for this book proved to be an excellent method of self-education, as well as being invaluable in the preparation of teaching materials.

In the midst of preparing this second book, I moved from UCL to a full-time post at the EUI. In principle this should have facilitated the completion of this research agenda. In practice, its effects were more diffuse and, as always, less predictable. As part of the competition for the post, I was required to give a public lecture. I chose to speak on the effectiveness of EC law. In the lecture I tried to elaborate a broad social and political as well as legal concept of effec-

---

[44] *New Directions in European Community Law* (Weidenfeld & Nicolson, "Law in Context" series, 1990). The essays in this book concerned all aspects of the charter, with one exception. Legal pluralism was omitted, for two reasons. First, I had not made up my mind how to bring the large theoretical literature on this topic to bear on EC law in the best way to exemplify a contextual approach. Second, I wanted very much to include an essay on the basic assumptions underlying the law of the Common Agricultural Policy, and chapter 4 turned out to be much longer than originally anticipated.

[45] *European Community Law,* 2 vols. (Dartmouth, "International Library of Essays in Law and Legal Theory" series, 1993).

[46] The book was published in English. However, my "Introduction" to each volume gives references to published work in other languages.

tiveness and also to show how two main EC institutions, the Commission and the Court of Justice, had sought so far to ensure the effectiveness of EC law in these related senses. In addition to its intrinsic interest, the analysis highlighted certain institutional and processual – in other words, political – gaps in the EC system. It intrigued me so much that, during the following year, I devoted considerable time to writing an article on the topic.[47]

This in turn led to a series of related papers on institutions, rules, ideologies and processes in the EC/EU.[48] Taken together, they pursued the first theme of the charter – institutions, rules, ideologies and processes – much more deeply and more widely than I had originally intended. However, apart from being intellectually interesting in their own right, they had the merit of providing a broad foundation for my current work on EU constitutional law, and in fact forcing me to think about whether, and to what extent, the Maastricht Treaty on European Union could be viewed as a constitution. This is part of what was nominally the third book within the framework of the charter.[49] The other parts of what was to be the third book were published separately, but because of their scope they are less contextual in approach.[50]

Since beginning to work in the field of EC law, I have always been interested in relations between EC institutional law and EC substantive law, that is, between constitutional law and economic law, or, to put it in a more general way, in relations between the characteristics of institutions and the content of decisions: not only the two separately but also how each influences the other. This was part of the rationale for the trade law book, a fourth plank in the charter programme. However, this concern also began increasingly to underlie

---

[47] See my "The Effectiveness of European Community Law: Institutions, Processes, Rules and Techniques" (1993) 56 *Modern Law Review* 19. Parts of this paper have been reprinted in *Democratic and Legal Problems in the European Community* (Seminar januar 1993, IUSEF Nr. 12. Senter for Europarett, Universitetet i Oslo) (Universitetsforlaget AS, 1994) 59–112; and in Daintith (ed), *Implementation of European Community Law* (Chancery, 1994).

[48] See my "Zuständigkeitsverteilung" in Monar, Neuwahl and Noack (eds), *Sachwörterbuch zur Europäischen Union* (Alfred Kröner Verlag, 1993) 381–384; "La Incidencia del Derecho de la Comunidad Europea en la Organizacion Administrativa del Reino Unido" (with A. Le Sueur), in Barnes Vazquez (ed), *La Comunidad Europea, La Instancia Regional y la Organizacion Administrativa de los Estados Miembros* (Civitas, 1993) 365–505; "Soft Law and Institutional Practice in the European Community", in Martin (ed), *The Construction of Europe: Essays in Honour of Emile Noël* (Nijhoff, 1994) 197–225; "Droit, symboles et politique méditerranéenne: Réflexions sur quelques décisions récentes de la Cour de Justice Européenne", in Bourrinet (ed), *La Méditerranée, Espace de Coopération: En l'honneur de Maurice Flory* (Economica, 1994) 303–309; "EMU – Metaphor for European Union? Institutions, Rules and Types of Regulation", in Dehousse (ed), *Europe after Maastricht: An Ever Closer Union?* (Law Books in Europe, 1994) 63–99; "Institutional Development in the European Union: Some Lessons from the Third Pillar, in Monar (ed), *The Third Pillar of the Maastricht Treaty* (College of Europe, 1994).

[49] It is intended to be published by Butterworths in the "Law in Context" series in 1995 as *Constitutional Law of the European Union.*

[50] The first comprised successive editions of the *Study Guide on EC Law* for the University of London External LLB (University of London, now 3rd ed. 1994). Starting from this base, I then wrote a substantially longer book on *Introduction to the Law of the European Union,* which though written in English was destined specifically for translation into Chinese for publication by Peking University Press in 1995.

my work on the CAP, economic regulation[51], and international economic law.[52] In turn, both of these latter strands have contributed to the development of a more general reflection on the nature of the EU and its law.[53] They have also helped to bring a new perspective on what will eventually be the fifth plank, the empirical case study still in progress on the making of the sheepmeat regime, an example of EC regulatory law.[54]

5. Dolce

After this repast, dessert might be too much, but something tantalising may not come amiss: hence a glance at the future. The kaleidoscope appears to crystallise around three main points.

The first point is the completion of the research agenda presaged by the charter. In addition to the case study, the main priority is the book on EU constitutional law. It is intended to arrive at an understanding and reinterpretation of EU constitutional law in various contexts.

The starting point is the idea of the Maastricht Treaty on European Union as the EU's written constitution. Due to be revised in 1996, the Treaty attempts to integrate diverse conceptions of the future of Western Europe. It also provides the basis for current and future enlargements of the EU, which themselves imply different models of EU law seen as a constitutional system. The basic hypotheses of the book, at this early stage, are two-fold. First, the EU legal system is coherent; and, second, this coherence cannot be understood adequately in terms of neo-functionalist theories of economic integration. I plan

---

[51] See "Europe after 1992: New Regulatory Strategies" (with R. Dehousse, C. Joerges and G. Majone and with the collaboration of M. Everson), EUI Working Paper Law No. 92/31 (1992), which was initially presented to the High Level Group ["the Sutherland Commission"] appointed by the European Commission to consider "The Future of the Internal Market"; see also "A Regulatory Framework for Foodstuffs in the Internal Market" (Report on the Conference, 6–7 May 1993, Florence, organised by Francis Snyder), EUI Working Paper LAW No. 94/4 (1994).

[52] On the former, see my *The Common Agricultural Policy of the European Economic Community* (Butterworths, 1990; reprinted from *Halsbury's Laws of England*, 4th ed. reissue, 1990) (Vol 1(2)) and especially "The Common Agricultural Policy in the Single European Market", in *Collected Courses of the Academy of European Law 1992* (Nijhoff, 1992) Vol. II Book 1, pp 303–336. On the latter, see my "The European Community's New Food Aid Legislation: Towards a Development Policy?", chapter 5 of *New Directions* but originally published in Snyder and Slinn (eds), *The International Law of Development: Comparative Perspectives* (Professional Books [now Butterworths], 1987); "European Community Law and Third World Food Entitlements" (1989) 32 *German Yearbook of International Law* 87, translated into Russian as "Pravo Evropeiskogo soobshchestva i prodol 'stvennaia politika stran 'tret'ego mira", in Danilenko and Ushakov (eds), *Mezhdunarodnoe pravo: sovetskii i angliiskii podkhody* (Institute of State and Law, USSR Academy of Sciences, 1989); and "European Community Law and International Economic Relations: The Saga of Thai Manioc", in Macdonald (ed), *Essays in Honour of Wang Tieya* (Nijhoff, 1993) 753–769.

[53] See also my "EMU – Metaphor for European Union?", already mentioned; "L'Economia mista e la nuova constituzione economica dell'Unione Europea", in Merloni (ed), *Quaderno sull'economia mista, oggi* (Il Mulino, 1994); "Integrità e frontiere dell'diritto europeo: Riflessioni sulla base della Politica agricola comune", EUI Working Paper LAW No. 94/6 (1994); see also Snyder (ed), *Constitutional Dimensions of European Economic Integration* (Nijhoff, forthcoming 1995).

[54] Some aspects of this work were published in *New Directions*; see especially chapters 2 and 3.

to pay special attention to several themes: the relationship between legitimacy and effectiveness; the relationship between constitutionalism and economic and political integration; the relationship between supranationalism and intergovernmentalism, particularly in the organisation of institutions and in decision-making processes; and the use of different types of norms and forms of regulation, as well as how they are related to the distribution of power among various levels of the EU legal and political system. My research has already touched on some of these themes; this book provides an opportunity to view the EU legal system as a whole.

A second point concerns EU external relations, in particular with China. I hope to carry out research designed to analyse and monitor the developing legal relations between the EU and China.[55] The core of the project will be trade law and commercial policy, in particular concerning textiles and anti-dumping. Attention will also be given to other aspects of EC–China relations, such as the implementation of the 1985 Co-operation Agreement.

As currently envisaged, the project has several aspects. It is designed to monitor legal developments, in particular with regard to trade. In addition, it is intended to consider how these developments affect the law of each of the parties. For example, on the EU side this involves the development of implied powers, the use of mixed agreements and the use of different types of legal instruments; on the Chinese side, it concerns the development of a market economy, the uniform application and transparency of trade laws, and the elaboration of different types of legal instruments in international trade. Finally, the project is intended to use the law as a learning device. This starts from the idea that changes in the content and the use of law affect the way each party views its partner, while the way each party views its partner may lead to changes in the content and use of law. The law provides a mirror of – and contributes to – changing relations between the two trading partners. The project thus represents a mutual attempt by each side to use *le regard de l'autre* to learn more about its own legal system, as well as about a complex and rapidly developing area of international economic law involving relations between the two major trading partners.

Both of these two projects thus are interdisciplinary, drawing not only on law but also on economics, politics, sociology and anthropology. Though similar in inspiration, the third venture is quite different in nature. It is the foundation of the *European Law Journal: Review of European Law in Context* (*ELJ*). In 1990, in my capacity as European Law Editor of the *Modern Law Review*, I edited a special issue of the *MLR* on "New Perspectives on European Law".[56] Subsequently I was

[55] The initial foundation for this project was provided by several elements: my acquaintance with Chinese law studies while a student at Harvard Law School; teaching EC external relations law at UCL and Bruges; supervision at UCL and the EUI of LLM and PhD research on the treaty-making power of the EC; my research on EC external relations law, including the honour of being able to contribute to the *festschrift* for Professor Wang Tieya, China's leading international law scholar; and preparation of the book on *Introduction to the Law of the European Union* for publication in Chinese translation, which includes a brief survey of relations between the EU and China.

[56] (1990) 53 *MLR* [September], Special Issue: "New Perspectives on European Law".

asked by Basil Blackwell Publishers to establish a new journal concerned with European law in context. After initially refusing, I gave the matter a good deal of thought and had numerous discussions with colleagues and the prospective publishers. Eventually, with the help of friends who agreed to serve on the Editorial Board[57], I decided to accept the challenge to establish the *ELJ*.[58]

The *ELJ* aims to represent (and also of course to institutionalise) a new approach to European law. Its main purposes are to express and develop the study and understanding of European law in its social, cultural, political and economic context. The future of the European Union is now on the agenda in the run-up to the 1996 Intergovernmental Conference designed to amend the Maastricht Treaty. EU law is in a phase of transformation, and substantial changes are bound to follow in teaching, research and law practice. The *ELJ* will be a forum for the debate on these changes. Among the themes to be given special emphasis in the *ELJ* are the emerging policy and legal system of the European Union, the legal and regulatory framework of the European economy, and social regulation, for example concerning consumer protection, equality law and the environment. Though its main focus will be on the EU, the journal will also concern the law of other western European groupings, the national legal systems of countries throughout Europe, and relations between western Europe and other parts of the world.

As with the creation of any new institution, the establishment of a new journal is a difficult but exciting undertaking. Since the beginning of my academic life, I have always enjoyed a very active role in the organisation and management of research within a faculty or in the university as a whole. The creation of a new journal seems, however, to be on different scale. Now, in addition to continuing my personal research, I expect to devote more time to creating an institution, fostering research networks, and encouraging research and writing in a more systematic way, especially by younger colleagues. Hence, for me the *ELJ* represents in many respects a significant change of direction.

6. Caffé or Green Tea

Caffé or green tea, anyone? Perhaps this excursus cannot be summarised in any other way. I began by stating that logic and linearity were less than useful here, yet the middle course of this account centred on a research agenda or intellectual charter. For the sake of convenience and credibility, not to mention any deference which may be due to the ideology of science, I would suggest that we simply agree that this device has served its purpose. It does not of course present the whole story, but the whole story (and who knows what is the real story?)

---

[57] In addition to myself, the Editorial Board consists of Brian Bercusson, Christian Joerges, Antoine Lyon-Caen and Joseph Weiler, with Renaud Dehousse as Associate Editor and Wolf Sauter as Managing Editor.

[58] The *ELJ* will be based at the EUI in Florence and will be published by Basil Blackwell in Oxford. The first issue appeared in Spring 1995.

would be far too long, involve endless disagreements about what was relevant and the criteria for deciding, and end up by confusing us all about what we thought we had agreed to be the nature and aims of academic research.

As Dr Spock once remarked[59], children seem to develop in phases which resemble the main phases of the adult life cycle but are shorter in duration. Academic research sometimes takes place in similar spurts. In addition, even though it is usually done by adults, its rhythm may often appear chaotic and unpredictable, as if it were not clear whether the child or the adult were the author. It may be suggested that, at least as represented in this account, my study of EU law in context has also occurred in phases, alternating between periods of concentration and periods of dispersion. Sometimes there was a single focus; at other times fragmentation or even loss of direction seemed to prevail. In fact, both concentration and dispersion are always present, but at any particular time one aspect has usually been dominant. Though further work would be needed to confirm the point, it might be suggested that this tension is not just a feature of my own research, but also of the development of the study of EU law in context as an academic field.

In my opinion, concentration and dispersion have constantly enriched each other. If we take the genealogical method seriously, and if we focus solely on the development of my own research on EU law in context, we can see periods of dispersion as a time of searching for new themes and approaches, of attempting to gain new perspectives by ranging widely in time and space, and even of working seriously in other disciplines. By contrast, periods of concentration may be viewed as a time for seeking to bring these new perspectives to bear on EU law, of trying to see what we can learn from them with regard to specific research questions, and of attempting to develop in a more or less systematic way the study of EU law in context. It should be obvious that this working method tends inevitably to pull one in a contextual direction; interdisciplinary and comparative work, as well as the study of legal doctrine, are all part of the genealogical structure. At the same time it is important to recognise that the relationship between concentration and dispersion is more complex than simply one of tension and alternation. Each period contains the germ of the other.

In this chapter I have presented a personal view. Though not necessarily representative, it may nonetheless provide some insights into the development of the study of EU law in context more generally. What factors have contributed most to the development of a contextual approach to European Union law? In addition to propitious institutional settings, several elements have been so important in my own work that I would not hesitate to commend them to students. A background in other disciplines is especially useful in suggesting new research questions and providing useful analytical tools in a field such as a law, which is often politically controversial. Work in comparative law, especially concerning radically different legal systems, societies and cultures, enables one to place EU law in a wider framework, to identify the characteristics which it

[59] I have not been able to locate the exact reference.

shares with other legal systems and to appreciate its distinctive features. The use of diverse research methods, in particular empirical field research and archival historical research, is indispensable in going beyond the purely doctrinal study of law. A focus on some of the most technical and complex areas of EC/EU law, combined with a concern for theoretical generalisation, ensures a constant tension between the particular and the general and between legal doctrine and theoretical explanation which can be very stimulating and productive. The highly topical nature of the subject means that one's working hypotheses are subject to comment and eventual correction in everyday life, because they touch matters which deeply concern many people.

The reader might well ask, however, "what is meant by 'law in context' and 'the context of law'?" This chapter has tried to indicate some of the possible answers to this question, but its basic message may well be that the answer depends on the purpose of the question. For example, social theorists, policy-makers, academic lawyers and lawyers in private practice or public service ask different questions and have in mind different criteria of relevance. In my view, such eclecticism is useful and, to some extent, inevitable in the development and consolidation of a new approach to the study of European Union law. Elsewhere I have drawn a sharper distinction between different ways of looking at law, legal institutions and legal processes. There I summarised the perspective of law in context as follows: "either law is viewed from the standpoint of other disciplines, using their theories and modes of analysis; or law provides the starting point but is situated in a broader context, whether social, economic, political or cultural: both strands aim ultimately to contribute to a social theory of law".[60] My own research so far has taken both tacks. Generalising from personal experience and some knowledge of the field, I would expect both to be developed more systematically with regard to EU law in the future.

Some other general points may also be drawn from this personal account. My work has not been situated solely within the sociology of law, and it has certainly drawn on other disciplines in addition to the sociology of law. But it has usually been concerned with either the relationship between law and society or the role of law in society. This is a classic distinction in the sociology of law. The first conception of law in context must not be concerned only, however, with relationships of cause and effect. Some relationships are undoubtedly causal, but other, non-causal relationships may also be extremely important. As I have written elsewhere:

> "... We must begin instead by recognising that in many different ways, as in numerous contexts, law is potentially – though not necessarily – significant.... The most profound influences may be in fact those which are the least obvious. For example, European Community law often has clearly defined, immediately instrumental implications. In addition, however, it may also influence [social life] by allocating important decision-making powers, by expressing otherwise implicit premises about

[60] See my "Soft Law and Institutional Practice in the European Community", in Martin (ed), *The Construction of Europe: Essays in Honour of Emile Noel* (Kluwer, 1994), at p 198.

> [social, economic, cultural or political relations], or by presenting a complex legal ideology of [for example] economic development or dependence."[61]

In contrast, the second conception of law in context considers that law is integral to society. Aspects of social life, such as interests for example, are embodied or crystallised in law. Law and society are inextricably intertwined, so that it makes little sense to conceive of them as separate. In other words, law is a constituent element in virtually all social relations.

With regard to this distinction, it is important for the future of the contextual study of EU law to bear three points in mind. First, the basic conceptual structure that is embodied in the distinction between law and society, on the one hand, and law in society, on the other hand, is not limited to sociology. It is also characteristic of studies of law which draw upon or are carried out within the framework of other disciplines, for example, economics, political science and anthropology. Second, these two alternatives are not of course the only points of departure for the study of EU law in context; indeed they are too restrictive. Other contextual approaches are likely to be equally if not more fruitful in the future. For the most part, however, they remain yet to be explored.[62] Third, any of these methods may – but does not necessarily – involve empirical research. In other words, I do not consider empirical research to be a defining characteristic of the study of EU law in context. Nor is it a necessary element in all research which falls within or can contribute to this field.

One may also ask how a contextual approach to the study of European Union law has opened up new areas of scholarship or helped to redraw conceptual boundaries. The study of European Union law in context has raised issues and identified relationships which have often been neglected by lawyers concerned only with legal doctrine. For example, they include relationships between law and legitimacy in the political and social sense, law as an expression of different types of economic and political integration, and law as an embodiment of local cultures within the European Union. Moreover, these issues are of interest not only to academic lawyers but also to policy-makers, politicians and ordinary citizens. In other words, I would suggest that the contextual study of EC/EU law has helped to redraw boundaries which extend beyond the academic world, and in particular beyond the world of legal scholars. They also encompass the world of policy-makers, practising lawyers, interest organisations, and academic specialists in other disciplines besides law.

---

[61] This paragraph is based on my "European Community Law and Third World Food Entitlements", (1989) 32 *German Yearbook of International Law* 87 at pp 109–110. See also my *New Directions in European Community Law* (Weidenfeld & Nicolson, 1990) 3.

[62] This paragraph is based on my (with Douglas Hay), "Comparisons in the Social History of Law: Labour and Crime", in our (ed), *Labour Law and Crime: An Historical Perspective* (Tavistock, 1987) 9–11; David Nelken, "Beyond the Study of 'Law and Society'? Henry's *Private Justice* and O'Hagan's *The End of Law*" (1986) *American Bar Foundation Research Journal*, and Boaventura de Sousa Santos, "Law: A Map of Misreading. Towards a Postmodern Conception of Law" (1987) 14 *Journal of Law and Society* 279. See also Massimo La Torre, "Formalism and Anti-Formalism in Modern Law – State Law and Beyond", in Krawietz, MacCormick and von Wright (eds), *Prescriptive Formality and Normative Rationality in Modern Legal Systems* (Duncker & Humbolt, 1994) 647–672.

Ultimately, in the study of law in context, as with a good meal, the proof of the pudding lies in the eating. We have skipped a heavy dessert, but one might point not only to publications and courses but also to colleagues, publishers and especially one's students as appropriate subjects for empirical enquiry. They indicate the extent to which the contextual approach has already made a mark in the study of law, as well as the extent to which it is likely to develop in the future.

Chapter 10

INTERNATIONAL COMPETITIVENESS AND EC COMPETITION POLICY

Professor Steve Anderman
University of Essex

For more than 25 years, EC competition policy has been consciously shaped by the two main aims of preserving workable competition in the internal market and helping to achieve the integration of Member States into a single market. The commitment to integration has been propelled by the desire to achieve the economic benefits of a single market but its legal foundation is Article 3 of the Treaty of Rome which provides that one of the principal means to be used to achieve the common market is "the institution of a system ensuring that competition in the internal market is not distorted". This has had the result that the basic system of competition rules which has long applied to private firms in the European Community, Article 85 of the Treaty of Rome which regulates agreements and concerted practices between private firms, and Article 86, which prohibits abuses of dominant positions, has been moulded by the Commission and the Community courts to give a high priority to the political-economic goal of integration.[1]

Similarly, the Commission's policy of preserving workable competition has not been pursued as a purely economic objective. Instead, it has been characterised by a concern to prevent the development of market structures which have the capacity to exclude competitors, particularly small and medium sized competitors, from markets within the EU. Economists, particularly those of the Chicago School variety[2], may complain that this is to preserve the inefficient at the expense of the efficient or to focus on competitive structures as opposed to the process of competition. Nevertheless, the Commission has steadily pursued the aim of preserving workable competition by protecting small and medium sized enterprises in its enforcement of Articles 85 and 86 and in its monitoring of mergers under the Merger Control Regulation of 1989.[3]

In recent years the growing awareness of the need for the European Com-

[1] See *e.g.* Whish, *Competition Law,* 3rd ed (Butterworths, 1993) Chs. 7 and 8.
[2] See *e.g.* Landes and Posner, "Market Power in Antitrust cases" [1981] 94 *Harvard Law Review* 937.
[3] See *e.g.* Whish, *Competition Law,* 3rd ed (Butterworths, 1993) Chs. 7 and 8.

munity to be more competitive in the face of stiffening international competition has introduced a new priority into the European Community policy agenda, one which makes the traditional preoccupations of EC competition policy appear rather inward looking. A growing understanding of the need to develop sufficiently high technological products in order to compete with Japan, the United States and the newly emerging dragons of Asia and Latin America has led to a recognition of the need to provide more incentives and support for the development of new technology. The European Commission's own White Paper, "Growth, Competitiveness, Employment"[4] points to the need to create a more competitive commercial and industrial structure in the EU in order to cope with world trade. Moreover, the Maastricht Treaty now provides specifically that the strengthening of the competitiveness of Community industry is one of the primary aims of the EU.[5]

The White Paper makes it clear that the only way for the EU to sustain its standard of living and raise its employment level through economic growth is to develop and maintain a lead through innovation in high technology industries. Existing policies have left the Union in an unfavourable competitive position vis-à-vis the United States and Japan, one which has "worsened as regards: employment; our share of market exports; R&D and innovation…".[6] EC industries "are not sufficiently well represented on expanding new markets, either in geographic terms or in terms of products" and EC firms are "sometimes at a disadvantage in the face of dominant positions held by certain innovative groups and the growth of strategic alliances.[7] The White Paper's recommendation for improvement is that "without eschewing competition, there is a need to foster co-operation and to have a legal…environment which allows strategic alliances, *i.e.* alliances that are necessary to counterbalance the weight of some US and Japanese competitors."[8]

It is not altogether clear, however, that the aim of enhancing international competitiveness can easily be introduced into European competition policy since some of its basic values are called into question by the main prescriptions for competitiveness. For example, in a world where co-operation between competitors is often the only way forward to sustained innovation in new technology and products, what is left of the traditional concern of EC competition under Article 85 to prevent collaboration between competitors? In a world where strategic alliances are needed to combat Asian and US trade champions, what is to become of the requirements written into the Merger Control Regulation that

---

[4] Growth, Competitiveness and Employment. The Challenges and the Way Forward 1993 Bulletin of the EC Supp 6/93.

[5] EC Treaty, art 3(1). See too Title XIII art 130 and Title XV arts 130f–130p.

[6] Commission of the European Communities White Paper, "Growth, Competitiveness, Employment", p 9.

[7] Commission of the European Communities White Paper, "Growth, Competitiveness, Employment", p 5.

[8] Commission of the European Communities White Paper, "Growth, Competitiveness, Employment", p 10.

appraisals of European takeovers and mergers be made without reference to an active industrial policy?

The argument has been made within the Commission that competitiveness in world trade can be achieved by the continuation of a policy largely devoted to maintaining strong competition within the EU, *i.e.* that international competitiveness presupposes a strongly competitive domestic market. It may well be, however, that the relationship between these two conditions is not quite so simple. It is true that strong competition on the home market may act as a spur to competitiveness in international trade in the sense of driving down costs and improving productive efficiency but more may be needed to ensure innovation at the higher end of the technology spectrum. As the White Paper points out, high technology innovation often presupposes co-operation between competitors and a certain degree of encouragement of "European Champions". Moreover, while in theory competition is supposed to act as a spur to firms to innovate to maintain a lead over rivals, as well as to cut costs, in practice, innovators often need to have incentives in the form of reductions in competition in order to minimise the risks inherent in investing in research and development of new products and processes. Implicit in the law of intellectual property is the idea that competition has a tendency to suppress innovation rather than to encourage it, which is why intellectual property laws confer monopoly rights in the form of exclusive rights to exploit patents, copyright and design rights.[9]

These issues raise questions about the way the Commission has been implementing certain spheres of competition policy in recent years. At the very least the new requirements for international competitiveness as spelt out in the White Paper, seem to call for a more careful balance to be struck between the values of co-operative investment and strategic alliances on the one hand and those of Article 85 and the Merger Control Regulation on the other, and this in turn requires some adjustment of policies by the Commission. The purpose of this paper is to examine certain aspects of current EC competition policy under the heads of (i) Co-operation Between Firms and (ii) The Creation of European Champions, to ascertain how and to what extent this adjustment is being made.

1. Co-operation Between Firms and EC Competition Law

The traditional view of EC competition law regarding co-operation between firms has been shaped by Article 85, which prohibits agreements and concerted practices which restrict or distort competition within the common market. One major concern of the Commission in implementing Article 85 has been with horizontal forms of co-operation, *i.e.* those between competitors in the same

[9] See *e.g.* Phillips and Firth, *Introduction* to *Intellectual Property Law*, 2nd ed (Butterworths, 1990).

market, in particular cartels or other forms of concerted practice which result in price fixing or market sharing. Under EC competition law, owing to a commitment to market integration, there has also been a concern to control vertical forms of agreement such as exclusive distribution, technology licensing and franchising. However, this aspect of Commission policy lies outside the scope of this chapter. The growing recognition that it is no longer tenable to expect a completely individualistic approach by firms to high technology product development and that complex new technologies can often only be produced through partnerships either in the form of R&D agreements or joint ventures has created pressure for a re-evaluation of traditional policies under Article 85.

Article 85(1) consists of a wide prohibition on agreements and concerted practices which potentially affect trade between Member States and whose object or effect is to restrict or distort competition within the common market. Article 85(2) provides that agreements which fall within the prohibition of Article 85(1) are void. Article 85(3) goes on to provide that an agreement can be exempted from the prohibition in Article 85(1) and the nullity provision in Article 85(2) if it meets four conditions: (i) it contributes to the improvement of the production and distribution of goods or the promotion of technical progress; (ii) it allows consumers a fair share of the resulting benefits; (iii) it imposes only restrictions which are indispensable to these objectives; and (iv) it does not eliminate competition with respect to a substantial part of the products in question.

The Commission has long been unwilling to balance the pro-competitive and anti-competitive features of restrictive clauses of agreements under Article 85(1), despite indications from the Court of Justice and the Court of First Instance that certain types of provision, including those in new technology agreements, could be treated in this manner.[10] Instead, it has preferred to give a wide interpretation to Article 85(1), bringing a great many agreements and practices within its scope, and requiring exemption under Article 85(3). This interpretation ensures that the Commission enjoys substantial power as a regulatory authority to approve or reject agreements under Article 85(3) because it alone has the power to grant exemptions under Article 85(3)[11]; although Articles 85 and 86 otherwise have direct effect, neither Member State courts nor competition authorities are able to grant exemption under Article 85(3). This interpretation also means that the parties to agreements are placed in a position of considerable legal uncertainty which can only be alleviated by notifying their agreements to the Commission to obtain exemption.

The Commission undoubtedly enjoys this position of control as well as the assurance of information from the steady stream of notified agreements but, with its limited number of personnel, it is not able to pursue a comprehensive policy of individual exemptions. To deal with the workload it makes use of

[10] R. Whish and B. Sufrin "Article 85 and the Rule of Reason" *1988 Oxford Yearbook in EC Law 1.*

[11] Forrester and Norall, "The Laicization of Community Law: Self help and the rule of reason" (1984) 21 *Common Market Law Review* 11.

informal "comfort letters" which indicate that an agreement is either not caught by Article 85(1) or that the file might be closed because it merits exemption. It has also adopted a series of block exemptions for certain categories of agreement.[12]

There has been some adjustment by the Commission in its administration and enforcement of Article 85 to allow for the need to accept certain forms of co-operative agreements between firms which promote innovation and competitiveness and this has taken two different forms. One has consisted of a policy of using the four conditions of Article 85(3) to shape the block exemptions. A good example is the block exemption for R&D agreements. A second type of adjustment by the Commission has been to create as more lenient policy allowing a balancing test of pro- and anti-competitive effects in the case of co-operative joint ventures. Let us look at each in turn.

2. Research and Development Agreements

Research and development are fundamental to the maintenance of growing, modern economies[13]; without adequate levels of research and development there can be little improvement in manufacturing processes or products and a trading block like the EU cannot expect to remain competitive with the United States, Japan and the other Asian economies. On the other hand, R&D agreements can be viewed as restrictive of competition in innovation and a possible front for the co-ordination of pricing, market sharing or production limits between competitors. Indeed, this risk is accentuated when the agreement moves beyond the first stage of basic research and development into the second stage of manufacturing the new product or the third stage of marketing the product. Nevertheless, there is an important balance to be struck between the advantages of shaping competition policy to encourage as much research and development as possible while at the same time allowing as few anti-competitive R&D agreements as possible. How has the Commission struck that balance?

Prior to 1992, the Commission's policy towards R&D agreements under the block exemption for Research and Development Agreements (Regulation No. 418/85) was characterised by a willingness to allow co-operation at the development stage of R&D. It was also prepared to allow its extension into joint manufacturing to a limited extent, thus acknowledging the need to carry joint R&D arrangements into the manufacturing stage simply to make the project as a whole economically viable. Joint manufacturing, however, was restricted to smaller and medium sized enterprises with less than 20% market share and limits were placed upon the scope of independent research, the possibility of building in no challenge clauses and allowing for third party manufacture.[14]

[12] See *e.g.* Bellamy and Child, *Common Market Law of Competition,* 4th ed (Sweet & Maxwell 1993).
[13] Whish, *Competition Law,* 3rd ed (Butterworths, 1993)) 437; Goyder, *E.C. Competition Law,* 2nd ed (OUP 1993) 184.
[14] V. Korah, *R&D and the EEC Competition Rules Regulation 418/85* (ESC, 1986).

In 1985, the Commission was unwilling to accept that the same logic required an entitlement to parties to R&D ventures to continue co-operation into the further stage of distribution or marketing of the product. The Commission insisted that any attempt by the parties to extend an R&D agreement into the marketing stage would cause the whole R&D agreement to lose its exempted status under the R&D Block Exemption Regulation. The difficulty with this approach was that if the parties to an R&D agreement consider that it is essential to extend co-operation beyond research and development and manufacture into the third stage of distribution the fact that they will be forced by law to end their co-operation and begin to compete at this stage will create a very strong disincentive working against their desire to enter into the agreement in the first place. The net result of an overly strict competition law regime under Article 85 will be to inhibit R&D co-operation. Indeed, because of its restrictiveness in these respects, Regulation 418/85 was not conspicuously successful as a stimulant to joint R&D agreements. The available evidence suggests that parties interested in obtaining exemption have felt it necessary to resort to the more cumbersome process of notification and individual exemption.

In 1992, the Commission finally acknowledged the need for a change by amending the block exemption to apply to joint R&D agreements which extend to the distribution stage, although this is subject to a market share limit of 10% of the relevant market for the parties to such an agreement.[15] This rather belated change in policy provides evidence that the Commission now recognizes that the balance it struck in the original version of the R&D block exemption was too restrictive of innovation and too protective of competition. However, the modesty of the change suggests that the Commission still prefers to err on the side of caution about internal competition than to go too far in giving support to innovation. In particular, the retention of market share upper limits with all their complexity and uncertainty continues to make resort to the R&D block exemption an unattractive option. In this respect, the Commission's concern with risks to internal competition has outweighed its impulse to adjust its policies to stimulate external competitiveness.

3. Co-operative Joint Ventures

Joint ventures often involve the creation of a separate company with a transfer of assets and allocation of specific responsibilities.[16] By comparison with R&D agreements, this form of business organisation offers the commercial advantage to parties of allowing a more flexible response to new and unforeseen problems in the development of new technologies, as opposed to the more restrictive framework created by an R&D agreement. It also allows co-operation without making the greater commitment of a complete merger of the two firms. In the

[15] Regulation 151/93 OJ 1993 L21/8.

[16] D. Goyder, *EC Competition Law*, 2nd ed (OUP, 1993) pp 186–7; see also Caspari, "Joint Ventures: The Intersection of Anti-trust and Industrial Policy in the EEC" [1985] *Fordham Corp. Law Institute* 449 at 453.

event, joint ventures are an important option for firms to resort to when undertaking risky investment in new technology. A policy of minimising the obstacles to access to joint technology ventures would appear therefore to be a way of promoting competitiveness.

On the other hand, joint ventures also create a potential risk of lessened competition in a given market. Inevitably, they reduce competition between the parties to the joint venture, including situations when the parties are operating in unrelated commercial areas. They can also have the effect of foreclosing opportunities for third parties to enter the market.[17] Again, the issue for competition policy in its new context is to draw a very careful line so as not to throw away the baby of innovative benefits for international competitiveness with the bath water of risks to internal competition.

Historically, joint ventures were analysed by the Commission under Article 85 as an agreement prima facie infringing Article 85(1) and requiring exemption under Article 85(3). During this period, the Commission was criticised for its seemingly inconsistent approach of applying Article 85(1) too strictly by focusing only on the anti-competitive features of the Joint Venture and then applying Article 85(3) quite generously to find the Joint Venture justified by its pro-competitive features. In the Thirteenth Report on Competition Policy, the Commission announced that they were prepared to bring a new realism to their assessment of the anti-competitive effects of a joint venture, in which the pro-competitive features of such a venture would be weighed in the balance before deciding whether or not Article 85(1) applies.[18] However, it took many years before this new approach could be discerned in Commission decisions. In *Odin Developments Ltd*[19], a joint venture between Tetrapak and Elopak, the Commission was prepared to acknowledge that some restrictions in joint venture agreements, such as exclusive knowhow licenses to the parties to the joint venture were justified because they were indispensable to the overall venture and if they were not allowed the venture might not proceed. Further, in *ECR 900*[20] the Commission was prepared to find a joint venture to be not restrictive of competition where co-operation at the distribution stage was essential because of the difficulties for either party acting alone to market the product. In both cases, the parents of the joint venture were not competitors.

In *Plessey* v *GEC and Siemens*[21] the Commission signalled a new approach to assessing joint ventures between competitors. The case involved a complex joint acquisition by Siemens and GEC of Plessey and an allocation between them of different sectors of Plessey's business: telecommunications, integrated circuits, acoustic wave devices, traffic control systems and defence electronics. The Commission analysed each sector separately concentrating on such factors as the market share of the Joint Venture, the existence of actual and potential compe-

---

[17] See *e.g.* Brodley, "Joint Ventures and Antitrust Policy" (1982) 95 *Harvard Law Review* 1521.

[18] Thirteenth Report on Competition Policy, p 50.

[19] *Odin Developments Ltd* [1991] 4 CMLR 832.

[20] *ECR 900* [1992] 4 CMLR 54.

[21] *Plessey Company plc* v *General Electrics Company plc and Siemens AG* [1992] 4 CMLR 471.

tition and the power of purchasers. It found that the anti-competitive effects of the joint venture were outweighed by its pro-competitive effects. The difficulties of high barriers to entry were accepted as a justification for an alliance. The existence of actual or potential competitors outside the EU was taken into account in evaluating market shares within the EU.

The significance of the *Plessey* case was that the Commission was prepared to concentrate its analysis upon the structure of a co-operative joint venture between actual and potential competitors almost as if it were a full merger in deciding the applicability of Article 85(1) to the joint acquisition. At a technical level, the Commission introduced the idea in *Plessey* that if the structural effects of a joint venture were not appreciable, the venture would not have to be justified under Article 85(3) because it was not caught by Article 85(1) in the first place. Moreover, the idea exemplified in *Odin Developments* that indispensable restrictive provisions to otherwise acceptable joint ventures would not be caught reinforced the more realistic approach of the Commission.[22]

Of course, where it could be shown that the joint venture would foreclose potential competition between the parties and/or third parties, exemption continued to be withheld[23] but it was clear that a more lenient legal regime for joint ventures had been ushered in by the 1990s.[24]

Much of this experience has been codified in the Commission's Notice on Co-operative Joint Ventures[25], in which the Commission indicated its concern with four main issues:

- To what extent are parties potential competitors?
- What are the effects of the joint venture upon the competitive position of third parties?
- Does the creation of the joint venture appreciably alter the conditions of competition on the relevant market? (*i.e.* the market for that product).
- Does the joint venture stand alone or is it part of a network of several joint ventures?

In the preparation of these criteria, as in the post *Plessey* caselaw, there is evidence of the Commission's willingness to give greater weight to the need to promote high technology alliances.

4. European Champions and EC Competition Law

Under Article 86 of the Treaty there is no impediment to a firm growing organically into a dominant position in a substantial part, or even the whole, of the

[22] Venit, "Oedipus Rex: Recent Developments in the Structural Approach to Joint Ventures under EEC Competition Law", *World Competition Law and Economics Review* 5–32.
[23] See *e.g. Eurosport* OJ 1991/L63.
[24] See Venit, "Oedipus Rex: Recent Developments in the Structural Approach to Joint Ventures under EEC Competition Law", *World Competition Law and Economics Review* 5–32.
[25] Commission's Notice on Co-operative Joint Ventures.

Common Market. The achievement of a dominant position is not unlawful per se: it is only when a firm in a dominant position commits an abuse of power that it behaves unlawfully. Under EC law the interests of allowing national firms to outgrow national markets have traditionally been given precedence over the more traditional anti-trust concern to prevent the creation of monopoly. This can be contrasted with the position in the United States where the Sherman Act makes achieving or attempting to achieve a monopoly unlawful.[26] The acceptance of this principle in Article 86 was intended to allow the growth of large European firms which would hasten integration of the Common Market.[27]

What is unlawful under Article 86 is conduct which amounts to an abuse of the power enjoyed by a firm which has already achieved a dominant position. A firm in a dominant position may not charge excessive prices, engage in predatory pricing, use discriminatory pricing to segregate markets and in certain circumstances refuse to deal with other firms arbitrarily. Such conduct is viewed as abusive because Article 86 has been interpreted to place upon the holder of a dominant position a special responsibility not to drive competitors out of the market or make it impossible for competitors to enter the market, *i.e.*, not to eliminate workable competition on the market by abusive conduct.

The jurisprudence of Article 86 provides the holder of a dominant position with a defence of justification for certain types of competitive conduct. Based on the German concept of competition based on performance (*Leistungswettbewerb*) or competition on the merits, it is possible for powerful firms to defend themselves against price cutting attacks by new entrants to a market, by matching the lower prices or even undercutting as long as costs are covered. Moreover, improvements based on internal research and development are lawful. In these ways, Article 86 allows firms to become and remain Eurochampions, almost as if the Treaty of Rome anticipated the White Paper.

In 1973, however, the Court of Justice made it plain in *Continental Can*[28] that it would not condone under Article 86 an attempt by a firm in a dominant position to extend its dominant position by a takeover or merger of a competitor. It did not matter whether the takeover was friendly or hostile; it was abusive conduct by a firm in a dominant position to use the device of a takeover or merger to strengthen its dominance in particular where in the process it created the prospect that competition would be substantially obstructed. At this stage, it did not appear to be unlawful for a firm to achieve a dominant position by merger or takeover. The abuse was limited to the reinforcement of a dominant position.

Shortly after the *Continental Can* decision, the Commission proposed to the Council that a regulation be adopted which would allow the Commission to

---

[26] T. Kauper, "Article 86 Excessive Prices and Refusals to Deal", 59 *Anti-trust Law Journal* 441; L. Gyselen, "Abuse of Monopoly Power within the meaning of Article 86 of the EEC Treaty: Recent Developments" [1990] *Fordham Corp. Law Institute,* Ch 29.

[27] *Ibid.*

[28] *Europemballage Corpn and Continental Can Co Inc* v *Commission* [1973] ECR 215.

assess all mergers which created or reinforced a dominant position and where the resulting merger would involve turnover of over ECU 200 million.[29] The Council, under pressure from the Member States, initially resisted this increase in the jurisdiction of the Commission at their expense and successively forced up the jurisdictional threshold. However, in 1988, the Commission's hand was dramatically strengthened when the Court of Justice ruled in *Philip Morris*[30], that the acquisition by a firm of an equity interest in a competitor could be caught by Article 85 where that acquisition could serve as an instrument for influencing the commercial conduct of the company so as to distort or restrict competition on the markets on which they conduct business. Within two years, a Merger Control Regulation was approved by the Council.

The Merger Control Regulation[31] provides that all mergers with an EC dimension, *i.e.* where the new firm would have at least ECU 5 million of worldwide turnover, have to be notified to and appraised by the Commission before the merger.[32] The Commission assesses the effects of the merger on competition within the Community and approves or disapproves the merger according to certain specified criteria. The jurisdiction of the Commission is exclusive: Community mergers are excluded from the application of the competition laws of the Member States (Art 21(2)), though provision is made for consultation with Member States in certain circumstances. In cases where the Commission finds that the merger would result in the creation or reinforcement of a dominant position in the Common Market, it must assess whether or not the merger created would significantly impede effective competition in the Common Market or a significant part of it. The drafting of the text of the Regulation was strongly influenced by the desire of the British and German governments to ensure that the assessment of mergers by the Commission would be based on strict competition grounds and would not be used as a back door for an EC industrial policy, along French, Italian or Spanish lines. Hence, it provides in Article 2(3) that once the Commission's appraisal results in a finding that the merger constitutes a significant impediment to effective competition, "it shall be declared incompatible with the Common Market". It is true that Article 2(1)(b) provides that the Commission should take into account the development of technical and economic progress as long as it is to consumers' advantage and does not form an obstacle to competition. However, this has not been interpreted to be a factor to be weighed in the balance once there has been a finding of significant impediment. At that point, Article 2(3) requires that the Commission must disapprove the merger.

Nevertheless, the experience of the Merger Task Force's appraisals of mergers suggests that industrial policy considerations, such as the need to foster European Champions, are not entirely ignored. The issue arises most often in

[29] OJ 1973 C92/1.
[30] *BAT* v *Commission of the European Communities* [1988] 4 CMLR 24.
[31] Council Regulation (EEC) 4064/89, art 1.
[32] The term merger (or concentration) includes concentrative joint ventures defined as JVs whose parents will not necessarily remain independent after the JV has been formed.

cases where mergers will result in a high degree of concentration in a market within the EU, effectively creating a new dominant position. In such a case, strict competition considerations should make the competition authority extremely wary about allowing the merger because it is likely significantly to impede competition within the Community. Yet, there are occasions when such a merger would produce a European firm better placed to compete against competitors outside the Community. How has the Commission dealt with such cases?

The starting point for the Commission's Merger Task Force has been the determination of the extent of market dominance of the new entity. Although it has not announced any formal market share guidelines, its experience in processing the almost 200 cases in its first four years, suggests that it applies an informal post merger market share test of dominance of about 40%. If the newly created entity would hold a market share of below 40%, then unless there was evidence of two firm (duopolistic) or multi-firm (oligopolistic) dominance in the common market or a substantial part of it, the new entity would generally be viewed as too small to amount to a dominant undertaking and the merger would be cleared at an early stage. If, however, the new entity would hold a market share of more than 40%, the merger would be given a careful investigation. There would be no automatic assumption that a merger of that size and scale would be incompatible with the common market, but care would be taken to ensure that competition in the post merger market would be sufficiently vital before the merger could be approved.[33]

In *ATR/De Havilland*[34], for example, an acquisition by two French and Italian turboprop aircraft manufacturers of a Canadian subsidiary of Boeing was blocked. The merger would have given the merged firm a post merger market share of 50% of the world market for commuter aircraft with a Community share of 71% of such aircraft in the 40–59 seat range and 55% of the Community market in the 20–70 seat range. The Commission was concerned that the dominant position on this mature market might lead to anti-competitive conduct partly because of the formidable barriers to entry to the market. Moreover, the nearest competitor, Saab, had a market share of only 19%, less than one half of the share of the proposed new firm. The case was controversial, with France and Italy voting against the Commission in the Advisory Committee. Their view was that the Commission should allow the creation of a European Champion to compete in world wide competition. One particularly controversial part of the decision was the way that the Commission dealt with the parties' contention that the merger would result in significant efficiency gains. Instead of viewing this as a factor mitigating the adverse competitive effects of the merger, the Commission used these claims to reinforce its view that the newly

[33] D. Ridyard, "Economic Analysis of Single Firm and Oligopolistic Dominance under the European Merger Regulation" [1994] *European Law Review,* 255 Vol 15; Neven, Nuttall and Seabright, *Mergers in Daylight* (1993) CEPR.

[34] *Aérospatiale, Aeritalia e Alenial De Havilland* [1992] 4 CMLR M2.

merged group would have a greater competitive advantage over their European rivals which could be misused.[35]

It would be wrong to conclude that *De Havilland* was indicative of an obsession with protecting the internal market at the expense of external competitiveness. What appeared to be the crucial factor in that case was the Commission's concern that there would be no substantial existing competitors in the market and there was no realistic prospect of potential competitors entering the market. In such a case the risks to internal competition were adjudged to outweigh the benefits to international competitiveness. However, where the Commission can find evidence of a competitive counterweight, it has been prepared to approve mergers resulting in high market shares. Even before *De Havilland*, in a case involving the merger of the helicopter divisions of Aerospatiale of France and MBB[36], a subsidiary of Daimler Benz, the resulting entity was estimated to hold 50% of the Community market. Nevertheless, the Commission cleared the merger after taking into account the openness of international competition and the existence of potential competition from the United States and Japan. It was persuaded that the level of post merger competition would be sufficiently high to ensure the new entity would not be able to behave independently of its competitors and customers.

After *De Havilland*, as well, there have been several cases where post merger market shares of over 40% have been viewed as compatible with the Common Market owing to the strength of the competition. For example, in *Mannesman/Hoesch*[37], a joint venture amounting to a merger between French and German stainless steel tube manufacturers which would have resulted in a market share of 60% in Germany and a Community market share of 36%, was cleared. The merger was allowed even though the new firm together with Sandvik of Sweden would hold 70% of the Community market. Though the Commission recognised that the new duopoly would create an incentive for restrictions of output and increased prices, it was prepared to clear the merger because of the existence of potential competition from British Steel and others within the EU and from Japan as well as Eastern Europe.[38]

Similarly, in *Rhone Poulenc/Snia II*[39], the Commission was prepared to clear a joint venture between the French producer Rhone-Poulenc and an Italian subsidiary of Fiat which would result in a market share of 42% of the European market for nylon textile fibres. The market share of its closest rival, Du Pont was only 23%, almost one half that of the new entity. Nevertheless, the worldwide resources and the reputation of Du Pont were such that the Commission considered that the post merger market would be sufficiently competitive to allow the merger to proceed.

These cases appear to indicate that industrial policy issues such as the

[35] Para 65.
[36] *Aerospatiale/Messerschmidt-Bölkow Blohm Gmbh* [1992] 4 CMLR M 70.
[37] *Mannesman-röhrenwerke/Hoesch AG* OJ 1993 L114/34.
[38] Para 25.
[39] Case IV/M 355 OJ 1993, L102/15.

creation of European Champions are coming into the merger appraisal test via the back door of the Commission's test of potential competition. However, it is a back door rather than a reversal of stated policy. The Commission appears to be rather consistently taking the approach of assessing the capabilities of the rivals of the new entity to determine the extent of competition that would be found in the post merger market regardless of whether that competition is from within or outside the Community. In cases where rivals to the post merger firm would be insufficient in size or scale to provide real competition, the Commission has required the parties to the merger to scale down the merger and in some cases help to create a new competitor to ensure that there is adequate competition on the internal market.

5. Conclusions

It is early days in the process of adapting competition policy to the challenge of competitiveness in world trade. In all three sectors of Commission activity looked at in this contribution there are some signs of change. However, in the application of Article 85 to Research and Development agreements there is evidence that the Commission is more anxious to maintain its grip on the process of regulating internal competition than to devise inventive means to stimulate innovation. In the case of Co-operative Joint Ventures, there has been a greater willingness by the Commission to treat the assessment process as a realistic appraisal of effects rather than a more formalistic examination of particular provisions in isolation from their effects. In that sense, the Commission has made a more promising adjustment towards a reconciliation of the new with the old policy goals. In the case of the Merger Control Regulation, the use of a widened concept of potential competition offers another example of an inventive adjustment, although it will take a legislative amendment to the Regulation to produce any more dramatic change in its administration.

Chapter 11

THE MORAL ECONOMY OF JUDICIAL REVIEW

Sir Stephen Sedley

The logic of history is only ever discernible in retrospect, and even then it can be perceived as anything from the workings of an ineluctable design to a series of human cockups; possibly both. Lawyers tend to spare themselves this pain by not thinking about legal history at all. In the age in which most of today's established lawyers were educated this did not matter because law itself was a body of data derived either from the will of Parliament or from the fogs of time, and the jobbing lawyer's and judge's role was to clarify and apply it. It is only in these last decades, when the genie of public law has got well and truly out of the bottle, that it has become apparent to even the stoniest of blackletter lawyers that legal history is happening and is going to go on happening under our noses, making us all – academics, judges and practitioners – either spectators or actors as we choose. I don't believe that there is any area of the English common law which has changed so much and at such speed as public law has done since 1970.

Why this should be so is not just a matter of intellectual curiosity. It bears on our constitutional future in a number of significant ways because the capacity for judge-driven change in the law by which government is governed is itself an artefact of time and situation. If it is so, what next happens to public law is likely to be a function of similar factors; but law is peculiar in this regard because it has its own imperatives of principle-seeking within movements of society and politics in which it is both a passive and an active force. The court which upholds or strikes down a ministerial policy as unlawful is, it hopes and believes, acting on nothing but legal principle; but its perception both of the nature of the policy and of its own power to intervene, and often too its choice between competing legal principles, is fundamentally conditioned by the moment of history at which it sits; and these perceptions in turn determine what legal principle is or is not to be deployed. Would the inexorable logic of the House of Lords' decision[1] that the employment rights of part-time workers fell short of enforceable European standards have been equally apparent to the Court of

---

[1] *Equal Opportunities Commission* v *Secretary of State for Employment* [1994] 1 All ER 910, HL.

Appeal which in 1925 decided[2] that it was perfectly all right for an education authority to sack its married women teachers because their domestic duties came first? Would one of today's Divisional Courts still hold that a local authority could lawfully use its cinema licensing powers to stop young people going to the pictures on a Sunday?[3]

So it behoves lawyers in thinking about the future to think about what I have called, for want of a more conventional phrase, the moral economy of judicial review. It was E.P. Thompson who coined the expression in his essay *The moral economy of the English crowd in the Eighteenth Century*.[4] By it he sought to draw attention to the lofty unsubtlety with which the term "riot" was conventionally deployed, as George Rudé had argued the term "mob" was, as a portmanteau account of reactive spasms of popular disorder calling, by its use, for no further inquiry. In truth, as Thompson went on famously to demonstrate, it is not the banal fact that people react to hardships but the uninvestigated complexity of why they react in the ways they do which is of real interest; and to lawyers there is – or ought to be – real interest in Thompson's thesis that far from being anarchistically bent upon crime and destruction, the eighteenth-century crowd could be seen frequently to be responding to a shared sense of historic legitimacy.

> "While this moral economy cannot be described as 'political' in any advanced sense, nevertheless it cannot be described as unpolitical either, since it supposed definite, and passionately held, notions of the common weal – notions which, indeed, found some support in the paternalist traditions of the authorities; notions which the people re-echoed so loudly in their turn that the authorities were, in some measure, the prisoners of the people. Hence this moral economy impinged very generally upon eighteenth-century government and thought, and did not intrude only at moments of disturbance."

In *Whigs and Hunters* Thompson went on to contend on a larger plane for the recognition of legitimacy as history's major prize, proposing the rule of law as an unmitigated good.

The rule of law in itself does nothing to determine by whom the law is to be laid down. That it should be done by an elected legislature is a political truth self-evident only to those societies in which democracy has shed its historical odium.[5] But while the legitimacy of parliamentary supremacy is for the present uncontroversial, the legitimacy of government has become heavily contested. It is here that modern public law has thrived. My argument is that this is not a historical accident but a development which is both a source of and a response to major changes in the functioning of the British State. These are throwing

---

[2] *Short* v *Poole Corporation* [1926] Ch 66, CA.

[3] As the puisne judge and Court of Appeal did in *Associated Provincial Picture Houses* v *Wednesbury Corporation* [1948] 1 KB 223.

[4] First published in Past and Present, No. 50, in 1971. See now E.P. Thompson, *Customs in Common* (Penguin, 1993), Chaps IV and V.

[5] See the entry on democracy in Raymond Williams *Keywords*. That election should be by universal adult franchise is still more recent, and what amounts to a free election remains a subject of serious controversy.

up contested issues of legitimacy in a context that corresponds with surprising relevance to Thompson's notion of a moral economy. My purpose, like his, is to get behind the notion that these things just happen.

I have suggested elsewhere[6] that the modern flowering of public law can only be understood against the backdrop of what has preceded it. A body of law which since its inception in the late 13th century has been almost entirely judge-made was adapted in protean fashion during the nineteenth to match the growth of Victorian state intervention and corporatism. By the time Dicey was rejecting administrative law as a foreign notion made unnecessary by the availability of resort to "ordinary" courts, the ordinary courts were developing a sophisticated series of controls over public administration; indeed Dicey himself acknowledged the existence of judicial "cross-currents" tending to disturb the symmetry of the legislative system which he took to enshrine the rule of law. These were real and sometimes fierce. Parliament spent much time first investigating some of the horrors of early industrialism and urbanisation and then, if the vested parliamentary interests were not too powerful, legislating either in the expectation that the courts would not interfere with the boards and inspectors who were put in office or, increasingly, making express provision for judicial non-intervention by means of preclusive or privative clauses.[7] These the courts circumvented by means which our generation has been taught to ascribe to a decision of the House of Lords in 1969[8], namely to hold that a decision taken without jurisdiction is no decision and therefore outside the protection of the privative clause.

It is perhaps too easy to put the process down to reactionary hostility to social legislation and regulation. But there were respectable grounds for insisting on judicial review: by removing the opportunities for paralysing inferior tribunals with endless lawsuits, it was pointed out, Parliament risked instead licensing oppression and injustice.[9] Moreover, it was not only the millowners who took advantage of the possibilities of challenge in the higher courts. It proved possible, for instance, to use mandamus to challenge the refusals of magistrates to convict factory owners.[10] By the third quarter of the century the legislative pendulum had swung towards acceptance of judicial control. The privative clause in the Coal Mines Inspection Act 1842 was not reproduced in the successor statutes from 1850 onwards, and the attempt in the Regulation of Railways Act 1873 to make decisions of the Railways Commission "final" had by 1877 been wrecked by judicial decision.[11]

Such histories tell us something important about legitimacy in the moral economy. Once the supremacy of the courts in construing statute law is

---

[6] "The Sound of Silence: Constitutional Law without a Constitution (1994) 110 LQR 270.

[7] Oats (ed), *The Factory Acts* (1862) 141–5, cited by Arthurs, *Against the Law* (Toronto, 1985).

[8] *Anisminic Ltd* v *Foreign Compensation Commission* [1969] 2 AC 147: it is in the speeches of Lord Pearce and Lord Wilberforce that the strong body of mid-Victorian authority emerges.

[9] See the comment cited in Arthurs, *op cit*, pp 146–7.

[10] See the opinion of the law officers to the factory inspectors, June 1848, cited by Arthurs, *op cit*, p 147, n 90.

[11] *London Chatham and Dover Rly* v *South Eastern Rly* (1877) 3 Nev. & Mac. 79, QBD.

accepted, as the rule of law demands that it should be, a second sovereignty exists in the state.[12] The division of constitutional labour between enactment and interpretation makes it unavailing for legislators to say they meant something else, for what Parliament means is what the courts say it means.[13] Moreover, by the middle of the 19th century the courts had established a power to supplement legislation, reversing the maxim *expressio unius exclusio alterius* by declaring that where Parliament had failed to prescribe fair procedures for administrators "the justice of the common law" would "supply the omission of the legislature".[14] Such interventions face a legislature with an insoluble problem: it cannot attempt to reverse them by amending legislation without in effect admitting that it is seeking to deny the justice which the courts are there to accord. The balance of legitimacy shifts accordingly.

Epochs are made when the same thing happens on the constitutional rather than the interpretative plane. It was not in the US Constitution but in Chief Justice Marshall's Supreme Court in 1803[15] that the power of judicial review of Congressional legislation was asserted – and, importantly for my thesis, not thereafter challenged. In Australia in this decade something similar has occurred with the decision of the High Court that it can interfere with primary legislation which frustrates constitutional values, even if these are not articulated in the constitution.[16]

When, with the Northcote-Trevelyan civil service in place and in charge, the judges of the early 20th century backed off and began to leave government to govern itself, they were acting out not simply a private idiosyncrasy but a widespread sense that government could be trusted to regulate both itself and the tribunals and agencies within its purview.

For the first time the departments of state were now headed by an intellectual meritocracy from the same schools and universities and clubs as the judges themselves. They could be trusted to advise ministers well and implement policy soundly. In the long sleep of judicial review which followed, the civil service acquired previously unimagined levels of unchallenged power. In particular it obtained a hold over the administrative tribunals which were intended to

---

[12] Lord Bridge has expressly asserted as much in *X* v *Morgan-Grampian* [1991] AC 1, 48: "The maintenance of the rule of law is in every way as important in a free society as the democratic franchise. In our society the rule of law rests upon twin foundations: the sovereignty of the Queen in Parliament in making the law and the sovereignty of the Queen's courts in interpreting and applying the law."

[13] The inroad made by *Pepper* v *Hart* [1993] AC 593 into this doctrine, permitting resort to *Hansard*, is limited to cases where the court can otherwise not make sense of the text. It brings in its train logical and constitutional problems which may well lead in years to come to the restriction of its ambit – if, for example, the construction of statutory instruments is not to be predetermined by the minister's affidavit of what he or she intended to achieve.

[14] Byles J in *Cooper* v *Wandsworth Board of Works* (1863) 14 CB(NS) 180.

[15] *Marbury* v *Madison* (1803) 1 Cranch 137.

[16] *Nationwide News Pty. Ltd* v *Wills* (1990) 177 CLR 1, and *Australian Capital Television Pty. Ltd.* v *The Commonwealth, ibid.* 106. The possibility of a similar move to judicial supremacism has been contemplated by Sir John Laws: "Is the High Court the Guardian of Fundamental Constitutional Rights?" [1993] PL 59, and "Law and Politics: a No-go Area for Judges?" (The Public Law Project Lecture, 1994).

balance the powers of the state against the needs and rights of the citizen, routinely dictating policy to them and developing a sense of proprietorship which it has been one of the major achievements of modern public law to dissolve. Here was a moral economy in which much of legitimacy had been consciously surrendered through judicial abstentionism to the executive, which by the post-war years was in effect, if not in constitutional theory, a third sovereignty in the state.

It is in the decades between then and now that something has stirred in the bowels of the polity, denying the claims of the executive and of ministers to sovereignty and calling for the protection of law against government. It is a striking fact that the bad press accorded to the judiciary since the later 1980s has been almost entirely related to miscarriages of criminal justice, and that the increasingly publicised interventions of the High Court and appellate courts in the process of government have been treated as proper interpositions of law between the people and the state. Although there is a simple and mechanistic political explanation for this – that the post-war corporate state has evoked the same judicial reaction as its Victorian ancestor – the evidence for it is thin and getting thinner. In particular, the decade of political deconstruction of parts of the state apparatus has also been a decade of increasingly intensive and extensive judicial review of ministerial action. The response, in this moral economy, is not to a particular structural form but to modes of government which upset a received sense of legitimacy. It can be seen very clearly to be a sense not of a monolithic parliamentary legitimacy but of a bi-polar sovereignty in which the courts are called upon to exercise a surveillance of executive government which Parliament is no longer equipped to perform.

I was called to the Bar in 1964. The first law centre – in North Kensington – was opened in 1969 and within a short time was encountering administrative tribunals which culturally had little idea of their quasi-judicial status and which politically were under the thumb of departments of state which believed, thanks to years of unchallenged practice, that these tribunals were instruments of departmental policy and behaved accordingly. In the same years the Child Poverty Action Group embarked upon a remarkably effective series of legal challenges, equipped with a specialised knowledge of social security law which made it more than a match for those it challenged. One of its discoveries was that the departmental response to the realisation that it was improper to dictate to independent tribunals had been to classify the directives as secret.[17]

Other challenges, on which I cut my public law teeth, were brought before the Divisional Court of Queen's Bench. Because my profession had been brought up to believe that there was no such thing as administrative law and so no recourse to the courts against unlawful administration, the court's lists were sparse. A further disincentive was that all judicial review applications went before a court composed of the Lord Chief Justice and two heavyweight judges, frequently Diplock LJ and Ashworth J, and – if leave was obtained – were

---

[17] See (anecdotally) Harlow and Rawlings, *Pressure Through Law* (1992) 172–3.

opposed by the Treasury Devil, Mr Nigel Bridge. For young barristers, who were the only ones rash enough to go there, this was a place of terror, made worse by the fact that there were almost no practice books[18] and by a corresponding inclination of the court to react to perceived merits rather than to look first for principles. But the perceived merits were sometimes in the citizen's favour, often because a decision had been taken without affording the individual a proper chance to be heard. What developed was a dialectic in which resort to principles set out in much earlier cases was supplemented by a growing willingness in the court to adapt and expand them to new and different administrative structures and procedural issues.

The great milestone cases along this path are well known. My own best experience was the run of prison cases by which, in the course of ten years or so, building on the initial breakthrough in the *St Germain* case[19], it was established that the exercise of disciplinary powers by governors is reviewable by the courts; that boards of visitors exercising their then disciplinary powers owed duties of fairness parallel to those owed by the courts; that prisoners could not be shunted from prison to prison in solitary confinement as a surrogate form of punishment; and that the Home Secretary must tell lifers what may influence him in setting their "tariffs".[20] Gipsies too gained from the courts a little of the protection which local government (by simply breaching its statutory duties) and central government (through the non-use of its enforcement powers) were denying them.[21]

Nobody supposes that judicial review has been changing the face of history, but it has changed the face of law and, with it, the constitution. For in a state which possesses an organic constitution, constitutional law is necessarily largely descriptive. What has been happening in the field of judicial review of government has been a realignment of the polarities of state power. It is not a realignment mapped out by any single body of consensual principle, for ours is not that kind of polity (at least not yet), but an organic readjustment of sovereignties within the state driven by the whole concatenation of forces which makes up the moral economy. For this reason, too, the future path of the process is never clear. It is possible that with or without a written constitution the courts may one day find themselves emboldened or provoked to strike down primary legislation as unconstitutional.[22] If they do, the outcome may be an interesting test of legitimacy in practice. What is more probable is that the strength of judicial review will continue to change with the perceived need and capacity of

[18] de Smith, *Judicial Review of Administrative Action* was first published in 1959; the second edition in 1968. Wade *Administrative Law* was first published in 1961. Neither was introduced to Bar students during their education and training during the 1960s.

[19] *R* v *Hull BoV, ex p St Germain* [1979] QB 425.

[20] See generally Livingstone and Owen, *Prison Law* (1993), esp. Chaps 7 and 8; Richardson, *Law, Process and Custody: Prisoners and Patients* (1993), Pt II.

[21] *E.g. R* v *Secretary of State for the Environment, ex p Ward* [1984] 1 WLR 834; *West Glamorgan CC* v *Rafferty* [1987] 1 WLR 457, CA.

[22] After all, not only the possibility but the existence of a fundamental law (the European Communities Act 1972) has been established *sub silentio* by the decision of the House of Lords in *Factortame (No 2)* [1990] 1 AC 603.

government to govern and of Parliament to control government. But, as before, it cannot be expected to be a simple reactive process, for the intrusion of legal principle into the exercise, while it can be seen historically to be less than determinative, ought nevertheless to make the judicial response more than arbitrary. What I do think is now in the past is the abstentionist theory which proposes that the courts, being unelected, must for that reason be expected to defer to government. We are now more at home with the antithetical proposition that governments are elected to govern within the law, and that what that law is is for the courts to determine on grounds of principle. The view of democracy which this represents is neither that which informed the Northcote-Trevelyan Report, nor that which informed the Haldane Report, nor that which informed the Fulton Report, but it may very well chime with two reports that, at the moment of writing, still lie in the future: the Scott Report on the Matrix-Churchill affair and the Nolan Report on standards in public life. Whether this is because the latter two are the work of senior judges, or whether senior judges are writing them because nobody else could be trusted to do so, is a question that can be debated without injury to my thesis. If the law is as the law does, then in public law the frontiers of legal knowledge are the frontiers of law itself, and our generation has seen these shift sharply to favour law at the expense of administration. An administrator's or minister's account of the recent history might not be factually very different, although it might well characterise the outcome in terms of judicial tanks on the departmental lawn. But it is, I would suggest, our moral economy which has clothed the new pretensions of public law with the legitimacy which is one of history's chief prizes.

Chapter 12

THE PATHWAYS OF PUBLIC LAW SCHOLARSHIP

Professor Martin Loughlin*
University of Manchester

What have been the main themes of recent academic writing on public law in Britain? Can distinctive methods be discerned and, if so, what might they reveal about the subject? These are the main questions which seem to present themselves when contemplating developments in public law scholarship over the last 25 years. Though I propose to focus on these questions, I feel that I cannot do so adequately without also trying to situate recent work within a tradition of writing on public law which has grown up over the last century or so. The reason for this is that so much of the recent writing in public law which seeks to project an image of what public law is (or to illustrate what academic public lawyers should be doing) may best be understood as an attempt to break free from the shackles of a Victorian frame of mind and to find a mode of speaking and writing about the subject which engages with contemporary concerns.

Since much of recent innovative writing may be understood in that light, I will begin by considering the broad outline of 19th century thought on constitutional law. I do so, however, not only to ground current concerns, but also to promote a controversial hypothesis; *viz*, that the emergence of the study of law in English universities has gone hand in hand with a progressive distortion of the constitution and a consequential inability to appreciate its character. This has occurred primarily because, in the exercise of seeking to establish law as an autonomous discipline worthy of university study, the relationship between law and constitution was cast the wrong way round. Instead of following Maitland's approach of studying the constitution in order to throw light on the character of English law, academic lawyers have generally thrown in their lot with Dicey who began by expounding a formal conception of law and then, armed with this weaponry, proceeded, through "legal analysis", to reveal the fundamental

* I should like to thank Neil Duxbury, Carol Harlow, Perry Keller, Tim Murphy, Anthony Ogus, Tony Prosser, Rick Rawlings and David Sugarman, all of whom kindly commented on an earlier draft.

principles of the constitution. Since these fundamental principles were all rooted in the law, Dicey was able to place law at the centre of our constitutional arrangements, to marginalise history and politics, and to project a conception of law as belonging to a distinct branch of academic inquiry.

During the 20th century, academics in the main adhered to this Diceyan method and it has only been since the 1960s that it has generally been questioned. One obvious reason for this is that the pace of change had had the effect of devaluing much of the common law wisdom which underpinned Dicey's framework, with the result that analytical public lawyers were obliged either to limit their inquiries to the analysis of the justificatory language of courts or to construct rather peculiar structures of constitutional rules which did not seem to correlate, even in a rudimentary fashion, to the imperatives of political life. The restrictions imposed by this tradition on what counted as legal knowledge simply meant that public lawyers were unable to reflect in profitable or imaginative ways about the relationship between law and government. Recent developments in public law scholarship can best be appreciated against this background and as attempts to generate new vocabularies through which public law might be reconnected with political life.

One specific impetus for such inquiry was provided by the expansion of higher education during the 1960s. The new universities (of which Warwick is exemplary) began to re-design the curriculum in a self-consciously modern form and thus set a teaching agenda which, especially in relation to public law, posed many basic questions for which traditional legal materials provided not only no answers but also virtually no guidance on how to discover an answer. In one sense, scholarly developments since the 1960s may be understood as the search along various pathways for answers to the sorts of questions which were raised in the classrooms of the 1960s mainly to provoke reflection and discussion. As a consequence, the period since the 1960s has been a highly creative one, in which a great body of excellent work by lawyers addressing issues of governance has been produced. In largely ignoring this work, my intention is not to detract from those achievements. Rather, my concern is to consider a set of more limited questions which seek to reveal something about the nature of the subject. Have new methods for a rejuvenated public law scholarship been set in place? In seeking to re-connect legal thought with political life, has a suitable characterisation of the law-society relationship been formulated? Are we able to fashion an adequate conception of the legal and thus to outline more appropriate boundaries for legal scholarship? Are we any closer to answering the question of what public lawyers should do?

1. The Age of Order

Scholarly study of the English constitution long predates the institutionalisation of law teaching in the English universities. Prior to the latter half of the 19th century, the constitution was conceived as forming an elaborate cultural heritage, the historical study of which provided a boundless source of prescriptive wisdom and comprised a vital element in the general liberal education of the English gentleman. And during the century, a grand tradition of constitutional history, embracing such figures as Stubbs, Freeman, Macaulay and Hallam, gradually evolved. This tradition encompassed what has since become known as a "Whig interpretation of history"[1]; a view rooted in the idea that the English past is to be revered as a "story of the triumph of constitutional liberty and representative institutions".[2]

One feature of the work of the Whig constitutional historians is that they regarded the lawyer's interpretation of the constitution with some distaste, inclining to the view that "our constitutional history has been perverted at the hands of lawyers".[3] The legal mind, they argued, seemed unable to grasp ambiguity, uncertainty and heterogeneity, and was thus incapable of sensitive historical understanding. In part, this was because the English lawyer's "love of precedent" was carried to unreasonable lengths; but it was also a result of the adoption of a legal method which tended to draw "acute and logical inference from given premises [which] will commonly be found to be historically worthless".[4] These failings, together with the fact that "the natural tendency of the legal mind is to conservatism and deference to authority"[5], rendered the lawyer's account of the constitution deficient. This was nowhere more evident than in relation to the apparently foundational concept of sovereignty. "[T]he whole ideal conception of the Sovereign", wrote Freeman, "is a purely lawyer's conception and rests upon no ground whatever in the records of our early history".[6]

When, during the latter half of the 19th century, law professors came to be appointed on any significant scale to the English universities, they were concerned to reconcile the quest for academic credibility with the need for professional legitimacy. In this endeavour, they were particularly influenced by the example of John Austin, whose work was seen as leading English law, in Austin's famous phrase, "from the empire of chaos and darkness to...the region of order and light".[7] Following the tenets of Austinian legal science, many law professors took the view that their role was "to reduce the mass of legal rules to an orderly series of principles" and "to set forth the law as a coherent whole".[8] Law, they asserted, was a science and the rational and systematic structure of this

---

[1] See, especially, Butterfield, *The Whig Interpretation of History* (Bell, 1931); id, *The Englishman and His History* (Cambridge UP 1944).

[2] Burrow, *A Liberal Descent. Victorian Historians and the English Past* (Cambridge UP, 1981) p 3. See also Blaas, *Continuity and Anachronism. Parliamentary and Constitutional Development in Whig Historiography and in the Anti-Whig Reaction between 1890 and 1930* (Martinus Nijhoff, 1978) Chap 2.

[3] Freeman, *The Growth of the English Constitution*, 3rd ed (Macmillan, 1876) x.

[4] *Ibid*, pp 127–8.

[5] *Ibid*, p 128.

[6] *Ibid*, pp 128–9.

[7] Austin, *Lectures on Jurisprudence* (Murray, 1885) 58.

[8] Dicey, *Can English Law Be Taught At The Universities?* (1883) p 18; quoted in D. Sugarman, "Legal Theory, the Common Law Mind and the Making of the Textbook Tradition" in Twining (ed) *Legal Theory and the Common Law* (Blackwells, 1986) 26 at 30.

legal science could be taught through textbooks which articulated the fundamental principles of the subject.[9] The task of addressing the issue of constitutional law fell to A.V. Dicey, Vinerian Professor of English Law at Oxford, who in his highly influential study of the law of the constitution went to great lengths to rescue the constitution from the historians' grasp.[10] Criticising the historians' "mere antiquarianism"[11], their limited understanding of the legal process[12], and their romantic attachment to the myth of the ancient constitution[13], Dicey sought to lay bare the legal fundamentals of the constitution.[14] Cutting through what Cobden had referred to as "that great juggle of the '*English Constitution*' – a thing of monopolies, and Church-craft, and sinecures, armorial hocus-pocus, primogeniture, and Pagentry!"[15], Dicey outlined an account of constitutional law which was both elegant and simple.

With the publication of *The Law of the Constitution*, Dicey achieved a remarkable success in reorientating the focus of constitutional scholarship. Though wrapped in the garb of analytical jurisprudence, Dicey presented a new version of the Whig interpretation of history; one which this time placed lawyers at the centre. "Our constitution", he asserted, "is a judge-made constitution"[16] in the making of which the lawyers had played a heroic role. As Collini has observed, Dicey not only forged an "improbable fusion of Whig interpretation of history, the Austinian analysis of law, and the individualist concept of the State" but was able to present "the whole amalgam...as a dispassionate conclusion of academic legal science".[17] When in 1910 Dicey wrote that Maitland's great achievement had been "to establish that English law lies at the basis of English politics, and at the centre of the development of the English constitution"[18] he was, in reality,

---

[9] On this movement see, especially, D. Sugarman, *ibid*; id, "'A Hatred of Disorder': Legal Science, Liberalism and Imperialism" in Fitzpatrick (ed), *Dangerous Supplements. Resistance and Renewal in Jurisprudence* (Pluto, 1991) 34.

[10] Dicey, *Introduction to the Study of the Law of the Constitution* [1885] 8th ed (Macmillan, 1915).

[11] "[T]he kind of constitutional history which consists in researches into the antiquities of English institutions, has no direct bearing on the rules of constitutional law. ... [I]t boots nothing ... to understand, if it be understandable, the constitution of the Witenagemot. ... It throws as much light on the constitution of the United States as upon the constitution of England; that is, it throws no light upon either the one or the other." (Dicey, *ibid*, p 14).

[12] "The supposition ... that the cunning of lawyers has by the invention of legal fictions corrupted the fair simplicity of our original constitution, underrates the statesmanship of lawyers as much as it overrates the merits of early society. ... For there are social conditions under which legal fictions or subtleties afford the sole means of establishing that rule of equal and settled law which is the true basis of English civilisation." (Dicey, *ibid*, pp 17–18).

[13] Dicey argues that "the illusion ... that modern constitutional freedom has been established by an astounding method of retrospective progress ["that every step towards civilisation has been a step backwards towards the simple wisdom of our uncultured ancestors"] ... conceals the truth both of law and of history." (*ibid*, p 17).

[14] "The duty ... of an English professor of law is to state what are the laws which form part of the constitution, to arrange them in their order, to explain their meaning, and to exhibit where possible their logical connection." (Dicey, *ibid*, p 31).

[15] Quoted in Greenleaf, *The British Political Tradition. Vol. II The Ideological Heritage* (Methuen, 1983) 39.

[16] Dicey, *op cit* n 10, p 192.

[17] Collini, *Public Moralists. Political Thought and Intellectual Life in Britain 1850–1930* (Clarendon, 1991) 287.

[18] Dicey, "Professor Maitland" 91 *Nation* 293 (29 September 1910). Quoted in Collini, *ibid*, p 298.

ruminating on his own influence.

Intellectual life in the Victorian era has often been characterised in terms of a struggle to reconcile two discordant trends: tradition and progress; faith and science; the lamp that illuminates experience with the mirror which reflects the world.[19] Could this tension between a positivistic, rationalistic, and scientific spirit be reconciled with a Romantic culture which expressed concern about the flattening tendencies of this modern temperament? Dicey's genius lay in the fact that, in his study of the constitution, he stumbled across a style which, though presented in a scientific idiom, served mainly to bolster the authority of traditional wisdom. The key was the idea of precedent. For Dicey, precedent was not the formalistic, backward-looking doctrine characterised by the Whig constitutional historians but was simply "a useful fiction by which judicial decision conceals its transformation into judicial legislation".[20] Precedent was the device which enabled us to reconcile continuity with innovation, order with progress. Though presenting itself as a mirror which would accurately and objectively reflect the fundamental principles of the constitution, *The Law of the Constitution* was in reality a lamp or beacon which proclaimed faith in the experience and wisdom of the common law.

2. The Age of Decline

During the 20th century, Dicey's approach rapidly established itself as the orthodox method of studying constitutional law. Its success may perhaps be gauged by the emergence of the textbook tradition. Despite the austere facade, these texts invariably comprised collections of legal fables and folk tales to rival those of the Whig constitutional historians. Keir and Lawson's *Cases in Constitutional Law,* first published in 1928, provides an illustration. After contending that the extensive use of Dicey's text was indicative of the fact "that some knowledge of the legal principles on which the English constitution rests is recognized as essential to its true understanding", the editors suggested that "this knowledge can best be acquired by a study of leading cases in constitutional law".[21] Such judgments create an "abiding impression ... not ... of historical change, but of the permanence of the Common Law"[22] and, being "replete with historical learning", "[o]nly the student who is prepared to read their judgments in the original form can fully appreciate the real genius of the constitution which they expound".[23] For Keir and Lawson, only by immersion in the leading cases – statutes were deliberately excluded[24] – could the student come

---

19 See Abrams, *The Mirror and the Lamp: Romantic Theory and the Critical Tradition* (Oxford UP, 1971).

20 Dicey, *op cit* n 10, p 18.

21 Keir & Lawson, *Cases in Constitutional Law* (Clarendon, 1928) v.

22 *Ibid.*

23 *Ibid,* p vi.

24 The editors explained that statutes "have for the most part only a fleeting interest" (*ibid,* p vi) and only three – the Public Authorities Protection Act 1893, the Petitions of Right Act 1860 and the Emergency Powers Act 1920 – were included in the collection (though the omission of Magna Carta and the Bill of Rights was explained on the ground that they were readily available in other collec-

to appreciate "a temper peculiar to persons who have been bred in the Common Law and impregnated with the characteristic traditions of ... English liberty".[25]

As the century unfolded, however, the difficulties with this Diceyan tradition began to reveal themselves. Dicey's work had been highly acclaimed at the moment of its publication. Since many of the great political issues of the day, such as the extension of the franchise or the question of Irish Home Rule, were being widely debated in the language of constitutional law, it was perhaps to be expected that a professor of law might be called on to offer guidance.[26] But there was more to it than that. His influence was to a great extent a reflection of the character of Victorian society and his own status within it. Dicey performed the role not simply of a legal scholar but rather, in Collini's terminology, that of a "public moralist". This role, being "predicated upon a degree of intimacy between critic and criticized", meant that Dicey felt "confident of having the ear of an important audience, confident of addressing concerns and invoking values which were largely shared with that audience, confident of an easy, intimate, even conversable, relationship with both Reason and History".[27]

By the turn of the century things were rapidly changing, as Dicey himself had acknowledged.[28] Political concerns were shifting away from constitutional issues and came to focus more directly on matters of social and economic reform, matters on which the constitutional lawyer could offer little guidance. Basic cultural changes resulted in a dissipation in influence of the "public moralist" and the emergence of scholars in a more professional and more limited role. But, perhaps most importantly, the transformation in the functions and institutions of government during the 20th century posed major questions for the Diceyan inheritance. The cultural changes which were taking place imposed major strains on the idea that the study of the common law provided an education in the distinctive cultural identity of the English nation. The changes in

---

tions). Though a general feature of common law culture, this approach was a particular characteristic of the Oxford method. See, *e.g.* W.T.S. Stallybrass, "Law in the Universities" (1948) J. of SPLT 157, 163: "I am sure that the Oxford Law School has been wise in excluding from its courses those branches of the Law which depend on Statute and not on precedent."

[25] *Ibid,* p vi.

[26] *The Law of the Constitution* was, for example, commended by Gladstone in the debates on the Home Rule Bill in 1885. See C. Harvie, "Ideology and Home Rule: James Bryce, A. V. Dicey and Ireland, 1880–1887" (1976) 91 *English Historical Review* 298.

[27] Collini, *op cit* n 17, p 58. *Cf* Sugarman, *op cit* n 8, p 54 who uses the term "conceptive ideologists" and who prefers it to Collini's "public moralists" on the ground that the idea that the role was peculiar to Victorian society is a claim that has yet to be demonstrated (personal communication with the author).

[28] See, especially, Dicey's extensive introduction to the eighth edition of *The Law of the Constitution* in 1915 in which he lamented the fact that over the previous 40 years "faith in parliamentary government had suffered an extraordinary decline" (p lvii), that the "ancient veneration of the rule of law has in England suffered ... a marked decline" (p xxxviii) and that the contemporary condition "greatly puzzles the now small body of surviving constitutionalists old enough to remember the sentiment of the mid-Victorian era, with its prevalent belief that to imitate the forms, or at any rate to adopt the spirit of the English constitution, was the best method whereby to confer upon the people of any civilised country the combined blessings of order and progress" (p xciii).

politics and governance rendered highly improbable the idea that the common law could any longer provide sensible solutions to the challenges of guiding, controlling and reviewing the exercise of governmental power.

As the impact of these changes slowly registered, a subtle change was effected in the style of public law discourse. The celebratory rhetoric in the texts began to disappear[29] and those working within the tradition fell back on the methodological aspect of the Diceyan inheritance. The niche which they sought in the academy may be illustrated by Paton's attempt in 1946 to classify studies concerning the State. There are, Paton suggested, three ways of concerning a theory of the State:

> "[W]e may examine the actual functioning of the State (as in political science), or the ideal of what a state ought to be (as in political philosophy), or the theoretical basis of the lawyer's approach to the State. The last method (the so-called juristic theory of the State) is not meant to present a complete picture of the actual workings of a state, but rather the theoretical conceptions around which the doctrines of the law are built."[30]

Public law was founded on a juristic theory of the State, formally distinct from political science and political philosophy, which concerned the structure of legal concepts relating to the workings of the state and which employed the method of legal analysis to lay bare that structure.

This attempt to repackage Dicey's construct as objective legal science seemed doomed from the outset. For Dicey, the analytical method was inextricably linked to – indeed, subordinate to – certain moral and political values which were reflected through the common law. The pretence of retaining the scientific method freed from those values would not wash. Dicey had packaged certain values and shared understandings of the Victorian authority structure as rules, a process most evident in his designation of particular understandings as "constitutional conventions". By formally separating these understandings from the political culture which sustained them, however, the constitutional lawyer was left only with a collection of habits to be enforced as though constituting a set of binding obligations. Being cut off from the sources needed to understand the processes of constitutional development, the analytical public lawyer was gradually pushed to the margins of social and political thought. Furthermore, with the suppression of those traditional values, the influence they exerted was more insidious: since these values were rarely identified and discussed explicitly, they tended to become absorbed as part of the ideology of the public lawyer.[31] And this process served only to confirm the conviction of many social

---

[29] Consider, *e.g.* the fourth edition of Keir and Lawson, published in 1954. The structure of the book was retained (and once again only three statutes were included). The paeans of praise to the common law had, however, been excised from their Preface.

[30] Paton, *A Textbook of Jurisprudence* (Clarendon, 1946) p 131.

[31] During the post-war period, the traditional values may most evidently be identified in the work of Sir William Wade. See, *e.g.* reviews of Wade, *Administrative Law* (Clarendon, 1961) by Griffith, 1962 *Cambridge Law Journal* 111, 113 ("I cannot say his creed. ... It seems to me that Professor Wade

scientists that, by inclination and training, lawyers were not merely conservatives but reactionaries.

By mid-century, the study of constitutional law was in a hopeless state. It could no longer be recommended as providing an acute insight into the genius of English culture and civilisation. Nor, since its analytical method was essentially a rhetorical device, could its discipline be recommended as providing rigorous intellectual training. And it had virtually nothing to offer either social scientists seeking an understanding of contemporary political phenomena or politicians trying to work strategically to realise their goals. It had been reduced in effect to a "meaningless collection of lifeless concepts".[32]

3. The Age of Science

During the post-war period the Diceyan approach had begun to strike an uncertain note, even amongst its most ardent adherents. It had, throughout the 20th century, been subjected to severe academic criticism.[33] It was not, however, until the establishment, during the 1960s, of new universities that the traditional approach was subjected to widespread challenge. The concern of the newly-founded law schools to project a self-consciously modern view revealed itself primarily in the attempt to re-connect public law to the concerns of political life. That the problem was widely recognised may be illustrated by W.J.M. Mackenzie's comment in the mid-1950s that "[i]n England so much of the practice of government is outside the law that lawyers hardly aspire nowadays (as did Bryce and Dicey and Anson) to teach realistically about public affairs".[34] Unless the new teachers were prepared to concede that their subject no longer had much to contribute to civic education, a substantial amount of rethinking was required.

One of earliest products of this movement was the publication in 1966 of Geoffrey Wilson's *Cases and Materials on Constitutional and Administrative Law.* This work was recognised as providing "a new departure in constitutional law"[35]

regards as descriptively accurate what in my view is traditional mythology.") and (in relation to the 5th ed) Loughlin, (1983) 46 *MLR* 666, 668 (criticises Wade's view that contemporary work adopts "a stance of fairly strict neutrality" and argues that it belongs "to the very era of self-satisfaction which Professor Wade believes is past"). It might be argued, however, that Wade simply articulates more clearly the values which underpin much of post-war public law writing.

[32] Geoffrey Wilson's evaluation of the fate of Roman legal scholarship at the hands of English scholars parallels this assessment of the impact of this tradition of public law: "English Roman law scholars and teachers gradually killed off the study of Roman law reducing it to a meaningless collection of lifeless concepts which had neither the systematic rigour of the Pandektists nor the classical scholars' understanding of it as an aspect of Roman civilisation nor the European historians' view of it as part of the foundations of the European legal tradition. Roman law was domesticated and Austinianised. By the beginning of the post-war period it was terminally ill." G Wilson, "English Legal Scholarship" (1987) 50 *MLR* 818, 830.

[33] See, *e.g.*, Jennings, *The Law and the Constitution* (London UP, 1933); Laski, *Studies in Law and Politics* (Allen & Unwin, 1932); Robson, *Justice and Administrative Law,* 3rd ed (Stevens, 1951).

[34] W. J. M. Mackenzie, "Political Theory and Political Education" (1955–56) 9 *Universities Quarterly* 351, 360.

[35] D. G. T. Williams (1966–67) 9 JSPTL 288.

primarily because "the constitution as a whole and the problems with which constitutional law has to deal have been ... taken as the focal point, rather than the courts and the concepts and rules used by them".[36] The book thus drew on a broad range of source material, including *Hansard*, official reports, biographies and newspaper articles in addition to statutes and cases, and, as if to underline the break with Keir and Lawson, no case was so much even mentioned until Chapter 4 of the book.[37] Wilson sought further to challenge "the frame of mind" which led to an exclusively "court-oriented approach" by ensuring that those cases which were included were set in their political and social contexts so as to emphasise the fact that "the way in which they are presented for decision in the courts [is] often only a small part of what is a much larger constitutional and social problem".[38] Here, then, is a text which symbolises the shift in public law scholarship that was pioneered in Warwick and at the new universities of the 1960s.

This new approach may be understood as marking an empirical turn in public law scholarship. In this form, attempts were made to re-forge a connection with the study of politics, which had emerged in the 20th century as a descriptive science engaged in a functional analysis of how government actually worked.[39] The new approach was marked by a shift in focus towards ends (outcomes) and away from means (processes); towards substance and away from form. How are decisions actually made in government, and what does this tell us about such constitutional doctrines as ministerial responsibility or Cabinet government? How do Parliamentary procedures operate in practice, and what questions might this pose for the idea of Parliamentary supremacy? To what extent can judicial decisions be seen to reflect their political or social class interests, and what implications might this have for the concept of the rule of law? Such questions became the meat and drink of many public law courses and, once adopted as teaching techniques, they tended also to compel academics to reorientate their work, not simply away from conceptual categories but also away from the general or universal and towards the particular and the local. Most of the innovative work in public law over the last 25 years has been of this type: that is, studies of how government works and of the roles which law can perform in regulating the conduct of government.[40]

---

[36] Wilson, *Cases and Materials on Constitutional and Administrative Law* (Cambridge UP, 1966), v.

[37] *Ibid*, p 76.

[38] *Ibid*, p vi–vii.

[39] This is, of course, greatly to simplify the evolution of political studies in the 20th century. See, *e.g.*, Crick, *In Defence of Politics* (Weidenfeld & Nicolson, 1962); Mackenzie, *Politics and Social Science* (Penguin, 1967); Johnson, *The Limits of Political Science* (Clarendon, 1989).

[40] There has been too much excellent work for me here to attempt to present an overview. We might note, however, that a significant amount of this work has been undertaken by scholars associated with Warwick, including: McAuslan, *Land, Law and Planning* (Weidenfeld & Nicolson, 1975); id, *The Ideologies of Planning Law* (Pergamon, 1980); Lustgarten, *Legal Control of Racial Discrimination* (Macmillan, 1980); id, *The Governance of Police* (Sweet & Maxwell, 1986); Hancher, *Regulating for Competition. Government, Law, and the Pharmaceutical Industry in the United Kingdom and France* (Clarendon, 1990); Snyder, *New Directions in European Community Law* (Weidenfeld & Nicolson, 1990) and the work of J.F. McEldowney on expenditure control: see McEldowney, "The National Audit Office and Privatisation" (1991) 54 *MLR* 933; id, "The Control of Public Expenditure" in Jowell & Oliver (eds) *The Changing Constitution*, 3rd ed (Clarendon, 1994) Chap 7.

But such work is not without its difficulties. Once the assumption of legal autonomy is questioned, scholarly work of this orientation, at some level or other, must not only explain the relationship between law and society but also must present an adequate characterisation of the idea of law. Wilson recognised as much when suggesting that the "study of constitutional law does not dissolve into a study of social facts by regarding them as relevant"[41], though it was perhaps predictable that such an acute commentator as de Smith should, in a generally positive review, observe that Wilson had made "no serious attempt ... to face up to the really difficult jurisprudential problems of British constitutional law".[42] Furthermore, notwithstanding Wilson's observation, it has often been the case that, in taking this empirical turn, public law scholars have too readily invoked mechanical metaphors to explain the law-society relationship and have tended to view law in essentially instrumental terms.

Empiricism in public law may be seen in its most extreme form in the work of J.A.G. Griffith. Starting from the assumptions that government is essentially about power, that legislators exist to promote particular interests and that it is only by stripping away the façade of constitutional doctrine that the true character of government might be revealed, Griffith contends that "law is not a moral concept", that "laws are merely statements of a power relationship and nothing more" and that "the constitution is no more and no less than what happens".[43] Though rarely expressed in such stark terms, Griffith's views are, in certain critical respects, shared by a number of eminent public lawyers, including Patrick McAuslan[44], Carol Harlow and Richard Rawlings.[45] The common pattern of their writing is that they challenge the myth that law is apolitical and seek to bring out the political dimensions of legal practice. In pursuing this line, they all tend to view the legal system as a power game in which competing interest groups vie for success. Furthermore, in that struggle, they treat law essentially as an instrument for realising particular political objectives.

Save in one important respect, the conception of law adopted by the empiricists is similar to that adopted by Lawrence Friedman. Friedman has argued that the legal system "works like a blind, insensate machine"[46] and that it may be likened to a rope in a tug of war in so far as it is simply the instrument through which the struggle between competing interests is expressed: "the game could not take place without the rope; it is the medium along which force moves" but the legal system "does not influence the outcome or the message".[47] Within British public law scholarship, the general theme of the empiricists has been

---

[41] Wilson, *op cit* n 36, p vii.

[41] S.A. de Smith, (1967) 30 *MLR* 349, 350.

[43] J.A.G. Griffith, "The Political Constitution" (1979) 42 *MLR* 1, 19.

[44] See, *e.g.*, P. McAuslan, *The Ideologies of Planning Law* (Oxford, 1980); id, "Administrative law, collective consumption and judicial policy" (1983) 46 *MLR* 1; id, "Public Law and Public Choice" (1988) 51 *MLR* 681.

[45] C. Harlow and R. Rawlings, *Law and Administration* (Weidenfeld & Nicolson, 1984); id, *Pressure Through Law* (Routledge, 1992).

[46] Friedman, *A History of American Law* (Simon & Shuster, 1973) 14.

[47] Friedman, *The Legal System: A Social Science Perspective* (Russell Sage, 1975) 156.

that, far from being a neutral medium, our legal system has in-built mechanisms which protect the status quo and subvert progressive social reforms.[48] Further, though retaining the game analogy, the empiricists have tended to replace Friedman's "rope" with a set of more fluid highway metaphors. Thus, in their text on administrative law, Harlow and Rawlings examine the tension between law as a control mechanism and law as a facilitator in terms of "red-light" and "green-light" theories[49] and, more recently, in a study of the way in which pressure groups use law as an instrument for achieving wider collective objectives, they articulate three models to explain how the judicial process may respond to these pressures: the drainpipe (restrictive); the freeway (accommodating); and the funnel (channelling).[50] In general, work in this vein has a tendency to treat law as an instrument for realising particular social objectives rather than as a cultural artefact which expresses the ways in which our tradition has been able to reconcile order with progress. Instead of studying legal concepts to obtain access to legal knowledge, this style of work generally regards concepts as tools to be employed by various actors to achieve certain political goals. Law is conceived as an instrument, the skills required by the lawyer to negotiate a way through the legal drainpipe, funnel or freeway are mechanistic skills, and the lawyer should be viewed essentially as a political fixer or social engineer.

The empiricist trend in public law scholarship since the 1960s has responded to Mackenzie's criticism that public lawyers no longer "teach realistically about public affairs"[51] essentially by bringing public law scholarship into alignment with the concerns of political science. In the process, however, not only has there been a tendency to imitate the empiricist methods of political science, but also to reduce the language of law to that of political science. In this respect they can be seen to be connecting with a radical, positivist tradition of British legal and political thought from which Dicey himself was but a highly selective borrower.[52]

---

[48] See, notoriously, Griffith, *The Politics of the Judiciary* (Fontana, 1977) in which, after challenging the "myth of neutrality" (pp 189–192), he states: "The judicial conception of the public interest, seen in the cases discussed in this book, is threefold. It concerns, first, the interests of the State (including its moral welfare) and the preservation of law and order, broadly interpreted; secondly, the protection of private property rights; and thirdly the promotion of certain political views normally associated with the Conservative party." (p 195). *Cf* C. Harlow, "Refurbishing the Judicial Service" in Harlow (ed), *Public Law and Politics* (Sweet & Maxwell, 1986) Chap 10 which argues that "the relative insulation of the English judiciary from the type of [empirical] research directed at other areas of the political process ... has obscured the basic similarity of political and judicial decision-making" and "that judges, like other actors in democratic society, must be representative of the community in which they function." (p 183).

[49] *Law and Administration, op cit* n 45, Chaps 1 and 2.

[50] *Pressure Through Law, op cit* n 45, Chap 7.

[51] *Op cit* n 34.

[52] I refer here to the philosophical radicalism pioneered by, amongst others, Bentham, the Mills and Austin. Bentham, an arch positivist, had sought to devise not simply a science of law but a more general science of legislation (or political science) based on a utilitarian balancing of interests. Though Dicey had followed Austin's idea of treating legal science as a discrete discipline based on a structure of rules, Austin had in fact largely followed Bentham's empiricist conception of law in determining the province of jurisprudence: law was the command of a sovereign identified by studying habitual patterns of obedience, which command imposed an obligation by the threat of a sanc

Though this empiricist movement provides an important and valuable corrective to a Diceyan construction based on the authority and autonomy of constitutional rules, it also raises certain problems. In treating law as a collection of myths which serve merely to block access to reality, the empiricists both fail to appreciate the function of myths and succeed only in replacing them with a new myth. In debunking such basic myths as those of neutrality and the rule of law, they seek to deprive law of the props which it needs in order to be able to function effectively. In seeking through demystification to obtain access to a "real" world, they fail to recognise that they have simply entered into a new world which is also socially constructed and which is likely to be built on premises which are just as contestable, irrational and mythical as the world which has been left behind.

4. The Age of Philosophy

From the mid-1980s, a number of public lawyers who were sensitive to the limitations of the Diceyan tradition but also were concerned at some of the implications of an empiricist orientation, sought to devise a more appropriate style of writing about public law. The primary concern of these writers was that the tendency of the empiricists to reduce law to an instrument of politics had grossly distorted the character of law. What this new style of writing shares is the need, in addressing the relationship between law and society, to start from an acceptance of the normative character of law. Constitutional law is generally, in a modern idiom, viewed as providing a foundation for the political order. The problem is that, given our peculiar history, we experience great difficulties in identifying the normative underpinning of the British polity. What these writers are seeking, then, is to find a way to reconstitutionalise the practices of government.

From this common starting point of seeking a juridical language in which to express the British tradition of constitutionalism, however, these writers take slightly different paths. In order to highlight these various pathways, I shall borrow Michael Walzer's idea that there are three general approaches to moral philosophy: the paths of discovery, invention and interpretation.[53] Walzer's framework is particularly helpful for this purpose because, as I shall argue, what this style of writing also has in common is the tendency to treat law as a branch of moral philosophy.

---

tion. Though Austin constructed his science of law as a structure of "rules" imposing "obligations", this normative terminology was used simply as a shorthand. The reality of law concerned commands (imperatives), habits of obedience (descriptive) and threats of sanctions (prudential) and law, for Austin, thus expressed the observable outcomes of conflicts between social interests. From this movement Dicey and his followers drew the idea that, if law is to be viewed as command, or the "infliction of an evil", there ought to be as little of it as was compatible with the preservation of the social order; whereas the empiricists drew on philosophical radicalism for their realist account of the character of law.

[53] Walzer, *Interpretation and Social Criticism* (Harvard UP, 1987) Chap 1.

The path of discovery

The path of discovery requires someone to "climb the mountain, go into the desert, seek out the God-who-reveals, and bring back his word."[54] The exercise is analogous to that of discovering a new continent, with the scholar being cast in the role of the explorer who brings back the first map of its contours. The scholar-as-discoverer must "wrench ... himself loose from his parochial interests and loyalties ... abandon ... his own point of view and look ... at the world ... from 'no particular point of view' ".[55] On the face of things, it seems an implausible role for any public lawyer to perform. But in the role of discoverer, I propose to cast Paul Craig who, in *Public Law and Democracy in the United Kingdom and the United States of America*, seeks "to establish a normative theory for the role of public law in a democratic society".[56]

Recognising that we can no longer assess the soundness of our system of public law simply by reference to such traditional canons as consistency and coherence, Craig suggests that our criteria of evaluation must include two broader ideas of "fit". First, we should consider public law in relation to the question of how the state actually functions, and thus assess the degree of fit between public law and the analyses produced by political science. Secondly, the conceptual framework of public law might be measured against the ideals which society espouses, and here we might assess the relationships between the norms implicit in public law and the value frameworks of certain political philosophies. After concluding that Dicey's theory is "inaccurate in descriptive terms" and has "prescriptive foundations [which] are questionable"[57], the book seeks to draw together some of the strands between public law, political science and political philosophy which, under the influence of positivism, have become severed from one another. That this exercise should be understood as a journey of discovery may be appreciated only once the comparative dimension is brought into the frame.

Public Law and Democracy in effect comprises four essays: an examination of work in political science on the character of American democracy and an assessment of its implications for thinking about US constitutional and administrative law[58]; a similar exercise undertaken in relation to the United Kingdom[59]; a critical examination of recent work in American political philosophy on liberalism[60]; and, finally, an explanation of the themes of civic republicanism and participatory democracy within recent American political theory and an assessment of their significance for public law thought.[61] Craig in fact draws his inspiration entirely from the United States. Though he seeks to justify this sim-

[54] *Ibid*, p 4.
[55] *Ibid*, p 5.
[56] (Clarendon Press, 1990). The quotation is taken from the book's blurb.
[57] *Ibid*, p 243.
[58] *Ibid*, Chaps 3 and 4.
[59] *Ibid*, Chaps 2, 5, 6 and 7.
[60] *Ibid*, Chaps 8 and 9.
[61] *Ibid*, Chaps 10 and 11.

ply on the ground that the United States "has a rich and sophisticated corpus of constitutional jurisprudence"[62], I believe that his work is best understood as a voyage of discovery.[63] If only we immerse ourselves in the sophisticated ways of American scholarship, the way ahead will be revealed.

Once viewed as an exercise in discovery, we may begin to make sense of the book's method. For although he analyses a broad range of writing, other than for his criticism of Dicey, Craig does not at any stage present his own views on those subjects. Notwithstanding the apparent objective of establishing a normative theory, there is neither an overarching set of critical principles nor any general conclusions. Though Craig argues that "it *is* a thesis of this book that some choice [between political theories] must be made" and that "[a]gnosticism is not possible"[64], we are left with the lingering impression that Craig is a committed agnostic. And this seems to make sense only if we presuppose the possibility of an objective analysis which lays bare the facts of the matter and leaves it to the reader to "discover" the appropriate way forward. This, however, is much too close to Dicey's analytical method to be comfortable. Craig seems in effect to be turning Dicey's method back on itself and in that sense he does so convincingly. But when he seeks to use the method reconstructively, problems arise. As we may see from Paton's schema[65], it was through an application of the analytical method that categorial distinctions came to be drawn between public law, political science and political philosophy. In seeking to build bridges – and to re-connect political science to public law and public law to political philosophy – Craig tries to utilise precisely the method which caused the problems in the first place.

In *Public Law and Democracy* Craig seeks to discover a new world of public law in American legal scholarship. He does so by utilising an analytical method which surveys the scene from "no particular point of view"[66] and seeks simply to "reveal" the way forward. That it cannot be done is borne out by the book's lack of conclusions. Though containing many skilfully executed analyses of contemporary public law themes, the book is unable significantly to advance the exercise of constructing a normative theory of public law. It is hardly surprising that one political scientist viewed the book as constituting "purposeless trespassing" in political studies and as signifying "a loss of faith in legal studies".[67]

The path of invention

Those who go down the path of invention generally begin with methodology, "a design of a design procedure" which is expected will eventuate in agreement.[68]

---

[62] *Op cit* n 56, p 10.
[63] These doubts are examined in detail in: M. Loughlin, "The Importance of Elsewhere" (1993) 4 *Public Law Review* 44.
[64] *Op cit* n 56, p 8 (emphasis in original).
[65] *Op cit* n 30.
[66] Walzer, *op cit* n 53.
[67] B. O'Leary, "What Should Public Lawyers Do?" (1992) 12 *OJLS* 404 at 405. For Craig's reply (which, rather ironically, focuses on the deficiencies of legal positivism), see: (1992) 23 *OJLS* 564.
[68] Walzer, *op cit* n 53, p 10.

The objective is to discover deeper laws of social interaction through which differences can be transcended. Within political theory examples of such work include such counterfactual techniques as Rawls' original position[69] or Habermas' ideal speech situation.[70] Of recent public law scholarship in a similar vein we might take note of Tony Prosser's attempts to project a view of public law in the light of Habermas.[71] But the most elaborate exercise in invention is to be found in the work of Ian Harden and Norman Lewis, who in *The Noble Lie* engage with a broad range of theoretical and practical matters concerning modern government.[72]

At a practical level, *The Noble Lie* examines the fragmented, informal, pragmatic and secretive nature of British government and explores the possibility of utilising American experience to reshape our arrangements into an open, integrated, principled and formal system. At the theoretical level it seeks to provide "a new descriptive and analytical model of constitutionally legitimate action in Britain".[73] The authors seek to achieve this by reworking the notion of the rule of law, showing it to be a "transcendent concept" and establishing it as a "master ideal", and then to show how "the gap between the master ideals and current political and constitutional practice can be bridged".[74] This reconciliation is to be achieved by exposing "a number of contradictions involved in the various strands of traditional constitutional theory" so as to demonstrate that "the claim to be a nation living under law cannot be rationally sustained" and then to outline a "programme of institution-building for the construction of rational discourse, for the construction of constitutional openness and accountability".[75]

That this exercise belongs to the path of invention is partially disguised by the fact that Harden and Lewis, in seeking to realise these ambitious objectives, invoke the method of "immanent critique"; a method which entails that of confronting "the existent, in its historical context, with the claim of its conceptual principles, in order to criticise the relation between the two and thus transcend them".[76] However, this method is not used at all rigorously.[77] The book is in fact short on historical analysis and long on grand claims. Take, for example, their treatment of Dicey. Though they declare that Dicey's "positivistic" version of the rule of law "has tended to highjack or colonize our larger constitution" and has been "instrumental in divorcing legal analysis from constitutional fundamen-

[69] Rawls, *A Theory of Justice* (Oxford UP, 1972) Chap III.

[70] J. Habermas, "Historical Materialism and the Development of Normative Structures" in Habermas, *Communication and the Evolution of Society* (Beacon Press, 1979) 116.

[71] See T. Prosser, "Towards a Critical Public Law" (1982) 9 *British Journal of Law & Society* 1; id, "Democratisation, Accountability and Institutional Design" in McAuslan and McEldowney (eds) *Law, Legitimacy and the Constitution* (Sweet & Maxwell, 1985) Chap 8. For a critical assessment of the use made of Habermas by academic lawyers see: W.T. Murphy, "The Habermas Effect: Critical Theory and Academic Law" 1989 *Current Legal Problems* 135.

[72] *The Noble Lie. The British Constitution and the Rule of Law* (Hutchinson, 1986).

[73] *Ibid*, p 7.

[74] *Ibid*, p 13.

[75] *Ibid*, pp 9, 11 and 13.

[76] *Ibid*, p 10; quoting Horkheimer, *The Eclipse of Reason* (Seabury Press, 1974) 182.

[77] For critical analysis see: M. Loughlin, "Tinkering with the Constitution" (1988) 51 *MLR* 531. See also, I. Harden and N. Lewis, "*The Noble Lie*: A Rejoinder" (1988) 51 *MLR* 812.

tals"[78] Harden and Lewis do not examine Dicey's views in any detail and thus are unable to capture the ambiguities and tensions within his work. Without this type of analysis, however, it is difficult to see how the immanent character of the rule of law could be identified. Instead, it is asserted that "there are immanent expectations of a system of open and accountable government which run deep in the British people and ... the rhetoric and claims made for our system of government foster such expectations"[79] or that the courts have "failed to respond in any principled fashion to the increase in the number and scale of governmental functions", largely because they "lack ... a clear understanding of the nature and purposes of judicial review" and "their role in the constitutional order of things".[80]

When we turn from analysis to prescription things become clearer. Harden and Lewis's hopes for public law are not at all immanent; they are transcendental. Their objective is to promote a rational political morality based on "a theory of 'an ideal constitution' "[81] in which "the law will need to partake of the flavour of a surrogate political process, not for engaging and arbitrating the claims of competing social values, but for assuming the larger constitutional values inherent in the rule of law to promote rational civic discourse".[82] And how is this to be achieved? The answer, quite simply, is by a range of reforms drawn from the United States, including freedom of information legislation, open access to all meetings of public bodies, formalised decision-making procedures of public bodies, the adoption by the courts of a hard look doctrine, and the establishment of a Standing Administrative Conference. Whether or not these reforms would improve our system of government is both open to debate and beside the point. The critical question is: how can we understand this package, drawn from different cultural and political traditions[83] and from a constitutional order based on federalism, the separation of powers and a tradition of judicial review, to form an immanent dimension of a system of parliamentary government rooted in the idea of sovereignty? Harden and Lewis's answer – that "[l]ight can be shed on some of these immanent expectations by examination of American constitutionalism ... because some of the British, dissatisfied by official lies, however noble, took the seeds of the rule of law and sowed them in the New World"[84] – is unlikely to convince those who find value in the methods of immanence. In the words of one political theorist of immanence:

> "The common law rights and duties of Englishmen were transplanted throughout the civilised world. ... In this process some of their flexibility was lost; the rights and duties were exported; the genius that made them remained at home. Peoples,

[78] Harden and Lewis, *op cit* n 72, p 52.
[79] *Ibid*, p 11.
[80] *Ibid*, pp 212–3, 202–3.
[81] *Ibid*, p 205.
[82] *Ibid*, p 263.
[83] See, *e.g.*, Hartz, *The Liberal Tradition in America* (Harcourt, Brace & World, 1955); Shafer (ed), *Is America Different?* (Clarendon, 1991).
[84] Harden and Lewis, *op cit* n 77, p 815.

> desirous of freedom, but dissatisfied with anything less than the imagination of an eternal and immutable law, gave to these rights the false title of Nature. Because they were not the fruit of their own experience, it was forgotten that they were the fruit of the experience of the British people. ... What went abroad as the concrete rights of an Englishman have returned home as the abstract Rights of Man, and they have returned to confound our politics and corrupt our minds."[85]

The Noble Lie is best understood as an exercise in invention. Harden and Lewis believe that "a vision of the Good Society is essential for social science" and that "such a vision can only be grounded ... through transcendental rationalism".[86] They are seeking to invent a political morality to "provide what God and nature do not provide, a universal corrective for all the different social moralities."[87] Though wishing to bring "an end to orthodox fairy tales"[88], they do so essentially by replacing the old tales with some new myths. Many will have good political reasons for embracing these new myths (this noble lie?). But we should not be distracted by the theoretical superstructure and fail to recognise the exercise as a political programme dressed in legal-constitutionalist garb.

The path of interpretation?

One basic problem with the path of invention is that it remains unclear why particular people situated in a specific culture should adopt that road. We might readily embrace Rawls' principles of justice behind the veil of ignorance but why should these newly invented principles "govern the lives of people who already share a moral culture and speak a natural language"?[89] Walzer argues that we must start from where we are. We do not discover the road because we have always lived there. We do not invent it, because it already exists:

> "No design procedure has governed its design ... It is also very dense: the moral world has a lived-in quality, like a home occupied by a single family over many generations, with unplanned additions here and there, and all the available space filled with memory-laden objects and artifacts. The whole thing, taken as a whole, lends itself less to abstract modelling than to thick description. Moral argument in such a setting is interpretative in character ... "[90]

What, then, of the path of interpretation in public law scholarship? During the last 20 years a significant amount of work of an interpretative nature has been

---

[85] M. Oakeshott, "Contemporary British Politics" (1947–8) 1 *Cambridge Journal* 474, 489–90.
[86] Harden and Lewis, *op cit* n 77, p 816.
[87] Walzer, *op cit* n 53, p 13.
[88] I. Harden and N. Lewis, "Sir Douglas Wass and the Constitution: An End to Orthodox Fairy Tales?" (1984) 35 NILQ 213.
[89] Walzer, *op cit* n 53, p 14.
[90] *Ibid*, p 20. Walzer here seems to be echoing both Wittgenstein and Geertz: "Our language can be seen as an old city: a maze of little streets and squares, of old and new houses, and of houses with additions from various periods; and this surrounded by a multitude of modern sections with straight regular streets and uniform houses." (Wittgenstein, *Philosophical Investigations* (Blackwell, G.E.M. Anscombe trans, 1953) 8. See also, Geertz, *The Interpretation of Cultures* (Basic Books, 1973) Chap 1.

produced in public law, much of it being influenced by the jurisprudence of Ronald Dworkin.[91] Work in this vein has been elaborated in public law most explicitly by Jeffrey Jowell and Anthony Lester[92], but the most systematic account of the character of our constitutional traditions in this light is to be found in a recent book by T.R.S. Allan.[93]

In *Law, Liberty and Justice* Allan takes up the familiar refrain that our traditions of constitutional law have become stultified largely as a result of a failure to look beneath the surface of some questionable dogma in the works of such writers as Blackstone and Dicey. His ostensible objective is to rework Dicey's ideas in order to re-establish a sense of balance between Dicey's key principles of parliamentary sovereignty and the rule of law and thereby to reach "the core of good sense"[94] in his writing, free from the distortions resulting from an adherence to Austinian legal positivism. Allan does so by resuscitating the doctrine of the rule of law, explicating its values, revealing these to be the values which are embedded in the common law and arguing that these values and that concept "serves in Britain as a form of constitution".[95] Drawing primarily on the work of Dworkin, Fuller and Hayek, Allan then seeks to re-interpret our traditions and to reveal "the legal foundations of constitutionalism" underpinning British political institutions.

Law, Liberty and Justice is an important and skilfully crafted treatise. But does it provide a faithful interpretation of the British constitutional tradition? My own view is that, in seeking to "re-interpret" Dicey so as to assert the primacy of the rule of law over the principle of sovereignty, Allan is in actuality re-inventing Dicey and, in the process, turning that tradition on its head. "Can it be supposed", Allan asks, "that Parliament has authority to legislate for purposes inimical to the peace, welfare, and good government of the United Kingdom?"[96] The answer, if the recent experience of the poll tax is anything to go by, must be given resoundingly in the affirmative.[97] The citizen, Allan asserts, "is entitled to assume that fundamental principles of law will not be altered lightly or obscurely".[98] But the beauty of this statement lies in its consummate obscurity and the fact that we may all agree on a principle which can never be precisely defined.[99] And in

---

[91] Dworkin, *Taking Rights Seriously* (Mass: Harvard UP, 1977), id, *A Matter of Principle* (Mass: Harvard UP, 1985), id, *Law's Empire* (Fontana, 1986).

[92] J. Jowell and A. Lester, "Beyond *Wednesbury*: substantive principles of administrative law" 1987 *Public Law* 368; id, "Proportionality: neither novel nor dangerous" in Jowell and Oliver (eds), *New Directions in Judicial Review* (Sweet & Maxwell, 1988); J. Jowell, "Courts and Administration in Britain: Standards, Principles and Rights" (1988) *Israel Law Review* 409.

[93] Allan, *Law, Liberty and Justice. The Legal Foundations of British Constitutionalism* (Clarendon, 1993).

[94] *Ibid*, p 1.

[95] *Ibid*, p 4.

[96] *Ibid*, p 76.

[97] See, *e.g.* N. Walker and C.M.G. Himsworth, "Poll Tax and Fundamental Law" (1991) *Juridical Review* 45. Allan might argue that the subsequent repeal of the legislation should be taken to indicate a lack of authority, but this would be to use the idea of "authority" in a much broader sense than the general thrust of his work suggests.

[98] Allan, *op cit* n 93, p 91.

[99] This technique is well-rooted in British constitutional discourse. See, *e.g.*, Hill, *The Century of Revolution 1603–1714* (Abacus, 1978) 65: "In 1641 Strafford was impeached, among other charges, for

viewing the common law as a distillation of a coherent set of principles whose force is "directly dependent on the dictates of reason"[100], Allan gives a rationalist reading of common law which turns the anti-rationalist tradition of the "artificial reason" of the common law entirely on its head.

These illustrations could be multiplied. The general point, however, is that this liberal interpretative theory of public law is not in fact an exercise in retrieving the meanings of our culture of public law but a further attempt, in Walzer's words, "to walk out of the cave, climb the mountain, [and] fashion for oneself ... an objective standpoint".[101] Allan's study is not an exercise in interpretation but, like Harden and Lewis' work, a disguised form of invention. At the core of Allan's argument lies a conception of law established *a priori* which provides the organising principle for a normative theory of public law. Allan thus argues that law must be understood as a structure of "'rules of just conduct', which regulate the ordinary relations between citizens, and which are independent of any particular purpose or policy".[102] Only once this conception is set in place, is he able to argue that law is categorially distinct from policy, that policy matters are for the executive or legislature while questions of right and principle are the province of the courts, and then to assert the primacy of common law over statute.[103] This entire framework, which Allan suggests "is fundamental to an understanding of modern public law"[104], is constructed on sets of self-sustaining equations. At one level we see this in the formulation: principles are foundational to law because law is rational and that rationality is revealed through the elaboration of principle. But more fundamentally it is rooted in the idea that law essentially is an expression of freedom. We are free when we act in accordance with reason; and this reason, which is revealed by principle, is constitutive of our essential nature. The more basic set of equations thus runs as follows: the legal is the rational, the rational is the free, the free is the natural, the natural is the legal.[105]

This conception of law is one which seems far removed from our own political and legal traditions. In postulating a view of the common law as being founded in Reason accessible to the individual, Allan in effect seeks to trans-

---

subverting the fundamental laws of the kingdom. The Commons were just about to vote the charge when the witty and malicious Edmund Waller rose, and with seeming innocence, asked what the fundamental laws of the kingdom were. There was an uneasy silence. No-one dared to attempt a definition which would certainly have divided a heterogeneous majority ... . The situation was saved by a lawyer who leapt to his feet to say that if Mr Waller did not know what the fundamental laws of the kingdom were, he had no business to be sitting in the House."

[100] Allan, *op cit* n 93, p 30.

[101] Walzer, *Spheres of Justice. A Defence of Pluralism and Equality* (Blackwell, 1983) xiv.

[102] Allan, *op cit* n 93, p 5.

[103] This primacy is asserted because: "legislation obtains its force from the doctrine of parliamentary sovereignty, which is itself a creature of the common law"; "statute is always necessarily subject to judicial interpretation"; "statute is necessarily more piecemeal and technical"; and it cannot "displace the common law by providing a rival vision of the constitutional order", especially since "the criteria of interpretation can hardly be supplied wholly by statute" (Allan, *ibid*, pp 10–11).

[104] Allan, *ibid*, p 6.

[105] *Cf* Hawthorn, *Enlightenment and Despair*, 2nd ed (Cambridge UP, 1987) 27.

form our system from a Catholic one based on the authority of the priesthood to a radical Protestant one "in which it is up to each member of the faith community who feels touched by God's saving grace to decide what the Word actually requires".[106] It is an interesting theory and one which, given contemporary circumstances, is deserving of serious consideration. But it is not "a practical philosophy grounded in existing constitutional tradition".[107] Allan here is seeking, rather in the manner of Harden and Lewis with their invocation of "immanent critique", to bolster a particular political theory with the authority of tradition and history. The technique is hardly novel; the Whig constitutional historians used a similar device in appealing to the myth of the ancient constitution.[108] But it is important also to recognise that these techniques simply exemplify the ability of human beings, while constructing the pathways on which they travel, to demonstrate in the course of building them that these paths were there all the while.[109]

5. The Age of Scepticism?

If the empiricists have tried to find answers to the problems of public law in political science, the rationalisers have sought solutions in political philosophy. The empiricists wish to strip away the myths of law to reveal a real world of pure fact, but have simply stumbled across a new world of social construction. The discoverers and inventors have tried to escape from the practical problems of law by finding some external, rational and universal measure of law and in the process have forgotten that law is pragmatic and not philosophical, is a political rather than a propositional discourse, and is a local, cultural practice rather than a universal system which works itself pure.[110] There can be no escape either in science or in philosophy. "Scientific" studies of political behaviour or normative theories of justice, democracy or liberty provide no substitute for a genuinely interpretative exercise of seeking to understand public law. And for

---

[106] Levinson, *Constitutional Faith* (Princeton UP, 1988) 25–26. See Allan, *op cit* n 93, pp 15–16. See also Dworkin, *Law's Empire, op cit* n 91 p 413: "Law's empire is defined by attitude, not territory or power or process. ... It is a protestant attitude that makes each citizen responsible for imagining what his society's commitments to principle are, and what these commitments require in new circumstances."

[107] Allan, *op cit* n 93, p 22. This attitude is, however, one which is often expressed by academics. See, *e.g.*, Stallybrass, *op cit* n 24, p 164: "[Y]ou cannot be a good lawyer unless you have a respect for property, life and order. Unless you have respect for these things you cannot possibly be entrusted to uphold our most precious British possession of freedom ... ".

[108] Consider, *e.g.*, Freeman, *op cit* n 3, who argued that the great constitutional documents – Magna Carta, the Petition of Right, the Bill of Rights – did not enact anything new: "All claimed to set forth ... those rights of Englishmen which were already old. In all our great political struggles the voice of the Englishmen has never called for the assertion of new principles, for the enactment of new laws; the cry has always been for the better observance of the laws which were already in force, for the redress of grievances which had arisen from their corruption or neglect." (p 57).

[109] See Fish, *There's No Such Thing as Free Speech and it's a Good Thing, Too* (Oxford UP, 1994) 156.

[110] See Fish, *ibid*, p 193. For the most recent illustration of the theme of purity see Dworkin, *Law's Empire, op cit* n 91, pp 400–407.

this it is essential that we "stand in the cave, in the city, on the ground" and engage in critical examination of the practice from principles which are internal to the practice.[111] The future, I hope, should belong to the sceptics.

The starting point for making genuine progress with this more sceptical approach to public law must be the manner in which studies of the State have been constructed and divided into the categories of public law, political science and political philosophy.[112] We might begin by recognising that advances in understanding may be achieved only by challenging the distortions which arise as a result of the formalism of that classificatory scheme. This challenge has mainly been posed by a hermeneutic approach to the human sciences, an approach based on the idea that explanation of human action must include an attempt to interpret the meaning of action from the point of view of those engaged in those actions. In accordance with this approach, the model we turn to for understanding is neither causation (the scientific model) nor logic (the formal philosophical model) but that of interpretation. This interpretative approach has in recent years been employed across the field of academic study, including the natural sciences[113], philosophy[114], history[115], anthropology[116], and political theory.[117]

The most relevant parallels for public law are to be found in developments in political theory. This new style of political theory differs from political philosophy in "being less formal and atomistic, less concerned to establish logical relationships between individual political concepts" and it "does not ... restrict itself to ... questions about the definition and use of the central terms of political argument".[118] What, in effect, recent political theory is doing is challenging the formal distinction between science and philosophy in the field of political studies. Here was a development that was potentially of great value to those public lawyers who were uncomfortable with the strictures of legal positivism and were not convinced by the claims of positivist social science or of analytical philosophy. Could the methods of post-empiricist political theory be used to address questions concerning public law?

In taking up this challenge, we might begin by rejecting an assumption,

[111] See Walzer, *op cit* n 101, p xiv; id, *op cit* n 53, p 21.

[112] See Paton, *op cit* n 30.

[113] Kuhn, *The Structure of Scientific Revolutions,* 2nd ed (Univ. of Chicago Press, 1970); more radically Feyerabend, *Against Method* (London, 1975).

[114] Quine, *From A Logical Point of View,* 2nd ed (Harvard UP 1961) 20–46 (criticising the empiricist argument that there is a categorial distinction between concepts and facts); Wittgenstein, *op cit* n 90 (the meaning of a statement is a function of its use); Rorty, *Philosophy and the Mirror of Nature* (Princeton UP, 1979) esp. Chap VII ("From Epistemology to Hermeneutics").

[115] Q. Skinner, "Meaning and understanding in the history of ideas" in Tully (ed) *Meaning and Context. Quentin Skinner and his Critics* (Polity, 1988) Chap 2.

[116] C. Geertz, *op cit* n 90; id, *Local Knowledge. Further Essays in Interpretive Anthropology* (Basic Books, 1983).

[117] Taylor, *Philosophical Papers. Vol. 2, Philosophy and the Human Sciences* (Cambridge UP, 1985) esp. Chap 1 ("Interpretation and the Sciences of Man"); MacIntyre, *After Virtue. A Study in Moral Theory,* 2nd ed (Duckworth, 1985).

[118] Miller and Siedentop (eds), *The Nature of Political Theory* (Clarendon Press, 1983) 1.

which is built in to the foundations of most forms of legal study, that public law constitutes an autonomous and objective field in which concepts acquire meaning through the application of some distinctively legal method. Concepts should not be viewed as forming discrete items of knowledge and neither should they be treated simply as myths which obstruct direct access to reality. Rather, they might be seen as tools which are used for particular purposes. The most obvious purposes for which concepts in public law are likely to be utilised are to realise certain political goals. From this perspective, then, public law might be viewed as a form of political discourse. Actors (lawyers, judges, politicians, scholars) use the concepts of public law (sovereignty, the rule of law, rights, natural justice, jurisdiction, proportionality etc.) to assist them in the realisation of their political goals. The language of public law is neither the language of essences nor simply the language of mythology; it is a fluid language which may be creatively employed by political actors in the light of their concerns.[119]

This type of interpretative approach seeks to open up the subject of re-connecting public law to the world of politics and governance. This form of contextualism is, however, more intricate, and also more ambiguous, than both the empiricist version rooted in a search for causal relations and the efforts of the inventors to find some formula which will unlock the mysteries of the subject. It differs from the liberal interpretative methods of Dworkin and Allan by adopting a "pluralising" rather than "singularising" hermeneutics.[120] Rather than seeking the one correct reading, it traces the various meanings within the texts and, through the exercise of relating language to experience and being attentive to the instabilities of meanings, seeks understanding by relating parts to the whole and vice versa in what might be called a "fusion of horizons".[121] It is thus an approach which might readily lend itself to a historical treatment of the subject since, by such study, we might begin to identify the way in which concepts change their meaning in the light of particular concerns and determine how the boundaries of the subject have been adjusted over time.

This type of approach might be labelled a sceptical method. Its primary objective is to bring to consciousness the value assumptions on which practices are built and it incorporates an evaluative dimension only insofar as it examines those assumptions and practices against such critical canons of rationality as consistency, coherence and contradiction. Even here there is a danger of going too far in imposing an inappropriate rationality on both the constitution and law. As Maitland noted, "the more we study our constitution whether in the present or the past, the less do we find it conform to any such plan as a philo-

---

[119] For an attempt to draw out some of these implications see: Loughlin, *Public Law and Political Theory* (Clarendon, 1992). Those interested in examining the (rather mixed) reactions of the empiricists, discoverers and inventors should see: C. Harlow, "Changing the Mindset: The Place of Theory in English Administrative Law" (1994) 14 *OJLS* 418; P.P. Craig (1993) 13 *Legal Studies* 275; T. Prosser, "Journey without maps" (1993) *Public Law* 346; and T.R.S. Allan (1993) 109 *LQR* 495.
[120] Marquard, *Farewell to Matters of Principle. Philosophical Studies* (Oxford UP, 1989) 120–124.
[121] Gadamer, *Truth and Method.* 2nd rev. ed (Sheed & Ward, 1989) 302–7, 576–7.

sopher might invent in his study".[122] Further, law does not work because it is grounded in God's truth, or a natural order, or an overarching set of rational principles, or through some logical calculus. Law is anti-foundational and functions "by deploying a set of ramshackle and heterogeneous resources in an effort to reach political resolutions of disputes that must be framed (this is the law's requirements and the public's desire) in apolitical and abstract terms (fairness, equality, what justice requires)".[123] And what is especially remarkable is that, as Stanley Fish puts it, "[n]ot only does the law forge its identity out of the stuff it disdains, it does so in public".[124] Law is distinctive essentially because it has a distinctive social function to perform. The ultimate test of law is that which is satisfactory in experience; law's truth is simply the truth that we can live by.

A further facet of this sceptical method is that it is, in a specific sense, anti-theoretical. That is, unlike the methods of the rationalists, this approach does not seek to use theory to yield new rational principles which point the way forward. My own view is that we have no need for new principles. There are already too many principles in the world and such principles do not provide answers to our problems, for the rather obvious reason that, since politics are the source of principle, we cannot avoid politics by appeal to principle. Furthermore, any normative theory of public law which we might devise would be unlikely to tell us much about the extant structure of public law and would, in all essentials, be indistinguishable from a political theory. Since public lawyers already have enough problems to grapple with, and since there is already enough moralising about the subject, why complicate matters further by invoking theory as an instrument of preaching?

Ultimately, all we have in public law is a set of shared understandings which go to make up our constitutional tradition and which come to be reflected in institutions, in texts, and in particular ceremonies and rituals. Common possession does not, however, imply agreement. In Walzer's words: "There is a tradition, a body of ... knowledge; and there is the group of sages, arguing. There isn't anything else. No discovery or invention can end the argument; no 'proof' takes precedence over the (temporary) majority of sages."[125] At this point, some will almost certainly invoke the spectre of relativism.[126] This issue needs to be addressed directly; not relativism which simply exists as part of the world but the fear of it which seems largely an exercise in shroud-waving. Because of this, it seems more sensible to challenge anti-relativism than to defend the view it

---

[122] Maitland, *The Constitutional History of England* (Cambridge UP, 1908) 197.

[123] S Fish, *op cit* n 109, p 209.

[124] *Ibid*, p 156. It might be noted that it is precisely because of law's anti-foundational character that I suggested that those in search of theory should seek a self-referential theory of law: Loughlin, *op cit* n 119, pp 250–260.

[125] Walzer, *op cit* n 53, p 32.

[126] See, *e.g.*, Harden and Lewis, *op cit* n 75, p 814: "[C]onstitutional lawyers can and should seek to identify the constitutional changes necessary to uphold the rule of law values ... not as an optional 'political' commitment, but as an essential aspect of their job. ... [F]or anyone who does not espouse relativism, 'the constitution' cannot be just whatever one wants it to be."

claims to be counter to.[127] "It was not relativism", Geertz points out, "that did in absolute motion, Euclidean space, and universal causation. It was wayward phenomena, wave packets and orbital leaps, before which they were helpless."[128] Nor was it relativism which has put paid to (insofar as it has) the Whig view of history, the Diceyan schema and the claim to have found objective, rational legal principles. It has been odd actualities – the socialisation of life, the pervasiveness of governance, the uncertain status of the states in a global economy, the changing social basis of modern politics – which have embarrassed their categories.[129] In the light of these developments, all claims to defeat relativism by placing law beyond culture and politics seem only to be fanciful.

The sceptical method which I am advocating may thus be viewed as an anti-foundational, anti-theoretical and anti anti-relativist method. And it is this positive method which I believe holds the best hope for the continuation of scholarly inquiries in public law.

6. The Pathways of the Scholar

It is a basic precept of hermeneutics that we might best understand something by seeking to understand it as an answer to some question. In order to highlight the objectives of this essay, then, I should return to the questions raised in the introduction. Academic writing on public law has, over the last 25 years or so, not only flourished but also adopted innovative approaches. For some, these developments might be viewed simply as an emblem of the times; a reflection of the need today for each academic lawyer to fashion a distinctive market niche. It seems to me, however, that innovation has stemmed primarily from the fact that our basic legal cultural orientations – those underpinning the Diceyan framework – are incapable any longer of providing us with adequate images of the world in which we live. Certainty inhibits exploration. Innovation in public law scholarship has mainly been a response to uncertainty and disorientation; it is a product of the attempt to continue work in public law without those certainties which gave birth to the subject.

But have new methods been devised which are able, not only to frame a suitable characterisation of the relationship between law and society, but also to formulate an adequate conception of the legal? What I have tried to show is that innovative writing has tended to follow one of two main paths – those of science and philosophy – and that each of these routes has tended to distort our experience. The scientific path has been taken primarily by those seeking to reconnect public law to the conduct of public life. In the process of portraying a more realistic image of law, however, these writers have often been seduced by the claims of political science, and have tended both to present law

[127] See C. Geertz, "Anti Anti-Relativism" (1984) 86 *American Anthropologist* 263.
[128] *Ibid*, p 275.
[129] *Cf* Geertz, *ibid.*

essentially in instrumental terms and to adopt an overly mechanical view of the law-society relationship. By contrast, those taking the route of philosophy, have repackaged law as an affair of reason, have invented a set of "constitutional fundamentals" or "fundamental principles of law" and have sought to re-order the world accordingly.

The former tends to eliminate the normative and reduce law to fact, whereas the latter asserts the primacy and purity of the normative sphere. While the idea of the constitution seems to disappear in the scientific account ("the constitution is ... what happens"), the philosophers claim to have uncovered the true principles on which the constitution is founded. Neither track seems adequate. We cannot eliminate the normative dimension from law without eliminating law altogether. But we should not assume that the normative discourse of law is philosophical rather than rhetorical and pragmatic. Legal method is governed neither by the laws of causation nor by the principles of logic; it is a creative process involving the deployment of a set of resources to negotiate differences in a manner which is capable of being framed in abstract and apolitical terms. Public law must be rooted in its political environment, but law shapes its identity by selecting from that environment and, far from working itself pure, it is the persistence of inconsistency that enables law to work. Only by accepting (*contra* the scientists) that law has a distinctive identity which is rooted in its unique social function and (*contra* the philosophers) that it is an uncertain, self-referential discourse will we be able to advance scholarly work in public law.

It is tempting to conclude the essay at this point. There is, however, one final question which has not yet been directly addressed and which is a source (albeit unacknowledged) of some of the disagreements amongst public lawyers. What should public lawyers do? This question is directed not so much to the character of law as to the relationship between academics and the practice of law. The issue is rooted in the existence of a basic ambivalence in the role of the academic lawyer; an ambivalence which may be expressed as a tension between the single-minded, rather monastic, pursuit of knowledge for its own sake and a nagging aspiration to act as a counsellor to princes and magistrates. How far should academic work be tailored to the contemporary problems of legal practice? Dicey had an answer: the function of the academic was to cut through the mass and reveal law as a set of orderly principles.[130] Through this exercise the academic could claim not only to be assisting the legal profession but also to be furthering the science of law. And it is this role which, during the 20th century, has been taken up by the textbook writers and is reflected in much of the academic output of law journals.

How, in the light of this question, should recent writing be measured? From this perspective, it would appear that the rationalisers are the true heirs of Dicey. Writers such as Dworkin and Allan may be viewed as working in the vanguard to perform the role of stuntmen to the judiciary: it is their role to try out some of the more dangerous tricks in advance which, if they can be shown

[130] Dicey, *op cit* n 8.

to work satisfactorily, might subsequently be adopted in practice. Thus, it is primarily the empiricists who have broken with the tradition of servicing practitioners and who have sought to address the rather complex question of law's place in the modern world. They might not have resolved the issue to our satisfaction but, in undertaking that exercise, they have at least managed to project a different, and perhaps more scholarly, role for the public lawyer. What this work serves to do, however, is, once again, to bring to the surface the problems of the role of the academic lawyer which have dogged us since the birth of the profession in the late 19th century. The tension was, for example, one which Maitland readily acknowledged in his inaugural discourse in 1888.[131] Reflecting on the rather vexed relationship between law and history, Maitland reminded us of the fundamental incompatibility between the professional approaches of the lawyer and the historian. The past for the lawyer must be a useable past and, while the process by which old principles are charged with new meaning may from the lawyer's point of view constitute "an evolution of the true intent ... of the old law", from the historian's viewpoint it is nothing less than "a process of perversion and misunderstanding".[132] Lawyers can get by with only "a little history", whereas "[i]f we try to make history the handmaid of dogma she will soon cease to be history".[133] And today Maitland's message extends beyond history, to embrace politics and the rest of the social sciences.[134]

Recent writing in public law may thus be understood as a search for an appropriate role for a public lawyer required to work with a constitution which is widely recognised to be intellectually bankrupt and against a background of a Diceyan tradition of scholarship which confined their work to the remote margins of the academy. And it is to those who wish to develop roles beyond those of handmaiden, stuntman or midwife to the judiciary to whom I appealed in suggesting that public lawyers might adopt as their "principal focus the examination of the manner in which the normative structures of law can contribute to the tasks of guidance, control and evaluation in government".[135]

---

[131] F.W. Maitland, "Why the History of English Law is not Written" in *Collected Papers* Vol. I (Cambridge UP, H.A.L. Fisher ed., 1911) 480.
[132] *Ibid*, p 491.
[133] *Ibid*, p 492.
[134] For an excellent discussion of the issue, see: W.T. Murphy, "The Oldest Social Science? The Epistemic Properties of the Common Law Tradition" (1991) 54 *MLR* 182.
[135] Loughlin, *op cit* n 119, p 264.

Chapter 13

INTERNATIONAL LAW IN A CHANGING WORLD

Professor Sol Picciotto
University of Lancaster

1. Introduction

The teacher of international law is faced with a multitude of challenges. Due mainly to the professional orientation of most law degrees, international law is normally an option in which students may indulge only after having been thoroughly grounded in the institutions of the national legal system and steeped in private law. Not only does this produce an inevitably parochial perspective, it reinforces commonplace ideologies of the nature of law. But the student of international law is abruptly forced to confront the limitations of comfortable positivist assumptions that a normative social process can only be called "law" if it consists of defined rules laid down by superior authority, within a system of compulsory dispute-settlement and backed by sanctions enforced by a specialist staff having a monopoly of the legitimate use of force. To conceptualise "international law" therefore requires a rethinking of the relationship between the law and power. This leads students, at least while in the heady air of the international law class, either to collapse law into a simplified and absolute notion of power and assert that international law merely legitimises the interests of the powerful; or to idealise law as the expression of popular needs or the embodiment of justice which is flouted by the powerful.

Rather than pursue the jurisprudence of international law in the abstract, it is at least pedagogically preferable to focus directly on the key concept, the "subject" of public international law, the nation-state. What does it mean to say that public international law regulates the relationships between states? The state is a highly reified concept, as can be seen from conventional approaches to international law (and international relations) which generally personify the state, treating it as a unitary entity. Thus, international society is seen as a community of states, the distinctive character of which is said to explain the peculiarities of its law. This appears to explain how international law is different: there is no overarching sovereign, so international law lacks centralised law-making and compulsory law-enforcement processes, and therefore it has to rely on reciprocity, mutual interest, or decentralised sanctions, for its binding force.[1] However, the personification of the state has two major distortive effects. On the one hand, it invites a comparison, essentially invidious, between the apparently peculiar nature of international law, and the implicitly superior or more advanced structures of the internal law of states. Furthermore, to view international law through this prism distorts its particular textures and characteristics. A better perspective for understanding not only international law, but more generally the dynamics of law in world society, is by relating it to the particular character of the nation-state, and its historical transformations.

De-personification and de-fetishisation of the state requires a theoretical and historical deconstruction of the state as a specific form of governance. This may include but must go beyond the conceptual deconstructionism which has become fashionable, since the state must be understood as a set of historically-developed social and political relations, and not merely, as one critic has startlingly asserted a "metaphysical entity".[2] Despite the challenging range and intellectual bite of some of the recent critical work in international law, much of it risks having a negligible impact, since too often "theory" seems to be an attempt to try to deal with the often harsh realities of the changing global landscape entirely through linguistic play with concepts.[3] Deconstructionist methodology has been in many ways very suggestive, in showing that behind the dualisms of international legal discourse, structured by the apparent opposition between naturalism and positivism, lies a common basis of liberal political ideas about international society, which assume that law is radically separated from politics and diplomacy.[4] However, this methodology puts great reliance on linguistic analysis, based on the view that "deconstruction of international legal argument will … inevitably relate that argument to that historically conditioned 'code' – or 'conceptual scheme'", since language is inseparable from the social life-process.[5] It is certainly helpful to understand that legal argument has a social character, so that it is both a product of history and helps to mould events; but even if language is the medium through which social relations are conducted and reality is understood, it is not the totality of the social life-process. It is putting too great a strain on linguistic deconstruction or ideologi-

---

[1] This leads to a behaviouralist approach attempting to answer the question "why do states obey international law?" *e.g.* Franck, *The Power of Legitimacy Among Nations* (OUP, 1990), which has been criticised as a tautology entailing anthropological self-validation (Purvis, "Critical Legal Studies in Public International Law" (1991) 32 *HarvILJ* 81).

[2] Anthony Carty, "Critical International Law: Recent Trends in the Theory of International Law" (1991) 2 *EuJIL* 66, p 94.

[3] Thus, for example, Philip Allott's starting-point, on withdrawing to a Cambridge cloister after a decade and a half of practice in the chancelleries as an international lawyer, was that "the international system itself is nothing other than a structure of ideas: and it has been made nowhere else than in the human mind" (Allott, *Eunomia. New Order for a New World* (OUP, 1990) xv).

[4] Koskenniemi, *From Apology to Utopia. The Structure of International Legal Argument* (Finnish Lawyers' Publishing Company, 1988), Intro.

[5] Koskenniemi, *ibid*, p xxii.

cal reconceptualisation alone to expect them to provide an adequate basis for understanding the relationship of the concepts of international law to economic and political power relations in world society.

Significantly, the new wave of debate in the 1980s, as writers from various perspectives have sought to rethink the nature and role of law in international affairs, pre-dated the major changes in inter-state relations which occurred in the 1990s. Much of the writing on international law in the 1970s had taken a functionalist and even instrumentalist view of law, arguing for an adaptation of law to the changed "realities" of international society, especially the creation of many new states by decolonisation. Equally major upheavals have transformed the political landscape since 1989: the collapse of state socialism in eastern Europe, the end of the Cold War, and the disintegration of the Soviet Union and of other states created in 1917–21. Yet the new concern with re-evaluating international law has not been a direct response to these changes in the character and number of states, but had deeper roots in the broader global crisis. Despite immense advances in productive potential in the international economy, we still do not have minimum tolerable standards of housing, sanitation, health, education or even food for the vast majority of the world's peoples. Even more agonisingly, continuing violence and even desperate warfare has symptomised the continuing disintegration of the European-inspired nation-state, in many parts of Europe itself as well as of Africa and Asia. Yet the sharpening of these contradictions has generated a widespread sense of powerlessness.

It is that which is reflected in the current ferment of intellectual debates about the possibility and limits of reason, order and justice in society. In earlier periods dissatisfaction with traditional perspectives and explanations led either to projects for a new world order, or at least to critiques of the existing bases of social power, aiming to empower the oppressed. In contrast, the post-modern pessimism of the recent period makes its challenge not just to the existing order but to the possibility of any order, or of any objective basis for universal or even generally acceptable principles of law governing conduct in international society.[6] In turn other theorists, such as T. Franck, also responding to the underlying pessimism of the age, have plunged more deeply than international lawyers are wont into the epistemological and ontological sources of theory, in order to replenish the wellsprings of liberalism. Yet in relation to the central issue of the changing nature of the state and of the global system, the limitations of some of the critical and theoretical approaches which are confined to the conceptual framework of international law have become apparent. Thus, Allott argues for dissolving the state as an illusion preventing the proper self-awareness of individual human beings as part of world society; whereas Koskenniemi has pleaded that we "take statehood seriously" and has opted for

[6] Carty, *The Decay of International Law. A reappraisal of the limits of legal imagination in international affairs* (Manchester University Press, 1986). Koskenniemi, *From Apology to Utopia. The Structure of International Legal Argument* (Finnish Lawyers' Publishing Company, 1988).

formal statehood as a necessary (although second-best) protection from the anarchy of global diversity.[7]

This new concern with the basis of normativity in international society has led to the rethinking of the conceptual structure and ideological effects of international legal rules, whether by those who wish to explain and justify their efficacy (Franck, Kratochwil), those who seek a reconceptualisation (Allott), or the deconstructionist critics (Kennedy, Koskenniemi, Carty), who reject the pretence or deception involved in maintaining the possibility of a universal system of rules. In general, however, there seems to be a large gulf between the debates within theory and any engagement with or attempt to understand the changes taking place in international society. As a first step, it is certainly important to abandon the simplistic positivist belief in law as rules, and view it as a social process, which helps to structure and mediate political and economic relations. Rosalyn Higgins has pointed out that at least in this respect some of the critical legal studies ("cls") perspectives resemble the "policy-science" school pioneered at Yale and of which she is an adept exponent. However, while the cls writers view law as radically indeterminate and contradictory, so that international legal arguments cannot be evaluated except by going outside the law, Higgins argues that legality entails ensuring "that decisions are made by those authorised to do so, with important guiding reliance on past decisions, and with available choices being made on the basis of community interests and for the promotion of common values".[8] However, this perspective offers little theory or analysis of society, viewing politics essentially as a process of decision-making based on values, without reference to social structure or organisation and therefore evading questions of inequality and power. Thus, especially in the hands of the dominant Yale theorists, it tends to result in apologia for the perspectives of authoritative decision-makers, cloaking their policies in value justifications based on generalised concepts of the human good.

Although traditional approaches, whether positivist or realist, can be criticised for treating international politics merely as an objective realm of "pure facts" which can be quarried to provide evidence of the observance or non-observance of international law[9], not all sociology or social inquiry is positivist. Theoretical reflection can provide a basis for understanding and intervening in social practices; while a critical interpretation of these practices in turn should contribute to the construction of a reflexive theoretical standpoint. An important adjunct to bridging the gap between social theory and practice is theoretically-informed empirical inquiry. Few today still accept the notion of a pure and disinterested objective empiricism: the very presence of an observer affects that which is observed, and systematic inquiry is usually inscribed within the social and political processes which include its object. Nevertheless, a social

[7] Koskenniemi, "Theory: Implications for the Practitioner", in *Theory and International Law: An Introduction* (British Institute of International and Comparative Law, 1991), p 42, and Koskenniemi, "The Future of Statehood" (1991) 32 *Harvard International Law Journal* 397.

[8] Higgins, *Problems and Process. International Law and How We Use It* (Clarendon Press, 1994) 9.

[9] Koskenniemi, "Theory", *op cit* n 7, pp 37–39.

science methodology based on a self-aware reflexive perspective can allow for that necessary interaction, and help the eventual audience to make its own intersubjective evaluation.

2. The Tension Between Statist and Universalist Perspectives

The underlying concern in contemporary debates about international law is what sort of legality is possible or appropriate in a world which has become increasingly diverse, complex and conflictual, and at the same time increasingly interdependent? Although this dual centripetal and centrifugal process has become increasingly acute in the past decade, it has marked the history of this century.

The attempt to grasp the tensions created by this dialectic of increased diversity and interdependence has also polarised international relations theorists. This relatively new discipline has, virtually since its inception, been broadly split between the realists or neo-realists who, continuing the tradition of diplomatic history, have focused primarily on interstate (meaning essentially inter-governmental) relations, and on the other hand a variety of neo-functionalists who have preferred to emphasise the "spider's web" of social relations in "world society" which cut across the "billiard-balls" of the territorially defined nation-states.[10] This latter approach has appeared in successive manifestations as interdependence theory, transnational relations, regime theory, and currently "policy networks", "epistemic communities" and "global civil society".[11] Others have argued, equally persuasively, that the increase in cross-border transactions has been more than matched by the increased density or intensification of economic activity and social relations internally within the state, and that the dominant tendency has been the consolidation of state sovereignty.[12] More recently, there has been the discovery by sociologists and social theorists generally of the issue of "globalisation". This term misleadingly implies a tendency toward global unity, but its more sophisticated advocates argue that the trend is rather towards an increased interconnectedness, which paradoxically fosters differentiation, or at least an increased awareness of diversity. The virtually instantaneous communication worldwide of commodities, artefacts, and cultural signs creates a "tension between cultural homogenisation and cultural heterogenisation".[13]

---

[10] This distinction was most clearly made by Burton, *World Society* (Cambridge UP, 1972), Ch 4, although he built on earlier work by Deutsch, Herz and others; see also Oran Young, "The Actors in World Politics", in Rosenau (ed.), *The Analysis of International Politics* (Free Press, 1972), 125.

[11] See *e.g.* (1992) International Organization 46:1, Special Issue on Knowledge, Power and International Policy Co-ordination, edited by P.M. Haas; Lipschutz, R.D. "Reconstructing World Politics: The Emergence of Global Civil Society." (1992) 21 Millenium 389.

[12] J.E. Thomson and S.D. Krasner, "Global Transactions and the Consolidation of Sovereignty", in Czempiel and Rosenau (eds), *Global Changes and Theoretical Challenges* (Lexington Books, 1989).

[13] A. Appadurai (1990). "Disjuncture and Difference in the Global Cultural Economy", in Featherstone (ed.), *Global Culture* (Sage, 1990); reprinted from (1990) 7 *Theory, Culture and Society* 295.

For international lawyers these debates strike a familiar chord, since for most of this century they have been wrestling between statist and universalist conceptions. On the one hand the state-centred view has retained its power, emphasising the autonomy and sovereignty of the nation-state, and therefore a strict dualism between international and municipal law and a reluctance to accept that international legal obligations restrict state autonomy unless very clearly emerging from the "consent" of sovereign states. Against this there has been a pull towards a new universalism, involving a close interaction or symbiosis between international and national law, accepting that international law can create rights and duties not only for states but also for individuals and transnational corporations, and arguing for global legal regimes covering matters as diverse as human rights, the protection of the natural environment, and international business or commercial transactions.[14]

The tension between these two perspectives underlies much of the theory and practice of contemporary international law. It also cuts across jurisprudential divisions such as divide positivists and naturalists, as well as the different political standpoints and economic interests of rich and poor, developed and underdeveloped countries. Thus, Hersch Lauterpacht, who accepted the Austinian view of law and therefore considered international law to be merely the law of an "immature society"[15], nevertheless took a neo-Grotian position. He envisaged the integration of public and private international law to deal with transnational transactions, "in proportion as international law is transformed from a body of rules governing exclusively the traditional aspects of the relations of states and assumes the complexion of an international law of mankind of which sovereign states are the principal but not the exclusive subjects and

[14] David Kennedy, in his re-evaluation of the writings of the "primitives", from Vitoria to Grotius ("Primitive Legal Scholarship." (1986) 27 *HarvILJ* 1), contrasts them with the "traditional" international legal scholarship of the post-Westphalia period, and the "modernists" of the 20th century. Indeed, although he is scrupulous to read the primitives on their own terms, his interest is to contrast their ideas with the subsequent perspectives: in his reading, the traditional scholars emphasise state sovereignty and make a sharp distinction between international and national law, while the "modernists" attempt in various ways to overcome this, without returning to the naive universalism of the "primitives". His essay itself thus attempts to chart modern concerns by re-reading the past.

[15] Lauterpacht, *International Law* (Cambridge UP, 1970) 12. On the 20th century neo-Grotian revival see Bull, Kingsbury and Roberts, eds. *Hugo Grotius and International Relations* (Clarendon Press, 1990). I choose Lauterpacht also because he reveals the tension between statist and universalist perspectives, as compared to an outright universalist and monist such as G. Scelle. Koskenniemi divides modern international lawyers into apologists for state power (realists) and utopians putting forward world order alternatives, but sees both as trapped by modernist illusions of the possibility of order based on universally applicable norms (see *From Apology to Utopia* (1988), more accessibly summarised in "The Politics of International Law" (1990) 1 *EuJIL* 4). His concern for conceptual differences seems to me to obscure what they have in common – an attempt to come to terms with the tensions and transformations of the nation-state. His own attempt to deal with the same phenomenon also seems trapped within these tensions: he opts for formal statehood, although as a second-best, since he considers that its bureaucratic rationality offers the possibility of a bulwark against the threat of authoritarianism which might arise from appeals to universal values, which in his view have no foundation and result in endless conflict and hence reaction ("The Future of Statehood").

beneficiaries".[16] Stepping rather more boldly in his footsteps came Wilfred Jenks, who fleshed out a vision of *The Common Law of Mankind* (Stevens, 1958), as

> "the law of an organised world community, constituted on the basis of States, but discharging its community functions increasingly through a complex of international and regional institutions, guaranteeing rights to and placing obligations upon the citizen, and confronted with a wide range of economic, social and technological problems calling for uniform regulation on an international basis which represents a growing proportion of the subject-matter of this law. The imperfect development and precarious nature of the organised world community is reflected in the early stage of development of the law but does not invalidate the basic conception. On such a conception, the law governing the relations between States is one, but only one, of the main divisions of the subject".

Jenks' choice of the issues regulated by this law reflected his experience as a long-serving international civil servant, and emphasised the role of international organisation (especially, with some prescience, of European integration), and covered Employment policy (his career had been mainly in the ILO), Atoms for Peace, and the then nascent international regimes for Antarctica and Outer Space. Other topics which today would be central to any work about global law, such as the environment, did not figure at all; and human rights received a bare three pages as a promising area of development. The concept of self-determination was also not mentioned, despite Jenks' emphasis on the increasingly universalist scope of international law during the 20th century with the acceptance of non-European states into the world community, and despite a whole chapter on "International Law and Colonial Policy", which dealt with international legal restraints on the treatment of the populations of dependent territories.

A rather different approach emerged from the United States, where teachers in the major law schools in the 1950s had begun to combine public and private international law, together with elements of comparative law and domestic public and private law, in so far as they applied to trans-national transactions. In his Storrs Lectures at Yale in 1956, Philip C. Jessup boldly fashioned these into something he was willing to call *Transnational Law*[17], although Steiner and Vagts preferred to entitle their influential casebook developed at Harvard Law School *Transnational Legal Problems*[18], since they did not purport to identify anything so systematic as a transnational legal system. Although these works included material on aspects of personal law, such as the applicability of constitutional rights to non-nationals, their main focus was on transnational business, and in particular the setting up of foreign operations through foreign direct investment, which had rapidly become the dominant mode of international business especially by giant US-based corporations in the postwar period. In the

[16] *International Law* (1970) p 42.

[17] Yale University Press, 1956. Jenks was also invited to deliver the Storrs lectures some years later in 1965, published as *A New World of Law* (Longman, 1969).

[18] 1st ed 1968, Foundation Press; they acknowledged their debt to earlier casebooks such as Katz and Brewster's *Law of International Transactions and Relations* (1960) and von Mehren and Trautman, *Law of Multistate Problems* (1965).

professionally oriented US law schools, courses based on the traditional topics of public international law at that time attracted only a handful of students; not surprisingly, the newer approaches dealing with international commercial or transnational business transactions were more attractive to the Wall Street bound students. It took only another decade or two for them to become staple fare and for all the main law schools to launch specialist journals on the law/politics/economics of inter- or transnational transactions.

By contrast, the process of emancipation of peoples and decolonisation which transformed the nature of the state system in the postwar period quickly led to a strong emphasis on state sovereignty. Although during the independence movements and in the first flush of the post-colonial dawn the principle of self-determination was seen by some to entail the rejection of imposed colonial boundaries, it quickly became apparent that the political basis of the nation-state owed more to the lengthy historical experience of administration of territorially defined entities than it did to ethnic ties. Thus, the African States quickly followed the historical precedent of Latin America in adopting the *uti possidetis* principle[19], and the grander projects of overcoming these divisions through a process of African unification were rapidly eclipsed by the consolidation of a nationalism which was both quick-growing and tenacious. The more recent experience of eastern Europe again emphasises that viable statehood requires a delicate combination of a culturally constructed national identity linked to a territorially-defined unit, even if this be an administrative unit of a previously federal or unitary state.[20] The long agony of former Yugoslavia shows

---

[19] Benedict Anderson has stressed the historical significance of the fragmentation of the Spanish empire into 18 states at the end of the 18th century. Although the geographical and economic factors which moulded Spanish policies helped turn the arbitrarily defined territorial units into economic zones, Anderson argues that the decisive force was the generation of a national consciousness involved in the formation of a specific creole culture: *Imagined Communities,* 2nd ed. (Verso, 1991), Chap 5. Although the 20th century nationalisms of the Asian and African colonies had their own distinct social roots (also since, following a century of state-formation, there was an established model for their aspirations), Anderson argues that the cultural patterns which formed the key strata of nationalist intellectuals were again rooted in the fatal racism of colonialism, which offered those intellectuals access to metropolitan civilisation, but only to a limited and circumscribed extent: *ibid* Chap 7.

[20] The principle of self-determination has operated most clearly to legitimise the independence of colonial territories, but the break-up of the USSR, Yugoslavia and Czechoslovakia shows that this may have a broader scope. Although the people of Eritrea had a longer struggle they also vindicated a right which was based on their long independent history, and the same claim can surely be made for others such as the people of West Sahara and East Timor. The detailed statement of the prin-ciple of self-determination contained in the 1970 Declaration on Principles of International Law Concerning Friendly Relations and Co-operation Among States strongly opposed "any action which would dismember or impair, totally or in part, the territorial integrity or political unity of sovereign and independent states"; however, this was subject to the important qualification, "conducting themselves in compliance with the principle of equal rights and self-determination of peoples as described above and thus possessed of a government representing the whole people belonging to the territory without distinction as to race, creed or colour". This recognised a link between the (non)-recognition of the rights to non-discrimination within a state and the right to self-determination as a separate state; however, unless this can be acceptably identified with an existing territorially-defined administrative unit, it is likely to spark off the vicious circle of inter-ethnic conflict seen not only in Bosnia but Cyprus, Northern Ireland and elsewhere.

the damage which can result from ethnic, racial or linguistic consciousness alone.

However, the granting of independent statehood to peoples who had been colonised and dispossessed also implied the creation of a more egalitarian international society and the ending of historical injustices which had been fostered or tolerated by a Euro-centric legal order. It also soon became clear that this was not simply a case of rewriting legal rules to catch up with social changes, but involved complex interactions between the law and political and economic power. The drive towards political self-determination was quickly reinforced or complemented by pressures for economic self-determination, which mainly took the form of the assertion of a right to sovereignty over natural resources, and then the broader programme for a New International Economic Order. Thus, the very strength of the pressures for national political sovereignty nevertheless engendered the paradoxical effect of a heightened awareness of international interdependence. Nevertheless, the political elites in poorer and weaker states, both those in power and the oppositional currents, have generally continued to stress the formalist legal concept of the sovereign equality of states. In a world in which social and political inequalities are also expressed as inequalities between states, national sovereignty is seen as a bulwark against the threat of political intervention from more powerful states, while the poorer states can try to rely on their numerical strength within international institutions to attempt to bring about the transformations in the international system which could overcome the massive international disparities and inequalities which were the heritage of colonialism.

The difficulty is that formal legal sovereignty without economic or political strength is an empty vessel, as is shown by the experience of over three decades of negotiations between the Group of 77 countries and the developed states, in various forums. For example, while the latter have been stubborn in protecting their markets against imports of manufactured goods in which poorer countries are competitive, notably textiles, they have insisted on liberalisation and removal of barriers even where there is total lack of reciprocity, for example patents and other intellectual property rights. The Uruguay Round and the setting up of the World Trade Organisation brings this to its logical conclusion, by tying together many of the key issues of international economic relations within an institutional framework dominated by the bargaining of market-access, which creates a ratchet effect in favour of the rich. States now find themselves very directly subject to the pressures exerted from the world economy, or "market forces", and even the most powerful sovereigns find themselves unable to impose national political controls which can stand up to the relentless tides of the global flows of commodities and finance.

3. Changing Forms of International Law

International law was born as a form of regulating relationships between sovereignties which were both autonomous and interacting. Hence, the tensions traced in the previous section in the post-war representations of international law between statism and universalism merely rearticulate in new forms issues and themes which go back to the very origins of the system. However, the personification of the state and the emphasis on a unitary concept of sovereignty have helped to conceal the very major changes that have taken place in the nature of states, and therefore in the character of their interaction and the role of law within and between states. The procedures, institutions and concepts of international law have undoubtedly become far more complex and diverse over the past few decades, as the expectations and demands on states have grown, while at the same time the range and variety of issues identified as global or international have also increased exponentially.

Probably the most significant change, but one strangely neglected by international lawyers, is the development of a vast international institutional framework for international relations.

Certainly, lawyers acknowledge the centrality of the United Nations system, but this is usually presented in the curious form of the debate about whether General Assembly resolutions are a "source" of international law. Beyond that, and a chapter on the "peaceful resolution of disputes", many international law books do not venture, although the practice of the discipline, certainly by state officials, now largely takes place in and through such organisations. This means not only the major and relatively visible intergovernmental organisations, of which there are now estimated to be many hundreds[21], but an even larger network of bodies ranging from relatively formalised institutions with written constitutions and a permanent secretariat, to committees of diplomats or officials meeting when required.

Such bodies now deal with matters involving a vast range of state functions, and their importance often varies inversely with their visibility or degree of formalisation. For example, in 1950 an informal Consultative Group was set up at the initiative of the United States, which has operated for several decades as a means of co-ordinating the embargoes on trade in military items and related technology by its members, consisting of the NATO countries with the exception of Iceland and the addition of Japan. The Group has apparently met rarely at Ministerial level, but has functioned continuously through the so-called Co-ordinating Committee, or CoCom, consisting of mid-level diplomats and technical military specialists, whose task was to establish and then revise and review the comprehensive lists of embargoed items. CG-CoCom is apparently not based on any treaty or other formal legal instrument, but operates as a "gentlemen's agreement", yet is nonetheless effective. An equally important and informal body is the so-called "Paris Club", which is simply a procedure for the multilateral renegotiation of government debt by creditor countries when they are in a situation of "imminent default". It has no fixed members, but consists of meetings convened and chaired by a French Finance Ministry official on the request

[21] H.K. Jacobson estimates that there were about 50 formal intergovernmental organisations in 1914, perhaps 80 by 1939, jumping to 600 by 1980; organisations described as nongovernmental he estimates at 330 in 1914, 730 in 1939 and over 6,000 in 1980: *Networks of Interdependence* (Knopf, 1984). Yet these are the tip of the iceberg; those with a formalised and visible existence.

of a debtor country and involving all its official creditors. As with the CoCom, agreements under its auspices are not considered to be legally binding, but establish a framework for formal bilateral pacts. Just as CoCom operates in the shadow of NATO, the Paris Club depends on the IMF, since its participants will only reschedule their bilateral debt following the creditor state's acceptance of the "conditionality" terms laid down by the IMF for its credits. Both bodies co-ordinate international negotiations on important issues of power (the one military/industrial, the other economic/financial), and utilise primarily technicist and bureaucratic techniques. Yet, although their formal status is quasi-legal at best, law also plays a part: there is precedent and reasoning by analogy, there are documents and rules and agreements to be drafted, and above all they deal with legal concepts and ideas such as liability, prohibition, obligation and sanction.

Thus, behind or below the highly visible and formal structures of the major intergovernmental organisations, the United Nations and its specialised agencies, the IMF, World Bank and others, there is a much denser network of less formal but in many ways more functional arrangements for co-ordinating state policies and actions. Their ambiguous status in international law is because they are established or operate essentially as an arena for the interaction, below the level of Foreign Offices and diplomacy, of officials or a more general policy community concerned with specific areas of state or quasi-state activity. Even Interpol, which facilitates international co-operation in a function as central to state sovereignty as policing, has long tried to resist formalisation as a treaty-based intergovernmental organisation, preferring to operate as a club for policemen without political "interference".[22] More easily accepted as a nongovernmental organisation is IOSCO (International Organisation of Securities Commissions): although its members are the official regulators of securities markets, in many cases from national Finance Ministries, they also include designated self-regulatory associations such as stock exchanges, which are not direct branches of the state.

Such bodies in any case often act not as a means of achieving formal international agreement but as a stage or arena for multilateral negotiation of standards or arrangements, perhaps supplementing or reinforcing networks of bilateral contacts and agreements. Thus, a working group of IOSCO's key body, the Technical Committee, produced two detailed reports in 1990 analysing the problems (mainly legal) experienced in developing international exchanges of information by the regulators on the basis of Memorandums of Understanding ("MOUs").[23] These arrangements are examples of the growth of international administrative co-operation involving officials, regulators, and policy communities of many kinds. Since they involve the interaction of national systems of law and administration, they attempt to resolve the often complex problems of conflict and co-ordination of national laws as applied to transnational transactions:

---

[22] Anderson, *Policing the World. Interpol and the Politics of International Police Cooperation* (Clarendon Press, 1989), esp. Chap 3.

[23] See Bulletin COB No. 253, December 1991 for the text of these reports. For examples of MOUs between securities market regulators see (1986) 25 *International Legal Materials* 1429.

for example, whether the enforcement powers of a national regulator may be used to collect evidence of breach of another state's laws. As international agreements, they are certainly drafted using legal forms and terminology, but explicitly disavow an intention to create legal obligations between the signatories, let alone their states.

Nevertheless, these MOUs illustrate very clearly that international agreements are today not merely pacts between rulers, but increasingly establish systems of co-ordination between national legal regimes. Due to the very wide range of state functions and activities with which they deal, international agreements can take a wide variety of forms, ranging from these MOUs establishing administrative co-operation among national regulators, to the comprehensiveness of the multilateral framework established to co-ordinate regulation of the uses of the world's seas by the 1982 UN Convention on the Law of the Sea (UNCLOS III). Indeed, the UNCLOS diverges from the standard image of a treaty as much, although in different ways, as the MOUs. UNCLOS does not establish a set of rules merely to be obeyed by states, but a framework of principles which have evolved over the 15 years it took to negotiate the Convention, as well as in the further dozen years until it entered into force, after receiving its sixtieth ratification, on 16 November 1994. Indeed, the post-signature period was one of continued negotiation, mainly due to the USA reopening the compromises embodied in the text, due to the Reagan government's opposition to the deep-seabed mining regime provided for in Part XI. Although this conflict was resolved by the adoption of an Agreement on Implementation of Part XI which effectively modifies UNCLOS[24], many of the principles both of the modified Part XI as well as of UNCLOS as a whole, will provide a focus for continued debate and bargaining. Thus, the requirement that the Enterprise set up under Part XI to conduct deep-seabed mining operations should do so in accordance with "sound commercial principles", or that the transfer of technology to it should be "on fair and reasonable commercial terms"[25], may establish some parameters but clearly still leave considerable scope for discussion and negotiation. This is even more obviously the case for other important issues, notably the delimitation of international maritime boundaries, which has exercised negotiators and adjudicators for several decades, especially since the rejection by the International Court of Justice of the equidistance rule and its affirmation that delimitation is based on "a rule of law which itself requires the application of equitable principles".[26]

4. Law, Power and Legitimation

This imprecision or indeterminacy of legal rules creates unease, especially

[24] Annex to UN General Assembly resolution 48/263 of 28 July 1994.
[25] Agreement Relating to Implementation of Part XI, s 2.2 and s 5.1.
[26] *North Sea Continental Shelf Cases* [1969] ICJ Reports 3, at 46–7; see generally J.I. Charney, "Progress in International Maritime Boundary Delimitation" (1994) 88 AJIL 227.

among positivists[27], for whom legal rules must be capable of clear and logical application to fulfil their function of providing certainty and predictability. On the other hand, it is the focus of critical legal scholars, who from their various perspectives seek to demonstrate that the indeterminacy of law means that the substantive content of legal rules is supplied from politics[28], and hence law's autonomy is a sham. As mentioned in the opening paragraph of this essay, international law is especially vulnerable to this charge, since the lack of compulsory adjudication leaves it without guaranteed procedures for the authoritative interpretation of its rules.

My own view is that it is important to understand and appreciate the relationship of law to politics and economics, and the particular role it plays in mediating social relationships. To say that those relationships are relations of power and often of exploitation, and that law generally helps to legitimise them, is neither to denounce law as illusory nor to deny its civilising role. After all, relations of power are of many sorts, and involve degrees of consent and coercion, and power legitimised through law is far better than that exerted by the barrel of a gun. It is nevertheless also important to probe and expose the limits of law's capacity to legitimise, and to see how this can be strengthened, as part of a more general process of achieving social and economic justice. In particular, merely to denounce liberal legal principles for their indeterminacy is perhaps to overlook that it is precisely this fluidity and flexibility that enables them to fulfil their role of mediating social relations of power.

The main problem for international law is the extremely weak nature of the international political system, which creates a great burden or dilemma for international law. If sovereignty, or political legitimacy, resides only in nation-states, then the content of international law can only be supplied by the reciprocal bargaining of "national interests" between government representatives. If, however, there are higher global interests at stake, in peace, in the preservation of the ecological balance, in economic development or at least the satisfaction of basic needs for the world's population, then how and by whom are those interests to be expressed? What is needed is a broader democratisation of international political processes, in which lawyers should also be involved, but for which law cannot substitute.[29] This, surely, is the dilemma of the international lawyer, which Koskenniemi has articulated as the alternative of becoming the apologist for power politics, or of projecting utopian designs for world order.

[27] See the discussion by R. Higgins of the ICJ's use of the doctrine of equity especially in the maritime boundary cases, *Problems & Process* 219–228; despite her orientation towards policy jurisprudence, Professor Higgins is also uneasy about the uncertainty produced by the ICJ's use of a notion of equitable principles, on the grounds that only a series of disparate criteria have been enunciated, with no evaluation of their relative weight: *ibid* p 227.

[28] See, *e.g.* Koskenniemi, "The Politics of International Law" (1990) 1 *EuJIL* 1, at p 28, where he specifically refers to UNCLOS as having no real rules but allocating decision-making power elsewhere by the use of equitable principles. For a discussion of cls views on indeterminacy see Kelman, *A Guide to Critical Legal Studies* (1987).

[29] I have developed this argument in relation to international business regulation in "The Control of Transnational Capital and the Democratisation of the International State" (1988) 15 *JLS* 58.

What needs to be recognised is that this is not a dilemma the international lawyer can solve alone, although there are certainly important contributions to be made from that perspective. A major step is to look behind the distorted or partial legalistic perspective, to try to understand law's relationship to broader social changes.

As I have tried to indicate in this short chapter, the central limitation of international law lies in the personification of the state, which draws a veil over the very real contradictions and changes that have been taking place in the nature of the state and the international system. What is more, it impedes an adequate appreciation of international law itself. I have argued that the main feature of the past few decades has been the increasing demands made on the state, while at the same time states have become increasingly interdependent. As a result, it is hardly surprising that there has been a process of fragmentation of the state, both internally and internationally. This can be seen also in the many changes that have been taking place in the role of law in international relations and activities. The horizontal and vertical axes of law have become intermingled, so that new categories of transnational and supranational law have been devised. Perhaps less often noticed, the very category of law itself has become more diffuse, and forms of quasi-law or "soft" law have come to play a part in mediating different aspects of international relations. However, underlying all these changes in the forms and functions of international law are the increasing pressures under which it has come in attempting to provide legitimation for the acute tensions in a world community characterised primarily by the very great inequalities within and between states.

Chapter 14

THE POLITICS OF HUMAN RIGHTS IN ASIA

Professor Yash Ghai*
University of Hong Kong

1. The International Context of Human Rights and Democracy

In recent years the salience of human rights in international political discourse has greatly increased. For the most part this has amounted to a berating of the governments of poor Third World countries for their disregard or oppression of human rights by the Western governments. In extreme cases sanctions have been imposed on governments which are deemed to have a particularly discreditable record; and in some other instances the dispensation of aid has been conditional on constitutional and economic reforms which serve to promote human rights. Financial or military dependence of many Third World governments on the West has prevented them from questioning Western views on rights, but the more favourable economic position of certain countries in East and South East Asia – particularly Singapore, Malaysia, China and Indonesia, have enabled them to challenge Western perceptions and policy prescriptions. A lively debate has ensued on the scope and relevance of human rights internationally as well as domestically. For the most part the protagonists on both sides of the debate are government leaders and diplomats, and consequently it is somewhat impoverished, being long on posturing and rhetoric and short on analysis. Nevertheless, governments regard issues raised by them as of great policy relevance and since their perceptions affect to a significant extent the relations between blocs of states as well as between the government and citizens, it behoves academics to pay attention to the debate.

Before we plunge into the so-called East–West debate, it is as well to remind ourselves that its very polemics are a measure of hypocrisy. The West, and

---

* I am grateful to the Hong Kong Research Grants Council which has supported my work on human rights. This chapter draws on my paper Human Rights and Governance: The Asia Debate published as an Occasional Paper by the Asia Foundation (1994).

the United States in particular, has cordial relations with the states which are the most outspoken proponents of the Asian position (and also some of them with a particularly poor record of human rights) – Indonesia, Malaysia, Singapore, and occasionally and in the past, Thailand and South Korea. The United States provides security for them both through its own troops and the sale of arms. There are extensive economic and trade relations between them and a wide measure of agreement on international issues. The globalisation of capital and the interlocking of markets enhance the interests and stakes of each side in the success of the other, and alliances are forged increasingly on transnational class lines. The rhetoric of confrontation hides this emerging transnational identity. The commitment of both parties to human rights has to be judged in this context of cordiality and fundamental common purpose.

The conception of the basis of human rights has varied from time to time, and from place to place. For a long time in the West, the belief that rights were derived from a divine ordering held sway, but it gradually gave way to the notion that rights originated from and were a response to the very nature of man. In that sense they are inherent and inalienable. This secularisation of the source of human rights arose under certain social and economic conditions which are said to mark the rise of market economic systems and consequently to emphasise individualism. In one way, it could be argued that basing human rights on the nature of man (and these days we must concede, woman) should lay the foundations for a universal regime. Unfortunately, for a variety of reasons, this has not been the case. At first the attacks came from those who believed that these rights, associated with the market, served merely to strengthen the dominance of one social class over others, and to result in the misery of the general public. The "man" of the market system was perceived to be acculturated in its peculiar values and dynamics, "disembodied" from the community. In societies where the dominance of the market over culture and community has not taken place or is incomplete, this view of human rights does not command universal acceptance. Similarly where the sway of religion or tradition is strong, the secular basis of human rights affects their acceptability, for which they must draw from the orientation of a particular religion or tradition.

The earlier differences were between the West which conceived of rights largely as civil and political and European socialist states which opted for the superiority of economic and social rights, representing the clash of liberal and Marxist ideologies. At the heart of the controversy was the role of the market in the organisation of the economy and the distribution of resources. The interesting point about contemporary controversies about human rights is that all the major contestants are committed to the market. An important aspect of the contemporary context is the collapse of the communist regimes in Europe, which was attributed to the inefficiencies of command economies and dictatorial political systems. Earlier pessimism about the crisis in capitalism was replaced by a surge in the legitimacy of markets. Much effort has gone into the establishment of markets in Eastern Europe and formerly Communist states in Asia. In some respects these efforts represent an extension of privatisation and structural adjustment policies that had been adopted by or imposed on various states in Africa, Asia and Latin America, the effect of which was to diminish the economic role of the state. The marketisation of domestic economies was paralleled by the globalisation of capital, markets and services, as national barriers to investments and trade were removed (under pressure from world economic institutions).

The case for markets was made principally in terms of the virtues of entrepreneurship, economic rationality and an efficient legal regime marked by security, predictability and transparency. The links of these developments to human rights and democracy were sought to be established through claims of increased choices for investors, consumers and workers, the restrictions on state power and the emergence or strengthening of civil society. So democracy, marketisation of economies, the promotion of human rights and the emergence of civil society were declared to be all of a piece. Further support for the emphasis on human rights and good governance was secured through arguments about their link to sustained economic and social development. At the same time there grew highly visible international non-governmental organisations (NGOs) which assumed a major responsibility for the scrutiny of the record of individual countries on human rights.

The result of the approach of the West was to bring out clearly the implications of the human rights work developed steadily through the United Nations and its agencies. It brought to the fore the responsibility of the international community for the protection of human rights everywhere, and thereby highlighted the ways in which national sovereignty has been qualified by the UN Charter and the human rights conventions. Relations between a state and its nationals were no longer a matter merely for that state; some fundamental norms of that relationship (enacted at an exponential rate, some claimed) were now defined in international law, and subject not only to the scrutiny of the international community but also to its sanctions. International relations themselves are increasingly mediated through human rights discourse and practice. Aid conditionalities, unthinkable a decade ago, have become commonplace. The legitimacy of international involvement was enhanced by the willingness of several countries to accept international assistance for establishing human rights and democracy (Eastern Europe, Russia, Nepal, Cambodia, South Africa, etc) and considerable public support in many countries for such intervention in their own case.

Several Asian countries, particularly in south east and east Asia, have offered a spirited rebuttal of this internationalisation.[1] They resent the interposition of

[1] In this paper I sometimes refer indiscriminately to "Asian Governments". Clearly not all governments subscribe to views that I attribute to "governments". So that my position is not misunderstood, I should say that my paper does not deal with the Middle East. It is also useful to try to make distinctions as among clusters of Asian governments. Issues and politics in south Asia (India, Pakistan, Nepal, Sri Lanka and Bangladesh) are often different from those in east Asia (China, Japan, the Koreas, Taiwan and Vietnam). The former are more plural with specific parliamentary traditions underpinned by ethnic politics, while the latter are influenced by Confucianism and a measure of authoritarianism. But even this broad generalisation needs to be qualified, since Japan may be said to have shed authoritarianism some decades ago, while Singapore could be included for this classification with east Asia, and Malaysia with south Asia. See Richard Cullen, "Protecting Individual Rights: East Meets West" (1994, mimeo).

the international community (and particularly the hegemony of particular countries within it) in their relations with their citizens, in an ever increasing number of areas. They also resent the leverage it has given these other countries (and international institutions) over their policies, and see the new approach as attempts to undermine their moral authority, disrupt their political stability, and retard their economic progress. They see in it renewed attempts at the assertion of Western hegemony. Rather than, as in some other regions, withdraw from the debate, they have sought to provide an alternative framework for the discourse of human rights and democracy. [2]

Secure in the economic success of their policies which owe little to democracy or human rights, they contest the claims of the positive links between democracy (and human rights) and economic development. Another plank in their argument is that most of the rights which the West is purveying are "Western" in origin, oriented towards an individualistic society and therefore inappropriate to Asia where the values of communal action are highly prized. Furthermore, the priorities as between different human rights vary from country to country and, certainly in their own states, the priority must be given to economic and social rights. On a more doctrinal but basic level, they challenge the legitimacy of international involvement in human rights and national political systems on the argument that the fundamental principle of international law and relations is state sovereignty (to which belong these questions). They also accuse the West of hypocrisy, since it has long been engaged in violations of human rights, from slavery to colonialism, and in view of the current decline of moral authority and public order in its own states.

The politicisation of human rights raises sharply familiar questions of theory and practice. What is the basis for international action on human rights? Why should a state's competence to deal with its citizens be circumscribed by reference to human rights or governance? At the heart of this debate lies the nature of human rights and the source of their authority. Are human rights determined by the culture or economic development of a country contingent on history, or do they represent universal values true for all time and places? Stemming from considerations of theory and strategies, are some rights more basic than others? How do civil and political issues relate to economic and cultural rights? Is there a sequence in the development and achievement of human rights? How do human rights, the rule of law, and democracy relate to each other? How are human rights and democracy linked to economic and social development? What is the role of civil society? The 1993 Vienna World Conference on Human Rights failed to resolve these hard issues, despite a "consensus" document. Consensus was achieved by genuflections to a series of contradictory positions, not an engagement with these issues.

[2] Perhaps the most articulate statement of this position is Bilabari Kausikan, "Asia's Different Standard", *Foreign Policy* 24–41 (Fall 1993).

2. Asian Governmental Perspectives on Human Rights

In contemporary debates, it is generally assumed that there is one Asian view of human rights, and that it is opposed to the traditions of individual human rights that first developed in the West. This in fact is the view of some governments, who speak as if they represent the views of the whole continent. This view is reinforced because they claim that their views are based on perspectives which emerge from Asian culture or religion or Asian realities.

Perceptions of human rights are reflective of social and class positions in society. What conveys an apparent picture of a uniform Asian perspective on human rights is that it is the perspective of a particular group, that of the ruling elites. What unites these elites is their notion of governance and the expediency of their rule. For the most part the political systems they represent are not open or democratic, and their publicly expressed views on human rights are an emanation of these systems, of the need to justify authoritarianism and occasional repression. It is their views which are given wide publicity domestically and internationally.

The unity of governments is more apparent than real. Although the Bangkok Declaration[3] was endorsed by all the Asian governments at the April 1993 Asian regional preparatory meeting for the Vienna World Conference on Human Rights, some of them have a firm commitment to human rights and their record is better than one might suppose from their endorsement of the Declaration (India and the Philippines being two examples). The reason for presenting a united front is not unconnected with a perceived North–South confrontation (as is evident from the Bangkok Governmental Declaration, which stressed the need to avoid the application of "double standards" in the implementation of human rights and its "politicisation"[4]).

The official view is a response to two circumstances: the imperatives of control, and confrontation with Western pretensions. Several ingredients constitute the official view. One which flows directly from both the circumstances is the assertion of "domestic jurisdiction" over human rights. Human rights are encapsulated within state sovereignty; the national treatment of human rights is no concern of other states or the international community. Self-determination, a concept which has been used to advance claims of human rights, is regarded as irrelevant to independent states. In its "White Paper" *Human Rights in China* (1991), the Chinese government stated that: "Despite its international aspect, the issue of human rights falls by and large within the sovereignty of each State".[5]

---

[3] The Declaration has been published in the *Law and Society Trust Fortnightly Review*, I May 1993 (3:57) pp 1-3.

[4] Note 2 above, at paragraph 7. These differences dominated the World Conference on Human Rights in Vienna in June 1993.

[5] Human Rights in China (Beijing: Foreign Languages Press, 1991). The paper was published by the State Council to refute the charges of human rights violations in China. The quotation occurs on p 11.

Indeed it has argued that human rights cannot be realised until a State achieves sovereignty.

Another element in the official view is the relativity of rights, determined by the economic, political and cultural circumstances of each country. The Bangkok Governmental Declaration "recognises that while human rights are universal in nature, they must be considered in the context of a dynamic and evolving process of international norm-setting, bearing in mind the significance of national and regional peculiarities and various historical, cultural and religious backgrounds".[6] This stance reflects the position in the Chinese White Paper which states that "the evolution of the situation in regard to human rights is circumscribed by the historical, social, economic and cultural conditions of various nations, and involves a process of historical development. Owing to tremendous differences in historical background, social system, cultural tradition and economic development, countries differ in their understanding and practice of human rights".[7] The Chinese use this framework to establish the priority of social and economic rights in their country, and much of the Paper is taken up with an account of the ending of pre-Communist regime practices of feudalism and other forms of human exploitation and the steady progress since in nutrition, education, health, the position of women and the disabled ("to eat their fill and dress warmly were the fundamental demands of the Chinese people who had long suffered cold and hunger"[8]).

If one implication of this relativist position is the primacy of economic development, the other is the specific conditions for political stability, with restrictions on civil and political rights. A forthright statement of this position is to be found in pronouncements of the Singapore Government following the detention of various social workers and activists in May 1987. I quote here from one such Statement (dated 24 June 1987 and addressed by the then Minister for Home Affairs, Mr. Jayakumar, to US Congressmen who had written to complain about the detentions). It contrasted the "resilience and cohesiveness" and shared values of the nation of the United States (which presumably makes possible the tolerance of human rights) to the fragility and heterogeneity of Singapore.

> "We are vulnerable to powerful centrifugal forces and volatile emotional tides. Like many other developing countries, Singapore's major problem of nationhood is simply to stay united as one viable nation. ... In our short history, Singapore has repeatedly encountered subversive threats from within and without. ... To combat these threats to the nation, the usual procedures of court trials, which apply in Singapore to most criminal cases, have proved totally inadequate. The very secrecy of covert operations precludes garnering evidence to meet the standards of the criminal law for conviction. In many cases of racial agitation, the process of trial itself will provide further opportunity for inflammatory rabble rousing. ... Singaporc cannot be ruled in any other way. ... Preventive detention is not a blemish marring our record; it is a necessary power underpinning our freedom."

[6] Para 8, n 1.
[7] P II, n 2.
[8] Pp 4–5, n 5.

These remarks were directed at a justification of administrative powers of detention without any kind of trial, but similar arguments have been used to justify other curtailments of civil rights, like the right to associate and assemble, of peaceful marches, of speech and expression. The Chinese Paper says that the people's right to subsistence will be threatened in the event of social turmoil or other disasters, and that it is the fundamental wish and demand of the Chinese people and a long term, urgent task of the Chinese government to maintain national stability and concentrate their efforts on developing productive forces.[9]

The emphasis these governments purportedly place on economic development has led them to support the right to development. This right is a matter of considerable international contention, with developing countries arrayed on the side supporting it, and most developed countries united in their opposition to it. It certainly does not have the quality of other kinds of rights, which inhere in individuals or groups and for the most part are entitlements against the state. Nevertheless the General Assembly of the United Nations adopted, in the face of abstentions by most Western states, a Declaration on the Right to Development on 4 December 1986.[10] The Declaration ties the realisation of human rights in the developing countries to international economic aid for them and gives to "peoples" (presumably meaning "states") the right to "participate in, contribute to, and enjoy economic, social, cultural and political development, in which all human rights and fundamental freedoms can be fully realised". In return for these, several concessions are made in emphasising the indivisibility of rights and the claims of individuals to full participation in development and in the fair distribution of the benefits resulting from it.

The Declaration is a fuzzy document, trying to be all things to all persons. So while there are sections of it which can be used to advance the (more traditional) cause of human rights, the gist of it seeks to establish reasons for the failure of the realisation of human rights in the international economic and political systems (including encroachments on the principle and practice of self-determination), while affirming that the primary responsibility for human rights is vested in states as part of their sovereignty. In other words, the rich countries must provide economic assistance to the poor countries, but must not question their human rights situation.

The Declaration is also an attempt to provide an alternative framework for the international discourse on human rights. It shifts the focus from domestic arenas (where most violations of human rights take place) to the international, and takes attention away from specific rights, for example, speech, assembly, social welfare to an ambiguous portmanteau right of development, for which, in

[9] P 8. There is of course no easy way to find out what the people of China want since there are no truly representative bodies or a free press - a point I return to later to establish the link between political rights and social rights

[10] The Declaration is reprinted in the *Compilation of International Human Rights Instruments* (Geneva: The Human Rights Centre, 1991). I have criticised the Declaration in *Whose Human Right to Development?* (London: Commonwealth Secretariat, 1989).

the nature of Third World affairs, the state must take the responsibility in defining and implementing. Through the Declaration, Asian governments seek to promote the ideology of developmentalism, which justifies repression at home and the evasion of responsibility abroad.

Another Asian initiative in changing the framework for the discourse on human rights is even more fundamental. The approaches discussed so far have taken the Western discourse as the main framework and have advanced qualifications to it or provided justifications for derogation from its values. Some governments have put forward the argument that the cultural matrix within which relations between individuals and the state are embedded are fundamentally different in Asia from that in the West. This matrix governs the nature and salience of human rights. This approach has been taken up aggressively in Singapore and Malaysia (less so in China, where the government's residual loyalty to Marxist thought is inconsistent with the adoption of this cultural approach, especially since so much of it is based on semi-feudal thought in Asia). [11]

I take as the basis of my discussion of this point an official statement of the government of Singapore, *Shared Values* (1991).[12] The context of this White Paper is a concern of the government that the cultural values of its people are under attack from foreign ideas and values. It poses the rhetorical question, "Can we build a nation of Singaporeans, in Southeast Asia, on the basis of values and concepts native to other peoples, living in other environments?" It goes on, "If we are not to lose our bearings, we should preserve the cultural heritage of each of our communities, and uphold certain common values which capture the essence of being a Singaporean".[13] It then finds certain perceptions and values which are common to the different ethnic communities of Singapore and which also distinguish them from society in the West. The key section of the Paper is devoted to a discussion of the relationship between the individual and society. Disputing the proposition that values are universal and common to all mankind, it states that there is a major difference between Asian and Western values in the balance each strikes between the individual and the community; Asian societies emphasise the interests of the community, while Western societies stress the rights of the individual. Singaporean society has always weighted group interests more heavily than individual ones. "This balance has strengthened social cohesion, and enabled Singaporeans to pull together to surmount difficult challenges collectively, more successfully than other societies. An emphasis on the community has been a key survival value for Singapore."[14] The core values of the Asian society are identified as placing society above self, upholding the family as the building block of society, and

[11] This sentence was written in 1993. As I revise it, today's *People's Daily* (19 September 1994, Beijing) starts the rehabilitation of Confucius, in several articles extolling the virtues of Confucianism as an aid to political stability and economic development.

[12] Shared Values Cmd. 1 of 1991 (Singapore: Singapore National Printers Ltd. (Government Printers)).

[13] Both these quotations appear on p 1, and are taken from a Presidential address to Parliament in January 1989.

[14] Para 26, p 5

resolving major issues through consensus instead of contention. There is a strong element of Confucianism in this elaboration, although the government denies that the values it propagates are purely Confucian. It, however, picks up an element of Confucian teaching as particularly relevant to Singapore: "The concept of government by honourable men (*junzi*), who have a duty to do right for the people, and who have the trust and respect of the population, fits us better than the Western idea that a government should be given as limited powers as possible, and should always be treated with suspicion unless proven otherwise."[15] The supremacy of political authorities is emphasised by the first of the Shared Values, "Nation before Community". Another aspect of Asian values, implicit though not explicit in the Paper, is the importance of duty as a counterpoint to right. The cohesion of society as well as the fulfilment of the individual is secured through a chain and hierarchy of duties. (The primacy of the notion of duty is emphasised elaborately both in the Chinese and Indian constitutions.)

The individual does not disappear altogether as a bearer of rights in the Singapore Paper. However, characteristically the concern with the individual is expressed more in terms of the obligations of the community to look after its less advantaged members. In Singapore there is a twist to this, in that the "community" in question is the ethnic community of the individual, not the State, "to avoid the dependent mentality and severe social problems of a welfare state as experienced in many developed states"[16], laying the foundations of a kind of community corporatism in the wake of declining popularity of the ruling party, showing how much these questions are viewed in that country from the perspectives of governance and management.

Cultural "embeddedness" is not the only justification for this view of the relationship between the individual and the community and the interposition of the family – which is also rooted in more pragmatic considerations. The White Paper hints at this, but it has been developed elsewhere. In at least Southeast Asia, there is a strongly held view that an authoritarian political system is the secret of its economic success, and the frequent Singaporean mocking of the democratic efforts of the Philippines (with a rather inefficient economy) is advanced as proof of it. But there is also the belief that it is not the individual but the family (tied in to a network of clan associations and relationships) which has been at the forefront of the phenomenal economic success of the region. There appears to be the view of a significant number of people (primarily but not only among the business community as is well evidenced in the debates in Hong Kong) that this combination of authoritarian rule and family and kinship networks lies at the root of economic success.[17] This model (which reverses the normal understanding of the relationship between the market,

[15] Para 41, p 8

[16] Para 38, p 7

[17] I have reviewed this literature (and examined its implications for the centrality or otherwise of the rule of law) in "Capitalism and the Rule of Law: Reflections on the Basic Law" in Wacks (ed.), *Legal Theory: China, Hong Kong and 1997* (Hong Kong: Hong Kong University Press, 1993).

individualism and the rule of law) is seen as threatened by democracy and human rights.

3. A Critique of Governmental Perspectives

Asian governments are right to insist that human rights must be located within the social and economic conditions of specific societies. So-called universal human rights of the West have evolved over a long period of European history, responding to the changing configurations of power and the tasks of each epoch of history. Claims of universality and indivisibility of rights are hard to sustain in the face of the West's history of the oppression of its own people and of others, with slavery which once enjoyed religious approbation, abuse of child labour, the exploitation of colonies and the other depredations of imperialism and racism. Nor is the process of the development of rights complete. Social welfare rights were acknowledged only in this century, and the appalling degradation of the environment has now set the stage for a new conception of rights and responsibilities, in which the community will have to be accorded a key position as a bearer of rights as well as duties. There is no reason why contemporary concerns and fads in the West should define the parameters of international discourse in and aspirations of human rights.

That is, however, not to say that the framework adopted by Asian governments is justifiable. I start with one element of that framework, religion, which has played a less important part in east Asia than in south and west Asia, but which is nevertheless supposed to give a uniform and distinctive character to Asian perspectives on human rights (although the invocation of religion is somewhat ambiguous since it is also argued that all religions are based on essentially the same values, and provide a common foundation for the primacy of human rights).

Religion

An immediate difficulty facing an exploration of the question whether a distinctive Asian perspective on human rights emerges from the religion of its people is that there are numerous religions in Asia, including all the world's major ones. Assuming that religion does indeed influence a people's perception of human rights, then one would have to concede that there would be a plurality of perspectives, not one. Even if we concede that for our enquiry what matters are "Asian" religions (Hinduism, Islam and Buddhism plus the influential set of beliefs represented by Confucianism), as reflecting more accurately Asian predispositions, they too vary in their beliefs and values. Nor does the same religion manifest itself uniformly in its discourse about human rights at all times and in all countries. Buddhism is militant and aggressive in Sri Lanka, asserting ethnic and religious superiority of one section of the population, while elsewhere, as in Cambodia, it has been a force for peace and the protection of the rights of all communities. Hinduism was once seen as tolerant and non-proselytising, providing a constitutional basis for secularism in India; today many of its adherents are militant and attack beliefs and institutions of other religions. The Hinduism of Nepal is more syncretised than of modern India, able to co-exist and even assimilate with other religions. In many east Asian countries, all religions seem to be mediated through Confucian thought and values, detracting from the specificity of the religion.

In many places religion takes its coloration from politics, woven into the apparatus of the status or claiming a special eminence in the affairs of the state. While Western states separated state and religion (whatever the influence of religion on human rights), the contemporary tendency in many parts of Asia (particularly south Asia) is to connect religion with state. In some instances this has served to diminish the scope for human rights. Sometimes religion acts as a conservative force, at other times it is a major factor for change (and the same religion can play these opposite roles if we compare Christianity in Latin America with that in Europe).

As to whether religions can provide a basis for a universal or pan-Asian regime of rights, it is always hard to say what the essence of a particular religion is, but it would seem that different values are enshrined in different religions. Some like Hinduism have sanctified social and caste distinctions, and others like Confucianism, established a social and political hierarchy. Nor is equality the hallmark of Islam, for despite its ideals, its practices cleaved to a tribal and unequal society of its origin. Christianity justified slavery for centuries, and Christian-based Western political systems did not accommodate the equal rights of blacks and women until this century. Not all Asian states (including the largest of them) encourage the holding or the exercise of religious beliefs (preferring, as in China, to base the source of rights in popular sovereignty). Religions would not appear therefore to hold the key to universalism. Indeed most religions in some sense deny the claims of equality: traditionally Hindus found people of other religion polluting, and most other religions have a notion of the "non-believer" to whom an inferior status is accorded in both religious and secular systems. Nor does religion provide a basis for a distinctive Asian perspective on human rights.

Culture

If an interest in religion is frequently motivated by the wish to find common roots for human rights, culture is explored to explain diversity and specificity. As noted above, some Asian governments claim that their societies place a higher value on the community than in the West, that individuals find fulfilment in their participation in communal life and community tasks, and that this factor constitutes a primary distinction in the approach to human rights. The Western preoccupation with individualism is explained by the alienation resulting from its economic system which has sapped the vitality of the community, and forced introspection on individuals as a means towards their identity. This argument is advanced as an instance of the general proposition that rights are culture specific.

The "communitarian" argument is Janus-faced. It is used against the claim of universal human rights to distinguish the allegedly Western, individual-oriented approaches to rights from the community centred values of the East. Yet it is also used to deny the claims and assertions of communities in the name of "national unity and stability". It suffers from at least two further weaknesses. First, it overstates the "individualism" of Western society and traditions of thought. Even within Western liberalism, there are strands of analysis which assert claims of the community (for example Rousseau and T. H. Green); and most Western human rights instruments allow limitations on and derogations from human rights in the public interest, or for reasons of state. Western courts regularly engage in the task of balancing the respective interests of the individual and the community.[18] Within liberal societies there are nuances in the approach to and the primacy of human rights, as becomes evident when one examines the differences among the United States, Canada, France and the United Kingdom. Furthermore, liberalism does not exhaust Western political thought or practice. There is social democracy, which emphasises collective and economic rights, and Marxism, which elevates the community to a high moral order, is also reflective of an important school of Western thought. There is much celebration in Western political thought of "civil society".[19]

Secondly, Asian governments (notwithstanding the attempt in the Singapore Paper to distinguish the "nation" and the community) fall into the easy but wrong assumption that they or the state are the "community".[20] Nothing can be more destructive of the community than this conflation. The community and state are different institutions, and to some extent in a contrary juxtaposition. The community, for the most part, depends on popular norms developed through forms of consensus and enforced through mediation and persuasion. The state is an imposition on society, and unless humanised and democratised (as it has not been in most of Asia), it relies on edicts, the military, coercion and sanctions. It is the tension between them which has elsewhere underpinned human rights. In the name of the community, most Asian governments have stifled social and political initiatives of private groups. They have destroyed

[18] See, for example, Kymlicka, *Liberalism, Community, and Culture* (Oxford: Clarendon Press, 1989).

[19] See Cohen and Arato, *Civil Society and Political Theory* (Cambridge, Mass.: MIT Press, 1992).

[20] Although, as I argue, that the lip service to the "community" is hypocritical, the real "community" which motivates politicians is parochial and clannish, pursuing its selfish interest at the expense of other communities, and is the basis of public corruption and graft - and therefore nothing to be proud of. An interesting light on "community" occurred in Hong Kong in April 1994, when two shoppers beat up a shop assistant, while her colleagues watched but did nothing to defend her. However, she bore no grudge against them, saying, "Even though I have known them for a long time what difference does it make? You cannot expect someone to help you. I am not their relative." (*Eastern Express*, June 11–12 1994). See Siu-kai Lau, "Utilitarianistic Familism: The Basis of Political Stability" in King and Lee (eds.), *Social Life and Development in Hong Kong* (Hong Kong: The Chinese University Press, 1981).

many communities in the name of development or state stability, and the consistent refusal of most of them to recognise that there are indigenous peoples among their population (who have a right to preserve their traditional culture, economy and beliefs) is but a demonstration of their lack of commitment to the real community. The vitality of the community comes from the exercise of the rights to organise, meet, debate and protest, dismissed as "liberal" rights by these governments. Nor is the tight regulation of society as in China and Singapore particularly Confucian. Confucius argued against reliance on law or coercion, and advocated a government of limited powers and functions.[21]

Another attack on the community comes from the economic, market oriented policies of the governments. Although Asian capitalism appears to rely on the family and clan associations, there is little doubt that it weakens the community and its cohesion. The organising matrix of the market is not the same as that of the community. Nor are its values or methods particularly "communitarian". The moving frontier of the market, seeking new resources, has been particularly disruptive of communities which have managed to preserve intact a great deal of their culture and organisation during the colonial and post-colonial periods. The emphasis on the market and with it individual rights of property are also at odds with communal organisation and enjoyment of property (and a further irony is that Asian leaders who allege their allegiance to communal supremacy and values are among the most ardent opponents of a Marxism that espouses the moral worth and authority of the community). Market policies have relied greatly on multinational capital and corporations, which have brought new values and tastes, and are increasingly integrating their economies and elites into a global economy and culture. Indeed it is these very considerations which prompted the Singapore White Paper, but the contradictions of official policies largely escaped its authors. It totally ignored the impact, indeed the onslaught, of modern technologies on traditional communities.

A final point is the contradiction between claims of a consensus and harmonious society and the extensive arming of the State apparatus. The pervasive use of draconian legislation like administrative detentions, disestablishment of societies, press censorship, sedition, etc., belies claims to respect alternative views, promote a dialogue, and seek consensus. The contemporary state intolerance of opposition is inconsistent with traditional communal values and processes. Contemporary state processes in Asia are less hospitable to community politics than the much derided adversarial processes of the West, which at least ensure a hearing for all parties.

Thoughtful Asians, who concede many of the above criticisms of a "communitarian" approach, nevertheless hold on to some important distinctions between the West and Asia, which they consider are rooted in culture. There is first the

[21] As with religion, Confucianism has been used for political purposes so that its essence has become somewhat obscure. It is undisputed, however, that Confucius was against tough laws and strong punishments, believing in the virtue of rulers and their sense of duty. See Rubin, *Individual and State in Ancient China* (New York: Columbia Univ. Press, 1976) and van der Sprenkel, *Legal Institutions in Manchu China* (London: Athlone Press, 1962) esp. 2 and 3.

distinction between duties and rights. An aspect of this is the tendency in the West towards formalism, the transformation of values as legal rights, and the consequent emphasis on the rights and prerogatives of an individual. Based on a theory of competition and suspicion of authority, this leads to demands rather than concessions, to confrontation rather than reciprocity and accommodation. An emphasis on duties on the other hand leads to honour and peace, as well as stability. It is argued that the rights-based emphasis leads to the impoverishment of society, so that in the search for the protection of the citizen against the state, the community collapses and non-state actors become the principal source of oppression and insecurity (making it unsafe to be on the streets of major metropolises after sunset). There is also the danger in formalisation of values as "rights" that the form may elude substance (so that the satisfaction of formal criteria hides realities that deny the values; as Professor Mazrui once said, the West may have abolished child marriages, but the number of teenage pregnancies has vastly increased).

However, in the hands of an intolerant government, the concept of duties can become a justification as well as an instrument of authoritarianism. This is perhaps not inherent in the notion of duties, because duties are also laid upon rulers (in the best Islamic and Confucian traditions), and indeed the notion of duty can be truly revolutionary. In practice, however, this is not often how it is, duties vary from person to person (persons at the top of the hierarchy having rights and those at the lower reaches, duties), reminiscent of feudalism. The emphasis on the fulfilment of duties, frequently betokening social, economic or political subordination, tends towards conservatism and the perpetuation of inequalities – antithetical to the claims of equitable development advanced by many Asian governments. Furthermore the conflation between the state and community serves to strengthen the tentacles of the government over society. The notion of duties transferred from the community to the state changes its nature from inter-citizen obligations and responsibilities to the much more problematic case of state-citizen relations. The West has to some extent separated civil society from the state, creating a "neutral" public area and space for communities (from which of course the commanding heights of the state may be controlled), while in Asia the tendency is towards the convergence of the two, regarded perhaps as necessary for the legitimacy of the state[22] but ultimately destructive of the community.

Even if we were to concede that Asian cultures or religions are distinctive and that these colour the perception and reality of rights, it is not clear why the global debate has taken the form of opposition of political and civil rights ("Western") versus economic and social rights ("Asian"). Why should the communitarian approach suggest that economic and social rights are more impor-

[22] The argument here is that in non-Western states, legitimacy does not come from the rule of law, constitutionalism and the neutrality of state institutions, but from their association with religion and culture—which in the mostly heterogenous states, means the culture and religion of the majority community. See for example Neelan Tiruchelvam, "Development and the Protection of Human Rights" (1993, mimeo).

tant than political? It may be argued that traditionally communities were hierarchically organised and that their cohesion depended on duties. But the communities were even less concerned with "development" which is undoubtedly more of a foreign concept than fair or accountable administration or harmony within the community. If human rights do not follow from Asian cultures, then no more does economic development. The same can be said of "Asian" religions, which are stereotyped as other worldly (like most religions), more concerned with salvation in the next world than economic prosperity in this. Ethics are more important than power, and asceticism and austerity are values approved by most of these religions. Apart from the somewhat ambiguous position of Confucianism (which is mistakenly today regarded as development oriented rather than as preserving the status quo as traditionally regarded), there is little in "Asian" religions to support a privileged position for economic development.

Political and civil rights vs. economic and social rights

If there is no substantial basis in community, culture or religion for economic and social rights, then why do Asian governments place such rhetorical emphasis on them? They sometimes say that civil and political rights are meaningless if the people are poor and illiterate. There is of course considerable truth in this, but there is reason to be sceptical about the sincerity of the governments for they have done little to establish economic rights or to promote civil rights in countries which have achieved great economic success. The more plausible reason is that the talk of economic and social rights is diversionary, an attack on civil and political rights. Governments are anxious to minimise challenges to their authority or legitimacy, which means (as it seems to them) the suppression or emasculation of political opposition. A preference for economic rights might also arise from the consideration that it is much harder to hold governments accountable for them. They are for the most part matters more of standards than precise rules and entitlements, their enforceability is problematic and they are widely regarded as contingent on resources. In fact these governments dislike talk of economic and social rights, except when engaged in global debates (many of them do not like talk of any rights). It is not easy to establish how civil and political rights threaten economic and social rights. The juxtaposition these governments play upon domestically is not between these different rights, but between civil and political rights and economic development. It is economic development, not economic rights, that they emphasise. They are, however, content to seek economic rights of states, the so-called developing states (as in their advocacy of the right to development). It is of course easy to understand why governments want economic development; it increases state resources, enables governments to establish larger armies, enhances the status of their leaders, and secures the support of the populace.

The dispute about the priorities of various kinds of rights had its genesis in ideological differences. However, its persistence between the West and east and Southeast Asia, where the market is the dominant matrix for the organisation of the economy, is, at first sight puzzling. The reason may be that each side has a different vision of the market. In Western theory the market is autonomous, and the safeguarding of that autonomy requires a number of civil and political rights (property, freedom of movement, association and organisation, expression, an independent and rational legal order, etc.). The control of the state (which provides the legal and administrative framework for the market) by the ruling group comes from its prior dominance in civil society (emphasising yet again the importance of civil rights). Asian markets are organised in a much more authoritarian and rapacious manner; there is widescale corruption; the state, more autonomous of social forces than in the West, is a means of control over economic resources and civil society; and many are still at the "primitive accumulation" stage. Administration is more important than the law; and the imperatives of control override those of economic rationality.

Although both the West and the Asian states are committed to the market, there is competition between them for the national or regional dominance of world markets. Quite how the market is organised may affect the interests of the states differently. The West has an interest in equalising the conditions of competition and in the opening up of markets, while Asian states are concerned with twin objectives – of increasing competitive edge and political control. It is thus easy to understand why the West would want to emphasise transparency, accountability, functioning legal codes and courts, etc. and a narrowing of the role of the state. It is equally easy to see why Asian states would resist these, using the shibboleths of economic, social and cultural rights. Culture becomes particularly functional as both providing a moral and popular mode of differentiating the East from the West, as well as in slowing down political mobilisation at home. But since the market remains the operating matrix, the process, as I have pointed out above, is not without deep contradictions.

Ideological justifications for the success of the markets in Asia, harping upon the Confucian values of authority, obedience and the salience of the family in economic affairs, are used to establish not the irrelevance of civil and political rights but their destructive qualities. Economic and social rights attempt to mediate between the market and the community, to soften the impact of market forces, to act as a safety net. Nothing in the present conjuncture enhances economic, social and cultural rights. On the contrary, the general acceptance of the market means that propertied and entrepreneurial classes have gained new salience, and that fresh restrictions on social and economic rights (including those of workers and as regards the environment) are placed in the name of global competitiveness. Asian governments may have some justification to see the emphasis by the West on workers' rights and the environment as attempts by the West to reduce the competitiveness of Asian economies, but the restrictions nevertheless point to the shallowness of their commitment to economic rights. It is therefore unlikely that we shall get useful purchase on the question of economic and social versus political and civil rights by examining the stance of Asian governments.

Economic, social and cultural rights are particularly valuable in uncovering the rationale for human rights. Human rights were part of the post-war agenda of the United Nations which emphasised their close connection with peace, development and human dignity. Unlike the "negative" liberties of political rights, these other rights raise a different framework and pose larger questions – that of the purpose of society and state, of social responsibility and social justice, of equity, and the potential of the human person. They suggest that a person is born full of potentialities – potentialities which find fulfilment through civil and political rights, that of expression, association, participation, but that these potentialities do not materialise without appropriate social and economic circumstances. [23] Undoubtedly poverty is the single most important cause of the violation of rights.

It is therefore necessary to move away from the polarities of civil and political rights on the one hand and social and economic on the other. Each has a bundle of rights which vary in their impact on the state and citizens and not all are individually oriented (for example the right of association serves political, economic and cultural functions). Their disaggregation and the purpose each serves may suggest different and more productive categorisations. The right of property is regarded as a civil right, yet it is pregnant with economic functions. It also suggests that no rights can be expended in favour of another; but the salience of each right may be contingent on circumstances. There is a great interdependence of rights. Since one's perception of rights is governed by the state of one's belly, it could be argued that a certain level of literacy and economic security are essential for the exercise and enjoyment of civil and political rights. Similarly, as Amartya Sen has argued, a society that proclaims the urgency of basic needs has first to have a democratic framework so that society can decide what the basic needs are. He has also suggested that basic needs can probably not be met in a society which is not responsive to public pressures or public accountability.[24] One might add that the transformative potential of human rights (and that must be their role in many authoritarian and unequal societies in Asia) lies in the rights of association, speech and other trade union rights, which have also the potential to expose and curtail a major public vice and waste of resources – corruption. Equally, economic prosperity and high literacy without the freedom of expression or the right of association fail to develop the full potential of the human person, and the denial of these rights can be humiliating and degrading[25] (this position is increasingly being taken in

---

[23] A. Beldon Fields and Wolf-Dieter Narr, "Human Rights as a Holistic Concept" (1992) 14 *Human Rights Quarterly* 1–20

[24] He illustrates his argument by a study of famines and shows that it was only when there was no freedom of expression or criticism that the governments were unable to anticipate shortages. He contrasts the relatively better position of immigrants in Britain, most of whom have the vote, with those in Germany, who do not. But he points to failures of democracy when preventing injuries or injustices in instances where it is not so easy to evoke human sympathy for them, unlike that in the case of major disasters. Sen, "Freedoms and Needs", *The New Republic* 10 (17 January 1994) p 31.

[25] The case of migrants provides an illustration. A large number of people migrate from the relatively democratic Philippines to work in States which are less protective of human rights, like Singapore, Malaysia and the Middle East, suggesting that they value economic advancement over rights. On the other hand, professionals from Singapore are emigrating to countries in the West where

recent international instruments on the rights of special groups – women, children and indigenous peoples, which have broken away from the bifurcation of the Covenants, being based on the understanding that real equality for women or indigenous people or the real protection of children's rights cannot be secured without major social transformations in their social and economic conditions).[26]

4. The Social Context for Human Rights in Asia

I conclude by renvoi to an earlier point of departure, to a distinction that is seen to flow from cultural differences – the role of the family. It is frequently said by Asian government representatives that the bedrock of Asian societies is the family, and it has become fashionable to ascribe social problems in the West to the breakdown of family life. It is claimed for Asia that mutual responsibilities within the family provide for the welfare of its members, ensure traditions of respect and rectitude, and promote social stability and economic development. The conversion of values into individual rights undermines the basis of family solidarity. However, countries which are not known for their practice of individual rights have found that the family may well be weakening under the pressure of other social and economic changes. A particular irony is that a legislator in Singapore, known to enjoy government support, recently introduced a bill to give parents the right to sue their children for maintenance (and the children the defence that the parents mistreated them when they were young!). It is hard to imagine that such a bill would achieve its objective of maintaining family solidarity!

---

personal and artistic freedoms are more highly valued, suggesting that economic wellbeing is not sufficient for human happiness and fulfilment. This example also illustrates another theme of my paper, that one's view of human rights is coloured by one's economic and social status.

[26] For example, the Convention on the Elimination of All Forms of Discrimination Against Women (CEDAW) (1979) guarantees not only the traditional political and civil rights and the general entitlement to equality before the law, but sanctions affirmative action, and requires States' parties to "take all appropriate measures (a) to modify the social and cultural patterns of conduct of men and women, with a view to achieving the elimination of prejudices and customary and other practices which are based on the idea of the inferiority or the superiority of either of the sexes or on the stereotyped roles for men and women; (b) to ensure that family education includes a proper understanding of maternity as a social function and the recognition of the common responsibility of men and women in the upbringing and development of their children ..." (art 5). States have to take all steps to suppress all forms of traffic in women and exploitation of prostitution of women (art 6). Special responsibilities have been imposed on States in respect of rural women; in particular they are to ensure that rural women participate and benefit from rural development; participate in the elaboration and implementation of planning; have access to adequate health facilities, including information, counselling and services in family planning; obtain all types of training and education, formal and non-formal; access to agricultural credit and loans, and marketing facilities and appropriate technologies; and enjoy adequate living conditions, particularly in relation to housing, sanitation, electricity and water supply, transport and communications.

The concern with the erosion of family values is instructive in a number of ways. At one level it minimises the Asian claim for cultural distinctiveness, and therefore relativity of rights. At another level it provides another basis for relativity. Societies are constantly changing, and with economic and social changes, there are also changes in the perception of what is important and valuable to a community or a group. In other words, an assessment of the priorities in human rights alters with the underlying economic transformations. The West too has had its "communitarian" phase (and the community is still important there), and the family is even now cherished, even if old solidarities are beginning to dissolve under economic pressures. Asian governments, which cheerfully and sometimes aggressively espouse "Western" notions of development and the market, find that they can no longer ward off its child, human rights.

The above analysis suggests that a useful perspective on human rights is drawn from history: the (dialectical) unfolding of rights, representing social achievements, etc. This in turn suggests that the development and understandings of rights are contingent on a variety of factors, moral ideas as well as material conditions, and that differences in their perception are attributable to them rather than to any inherent ideas of culture, community, etc. This approach does indeed provide a basis for reconciling so called "Western" and "Eastern" perceptions of human rights. In my view this provides a better basis for global debates on this subject. The notion that distinct "Western" and "Asian" perspectives exist is inaccurate, ahistorical, and leads to unfruitful polarities (ignoring for example that the West also has a notion of duty (limitations on rights/freedoms). Equally it distorts the debates on human rights, by suggesting that the key conflict is between the East and the West, rather than that it is within each. It detracts from the relevance and urgency of human rights discourse in Asia, the keen debates on the appropriate models for representation, governance and accountability, and equity. Asian intellectuals and activists need to rescue the debate from the present sterile phase to place it at the centre of national and regional politics.

If human rights have to be located in their social and economic contexts, what are the appropriate features that constitute the context for them in Asia?[27] If one may generalise (keeping in mind the simplification that this may involve), the following specifics of the Asian situation stand out. The first point is that the function of human rights (and discourse on them) in Asia is quite different from that in the West. Human rights in the West have responded to the configurations of power and economic relationships as they have evolved over a long period. They are consequently consistent with the patterns and structures of authority, and people's aspirations as well as expectations. There are no serious competing paradigms of political organisation. The role of human rights is to fine tune the administrative and judicial system and fortify

[27] A useful beginning is made in a reflective and insightful essay by Upendra Baxi, "The Right to be Human" 13:3 and 4 (December 1986) *India International Centre Quarterly* 185. The essay has been reprinted in Kothari and Sethi (eds.), *Rethinking Human Rights: challenges for theory and action* (New York: New Horizons Press, 1989).

rights and freedoms that are largely uncontroversial. In Asia, on the other hand, human rights have a transformative potential. They are a constant challenge to vested interests and authority in societies riven by enormous disparities of wealth and power, with traditions of authoritarianism and the helplessness of disadvantaged communities, of militarisation and the conjunction of corrupt politicians and predatory domestic and international capital. Human rights are therefore a terrain for struggle for power and the conceptions of good society. It is for this precise reason that Asian governments have engaged in the debate with the West; the real audiences are their own people.

The second point is that there are massive violations of human rights in Asia; of women and children, of lower castes and otherwise disadvantaged communities, of ethnic minorities, of workers. Violations range over the whole conspectus of human rights; civil and political rights, as well as cultural, social and economic; there are mass killings and widespread disappearances; torture; wide displacements of communities from their traditional abode; arbitrary detentions and extensive censorship of thought and expression. The state is a major culprit, brutalising whole populations, but massive violations also take place in and through civil society, sometimes with the connivance of the state, and frequently reflecting feudalistic and patriarchal dimensions of culture. Social conflicts, particularly those stemming from ethnic or caste differences, have politicised and militarised civil society in many states. These developments should caution us against over-romanticisation of civil society (which in India, for example, is a major source of the oppression of millions of people, through murder and rape, bonded labour, and a web of discriminatory and punitive customs and practices).[28]

The third point is that despite these violations, human rights consciousness is low. Explanations for this paradox may lie in the weight of oppression over centuries, a fatalistic acceptance of one's miseries,[29] obstacles placed in the way of those who would seek to make explicit to the downtrodden the causes of their oppression. It certainly lies in the ethnic divisions of societies; ethnic consciousness can dull human rights consciousness, distinguishing us from "others" and facilitating justifications for their oppression. A major challenge to human rights workers is undoubtedly this ethnic consciousness which compels a perception of outsiders as less than human. Another cause of low human rights consciousness may be widespread poverty. Poverty is a great cause of the denial

[28] The framers of the Indian Constitution were well aware of these problems of civil society. Article 15 declared illegal discriminations on the ground, *inter alia*, of caste, in, for example, access to wells, tanks, bathing ghats, roads and other places of public resort. Article 17 abolished untouchability and its practice in any form. Article 23 prohibited traffic in human beings and forced labour, particularly the traditional form of bonded labour known as "*begar*". There are various laws at the central and state levels to implement these provisions, particularly the Civil Rights Act of 1955 (expanded and renamed as the Scheduled Castes and Scheduled Tribes (Prevention of Atrocities) Act in 1989). Despite these attempts, the social and economic position of these disadvantaged communities shows little improvement.

[29] It is interesting to note that the first generation of women to realise the oppressiveness of the system under which they have been brought up have singular difficulties in behaving in a manner less servile than their mothers!

of human rights. The international system refuses to accept this reality – for largely political reasons. It refuses to acknowledge that poverty destroys human dignity and renders alienable what we proclaim are inalienable rights (the very freedom of the person, as in bondage or sale of children). Without human dignity there can be no human rights; or indeed the capacity to challenge the system of oppression. To serve their transformative potential rights must be linked to power and consciousness.

A further point about human rights in Asia is that challenges to their violations are not individual based but group or class based. This is particularly the case in multi-ethnic states. The protection of human rights is therefore pursued through the group. This fact, and that the state is a major violator of human rights, suggests strategies that are different from the traditional Western approaches, which are legalistic and court centred. Asian strategies cannot realistically be court centred, however favourably the judiciaries may be disposed towards human rights (and for the most part they are not). Human rights conscientisation and mobilisation based on connections between them and their oppression are a fundamental starting point (connections which neither local governments nor the West are anxious should be made).

Nor must the terrain of struggle be purely domestic. Despite the resistance of governments, the realisation of human rights in each country is intimately tied to wider global forces (particularly in the contemporary worldwide pursuit of marketisation). Even today many governments in the Third World are surrogates for external economic and political interests, and it is necessary to take the battle to the homelands of these interests, just as it is necessary to recruit foreign interests to put pressure on domestic governments which deny their people the right to participate in decisions affecting their own destiny.

For Asians concerned with the welfare and dignity of their fellow citizens, the right strategy should embrace the universalism and indivisibility of human rights. The implication of universalism and indivisibility is that human rights can no longer be seen in national terms or responsibility or as contingent on particular economic systems. They raise global issues which highlight the responsibility of people in one state to peoples in others. They imply that consumers in the rich Western countries owe a duty to present generations in other parts of the world and to future generations everywhere. They necessitate the closure of the armaments industry. They require a more equitable international economic system. They import a more democratic international system. Consistent with the dominant role of human rights in history, they raise a truly revolutionary agenda, sufficient to discomfort the West.

Finally, I turn to a brief consideration of the connections between rights and democracy, in the context both of established democracies and other countries which have recently attempted a transition to democracy (Thailand, Nepal, Cambodia, Taiwan, etc.). The process towards better governance and democracy is extraordinarily complicated (even if governance and democracy had similar pre-conditions, which they may not), for it involves issues, which although they are often regarded as of a piece, have different dynamics and consequences – the development of civil rights, the Rule of Law and a liberal culture, democratic reforms through the extension of the franchise and other political rights, the securing of economic and social rights, and fair and transparent governance (to which in some instances we should add marketisation). One problem is that in contemporary constitutionalisation, all these goals are being sought simultaneously. In any circumstances such a task would be daunting, but it becomes even more problematic because there may well, at least in the short run, be a conflict between them. In the 19th century, for example, the rule of law was considered to be under threat from democratisation. Many countries in the transition to democracy in this century have built in a deliberate "democracy deficit", in part to placate its former enemies but also to create the capacity to absorb the social and political consequences of democratisation.

There is space only for some general comments. Let me first take the relationship between democracy and the market. The supporters of the market argue that it inevitably leads to democracy. The argument might be made on both logical and historical grounds. The market is a system of private economy, in which there is a massive decentralisation of decision making and a wide scope for choice. Central to the market are private property, which ensures a measure of autonomy for individuals and groups, and the freedom of contract, which enhances choice and secures rights (and limits the powers of the state). Predictability and legal security, which are also essential to the market, lead to an expert and independent judiciary, and thus to the separation of powers. The market gives rise to or strengthens civil society, and provides a countervailing force to that of the state. In this analysis, the market is more dependent on rights than on democracy.

The historical case, however, is that the development of democracy in the West followed the rise of the market, and that parallel processes are underway in east Asia (in particular Taiwan and Korea). It would be argued that the market leads to certain forms of social formations which stimulate pressures for democracy. In particular it undermines traditional forms of economy and their corresponding forms of political authority, and frees labour from its previous constraints ("from status to contract"). It gives rise to a middle class with its specific interests, connected with rights and democracy, and the economic and political clout to protect them. It also facilitates the organisation of labour, leading to a competitive and pluralistic political order.

However, neither the logical nor the historical evidence is conclusive. Drawing from a model of consumption, the former disregards the process of production (where economic coercion prevails and the mode of organisation is hierarchical). It also assumes a false dichotomy between the state and the market, ignoring their inter-penetration. The market favours a few and does not universalise rights, except perhaps at a formal level. The market oriented civil society substitutes economic pressures for direct political authority, but by that very fact removes accountability, and introduces a different mode of subordination. Similarly, the historical process may be no guide, since it was the market which shaped the state in the West, but it is the state which has shaped the market in Asia. Nor is the globalisation of capital and markets likely to be conducive to rights or democracy. Freed from a territorial nexus, capital may become even more irresponsible and less accountable – less responsive to public opinion and more accommodating of state restrictive practices in its pursuit of profit (as is demonstrated by the way in which both Murdoch and Turner have bent their communication empires to the censorship by China). The growing global dominance of the power of capital over political authority and structures diminishes rather than increases prospects of rights and democracy. The progress in rights and democracy has been achieved by the struggles of the workers and other disadvantaged communities, and not by the advocacy of capitalists.

Let me, finally, explore some conflicts between human rights and democracy. The formalisation and juridification of rights have thrust courts and tribunals to the centre of their definition and enforcement and their discourse has become increasingly specialised. This detracts both from the responsibility and capacity of elected bodies for human rights. The globalisation of human rights detaches specific rights from the national context and relevance. The transformative consequences of economic and social rights (for example, the revolution in the position of women or the shift of power from one caste to another in rural Nepal) may be threatening to an infant democracy because of the interests of incumbent leaders and influential groups.

It is true that certain kinds of rights may be prerequisites to democracy – franchise, expression, and association. It is also true that certain rights may be better protected in a democracy than in other political systems. But the logic of rights is different from the logic of democracy. The former are individual centred (even when they concern social rights), while democracy is majority-centred. The scope of rights is drawn from the nature of the human person; the scope of democracy from the general will. Rights serve to limit state power, while democracy justifies its expansion. Rights may be said to be "rational" and purposive, but democracy is frequently messy and manipulative.

When there are conflicts, rights are likely to give in to democracy.[30] Although rights are now prescribed in considerable detail, and democracy is still nebulous (no international instrument defines or protects it), democracy seems to command greater legitimacy, at least in Asia. Rights are harder to enforce than democracy, in part because of the differing precision of definitions. They may also threaten existing power structures. For that reason democracy may be used to suppress human rights. Politics are viewed largely as a formal business of professional politicians, as a kind of joust (to the finish) rather than as discourse, questioning the legitimacy of academics, journalists, social workers, etc. who wish to express opinions on policies (even in the areas of their own expertise). Democracy, seen largely as an electoral process, becomes plebiscitary. Democ-

[30] The inability of the US government to maintain a consistent policy regarding human rights conditionalities, especially in relation to China, is itself the result of US democracy, as the administration feels compelled, for electoral reasons, to take into account views of corporations and workers who benefit from investments in and trade with China.

racy, seen as the access to state power, becomes manipulative and corrupting. Yet it is presented as the voice of the people; a talisman to ward off domestic and foreign pressures for rights and equity.[31] But for that very reason it increasingly relies on, and caters to, sectional interests.

In the south Asian context, ethnicity has frequently provided that sectional interest. Ethnicity, linked to the democratic or at least the electoral process, has had, for the most part, a negative effect on governance and human rights. Political parties have aggregated and articulated ethnic demands, the majority community has imposed its cultural forms on the state, and the rights of minorities have been trampled upon. The result has often been the militarisation of both the state and civil society and the application of oppressive legislation which has denied a whole array of political, civil, economic and social rights. And yet democracy of a sort has flourished and fed the process of the attrition of democratic values.

[31] Consider the following statement of Dr. Mahathir, Prime Minister of Malaysia, in an attack on the power of judges to interpret and decide on the validity of laws: "If the people want the Government to be restricted so as not to be able to draft certain laws, the people will cause the downfall of the Government...". Quoted in Hickling and Wishart, "Malaysia: Dr. Mahathir's Thinking on Constitutional Issues" (1988–89) *Lawasia*, pp 27–79, at p 57.

Chapter 15

ENRICHING THE STUDY OF LAW

Professor Geoffrey P. Wilson
University of Warwick

Warwick's initial development was based on challenging assumptions. In recent years it has not been necessary to make a conscious effort to challenge assumptions. They have been challenged by events. Two in particular stand out. In the universities there has been a major shift of emphasis from education to research. In the world at large Britain has joined the European Community. Beyond these are changes in technology whose implications we are still not in a position fully to grasp.

The changes at Warwick had focused on the curriculum because, at the time at which it was established, legal education was seen as the main function of a law school, and it is hardly an exaggeration to say that for most legal scholars it was the curriculum that lay at the heart of legal scholarship. All that has now changed for Warwick, and law schools generally. Undergraduates and graduates are no longer the primary customers of law schools. Research has not only been given an identity distinct from that of legal education, it has also been given a new priority. There may still be incentives of convenience to keep the two in harness, and there may still be benefits in feeding the experiences of the one into the other, but the curriculum no longer provides the basic framework for legal scholarship. Enriching the study of law no longer means enriching the curriculum.

The results of British entry into the European Community have been even more dramatic. In 1968 it was still possible to assume that the study of law meant primarily the study of English law, a view reinforced by the pressure of the professions to include in the curriculum what they regarded as the basic elements of English law. It did not need a wizard to see that as a result of British membership of the Community both legal education and legal scholarship would need to take on board the study of Community law. This followed the traditional patterns of English legal scholarship following English law wherever it leads. And, whatever may have been thought at first, it soon became clear that the implications of British membership would not simply be a matter for specialists but, because of the wide scope of Community law and the reverberations it was having in the legal system, would result in a general shift in the orientation of English legal scholarship at large. And it does not stop with Community law itself. Those who shape and administer Community law do not get their ideas out of the blue. They derive them from their experience of, and education and training in, their own systems. This is not just a question of ideas about the substance of the law. It also includes basic assumptions about such matters as the role of law and of different forms of law, the use of alternatives to law, the balance between rule and discretion, the role of judges and lawyers, what constitutes good and bad, relevant and irrelevant, legal reasoning, legal argument and legal justification. As a result, getting to grips with Community law leads easily on to looking at the national systems of Member States from which these ideas and assumptions come. The need simply to understand would lead to this. But the challenge presented by British membership may not simply be a challenge to our understanding. As pressures grow to develop a common European prototype, it may also be a challenge to English law and the English legal system, and even English legal scholarship itself, and the assumptions underlying them and the values they enshrine.

Our responses as individuals to these developments will vary with our reasons for being there at all. It is one of the benefits of the release of legal scholarship from the constraints of the curriculum that it is no longer a question of either/or. There is room for those who see it as a means of servicing the legal system or carrying on practice from a scholarly base; for those who see it as a way of doing good, of using law as an instrument of social change or simply giving effect to the values that are regarded as implicit in the very idea of law; and even for those who see it as a series of challenging puzzles or a giant crossword that will never be solved. There is greater scope than ever before for new developments, new specialisations and more intense developments of old favourites, such as black letter law, though perhaps in a new and more sophisticated guise.

Most of these activities will take place automatically and will require no positive action on our part. But there are two matters which may need special attention. One concerns the foundations and scope of the whole enterprise itself. So many assumptions have been challenged in the world at large and in the universities in which most of us work, that we can no longer take for granted that a pattern set by our predecessors in the 19th century, and in which legal education and the curriculum have played such an influential role, should hold sway into the 21st century. Pollock, Dicey, and Maitland, and their successors, who over the years have shaped the development and direction of English legal scholarship, are not only buried, they no longer rule us from their graves. The loss of the curriculum as a unifying factor and as something which provided a sense of common purpose has left a vacuum. We are in uncharted waters and one question is what use are we to make of our freedom? Secondly, some activities may need a little more encouragement and even protection if they are to develop or even survive. They do not fit so easily into current preoccupations or pressures, and, if care is not taken, they may simply disappear by default. These are questions which not only affect legal scholarship – they directly affect the life of the legal scholar.

The first thing to notice is that we may be more free than legal scholars elsewhere. Everyone takes for granted the fact that law and legal systems differ in different countries. But it is also true of legal scholarship. One reason for this is the different responsibilities legal scholars have in different countries for the maintenance and development of the local law. Every system needs a research arm, but in some countries legal research and scholarship have a far more direct role to play, and legal scholars have a more direct responsibility for the successful working of the system, than in others. One result is that legal scholars in different countries may have different agendas and this may affect the subject-matter, scope and even the form and style, of the local legal scholarship. Even in a common law country like the US legal scholars have played an important role in developing principles of law that would rise above the variations in the courts throughout the country. But the contrast with England is most noticeable in countries like France and Germany where not only do the codes and constitutions provide a basis for the development of the law that is independent of the decisions of the courts, but there is a long-standing tradition that the work of legal scholars has an independent authority within the system. In Germany, for example, the role of legal scholars is neither inferior nor subordinate to that of the judge, even though German legal scholars have increasingly to refer and even to defer to decisions of the higher courts. The character of the BGB which still sets the tone for much of the system is symbolic of the scholarly character of German law and German legal scholars still play the role of architects, inventors or composers, albeit within an existing tradition.

In England the role of legal scholars often looks more like that of parents clearing up clothes left lying around by wayward and careless judges. Citation of, or reliance by the courts on, works of legal scholarship are still hailed as achievements or breakthroughs, which add distinction to the scholars cited rather than the judge. The role of the legal scholar remains much nearer that of a mechanic or bibliographer. The absence of a code, like the absence of a written constitution, means that there is no legal authority higher than the courts to which scholars can appeal, and from which they can develop principles independently and ahead of the courts. Every pronouncement of legal principle by an English legal scholar is provisional and principles largely owe their authority to the fact that they seem to explain successfully the decisions of the courts rather than that they form a body of doctrine founded on a commonly recognised authoritative text. A single decision of the judges of the superior courts can overturn the learning of years derived from and based on their own past decisions. More can be achieved by a generation change or a simple change of composition in the House of Lords than years of intellectual and scholarly argument. In England the case by case approach in which precedents play a larger role than principles, and a strongly centralised system of courts, in which the House of Lords has the last word, gives the legal scholar a less important, less necessary and, ultimately, a less satisfying role to play.

There is another feature of the continental systems, particularly the German, which may affect attitudes both to law and legal scholarship. Codes are usually accompanied by a claim to be comprehensive. And this transfers to the law in general. It results in a model of law as a unity, an overarching whole which in principle is complete. Legal scholarship can be presented as a truly legal science, with the universality of a science, the science of a scientifically based system. This notion of a gapless system may begin simply as a question of technique relevant only to the limited role that law has to play in the society at large. But it is easy to move from the claim that law is comprehensive within the sphere allotted to it to a claim to be comprehensive as a dimension of and as a means of regulating society as a whole, so that law is seen as something of value which provides a comprehensive framework for the whole of society, and not simply as a general ideal but in detail. In spite of its doctrinal and conceptual character the study of law becomes a science of society as a whole and not just part of it and there is a commitment to its use as a value. In some cases this transition or confusion may be reinforced by local circumstances. The German *Grundgesetz*, for example, does not simply set out the legal parts of the Constitution. It provides the basic framework for making democracy a success in Germany and the foundations of a *Rechtsstaat*. It is the core around which a political tradition can grow. Here again the universality attributed to it within the law itself easily becomes a claim to universality of the role of law within society at large, especially when it is a reaction to arbitrariness uncontrolled by law. Scientific commitment is backed up by political commitment and there is a political as well as a technical ground for the dominance and exclusivity of doctrine and for legal scholarship following suit, and for seeing the foundations of the legal system and the foundations of legal scholarship as the same.

English law operates on the basis of a completely different principle. It is open-ended and incremental. Each new decision can in principle alter the shape of the whole and nothing other than a precedent or an individual piece of legislation is sacred. So far as its public law is concerned, in Britain it is the political tradition which is central and not the law. There is not the same incentive to make the coherences and subject-matter of legal scholarship the same as those of the legal system.

Of course, if one was operating as an English legal scholar within these other systems, one might not take the claims for the dominance of a doctrinal approach or comprehensiveness quite as seriously as they are presented here. Even a code based system can be broken up in a quite different way when one looks at law not in terms of its own categories but in the light of the social problems with which it has to cope, with all that means in terms of breaking down traditional internal categories, taking into account the way the system works in practice and looking at alternatives to law in the solution of social problems. Nonetheless a readiness to look beyond the legal system for the subject-matter of legal scholarship and to adopt a style and technique that does not simply reproduce the style of the legal system, may come more naturally to scholars working in a system which does not claim to be comprehensive and which relies on convention in the most basic parts of its constitutional law, just as a readiness to look outside the law at the social problems with which it has to deal may come more naturally to those whose scholarship and legal system do not give such weight to doctrine and Dogmatik, and for whom the Rule of Law does not mean the rule of law.

Some of these differences may lose their force in the future. Although some of the reasons for the different emphasis on doctrine and the contribution of legal scholarship may reflect a difference of principle, others may be the result of mere convention or habit, or even laziness, with English judges at one extreme being content to rely on precedent, or at the other enjoying the exercise of discretion untrammelled by rule. Exposure to Community law, with all the assumptions and learning that go with it, and to lawyers who have been trained in or have studied other systems, may lead to changes, just as the direct impact of Community law has already led to changes in what had hitherto been regarded as fundamental principles of the legal system, such as the doctrine of the Sovereignty of Parliament and the practices of statutory interpretation. If the United Kingdom ever incorporated a Bill of Rights this too would not only judicialise what has until now been regarded as a matter of largely political concern and increase the range of considerations that were relevant to legal argument and judicial decisions, but it might also encourage a move towards a more "rights based" system which would increase the pressure to place more reliance on doctrine and to see the law as a comprehensive and scientific whole.

In any event the task of getting to grips with Community law, let alone the national laws that lie behind them, has enormously increased the scope even of an English legal scholarship that is focused exclusively on English law. A whole new body of learning has suddenly become relevant including not only the substantive law but also the contributions and commentaries of representatives of quite different traditions and ways of going about things, which rest on assumptions and understandings that go well beyond the rules of Community law themselves. Neither practising lawyers nor judges can be expected without help to identify or comprehend the challenges and the alternatives that lie out there. And there is not only a task of assimilation. Legal scholars are ideally placed to go further and to examine critically what is being offered, spelling out the advantages, implications, pitfalls and side effects. This is particularly important where the arrangements elsewhere are regarded as having not just relative but scientific validity and where there may be a commitment to the local and national that goes beyond its mere usefulness.

Merely pointing to differences between the present role of legal scholars in Britain from those elsewhere does not lead inevitably to the conclusion that English legal scholarship should go its own way. However, it does open up a small crack, the possibility that there might be an English legal scholarship which is different because it reflects the different character of the English legal system. This crack becomes wider if one looks not merely at the differences between the national legal systems but at the notion of legal scholarship being focused on the local legal system in the first place. The different role of legal scholarship in England is one reason for thinking that it should not be focused exclusively on the English legal system – but it is not the only one. There is an even stronger case to be made than this and it too is in part a product of the pressure to become more European, but with even more dramatic results.

Instead of simply accepting the need which has resulted from Community membership to get to grips with Community law and the national systems that lie behind it, Warwick has gone one step further and seized the opportunity, not simply to become more European, but to become more international. Its current view is that up until now law schools throughout the world have been guilty of offering something approaching a fraudulent prospectus. They have offered their students the opportunity of studying law but have ended up, usually without any apology or explanation, teaching them for the most part the law of their national system, with all the assumptions and values that go along with it, and legal scholarship has followed suit. Looking at foreign systems has been seen as the work of specialists in comparative law and not included within the scope of everyday legal scholarship. Even they have had a strongly national orientation and have tended to spend their time either explaining their own systems to people outside, or studying foreign systems mainly with a view to improving their own. In each case the intellectual and practical orientation has remained national. The current view at Warwick is that legal scholarship is an intellectual enterprise which ought not to be defined by reference to national frontiers and national jurisdictions and that in future, if anything needs to be justified, it is the focus on English law. Interest in foreign legal systems should no longer be seen as a specialist activity or even as comparative, if comparative means comparing other systems with one's own, but as the natural subject-matter of legal study, whatever the practical reasons, linguistic difficulties, national and local pressures, desires to earn a living within the national legal system, or simple preference, that might lead someone to concentrate on the English legal system. Like so many other preconceptions the emphasis on English law in the past has been rooted in the notion that the function of legal education was to prepare English lawyers to work in the local system, and that this was best done by taking English law as the focal point of the programme. Whether or not this is right in terms of legal education, once legal scholarship is freed from the constraints of the curriculum this reason falls away. The fact is that places like China, Japan, Peru, South Africa or India are no longer the stereoscopic curiosities that they were in Victorian times, when English law was introduced in to the universities. They are part of the immediate world in which we live and, to the extent that legal scholarship is concerned with the role of law and lawyers in daily life, it is their law and life which is relevant as much as ours. And this would be true even if our goal were limited to becoming more European. The definition of Europe is not simply a question of its internal arrangements. Part of its identity is a question of where it fits into the world at large, including other legal systems and even other traditions of legal scholarship.

Taking an international view does not mean the abandonment of a national perspective. Other systems will still be looked at from national cultural, intellectual and even national legal system perspectives, and in the light of national traditions of scholarship in general, and of legal scholarship in particular. Some of this is inevitable but some of it may also be desirable. It may reflect not only unavoidable limitations on outsiders' attempts to understand the society and legal system of another country. It may also reflect a choice. Just as different national legal scholarships may have different agendas, they may have different ways of looking at things, different priorities and concerns, and this applies as much to the ways in which they look at other legal systems as it does to looking at anything else. Although one of the aims may be to reduce the local or insular quality of the perspective, as part of the process of getting a better understanding of law as a whole, nonetheless the scope and purpose of the exercise, the way of going about it, what is seen as significant, may well differ from one national scholarship to another. Even if the purpose of looking abroad ceases to be to service one's own legal system, the object may still be to service one's own legal scholarship, to increase that scholarship's understanding of law and the problems with which it has to cope, the variety of methods available to it, the alternatives to them, the conditions of their effectiveness, and the causes of their failure.

Emphasis on the national perspective is important for another reason. If we are talking about the development of the foundations of English legal scholarship as a whole and expanding the shared perspectives of those working in it, and not just adding specialisms to it, we need to take account of our present national position. Because the transition from national to international is so recent and so sudden we know little collectively about the world at large. And we are talking here of our collective ignorance which has resulted from the ways in which the boundaries of expectation have been drawn in the past and not of individual ignorance, which will vary from one individual to another. There is, if we accept the challenge, a good deal of ground to make up. One result of this is that the first steps may have to be very elementary. We start in some respects from so far back that even rather simple facts may make major additions to our understanding, facts that may be readily available but which we have never seen as relevant. It is important that we should not be deterred from taking these steps by the fact that they do not match up to the most sophisticated standards of the existing traditions of legal scholarship or that they may not be seen as original research. As will be argued later it is important that what counts as innovation should take into account the relative state of different groups and audiences and this is a good example of a step that we should not hesitate to take because of a fear that it will not at first be path-breaking in some general world-shattering way.

The way in which we make the move from foreign systems being seen as a subject only for specialists to the position in which they become part of the natural subject-matter of legal scholarship will vary. Different scholars will have different routes of access depending on interests and accident, on skills and opportunity. Two lines of approach may, however, be particularly useful. It is probably wise in the first place to think in terms of total legal systems in the context of total communities, where everything is seen as potentially relevant rather than going straight to investigating what seems to be the nearest legal equivalent to something with which we are familiar from our own legal system. This is perhaps more obvious when one is looking at a country and legal system that is as remote from an average English legal scholar's consciousness as Japan. It may, however, be equally wise when looking at countries with which we may think we are more familiar. Looking at Germany, France, Italy, and Greece, raises in principle the same general problems. This first approach is itself assisted if, secondly, when looking at the law and the legal systems of other countries, we do not start with the substantive law, but begin by looking at the way the society deals with the problems which face legal systems generally, whether they be structural problems of the legal system itself such as the constitutional framework, sources of law, the appointment, role and status of judges, divisions of jurisdiction, the role of lawyers, accessibility to advice and remedies, or social problems such as the maintenance of order, the organisation and regulation of business, the environment, the organisation of the family. The latter approach is one which is facilitated at Warwick by its now traditional focus on major social problems rather than rules of law. Although the social problems were chosen for the purposes of the new curriculum with British society in mind, the notion of orienting the study of law to social problems makes even more sense as a method of international study. If the problems chosen are problems common to most communities, it becomes possible to make comparisons by looking at the different ways in which different legal systems tackle them, breaking across the internal divisions of law and jurisdiction, which may otherwise hinder an understanding of other systems of law, and yet at the same time highlighting the methods, approaches and concepts that are peculiar to them.

Looked at in this light the shift of emphasis from England to Europe and from Europe to the international scene has been almost entirely positive. The shift in emphasis from legal education to legal research has been more of a two-edged sword. On the one hand it has liberated legal scholarship once and for all from the constraints of the curriculum. At the same time the way in which it has been effected and the motivations behind it have posed a serious threat not only to legal scholarship but to scholarship at large. This is because the shift was not primarily driven by intellectual concerns. It was part of an attempt to redefine what universities are or ought to be about. It was a response to pressures to make universities justify themselves, to make them more accountable, to make them pay their way, which have then been passed on to the departments within them. Although they come to the departments from the universities they are often simply undiluted translations or expressions of the pressures put on the universities themselves. Even the language they use often pays little regard to the special characteristics of universities or the work that goes on in them. They could as well have been sent out by the manager of a water company, biscuit factory or national trust hospital as by the current guardians of the intellectual heritage and enterprise. The image of the transferable manager, tractors one week, prison services the next, has reached the universities, if not in fact, then in terms of personal aspiration. Vice-Chancellors seem to have welcomed the opportunity of presenting themselves as captains of industry just as they have welcomed the restoration of hierarchical, top down management, presented as the most efficient way of making use of scarce resources. It would be foolish for legal scholars who have escaped from the curriculum and the limitations of the national legal system to accept a poisoned chalice from their own managers. If universities have ceased to act as shields or filters and scholars have lost the power to influence the roles and goals of universities, it will be for scholars themselves, in the areas of autonomy which they still possess, to separate out those pressures which may affect the extent to which they will in practice be able to do what they think is right and best from those which should shape the intellectual foundations, scope and direction of their work. Although the pressures will always be on the agenda they should never be allowed to dictate it.

A first step is to escape from the crude use of the word "research" to describe everything that counts as scholarly activity. The use of the word "scholarship" is important in this respect. It is one of the weaknesses of the word "research" that it carries with it a notion of novelty and originality which involves someone discovering something that no one ever knew before. "Scholarship" is more open-ended and covers other ways of making advances which may often be more radical than new discoveries, such as challenging assumptions, explaining, interpreting, adapting, making new associations, classifying, organising and reorganising. Research as discovery also fails to take into account the ways in which audiences are fragmented. Behind it lies an image of something once discovered having a universal validity, and of a single scientific community so organised that the knowledge of one soon becomes the knowledge of all. But there is a good deal of understanding that is not as widespread as that model suggests. Quite apart from the barriers of geography, publication and language, knowledge and understanding are in practice also fragmented by and between disciplines so that what is known to one audience, scholars in one discipline or subject area, may not be known to another and may not even be seen as relevant, because of the way in which they have defined their expertise and sphere of interest. One task of scholarship is to bridge the gaps that exist as a result, even though this is not research in the discovery sense. And the recognition of the fragmentation of knowledge by disciplines is not only relevant to the definition of what counts as scholarship, it is also relevant in another way. It raises the question whether the existing boundaries are drawn in the right place. There have been suggestions in recent years that, at least for the purposes of education, they may be too tightly drawn. It is implicit in the notion of a university that it offers a wide range of courses. Actual choice often, however, cuts off options and, because of the narrow way in which subjects and disciplines have come to be defined, a decision to take a particular subject excludes more than it includes. One response has been the proposal of proponents of modularisation to give students a wider choice of topics from more than one discipline. This has run into the criticism that it may lead to a pick and mix approach which ignores the virtues of coherence and progressive understanding of a subject area from year to year. An alternative response has been for those working in individual subject areas to counteract the worst effects of fragmentation by providing something nearer the rounded experience that the idea of a university conjures up, maintaining coherence by grouping courses within a single discipline but taking a broader view of the discipline itself. This was the approach that Warwick adopted in relation to legal education. At Warwick it was argued that, even if one took an established discipline like Law, there was scope for a broader approach than that which was traditional. Boundaries, it was said, were being drawn in the wrong place. In adding a consideration of social problems to the traditional black letter law the new additions were not recommended as extra-curricular or as law plus another discipline. They were recommended as an essential part of the systematic understanding of law, but with a more expansive view of what that involved. The range of issues was increased as well as the range of relevant literature. And different kinds of coherences and relevances were added to those to be found in judgments in decided cases.

The fragmentation of audiences and groups into disciplines and departments is not confined to education. Its real home is in the field of scholarship where one can also put the question whether the boundaries are drawn in the right place, and whether in particular the existing conventions regulating the scope and content of English legal scholarship should be revised. Here it is important to remember that when we talk of boundaries we are not talking of boundaries like those of territories drawn on a map, of boundaries "between" disciplines, but of boundaries of "disciplines". If one expands one it is not at the expense of another. Each discipline is in effect operating in a world of its own and its scope is for itself to determine. Although we cannot recreate the idea of a university at the level of legal scholarship any more than we can at the level of legal education, we can get nearer to it, and see whether legal scholarship has not cut itself off too soon and too much out of the wider picture. This does not mean that change will be easy. Existing patterns are often strongly entrenched. They are reinforced at the level of education by such things as examinations and the criteria of relevance used in them and are supported at the level of scholarship by such things as criteria for appointment and promotion. Paradoxically with all its connotations of novelty the new emphasis on research with its reliance on peer review and its evaluation in terms of publication in refereed journals and fundraising may often reinforce traditional conceptions of the scope of particular subjects and views of what constitutes excellence in them, and help to keep wanderers in line. Expectations can, however, change. At one time it was enough to know the leading cases and basic principles in a subject as narrow as the law of tort, as a result of the accident that English law does not have a separate category of obligations, and to know only domestic English law. Even a profession-oriented view of legal education would change if one thought less in terms of the production of private lawyers and more in terms of lawyer-administrators. The existing patterns were changed at Warwick and many other scholars followed suit. And even if the final vote is against any change, expansion or realignment, it is arguable that this is at least an opportune moment for exploration.

In exploring the possibilities two connections seem worth looking at. One is the relationship of legal scholarship with both other forms of scholarship and with the world of scholarship at large. Here it is probably time for a change. Back in the 1960s there was a good deal of talk about the incorporation of social science perspectives and methodologies into the study of law. In the late 1960s social scientific tended to mean sociological as sociology was enjoying a reputation of adding exciting new dimensions to the study of society generally, and therefore law within it. On the one hand it was hoped that empirical research would reveal how the law worked in practice and bridge the gap between the law in books and the law in action. On the other sociology seemed to have developed a number of theories which facilitated an in-depth critique not only of law but of the whole of society and of the economy of which it was a part. This was the period in which the notion of socio-legal studies came into common use, epitomised in the (then) SSRC's support of research and post-graduate studies, the setting up of a Law and Social Sciences committee in the SSRC with, what was at the time unusual for that body, a remit to be proactive and encourage the growth of interest in and the conduct of socio-legal research, and the experiment of a socio-legal studies centre in the unlikely location of Oxford. There were courses on socio-legal methods for lawyers like those sponsored by the Nuffield Foundation, which also set up its small grants scheme for socio-legal research. The close association of legal scholarship and the social sciences was seen to be a natural consequence of the fact that they were all concerned in some way with society or simply that they used the word law somewhere along the line. In this sense it could be argued that the attempt to integrate the study of law into the social sciences was more than a response to the attraction of the fashionable and was in part because it offered the possibility of making it part of larger systematic programme.

There is both a negative and a positive case for a change. Although parts of legal scholarship will always resemble parts of the social sciences and will benefit from a knowledge of the subject-matter and methods used in them, the study of law never was and never will be reducible to a social science. In practice sociology proved more attractive for its theoretical and ideological writings than its empirical methodology. Disappointment about the costs in terms of time and the yield in terms of results left that work to specialists. Legal scholars remained indoors but read Marx instead of Maitland. Economics has offered useful insights but can never cover the whole ground.

It is not just a question of the social sciences being a disappointment. There is also a positive argument for a change. Attachment to the social sciences, seeing them as in some sense neighbouring has ceased to be liberating and has become an inhibiting factor. If the study of law needs a home in one of the super-categories into which disciplines are traditionally divided it is perhaps time to see itself as one of the Humanities. This would help to emphasise that law and the study of law are about the quality of life and not just about the mechanics of living and a method of dispute resolution. They are part of the cultural heritage. Legal scholars, like lawyers themselves, need to be more than social engineers, if they are to reflect the values implicit in the idea of law. In fact, rather than make a new attachment, there is probably a stronger case for complete detachment, with no standard alignment at all, no special relationships, no "neighbouring" disciplines. Part of the attraction of the notion of integrating the study of law and the social sciences was that it suggested something systematic, even organic, as if the study of law was to become a major branch of a larger tree. In fact, even within the social sciences, the way in which topics and famous names have been leapt on with enthusiasm by legal scholars looking for new directions, new insights and new stimuli has been fairly random. Fashion, and opportunism, as well as the glamour that comes from identification with a famous name or tradition, have always played an important part in the development of interests. Even the accidents of translation helped to push the work and particular works of Renner, Pashukanis and Habermas to the fore. This randomness in the shaping and direction of scholarship is not confined to the use made of the social sciences. Motivations generally for taking a particular path or perspective have also been random. At an individual level personal interests have been transformed into an intellectual interest. Aspiring solicitors have stuck to doctrine, political activists have studied basic rights and discrimination, women have studied women, mothers have studied family law. The randomness works in a negative way as well. Areas are avoided for which a skill is needed that is not there – languages are a prime example. None of this is reprehensible. It is important that legal scholarship takes into account the life of the legal scholar, but it casts doubt on the desirability of a systematic alignment with any other particular disciplines. There are other reasons for detachment. Intellectual progress seems to take place at different rates and in different ways in different subjects of study at different times. Attention seems to home in on a particular area so that it is not the subject area that is important but the intensity and concentration of clever minds. The breakthrough may occur anywhere and lead to a minor renaissance in one particular field which then provides a stimulus for others, and it does not have to be in the social sciences. Even a fashion may set off a reaction and stimulate a concentration of this kind. Gender is a recent example. Often stimulated by personal concern, as well as objective concerns about inequality and identity, it has also become a fashion. The focus of attention has lead to it being used as a lever to expose assumptions far removed from the original interest in the way that a Marxist approach had done earlier. Scholars have constantly found stimulus as a result of reading books written by non-lawyers and there is no need to cut them off from the parts of the library in which books written by non-social scientists are found. This is particularly true at Warwick which has always had a raiding and expansionist mentality.

Looking at the connection between the study of law and the work of other disciplines is clearly one strategy for looking to the future. The second involves a more direct approach than one prismed through other disciplines. It is more radical and more wide ranging because it does not begin with law or even legal scholarship and ask what out there is relevant to it. It starts with what is out there and asks what is the relevance of legal scholarship to it. It is the same approach that was adopted at Warwick in relation to legal education but on a much larger scale and not limited to social problems.

The original message of Warwick was that it was time to take a broader view of the scope of legal education and scholarship. One of the ways in which new issues were raised, and the scope of legal education expanded, was to take self-evidently important problems facing individuals in their daily lives that could be generalised into problems facing society as a whole, and to ask what was the relationship of, not only law, but also lawyers and the legal system to them. The law "of" became the law "and", law and the consumer, for example, rather than the law of the consumer, or more often the law of the sale of goods, law and the environment, law and the family, law and employment. This expanded the scope of the study of law not only by setting up links with the problems with which law was designed to deal but also with other things which were also relevant to the problems. It expanded the study of law to include the study of not-law, the alternatives to law whose use may be more effective or more appropriate than the use of law, or may be an essential condition of the success of the use of law or which may be needed in addition to and alongside of law. In putting social problems first it raised questions about the role of law instead of simply taking it for granted and opened up discussion of the different roles of law and lawyers in relation to different kinds of problem. It cut across the traditional boundaries between different forms of law, civil, criminal and administrative, and different areas of law, tort and contract, and added problems like accessibility, jurisdiction, cost, and effectiveness to the study of law and procedure. It also made it clear that the study of law was meant to concern itself with matters of obvious importance. It was not simply a mental exercise or discipline or to be studied merely to qualify to be a lawyer or simply to monitor and respond to the accidents and incidents of litigation.

All this was a radical advance but it was still only a limited one. In taking social problems as a starting point it was only necessary to take some of the most obvious and there was a limit to the number that could be considered because of the pressure on the curriculum from the professional bodies and the limits of a three year course. There were major omissions which are not only Warwick omissions but blind spots which seem to have affected English legal education and scholarship generally. In spite of the importance of agriculture, for example, in the European Community, in the development of individual countries, in world trade, and in relation to the environment, the mainstream tradition of English legal scholarship has been resolutely urban. It has also been resolutely secular, showing little interest in religion. It has been philistine in its neglect of the cultural heritage, as if using conveyances as lampshades was the best that one could hope from law as a means of illuminating the quality of life. When one considers how large a problem the armed forces can create for constitutional government it has given little prominence to the armed forces. None of these omissions is likely to survive the shift from education to research or from the national arena to the world stage.

It is now time to go beyond social problems in considering the future scope and orientation of English legal scholarship, but the basic strategy remains the same. First comes the identification of something that is important which derives its importance from some other source than its direct legal significance. Then comes the question about the relationship of legal scholarship to it. Here too we are speaking in the first instance of the obviously important, but this time not limited to readily identifiable social problems but extended to events, ideas, understandings, institutions, even artefacts, that are generally accepted as being important in their own right, the neglect of which seems to call for some explanation; the kinds of thing which are said to form part of or to have helped to shape the cultural, intellectual, political economic or physical environment; things which are part of one's consciousness without their having been studied, or because they formed part of a general education and socialisation now half forgotten; things of which one can say that one really ought to know about them especially when failure to do so is derived from the current expectations of what a legal scholar should, or need not, know, where the suggestion that legal scholarship has nothing to do with or say about them casts doubt on its own importance and relevance. Something must give way, either their claim to importance or legal scholarship's refusal to acknowledge any concern about or relationship with them.

Europe may serve as an example. The question has already been raised as to how much does one need to know about Europe to be a legal scholar? The minimalist response is, of course, a knowledge of the structure of the Community and Community law. But it was suggested earlier that the need to get to grips with Community law can easily lead on to the wider study of the legal systems of Europe and even of the world at large. But what of the Europe that is not Community law and which is not law at all? What of Europe's past? How much of the past and what parts of the past do we need to understand if we want to understand Europe as an aspect of legal scholarship, not as a specialist topic, but as part of the definition of legal scholarship itself. What is and ought to be the relationship between English legal scholarship and those events and developments in the past which are widely assumed to have influenced the present and indeed which can be said to be part of the living past, which are said to have shaped and continue to shape our conceptions of Europe and our European conceptions, and even the fact of Europe; which are said to be part of our European heritage including our traditions of scholarship in general and legal scholarship in particular? What of the legacy of Greece and Rome, for example the Reformation and the Renaissance, the expansion of Europe and the Spanish conquest of the Americas, colonialism and the growth of European-centred learning, the Enlightenment, the American, French and Russian revolutions, Mussolini's Italy, the Nazi regime, and the German *Grundgesetz*? Can an understanding of the context in which legal scholarship is carried on ignore the revival of learning in Bologna in the 12th century and in Berlin in the 19th century? Can even Europeans ignore events outside Europe such as the civil rights movement in the United States, not to speak of Akbar and Ashurbanipal?

Europe and the past are just one small example of the challenge. The strategy of questioning the relationship between legal scholarship to matters of importance is both flexible and dynamic. It not only involves remapping, rethinking the place of legal scholarship in relation to matters of established importance. It also involves looking at new developments in the present and the future; the breakdown of central and eastern Europe, for example, the problems facing developing countries, the organisation of world trade, the impact of developments in South East Asia, the future of the European Community, the role of women, and as well as narrower topics such as corruption in Italy, Europe and the world at large, down to objects of importance in everyday life, and asking what is the relationship of English legal scholarship to them. The first step puts legal scholarship on the wider map. The second is designed to keep it there. It is not only a way of keeping legal scholarship up to the mark. It also provides a perpetual source of challenge and enrichment, parallel to, but on a different planet from, that provided by new judgments for the traditional common law scholar. How much of a challenge and how great the enrichment depends on the spirit in which the task is undertaken, if it is undertaken at all. There is an argument for boldness, for a realignment and a reorientation which will provide some assurances that legal scholarship will be and remain near to the mainstream of important developments, and which will prevent legal scholarship becoming too boxed in by its own traditions, becoming too introverted. Here the emphasis on, and the opportunity of looking directly at, the world at large rather than at or through other disciplines may be of particular help. We can afford to be bold because we are not being prescriptive as we were forced to be when discussing what should be included in a limited curriculum. The search is not for a new orthodoxy. It is a search for greater variety not less, a broader scope not a narrower and not simply at the edges and the frontiers but as part of the foundations of the enterprise and for something more systematic than the random nourishment of the legal imagination.

It cannot be claimed that the coherences and the relevances that are created in this way will have a universal validity, true for all times and places of the kind which the natural sciences have to offer. Nor are the links there to be discovered. Just as what is European is something to be defined not simply observed, tracing out the links and seeing whether and in what way the new features are to be integrated into the total picture is a creative enterprise but probably no more so than the invention of Law as a subject of education and scholarship was in the first place. Acceptability of any proposal for change will depend far more on the goodwill and enthusiasm and imagination of the listener than any knock-down argument, and on an appeal that goes deeper than surface logic. The principal argument for it must be that it offers a more useful, stimulating, satisfying framework for legal study, something that will tap the full potential of legal scholars, and which ensures that legal scholarship has a more mainstream role to play both in the world of scholarship and in the world at large than it has permitted itself in the past.

In drawing new boundaries, making new links, and expanding the criteria of relevance and coherence, legal scholars can afford to be less rigorous than lawyers working in the legal system. And this is true not only of the drawing of the boundaries of the scope and subject-matter in the first place. It is also true of the practice of legal scholarship once the new boundaries have been drawn. The discipline of the law, even the relatively lax discipline of English law, and the discipline of legal scholarship, are not the same. There may still be the need on occasion to adopt or ape the formal style of legal argument and language used in the legal system but this need not and should not cover the whole ground. There is even more of a need to preserve styles, means, levers, tools, criteria, values and forms of language and expression which go beyond the characteristic language, logic and methods of the law, even English law. Here again, English legal scholarship may be a special case. It may be more plausible for a more limited range of styles of reasoning and criteria of relevance to dominate the language of legal scholarship where and when the main function of the legal scholar is to service the legal system. English legal scholarship, however, can afford openly to acknowledge techniques and qualities which are outlawed from the public face of the legal system. It can exploit chance, serendipity, randomness, opportunism, curiosity, speculation, imagination, intuition, hunch, impulse, spontaneity, experimentation, risk, boldness, excitement, adventure, surprise, eclecticism, plausibility, ambiguity, imprecision, simplicity, naivety, open questions, hesitations, uncertainties, doubts, alternative views, contradictions, inconsistencies, mistakes, flair, elegance, style, sensitivity, learning, iconoclasm, idiosyncrasy, irreverence, irony, satire, variety, renewal, revival, colour, shape, vibrancy and infection. All these may, of course, in practice be features, even desirable features, of the legal system itself, but there the façade of logic that hides them is an important part of the formal discipline which contributes to the legitimacy of the law, and its special methods of creativity and development. But neither legal scholars nor legal scholarship should be too quick to put on a suit and a wig.

This list is random and casual. It is simply to make the point that it is important to keep open and available a wider range of styles and methods than is permitted to judges or commonly find their way between the covers of a legal textbook. But there are two values which may need special consideration, one because it may disappear by default if no special attention is given to it, the other because it seems to have escaped general notice altogether.

The particular mode of expression, communication, reasoning and understanding that may need special attention is the oral. It is a noticeable feature of much of the new pressure to put research as a top priority that it emphasises, not so much research as such, but publication, and publication in written form. Developments in technology push in a similar direction, though this may be temporary, until they cease to rely so heavily on written communication and give equal emphasis to the visual and oral. It is no longer as fanciful as it was to imagine a law school as a location of machines with no one present but the technicians needed to service them. There need not even be law schools. One would be enough, with any separate contribution that different law schools might have made in the past being reduced to channels of choice, if variety is still seen to be desirable, with scholars writing programmes for them and adding to the menu, communicating with one another from deepest Norfolk, the south of France or far-flung California. No one need meet or speak again. It is at least a moment to pause and ask whether we should mind if publication and communication in written form were to characterise the whole of legal scholarship or whether it should preserve other styles of expressing and communicating understanding.

Oral communication, in particular when it is face to face communication, has distinct features. The lecture, when seen as a distinct genre and not simply as a means of conveying written information, can stand as a shorthand for some of them, though discussion and dialogue may have others. More acutely than in the case of something written the lecture requires the presenter to take into account the limitations of the attention, endurance and comprehension of his audience. It must also take the relativity and fragmentation of knowledge and understanding into account by responding to the different characteristics and needs of different audiences. It often involves simplification. It cannot rely on footnotes. If it has any regard for the audience it must be phrased in a particular way. If it is to be persuasive it may have to sugar the pill. It may have to adopt forms of communication which appeal to the imagination. It becomes even more distinctive when everyday language is used. There is a special quality about an argument that uses everyday language and in which rhetoric, the striking phrase or analogy is an important element. It serves to reduce the mysticism both between specialists and between specialists and the wider public and increases the chances of the contents of the lecture becoming part of a wider common currency, albeit with the attendant risk of degeneration into communication by soundbite. Like the formulation of new coherences it is then a step towards the idea of universality. It is particularly useful for particular purposes such as setting goals and aspirations, formulating programmes, challenging old and setting up new assumptions. As a face to face occasion, too, the lecture includes the possibility of communication and persuasion by gesture, demonstration, presentation and accompaniment. It also has the potential of being an event, a decisive moment, though the connotations here are more often negative than positive, especially when the oral becomes part of a staged multi-media event, when persuasion is carried to an extreme, presentation becomes propaganda and audience response hysteria, though its very significance in this respect calls for attention. What is even more important than its special characteristics as a means of conveying understanding is that it conveys a special kind of understanding, that which can be expressed orally just as it is a special kind of understanding, which can be taken in aurally. Oral communication sets itself apart from all kinds of mechanical communication and the kind of machine learning which can escape the emotional commitment that constitutes true understanding, when we internalise something and make it, or some version of it, our own and which distinguishes it from mere knowledge. It preserves the notion that communications have communicators, and that, at the end of the day it is they who are the important players, something that is obscured when communication is entirely by E-mail. It reflects a distinctive view of the structure and quality not only of the world of scholarship but of society at large and the relationships within it.

The fact that in addition to being distinctive the oral has also been a feature of the English legal system may also be important, not because it has been a feature of the system but because it may be seen as characteristically English. The English legal system has long placed a value on oral argument and presentation and judgment, and shown reluctance to rely on written briefs, allowing even superior courts to give judgments in a style that would not be accepted for an article in the Harvard Law Review.

If orality is under threat the visual is hardly seen as a value at all. The visual as subject-matter can be found in strictly legal contexts in relation to questions of intellectual property, or the sale of art works, and in the international arena as a claim to the recovery of items of cultural heritage taken from their countries of origin. But the challenge of the visual to legal scholarship is not a question of the circumstances in which visual objects or images may become important or relevant in law. It is a question of how far legal scholarship can ignore the visual as such. A deep imbalance has grown up between the use of the visual as a means of communication in the outside world and in everyday life, and its use in universities in general, and in legal scholarship in particular. The visual appears in a multiplicity of guises: photographs, films, drawings, prints, buildings, sculptures, paintings, posters, scenery, demonstrations, rituals, processions, ceremonial, dress, emblems, banners, flags, uniforms, illuminations and artefacts. It plays a variety of roles. Visual images are part of the cultural heritage and the environment; they help to shape our perceptions and conceptions; our views of presidents, prime ministers and products. They appear as propaganda, they present authority, hierarchy and power. They are used to instil terror and inspire belief. They clearly make up an important element of daily life and societies the world over and are important means of communication. Their importance is so great and diverse that it must raise a question about a scholarship that can think of them only in terms of visual aids or the subject-matter of regulation or litigation or the concern of the, rare, specialist. Like the oral, the visual is not simply a neglected form of communication. It is a neglected form of understanding. The concept of Europe, for example, is not simply illustrated by the visual. It is partly visual. Nazism or colonialism are not simply illustrated by their architectural and other visual manifestations. These are part of what they were, just as crowns and wigs are not illustrations of monarchs and judges. They are worn to be a part of our conception of what being a monarch or a judge is. Like the oral the visual is another particular case where the starting point is that it is something of importance in its own right, as a general category and not simply in its individual forms, and poses the same question: what should the link be between it and legal scholarship?

If English legal scholarship were to take on two further features then the wheel would have come full circle, from detachment from the English legal system to some kind of rapprochement with it, for attachment to concrete situations and a pragmatic approach have been regarded as even more characteristic of the English legal system than its attachment to the oral. One feature of the Warwick approach as originally conceived was that its ultimate reference point was to factual situations, not in the sense that it emphasised empirical research, though it has come to do so increasingly in recent years, or even that it focused its attention on the way in which the system worked in practice, though this has always been one of its concerns, but in the sense that its major criterion of relevance and importance was the experience of people in their daily lives. The social problems to which it referred were common basic problems facing individuals on a continuing basis. Housing, employment, shopping, social security as well as what lay behind them, the organisation of businesses and commerce and of government. All else was instrumental. Housing law did not start with a statute on housing. It started with the need for housing and how that was to be satisfied. The law of negligence became the means for dealing with the prevention, and compensation, for accidents. *Donoghue* v *Stevenson*, the paradigm case in legal education at the time, became simply an example of one means of tackling the problem, both at the narrow level of the tort of negligence and the broader level of judicial decision-making within the framework of the doctrine of precedent.

The wider the frame of reference the greater the need for a clear set of reference points. There are still strong arguments for using concrete situations, even artefacts, as reference points, as points of departure and return and for using impact on people as a test of importance and relevance. However remote the links between the Renaissance, for example, and the experience of the individual may seem, the assumption is that a link can be found or created. It is not simply part of a closed world of scholarship. Not only do concrete facts provide a measure of importance and a reference point, a discipline, they may also act as catalysts, as keys to open up and deepen understanding, and this applies to objects from fish and bananas to the frieze of the Parthenon and the lord of Sipan.

In the English legal system the emphasis on concrete factual situations is part of a more generally pragmatic case-by-case approach to the administration and development of the common law. It is a feature of this approach that it leaves gaps. It does not attempt to fill in all the open spaces. It gives at least some credit to the peculiarities of individual cases and in this way attempts to reduce the gap between them and the principles which are used to describe, define or deal with them. Here English legal scholarship may have something to learn from the English legal system. There are virtues in the latter's hesitation to become abstract too quickly and its reluctance to use abstractions which cannot readily be traced back to concrete, or, at least, realistic hypothetical, cases, and its preference for reacting to the stimulus and variety of concrete cases. There is a special quality too about a legal scholarship which has its ultimate roots in everyday life, where behind the abstraction is a concrete image and a thread which leads back to a typical concrete situation; where the relevant principles are not sealed off in an enclosed body of doctrines, concepts and principles where there are multiple direct relationships of its parts to the real world, and in which the principles themselves are renewed by the pressure of concrete facts and result from and are tested against concrete issues. It is quite different from an approach which sees theory and theorising as the purpose and foundation of scholarly activity or which aims to build up scientific theories which purport to explain results in terms of causalities of a recurring kind.

There are constraints on our freedom to choose. It is important to recognise and understand them and also to recognise them for what they often are: institutional, structural, often self-imposed but not, in the end, intellectual and not allow them to obscure the real or possible nature of the enterprise, even though they may shape what can actually be done at any particular time. One can stand for the rest. Just as it was easier to introduce a new curriculum in a new institution rather than an old one, some of the goals of legal scholarship may not be attainable or not so easily attainable unless some existing structures and traditions are changed. The tradition of the lone scholar in particular may prove inadequate. It is difficult to see how individuals scattered in different institutions can realistically tackle the problems caused by major institutions such as governments or multinational corporations, or widescale problems such as the pollution of the environment or the common agricultural policy, or the problems facing the desire for more constitutionalism in Europe, let alone the wider world. It has always seemed odd that lone legal scholars should even attempt to take on single-handedly the combinations of talent and resources that one finds in corporate firms or government departments or to compete with scholars elsewhere who have a more authoritative status and more resources, with fewer resources than are available to a team of journalists engaged in the same task, and not even back up from assistants or doctoral students. We may have to look for more co-operation between individuals and between law schools and not only between British law schools but between law schools across Europe and beyond. The advances of technology may here make a vital difference and this is important because there is a natural tendency to refuse to consider any development which goes beyond one's present skills, capacities or current agenda, a danger that the definition of the field as a whole will resemble a collective projection of what each individual feels is within his present capacities at a time when one of the basic issues is whether the skills, capacities and agenda should be expanded.

Even if the end conclusion is that nothing needs to be done, the strategies suggested here are at least a means of questioning existing assumptions about the scope and orientation of legal scholarship. Even the exploration rests on assumptions; that the curriculum, the legal system, other disciplines should not be allowed to provide the whole of the context in which legal scholarship is carried on, that there is a case to be made for a more rounded and more wide ranging conception of its foundations and for a more rounded and more wide ranging conception of the life of a legal scholar.

THE CONTRIBUTORS

Professor Steven D Anderman

B.A., (Econ) (Queen`s College, CUNY) LL.B. (Yale), MSc (Econ) (London)

Professor of Law, Department of Law, University of Essex

Previous posts

Research Fellow, Law Faculty, University of Stockholm (1960-61)
Staff Tutor in Industrial Relations, Delegacy for Extra-Mural Studies, Oxford University (1966–68)
Lecturer in Law (1968–73); Senior Lecturer in Law (1973–77); Reader in Law (1977–90); Chairman, School of Law (1979–82), University of Warwick Law School

Other appointments and qualifications

Visiting Professor, New York Law School (1983 and 1985)
Visiting Professor, University of Pennsylvania Law School (Spring 1988)
Distinguished Visitor in the University of Connecticut School of Law, Distinguished Visitor Programme (1985)
Adviser to Department of Employment on Labour Legislation (1968–70)
Expert adviser to the Economic and Social Committee of the European Community (1984–current)

Selected publications

Trade Unions and Technological Change (1967) George Allen and Unwin
Unfair Dismissals Procedures and the Industrial Relations Act (1972) PEP
Employment Protection: a Legal Framework (1976) Butterworths
Law of Unfair Dismissal (1978) 2nd ed (1985) Butterworths
Law and the Weaker Party, an Anglo Swedish Comparative Study of Housing, Consumer and Labour Law (Joint General Editor) (1981–90) Butterworths
Labour Law: Management Decisions and Worker Rights (1992) 2nd ed (1993)
EC Competition Policy and Intellectual Property Rights (in preparation) OUP

Professor Patrick Atiyah

B.C.L, D.C.L (Oxford), LL.D (Hon.) (Warwick)

Emeritus Professor of English Law, University of Oxford

Previous posts

Lecturer, Senior Lecturer, University of Khartoum (1955–59)
State Attorney, Attorney-General's Chambers, Ghana (1959–61)
Legal Assistant to the Board of Trade, London (1961–64)
Fellow, New College, Oxford (1964–70)
C.U.F. Lecturer, Oxford University (1965–1970)
Professor of Law, Australian National University (1970–73)

Professor of Law, University of Warwick (1973–77)
Professor of English Law, Oxford University (1977–88)
F.B.A. (1978)

Other appointments and qualifications
Visiting appointments, Yale Law School (1968); University of Texas (1979); Harvard Law School (1982–83); Duke University (1985)
Public lectures: Lionel Cohen Lecture, Hebrew University of Jerusalem (1978); Oliver Wendell Holmes Lecture, Harvard (1981); Chorley Lecture, London School of Economics (1984); Hamlyn Lectures (1987)

Selected publications
The Sale of Goods, 1st ed (1957) (9th ed (by John Adams) 1995) Pitman Publishing
Introduction to the Law of Contract, 1st ed (1961) (5th ed 1995) OUP
Accidents, Compensation and the Law, 1st ed (1970) (5th ed (by Peter Cane) 1994) Butterworths
The Rise and Fall of Freedom of Contract (1979) OUP
Essays on Contract (1983) OUP
Form and Substance in Anglo-American Law (1987, with R S Summers) OUP

Professor Michael Chesterman

B.A., LL.B (Sydney), LL.M (London)

Professor of Law and Dean of the Faculty of Law, University of New South Wales

Previous posts
Solicitor (1965–87); Barrister (1987–current), Supreme Court of New South Wales
Lecturer in Law, King's College, London (1966–73)
Senior Lecturer in Law (1973–77); Professor of Law (1977–78), University of Warwick
Commissioner, Australian Law Reform Commission (1983–92)
Commissioner, New South Wales Law Reform Commission (1993–current)

Other Appointments
Barrister-at-Law, Lincoln's Inn, London (1969–current)
Visiting Senior Lecturer in Law, University of Nairobi (1972–73)

Selected Publications
Specialist Contributor, *Gore-Browne on Companies* (ed A J Boyle), 42nd ed (1972), 43rd ed (1977) Jordan & Sons
Specialist Editor (Conflict of Laws), *Benjamin's Sale of Goods* (ed A G Guest), 1st ed (1974), 2nd ed (1981) Sweet & Maxwell

Law of Business Associations in East and Central Africa (1976, with J Katende, P Thomas, S Mann) East Africa Literature Bureau
Small Businesses, 1st ed (1977), 2nd ed (1982) Sweet & Maxwell
Charities, Trusts and Social Welfare (1979) Weidenfield & Nicolson
Australian Law Reform Commission Report 27, *Standing in Public Interest Litigation* (1985) and Report 35, *Contempt* (1987) Australian Government Publishing Service
"Legal Scholarship in Australia", MLR 50 (1987, with D Weisbrot)
Trusts Law: Texts and Materials (1988, with G Moffat) Weidenfield & Nicolson
"The Money or the Truth: Defamation Law in Australia and the USA", (1995) 18(2) University of New South Wales Law Journal 300

Professor Ross Cranston

LL.B (Queensland), LL.M (Harvard Law School), D.Phil (Oxford)

Cassel Professor of Commercial Law, London School of Economics

Previous posts
Lecturer in Law, University of Warwick (1975–77)
Lecturer, Australian National University (1978–86)
Dean and Director of Centre for Commercial Law Studies, Queen Mary and Westfield College (1986–92)

Other appointments and qualifications
Barrister, Gray's Inn (1976)

Selected publications
Consumers and the Law, 2nd ed (1985) Weidenfeld & Nicolson (*Law in Context Series*)
Regulating Business (1979) Macmillan (*Oxford Socio-Legal Studies*)
Legal Foundations of the Welfare State (1985) Weidenfeld & Nicolson *(Law in Context Series)*
Law, Government and Public Policy (1985) OUP
Legal Ethics and Professional Responsibility Clarendon (n.y.p.)

Professor John Dewar

B.A., B.C.L., M.A. (Oxford)

Professor, Faculty of Law, Griffith University, Brisbane, Australia

Previous posts
Lecturer in Law, University of Lancaster (1981–83)
Lecturer in Law, University of Warwick (1983–88)

Head of Education and Training, Allen & Overy, London (1988–90)
Fellow and Tutor in Law, Hertford College, Oxford (1990–5)

Other appointments and qualifications
Barrister-at-Law, Gray's Inn

Selected publications
Law and the Family 2nd ed (1992) Butterworths
Cohabitants (with S. Parker) 4th ed (1995) FT Law and Tax
"Concepts and coherence in Family Law" in P.Birks (ed) *Examining the Law Syllabus: Beyond the Core* (1994) OUP
Family Law: Theory and Policy (draft title) with S. Parker OUP (n.y.p.)
Media Symposium Presentation (1993)

Professor David Farrier

LL.B. LL.M. (London), Dip.Crim. (Cambridge)

Professor of Law; Co-Director of the Centre for Natural Resources Law and Policy, University of Wollongong

Previous posts
Ford Foundation Fellow, University of Columbia (1970–71)
Inter-University Council Fellow, University of Ahmadu Bello, Nigeria (1975)
Lecturer in Law, University of Warwick (1971–78)
Visiting Senior Fellow, University of Warwick (1985–86)
Senior Lecturer in Law, University of New South Wales (1979–91)
Visiting Research Fellow, Natural Resources Law Center, University of Colorado (1994)

Selected publications
Drugs and Intoxication (1980) Sweet & Maxwell
Environmental Law Handbook: Planning and Land Use in New South Wales (1988) 2nd ed (1993) Redfern Legal Centre Publishing
Criminal Laws (with D. Brown, D. Neal and D.Weisbrot) (1990) Federation Press
"Conserving biodiversity on private land: incentives for management or compensation for lost expectations?" (1995) 19(2) *Harvard Environmental Law Review* 303–408
"In search of real criminal law" in Bonyhady, *Environmental Protection and Legal Change* (1992) Federation Press 79–124
"Regulation of rural land use: coercion or consensus" (1990) 2(1) *Current Issues in Criminal Justice* 95–124
"Criminal law and pollution control: the failure of the Environmental Offences and Penalties Act 1989 (NSW)" (1990) 14(5) *Criminal Law Journal* 317–341

"The distinction between murder and manslaughter in its procedural context" (1976) 39 MLR 414–431

Professor Yash Ghai CBE

B.A., D.C.L. (Oxford), LL.M. (Harvard)

Sir Y K Pao Professor of Public Law, University of Hong Kong
Honorary Professor of Law, University of Warwick
Honorary Doctor, University of the South Pacific

Previous posts
Lecturer, University of East Africa
Uppsala University
University of Warwick
National University of Singapore
Yale Law School
Professor of Law, University of Warwick (1978–92)

Other appointments and qualifications
Barrister-at-Law, Middle Temple
Visiting Professor, Indian National Law School
Adviser to various governments and political parties on constitutional matters
Consultant on the independence constitutions of Papau New Guinea, the Solomon Islands, and Vanuatu
Member, Advisory Council of the Commonwealth Human Rights Initiative
Member, Advisory Council of Interights
Member, Law Reform Commission of Hong Kong

Selected publications
Public Law and Political Change in Kenya (1970), with Patrick McAuslan OUP (Nairobi)
Law in the Political Economy of Public Enterprise (1977) Nordic Institute of African Studies (Uppsala)
The Political Economy of Law: Third World Perspectives (1987, co-ed) OUP (Delhi)
Law, Politics and Government in Pacific Island States (1988) University of the South Pacific (Suva)
Heads of States in the Pacific: A Legal and Constitutional Analysis (1988), with Jill Cottrell, University of the South Pacific (Suva)
The Law, Politics and Administration of Decentralisation in Papau New Guinea (1992), with Anthony Regan,University of the South Pacific (Suva)
The Hong Kong Bill of Rights: A Comparative Approach (1993, co-ed) Butterworths (Singapore)

Professor Martin Loughlin

LL.B. (London), LL.M. (Harvard), LL.M. (Warwick)

Professor of Law, University of Manchester

Previous posts

Sessional Lecturer, Osgoode Hall Law School, York University, Toronto (1977–78)
Lecturer in Law, University of Warwick (1978–84)
Lecturer in Law, London School of Economics (1984–88)
John Millar Professor of Public Law, University of Glasgow (1988–91)

Other appointments and qualifications

Visiting Assistant Professor of Law, University of Oklahoma (1978)
Visiting Fellow, School for Advanced Urban Studies, University of Bristol (1982–83)
Visiting Professor of Law, Osgoode Hall Law School, York University, Toronto (1987)

Selected publications

Half a Century of Municipal Decline 1935–1985 (1985) Allen & Unwin, co-ed
Local Government in the Modern State (1986) Sweet & Maxwell
Public Law and Political Theory (1992) Clarendon Press
Administrative Accountability in Local Government (1992) Joseph Rowntree Foundation

Professor Martin Partington

LL.B (Cambridge)

Professor of Law and Pro-Vice Chancellor, University of Bristol

Previous posts

Lecturer in Law, University of Bristol (1966–69)
Lecturer in Law, University of Warwick (1969–73)
Lecturer in Law, London School of Economics (1973–80)
Professor of Law and Head of Law Department, Brunel University (1980–87)
Dean of the Faculty of Social Science, Brunel University (1985–87)
Dean of the Faculty of Law, University of Bristol (1988–92)

Other appointments and qualifications

Barrister-at-Law, Middle Temple
Chairman, Coventry branch of Child Poverty Action Group (1971–73)
Member, Executive Committee of the Legal Action Group (1982–83)
Member, Law and Social Sciences Committee of the SSRC (1980–83)

Member, Lord Chancellor's Advisory Committee on Legal Aid (1988–91)
Member, Law Society's Training and Academic Consultative Committees (1989–91)
Member, Tribunals Committee (1988–95) and main board of the Judicial Studies Board (1992–95)
Chairman, Committee of Heads of University Law Schools (1990–92)
Chairman, Socio-Legal Studies Association (1993–95)
Member, Council on Tribunals (1994–current)
Visiting appointments, Osgoode Hall Law School, York University, Ontario (1976) and University of New South Wales (1980)
Director, Centre for the Study of Administrative Justice, University of Bristol (1994–current)
Social Security Editor, *Industrial Law Journal*
General Editor, *Anglo American Law Review*

Selected publications
Landlord and Tenant (1975, 2nd ed, 1980) Weidenfeld & Nicolson
Claim in Time (1978) Francis Pinter (2nd ed, 1989, 3rd ed, 1994) Legal Action Group
Housing Law (1983) (with A. Arden) (2nd ed with A. Arden Q.C. and C. Hunter, 1993) Sweet & Maxwell
Housing Law (1991) (with J. Hill) Sweet & Maxwell
Secretary of State's Powers of Adjudication in Social Security Law (1990) School for Advanced Urban Studies, University of Bristol

Professor Sol Picciotto

B.A. (Oxford) J.D. (Chicago)

Professor of Law, University of Lancaster

Previous posts
Lecturer in Law, University College, Dar es Salaam (1964–68)
Lecturer in Law (1968–79); Senior Lecturer (1979–92); Chairman, School of Law, (1982–85), University of Warwick
Head of Law Department, University of Lancaster (1992–95)

Other appointments and qualifications
Visiting Professor, Nagoya University, Japan (May–June 1986)
Jean Monnet Fellow, European University Institute, Florence (1991–2)
Joint Editor, *International Journal of the Sociology of Law* (1988–91)
Founding Joint Editor, *Social and Legal Studies, an International Journal* (1992–current)

Selected publications
Negotiable Instruments in East Africa: Text and Materials (1967)

"The International Firm, International Law and the Nation-State" (1973) 6 *Eastern Africa Law Review* 1
"Capital, Crisis, and the State" (with John Holloway) (1992–95) University of Lancaster (1977) 2 *Capital and Class* 76–101
Jurisdictional Conflicts, International Law and the International State System" (1983) 11 *International Journal of the Sociology of Law* 11–40
"Nuclear weapons, state power and legitimacy in international law" in Dewar, Paliwala, Picciotto & Ruete (eds) *Nuclear Weapons, the Peace Movement and the Law,* (1986) Macmillan at 3–24
International Business Taxation (1992) *Law in Context Series,* Weidenfield & Nicholson/Butterworths
International Taxation and Intra Firm pricing in transnational corporate groups (1992) 17 *Accounting, Organisations & Society* 759–792
"Transfer pricing and the antinomies of corporate regulation" in McCahery, Picciotto, Scott (eds) *Corporate Control and Accountability* (1993) OUP
"The regulatory criss-cross: interaction between jurisdictions and global regulatory networks" in Bratton, McCahery, Picciotto and Scott (eds) *International Regulatory Competition & Coordination* OUP (1996)

The Hon Mr Justice Sedley

B.A. (Cambridge)

Judge of the High Court of Justice, Queen's Bench Division
Honorary Professor of Law, University of Warwick

Previous posts
Visiting Fellow in Law, University of Warwick (1981)
Visiting Fellow, Osgoode Hall Law School (1987)
Distinguished Visitor, University of Hong Kong (1992)

Other appointments and qualifications
Bencher, Inner Temple
Chairman, Bar Council Sex Discrimination Committee
Founding Director, Public Law Project
Honorary Professor of Law, University of Wales at Cardiff

Selected publications
A Spark in the Ashes: The Pamphlets of John Warr (1992, edited with introduction)
Articles in *Public Law, Modern Law Review, Journal of Law and Society, Civil Justice Quarterly, London Review of Books, Law Quarterly Review, Industrial Law Journal*

Professor Avrom H. Sherr

LL.B (London), Ph.D (Warwick)

Woolf Professor of Legal Education, Institute of Advanced Legal Studies, University of London

Previous posts

Lecturer in Law (1974–90), Director of Legal Practice (1977–90), University of Warwick

Professor of Law (1990–95); Director of Centre for Business and Professional Law (1991–95), University of Liverpool

Other appointments and qualifications

Higher Education Funding Council Reporting Assessor for Teaching Quality Assessment in Law Faculties (1993–94)

Selected publications

Lawyers—The Quality Agenda, Vol 1: *Assessing and Developing Competence and Quality in Legal Aid—The Report of the Birmingham Franchising Pilot.* Vol 2: *Assessing and Developing Competence and Quality in Legal Aid—Transaction Criteria* (1994) HMSO

The Skills of Advocacy (1993) Blackstone Press

Transaction Criteria: Quality Assurance Standards in Legal Aid (1992) HMSO (with R. Moorhead, A. Paterson)

Solicitors and their Skills (1991) Law Society

Freedom of Protest, Public Order and the Law (1989) Basil Blackwell

Client Interviewing for Lawyers: an Analysis and Guide (1986) Sweet & Maxwell

The Welfare Officer in the Birmingham County Court (1984) Citizens Advisory Bureaux (with J. Richards)

Professor Francis Snyder

B.A. (Yale), Fulbright Scholar, J.D. (Harvard), C.E.D.P.A. (Paris) Doctorat de Specialite (Paris)

Professor of European Community Law, European University Institute, Florence

Professor of Law, College of Europe, Bruges

Honorary Visiting Professor of Law, University College, London

Previous posts

Fellow, Programme in Law and Modernisation, Yale Law School (1970–71)

Assistant Professor, then Associate Professor, Osgoode Hall Law School and Division of Social Science, York University, Toronto (1971–78)

Senior Lecturer in Law (1978–82); Reader (1982–87), School of Law, University of Warwick

Reader, Professor of European Law, University College, London (1987–92)

Other appointments and qualifications
Member of the Bar of Massachusetts
Visiting appointments, Afrika-Studiecentrum Leiden (1977), Institute of Development Studies, University of Sussex (1978), Universite d'Aix-Marseille III (1987)
Officer de l'Ordre des Palmes Académiques
Founding Editor, *European Law Journal*
European Law Editor, *Modern Law Review*

Selected publications
One-Party Government in Mali (1965) Yale University Press
Capitalism and Legal Change: An African Transformation (1981) Academic Press
Law of the Common Agricultural Policy (1985) Sweet & Maxwell
Droit de la Politique Agricole Commune (French translation) (1987) Editions Economica
Diritto Agrario della Comunita Europea (Italian translation) (1990) Giuffre Editore
Labour, Law and Crime: An Historical Perspective (1987) Tavistock (co-ed with P Slinn)
The International Law of Development: Comparative Perspectives (1987) Butterworths (co-ed with P Slinn)
The Political Economy of Law (1987) OUP (co-ed with Y Ghai and R Luckham)
Policing and Prosecution in Britain 1750–1850: Essays in the Social History of the Criminal Law (1989) Clarendon Press (co-ed with D Hay)
Common Agricultural Policy of the EEC (1990) Butterworths
New Directions in European Community Law (1990) Weidenfeld & Nicolson (*Law in Context series*)
European Community Law (ed) (1993) Dartmouth Publishing Company
Constitutional Dimensions of European Economic Integration (ed) (1995) Kluwer
Introduction to the Law of the European Union (in Chinese, translated by Y Song) Peking University Press (n.y.p.)

Professor William Twining

D.C.L (Oxford), J.D. (Chicago), LL.D (Hon.)
(Victoria, B.C. and Edinburgh)

Quain Professor of Jurisprudence, University College, London

Previous posts
Lecturer in Private Law, University of Khartoum (1958–61)
Senior Lecturer in Law, University College, Dar es Salaam (1961–65)
Senior Fellow in Law, Yale University (1965)
Visiting Lecturer in Law, University of Chicago (1964)
Professor of Jurisprudence, Queen's University, Belfast (1966–72)
Professor of Law (1972–82), Chairman (1977–80), University of Warwick

Other appointments and qualifications
President, Society of Public Teachers of Law (1978–79)

Commonweath Legal Association: Chairman (1983–90); and Executive Chairman (1990–93)
Chairman, Bentham Committee (1982–current)
General Editor, Law in Context series (1966–current)

Selected publications
Karl Llewellyn and the Realist Movement (1973, 1985) Weidenfeld & Nicolson/ University of Oklahoma Press
How To Do Things With Rules, 3rd ed (1991) (with D Miers) Wiedenfeld & Nicolson
Theories of Evidence: Bentham and Wigmore (1985) Weidenfeld & Nicolson/ Stanford University Press
Rethinking Evidence (1990, 1994) Blackwell/Northwestern University Press
Analysis of Evidence (1991) (with T Anderson) Weidenfeld & Nicolson/Little, Brown
Legal Records in the Commonwealth (1994) with E V Quick, Dartmouth
Blackstone's Tower: The English Law School (1994) Sweet & Maxwell

Professor Geoffrey Wilson

LL.B (Cambridge), LL.M

Professor of Law, University of Warwick

Previous posts
Fellow of Queens' College, Cambridge (1953–67)
Lecturer in Law, University of Cambridge (1955–67)
Founding Professor of the Warwick Law School (1967)
Chairman, Warwick Law School (1967–75)

Other appointments and qualifications
Barrister-at-Law, Gray's Inn
Harkness Fellow, Universities of Yale and Berkeley (1960–61)
Alexander von Humboldt Fellow, University of Freiburg (1974–75)
Visiting Professor, University of Augsburg (1979)
Law and Social Sciences Committee of the SSRC: Member (1971–78); Chairman (1975–78)
Research Initiatives Board of the SSRC: (1976–78)
German Exchange Panel of the SSRC: Chairman (1975–78)
International Academy of Comparative Law: Associate Member (1995–current)

Selected publications
Cases and Materials on Constitutional and Administrative Law (1966) CUP
Cases and Materials on the English Legal System (1973) Sweet & Maxwell
"The Concept of a Law Degree: Getting On With The Job", Jo.SPTL X (1968–69)
Socio-Legal Research in Germany (1980) SSRC
"English Legal Scholarship" (1987) MLR 50
"Europeanising the English Law School", *SPTL Reporter* (Spring 1994)